Rich Client Programming

Rich Client Programming

Plugging into the NetBeans™ Platform

Tim Boudreau

Jaroslav Tulach

Geertjan Wielenga

PRENTICE
HALL

Upper Saddle River, NJ • Boston • Indianapolis • San Francisco
New York • Toronto • Montreal • London • Munich • Paris • Madrid
Capetown • Sydney • Tokyo • Singapore • Mexico City

This Book Is Safari Enabled

The Safari Enabled icon on the cover of your favorite technology book means the book is available through Safari Bookshelf. When you buy this book, you get free access to the online edition for 45 days.

Safari Bookshelf is an electronic reference library that lets you easily search thousands of technical books, find code samples, download chapters, and access technical information whenever and wherever you need it.

To gain 45-day Safari Enabled access to this book:

- Go to http://www.prenhallprofessional.com/safarienabled
- Complete the brief registration form
- Enter the coupon code 32IE-M6EH-YU9W-QRHE-V51D

If you have difficulty registering on Safari Bookshelf or accessing the online edition, please e-mail customer-service@safaribooksonline.com.

Visit us on the Web: www.prenhallprofessional.com

Library of Congress Cataloging-in-Publication Data

Boudreau, Tim.
    Rich client programming : plugging into the NetBeans platform / Tim Boudreau, Jaroslav Tulach, Geertjan Wielenga.
        p. cm.
    Includes bibliographical references and index.
    ISBN 0-13-235480-2 (pbk. : alk. paper)
1. Java (Computer program language) 2. Computer programming. I. Tulach, Jaroslav. II. Wielenga, Geertjan. III. Title.
    QA76.73.J38B672 2007
    005.13'3--dc22   2007007068

ISBN 0-13-235480-2
Text printed in the United States on recycled paper at Courier in Stoughton, Massachusetts.
First printing, April 2007

Contents

Appendix A Advanced Module System Techniques 551

Appendix B Common Idioms and Code Patterns in NetBeans 569

Appendix C Performance 575

Index 583

Foreword

by Jonathan Schwartz

Great technology stays just that—great technology—without great tools. Great tools enable great technology to reach global audiences, transform industries, and, quite literally, change the face of the Internet. And now you understand our view on the importance of NetBeans—to Sun, to the Internet, and to the user community at large.

Now, every product or network service starts with an idea. Turning ideas into reality is what NetBeans has been all about, ever since a very small team in Prague joined a bigger team in Menlo Park, California—and an even bigger team across the globe. From that small beginning, among a small but loyal community of users and developers, NetBeans has become the fastest growing multiplatform development environment we've ever seen.

The growth has been tremendous—a result of fierce competition, innovation, reinvention, and commitment; and we see no limit to the growth across the world.

As I said back in the days when I was running Sun's Developer Tools group, there are two ways to understand the strategy of a technology company. The first is to see how they compensate their sales force, to understand their immediate tactical priorities. The second is to look at the roadmap for their developer tools, to understand their longer-term, strategic priorities.

To that end, there is no product at Sun that better represents the future we envision than NetBeans. And on behalf of Sun, as just one member among many in the community now chartered with its evolution, and as one among many in the corporate user communities, I can say without reservation that it's a thrilling future indeed.

Jonathan Schwartz
Chief Executive Officer and President of Sun Microsystems, Inc.
`blogs.sun.com/jonathan`

Foreword

by Jan Chalupa

I started using NetBeans Developer 2.0 in the late 1990s, but I didn't care about its internals until I joined Sun and the NetBeans team in 2000 to work on NetBeans 3.0. I was coming from the world of Win 32 APIs, MFC, and COM, was moderately familiar with Java libraries and Swing, read the "Gang of Four" bible and all kinds of other books on design patterns and object-oriented programming. In many aspects, what I found in the NetBeans APIs didn't resemble anything I was used to. "What kind of pattern is this `Cookie` thing?" I wondered. "Why is the class that represents a simple view or window called `TopComponent`?" "What is the difference among `FileObjects`, `DataObjects`, and `Nodes`?" "`SplittedPanel`? Doesn't sound like correct grammar to me." And surprisingly, despite the prevalent code hacking and antiauthority culture inherent to the NetBeans core team, almost everything in NetBeans was accessible through a singleton class called `TopManager`.

However, soon I started to find out that no matter how weird some of the names or concepts could seem, NetBeans was architected with reusability and extensibility in mind and allowed developers to add new features easily—or even build their own applications by reusing NetBeans core classes as a framework. I came to realize that NetBeans wasn't just an IDE, but also a very powerful concept that could save application developers years of development time. NetBeans was a platform.

I also figured out why some of the building blocks looked unfamiliar and a little awkward at first glance. NetBeans started as a students' project in the mid-nineties. Most of the developers, including the architects, were university students or fresh graduates with very little experience in software design. They worked extremely hard while learning on the fly. Sometimes inventing the wheel, sometimes introducing new names for existing things, and sometimes, admittedly, making design mistakes. In spite of all this, the original idea of an extensible application platform implemented in Java turned out to be very smart, innovative, and forward-looking.

NetBeans™: The Definitive Guide (O'Riley), written in 2001–2002 and the only comprehensive book on NetBeans APIs to date, was the first attempt to make the NetBeans Platform available to a wider developer audience. Unfortunately, it was the time when the most serious architectural flaws began to emerge and became blockers for future development of the platform. By the time *NetBeans™: The Definitive Guide* was published, some of the APIs described in the book were gone and new APIs were introduced. The primary focus had shifted to making a really solid IDE, while the platform evangelization had been put on the back burner, known only to those who were really close to the NetBeans developer community.

Nevertheless, the NetBeans Platform did not disappear. Over several years, it just got better and more mature. `SplittedPanel` got deprecated. So did `TopManager`, replaced with the `Lookup` concept allowing for feature discoverability and intermodule communication in a distributed and loosely coupled modular architecture. Many APIs got polished and stabilized. NetBeans IDE 5.0 added extensive support for developing modules and building applications based on the NetBeans Platform. Creating a new module became simpler than ever before. The `platform.netbeans.org` site was established and became a valuable source of documentation, articles, and tutorials about the platform.

The only thing that was still missing was a new book. I would like to thank Tim, Jarda, Geertjan, and many other contributors for filling this gap. I believe it will make the NetBeans Platform accessible to many new developers.

Jan Chalupa
NetBeans Director

Preface

Welcome to the world of rich client development on the NetBeans Platform.

Though the Internet boom pushed much programming effort to the server side, the demand for quality desktop software remains and is arguably increasing. Some of the reasons include

- Web pages, which are generally the interfaces for server-driven applications, often are insufficient for the needs of the end user.
- Not every application requires a constant Internet connection, and some applications need to function offline.

In this book, we will focus on using the NetBeans Platform as a framework for creating rich client applications that can be written once and then run on any operating system. The NetBeans Platform is the foundation of the NetBeans IDE, which helps hundreds of thousands of programmers develop applications of all sizes and complexity. As such, the platform is a very powerful and robust base that you can use for your own applications, whether they are commercial applications or in-house solutions. In addition, we will show you what you need to know to create modules to plug into the NetBeans IDE itself.

Rich Client Applications

What do we mean by the term *rich client application*? A rich client application is simply a piece of software where a good portion, if not all, of the application's features work on the user's local system. This is in contrast with a Web application, where the features are entirely dependent on code that is run from a remote server and (usually) accessed by the user through a Web browser. More or less, the term *rich client* is a fancy new moniker for "desktop application." For example, NetBeans IDE itself is a rich client application.

What Is NetBeans?

NetBeans is best known as a popular and award-winning integrated development environment (IDE) for developing Java applications. At the IDE's core is the NetBeans Platform, a modular and extensible application framework. The IDE is a well-orchestrated combination of the platform and a vast array of modules.

At a very early stage in the history of the IDE, the IDE's architecture was modularized to make development of the IDE more flexible. The IDE's modular architecture has the following advantages:

- It simplifies the creation of new features.
- It makes it easy for users to add and remove features.
- It makes it easy to update existing features in a user's installation without disrupting the rest of the application.

The modularity of the NetBeans Platform has made it very attractive to software developers around the world, who have created a large number of different applications on top of it. The NetBeans IDE is the most well-known of those, but the NetBeans Platform has been used as the basis for applications in many domains, from speech processing to geological mapping to stock trading.

Why NetBeans?

There are many reasons to build NetBeans Platform-based applications, not the least of which is the fact that NetBeans-based applications are truly cross-platform. It is possible to develop cross-platform rich client applications in a variety of ways. For example, you can use Swing components and write all of the plumbing of a desktop application yourself. Using the NetBeans Platform, however, gives you powerful building blocks and back-end infrastructure that your applications need, so that you do not have to code those parts yourself. This can save you a significant amount of time. You add the Swing components to the NetBeans Platform that are needed for your application logic, and optionally use other libraries such as JGraph, JFreeChart, etc. So, overall, NetBeans has a great deal to offer when it comes to rapid development of robust and scalable applications. You can focus on the essentials that are specific to your application. Put another way, the NetBeans Platform is to Swing development what JavaServer Faces technology and Struts are to Web development.

The following are some of most important benefits of the NetBeans Platform:

- *NetBeans is free and its code is freely reusable*, whether you are developing commercial or noncommercial software.

- *NetBeans is a mature and feature-rich application framework.* The components of the NetBeans Platform have been developed to serve the needs of the NetBeans IDE, an application that is used by hundreds of thousands of demanding software engineers—yet they are optimized for the production of any sort of desktop application, not just IDEs or IDE-like applications. With the NetBeans Platform, you have a great basis for a production-quality application.

- *NetBeans is truly a "write once, run anywhere" platform.* NetBeans is based on Swing, the pure-Java visual toolkit which is part of every desktop Java installation.

- *NetBeans technology is standards-based and open source*, which means that you will never be a victim of proprietary lock-in when developing on the platform.

- *Plugins for NetBeans IDE have a massive potential audience.* If you are looking to showcase your own technologies, creating a plugin module for NetBeans IDE and making it available through the NetBeans Plugin Portal (`http://plugins.netbeans.org/PluginPortal`) is a great way to reach a wide audience of developers.

- *NetBeans has a vibrant developer community.* The NetBeans Platform benefits from a strong community of developers who are eager to share their experiences. If you have questions about a particular problem, chances are that someone will have had the same issue and will be able to help you.

What Does the Platform Provide for Me as an Application Developer?

When you develop on the NetBeans Platform, you get a rich set of base features, extensive APIs with which you can create your own features, and a powerful set of tools to help you in development.

The following are some of the most important things that you get when you start programming on the NetBeans Platform:

- A Window System that greatly simplifies the manipulation of multiple components within a single frame.

- An Actions system that makes it easy to declaratively install and uninstall menu items, toolbar items, keyboard shortcuts, etc.

- The Auto Update mechanism, which provides a way to dynamically update a user's installation of your application.

- The whole range of NetBeans IDE features that simplify application development, such as code completion and an advanced GUI builder (formerly code-named Matisse), in which you can visually design your user interfaces by dragging, dropping, and rearranging components. In addition, you get special module-development features such as module templates and the ability to test modules on the fly by installing or reloading them into the currently running IDE.

- The architecture of your application is likely to become more robust when using the modular coding techniques encouraged by the NetBeans Platform.

Why This Book?

With the increasing popularity of the IDE and the recognition of the platform's convenience for creating the basics of any application, a book is sorely needed. Much information about the NetBeans Platform is already available, but there is no single up-to-date source that demonstrates how to make use of the whole platform. This book pulls together years' worth of accumulated wisdom, best practices, and practical information, and presents it all in one place.

This book will get you started quickly with module development and guide you through the most important APIs. Along the way, you will learn some of the programming practices that have made NetBeans such reliable and scalable software.

How to Use This Book

This book is divided into twenty-two chapters, two use cases, and three appendices.

- Chapter 1 gets you set up and shows the basic process of creating a module.

- Chapters 2 and 3 discuss the benefits of modularity and provide an overview of the modular structure of the NetBeans Platform.

- Chapters 4 and 5 explain the concepts behind the way NetBeans modules work together and show you the platform's mechanisms for making modular applications cohesive.

- Chapter 6 introduces you to the Filesystems API, which is the NetBeans Platform's base construct for handling both user data and system configuration data.

- Chapter 7 consolidates information from previous chapters and shows you how to create a simple Navigator component for the platform.

- Chapter 8 explains and demonstrates the NetBeans building blocks and features for creating mature multiwindow applications.

- Chapter 9 shows you the Nodes and Explorer APIs, which give you rich ways to present data structures to users.

- Chapter 10 highlights the Datasystems API, which gives you ways to easily programmatically manipulate files of a given type.

- Chapter 11 shows off the IDE's GUI Builder and how it simplifies developing user interfaces for NetBeans Platform applications.

- Chapter 12 builds upon the previous chapters and shows you how to provide multiple types of representations of a file's contents.

- Chapters 13 and 14 show you ways to add editing features for a file type.

- Chapter 15 explains how to create a palette of objects and provides an example for enabling drag-and-drop of code snippets from the palette to a text editor.

- Chapters 16 and 17 show how to develop more editing features.

- Chapter 18 shows you how to add user-configurable options to your application.

- Chapter 19, using Wicket as an example, shows how you can create IDE support for a Web application framework.

- Chapter 20 shows how you can use Web services with a NetBeans Platform application.

- Chapter 21 demonstrates how to integrate help documentation into your application.

- Chapter 22 shows you how to make updates of your modules (and totally new modules) available to users in a dynamic update center.

- The two final chapters are use cases presented by users of the NetBeans Platform. In Chapter 23, you get an example of integrating an existing developer tool into the IDE. In Chapter 24, you can see an example of creating a specialized desktop application, in this case for editing audio files.

- The appendices provide extra information that you might find useful for optimizing the robustness, readability, scalability, and performance of your code.

This book does not cover the features of the IDE so much as the APIs that make those features possible. If you are interested in using the IDE for development of standard Swing, Web, enterprise, mobile, and other Java applications, there are a number of other excellent resources available, such as the *NetBeans™ IDE Field Guide* (also available from Prentice Hall) and the documentation available in the product and on the www.netbeans.org and http://wiki.netbeans.org Web sites.

No tutorial is a complete substitute for reference documentation, and this book is no exception. Full documentation for NetBeans APIs can be found on the NetBeans Platform Web site[1] or downloaded directly into the IDE from the Update Center. The Developer FAQs[2] are a good resource for getting answers to both eternal and newly arising frequent questions. The NetBeans mailing lists, particularly the dev@openide.netbeans.org mailing list, are invaluable for getting answers to less frequently arising questions. If you are going to develop modules, we strongly encourage you to sign up for this list. Through it, you can reach the entire NetBeans development team and extended community, including the authors of this book.

Before beginning to develop NetBeans modules, it is worthwhile to check the Update Center (on the **Tools** menu) and make sure you have the latest version of the NetBeans module development tools. These tools contain templates and other special support to simplify module development.

---

1. http://platform.netbeans.org

2. http://wiki.netbeans.org/wiki/view/NetBeansDeveloperFAQ

Staying Up-to-Date

Check the home page for this book[3] for updates and extra content.

This book is written to version 5.5 of the NetBeans Platform, which is currently the most recent release. Future versions of the platform will surely follow. Version 6.0 is currently in progress and will be final later in 2007. Though information in this book will be valuable for version 6.0 and well into the future, you will probably still find it worthwhile to check the Upgrade Guide[4] to find out about any API changes, improvements, and deprecations occurring after 5.5. Where we know about changes for 6.0, we have noted them.

---

3. www.netbeans.org/books/rcp.html

4. www.netbeans.org/download/dev/javadoc/apichanges.html

About the
Authors and Contributors

Authors

Tim Boudreau

Tim Boudreau had his first startup when he was 13, and has been hooked since, with brief departures to play rock and roll, write and play music, and do graphics and photography. He is the coauthor of the original NetBeans Platform book, *NetBeans™: The Definitive Guide*. Tim was part of the team that opensourced NetBeans, worked on the NetBeans core team, and currently works as a NetBeans evangelist teaching NetBeans APIs and modular design.

Tim Boudreau

Jaroslav Tulach

Jaroslav Tulach is one of the founders of NetBeans. He is proud to see it thriving ten years later. He says: "I partially attribute this to the base architecture we chose when we designed NetBeans in 1997. I am glad I could coauthor this book and help more users build systems on the solid basis that is NetBeans."

Jaroslav Tulach

Geertjan Wielenga

Geertjan Wielenga is the technical writer responsible for NetBeans documentation relating to module development and rich client application development. He has been a technical writer since 1996, focusing mainly on software documentation, with a special emphasis on IDEs. Geertjan holds an Ll.B degree from the University of Natal in Pietermaritzburg, South Africa. He is an active blogger at `http://blogs.sun.com/geertjan`.

Geertjan Wielenga

Contributors

John Jullion-Ceccarelli

John Jullion-Ceccarelli studied Central European politics and history in college and moved out to the Czech Republic in 1996. He joined Sun Microsystems around the time of the NetBeans acquisition in 2000. For the last five years, he has been documenting Java and the NetBeans IDE. He recently became the manager of the NetBeans documentation team, but as you can see from this book, he still likes to write occasionally.

John Jullion-Ceccarelli

Patrick Keegan

Patrick Keegan has been writing tutorials and help for NetBeans IDE since 1999. He is also the lead author of the *NetBeans™ IDE Field Guide*, which is also published by Prentice Hall. He lives in Prague, Czech Republic.

Patrick Keegan

Jens Trapp

Dr. Jens Trapp works as a software architect for Sun Microsystems in Hamburg, Germany. He does consulting for Java-related technologies and products as well as for architectures and proofs of concepts in customer projects. His main areas of interest are rich and Web clients in enterprise environments using Java and XML technologies.

Jens Trapp

Rich Unger

Rich Unger is a long-time NetBeans contributor and member of the NetBeans governance board. He has spoken about NetBeans RCP development at JavaOne and OOPSLA, and written several articles, tutorials, and samples on the subject. Until recently, Rich was a software developer at Nuance Communications. There he worked on one of the first VoiceXML interpreters as well as the V-Builder VoiceXML development tool.

Right now, Rich is traveling around the world. He'd like to take this opportunity to mention that he'll be job shopping when he gets back.

Rich Unger

Acknowledgments

The authors and contributors would like to thank staff at Sun Microsystems and Prentice Hall for making this book possible. We are especially grateful to Judith Lilienfeld, Jan Chalupa, and David Lindt for their support and encouragement, but mainly for giving us time away from our normal duties to concentrate on the book.

For a book this technical, thorough review is essential. Many users from the NetBeans community, as well as internal Sun staff, helped out in reviewing this book. Of the many whose insights were beneficial, below is a list of those whose review comments particularly helped us maintain focus, perspective, and accuracy:

Andreas Andreou, Stanislav Aubrecht, Andrei Badea, Dusan Balek, David Beer, Emilian Bold, Sandip Chitale, David Coldrick, Roderico Cruz, Marek Fukala, Jesse Glick, Troy Giunipero, Michel Graciano, Arun Gupta, David Havrda, Charlie Hunt, Lukas Jungmann, Jiri Kopsa, Jiri Kovalsky, Milan Kuchtiak, Jan Lahoda, Pierre Matthijs, Miloslav Metelka, Chuk Munn Lee, Gregory Murphy, Tomislav Nakic-Alfirevic, Tor Norbye, Soot Phengsy, Petr Pisl, Winston Prakash, Tomasz Slota, Gregg Sporar, Roman Strobl, Chris Webster, and Tom Wheeler.

The creation of the book involves much more than writing and reviewing. Huge thanks go to Greg Doench, for guiding us through the project from concept to printing; to Elizabeth Ryan for her patience and thoroughness in handling the production details; to our expert copy editors, Dmitry Kirsanov and Alina Kirsanova (bonus points for being able to handle the copy in our preferred format, DocBook XML); and to Rudolf Balada, for extraordinary patience in helping us to assemble the CD accompanying this book.

Some personal gratitude from Tim: "First I'd like to thank Geertjan for dragging me into this project ('Would you like to contribute a chapter or two?'

Six chapters and two appendices later . . . in for a penny, in for a pound!);
Patrick for herding us cats, Jarda for being a worthy intellectual sparring
partner, and Jesse for his usual blunt wisdom. Judith for putting up with my
crabbiness as I scrambled after deadlines; Karel Z. and Lilka for letting me in-
habit their living room in Prague where my first chapters were written; Charlie
Hunt for his helpful feedback; and the whole NetBeans evangelism
team—Roman Strobl, Brian Leonard, Gregg Sporar, Ashwin Rao, David Bot-
terill, and Bruno Souza—for cutting me enough slack to get this done while
holding down a day job; Henry Story for distracting me with Very Interesting
Problems and much enjoyed opportunities for procrastination; Hans and
Sarah, the delightful and tolerant owners of the Coronet Motel in Palo Alto,
who put up with my eccentricities while banging out more chapters and edits.
And to the countless members of the NetBeans community who offered
feedback and insights, particularly to the many Java User Groups in
Brazil—much of the organization and presentation of the material in my
chapters was conceived while doing a whirlwind teaching tour in that lovely
country. And especially to my parents, Hal Boudreau and Mary Scarcliff, who
have been supportive of my wanderings, and who endured my bringing a book
project home for the holidays."

On a personal level, Geertjan would like to thank the following: "Of course,
first and foremost I'd like to thank my fellow authors Tim and Jarda for their
patience and dedication to this task. Also many thanks to Patrick for being
constantly available and ever willing to bounce random ideas around. A lot
of gratitude to Andrei Badea and Sandip Chitale especially, for being incredibly
thorough technical reviewers. Jens, John, and Rich—thanks for contributing
to this book, your involvement has really raised the level of usefulness of
this tome."

In thanks, Jens wants to share the following: "It has been a great pleasure
working with the NetBeans team and contributing to this book. Thanks to the
team for their help, especially to Geertjan and Troy. I would also like to thank
my wife Katrin for her patience and support."

Finally, in addition to his essential review comments, Jesse Glick also
provided important bits of technical and logistical assistance, such as helping
us with the repository for the manuscript.

CHAPTER ONE

Getting Started with the NetBeans Platform

When you develop applications on top of the NetBeans Platform, you will probably want to use the NetBeans IDE to simplify development. The IDE contains the platform itself, plus an array of useful development tools. You might think of the IDE as the Software Development Kit (SDK) for the NetBeans Platform. This chapter contains a quick survey of some important features of NetBeans IDE that will greatly ease the development process.

1.1   Setting Up the IDE

You can install the IDE directly from the CD that comes with this book, or you can download the latest version of the IDE from www.netbeans.org.

Another indispensable tool is the API documentation for the platform and IDE. You can download this documentation using the IDE's **Update Center** (choose **Tools | Update Center** in the IDE).

The samples that you will read about and build in this book are found in a NetBeans Module file (NBM) on the CD. After you install the NBM file and open the projects in the IDE, you should see a list of NetBeans projects, as shown in Figure 1.1. The projects are found in the **New Project** wizard, as

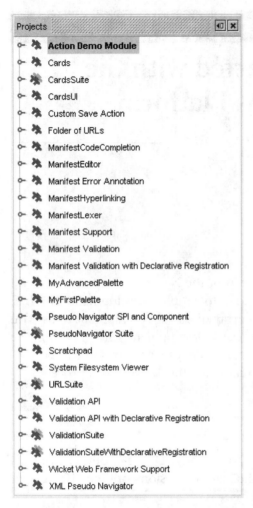

Figure 1.1: List of samples in the **Projects** window

shown in Figure 1.2. Open the **New Project** wizard by choosing **File | New Project** from the main menu.

In the remainder of this chapter, you will learn about the most important tools for development on the NetBeans Platform. In the process, you will learn the most important steps of the development process, which are discussed in greater detail throughout this book.

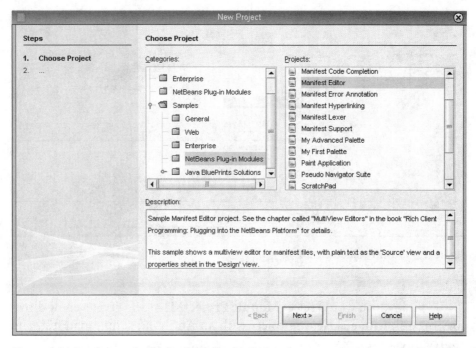

Figure 1.2: Book samples in the **New Project** wizard

1.2   NetBeans IDE Basics

In this section we provide a bare-bones description of the minimal tasks needed to develop NetBeans modules and applications. In addition to the description below, there are many other references for using the NetBeans IDE. The built-in help is a good place to start. The information below is meant to make this book intelligible to someone who has not yet started using the NetBeans IDE to develop applications on the NetBeans Platform.

1.2.1   Creating a Module

Many exercises in this book start by instructing you to create a new NetBeans module. This means you should go to the **File** menu, invoke **New Project**, and select **NetBeans Plug-in Modules**, as shown in Figure 1.3.

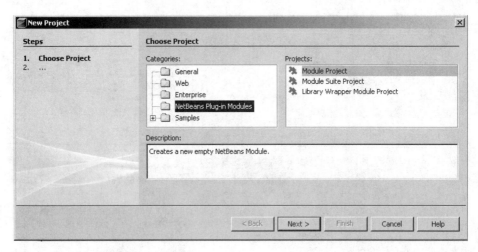

Figure 1.3: **New Project** wizard

Typically, you would select **Module Project**. That will create a new directory on disk with a skeleton project with an Ant build script, manifest, and
source directories.

At its most fundamental, a module is just a plain old Java JAR file, with a
few special entries in its manifest. In fact, any JAR can be made into a module
simply by adding the correct metadata to its manifest. This approach is
sometimes useful when migrating existing applications to the NetBeans Platform. An NBM (NetBeans Module) file is simply a signed JAR that contains
a module's JAR file, some auxiliary files, and some metadata that describes
the module and its dependencies.

1.2.2   Creating an Application

When creating applications on top of the NetBeans Platform, use the **Module
Suite Project** template in the **New Project** wizard, shown in the previous section. This template gives you a complete framework for your application. It
consists of the core of the IDE, together with all of the IDE's modules. Unless
you are creating some kind of editor, you will not need the IDE's modules. As
shown in Figure 1.4, if you right-click the node of a module suite project and
choose **Properties**, you can exclude the IDE's modules by choosing **Create**

Standalone Application in the **Application** panel. Then the IDE will ask you to confirm that you do not want the IDE's modules.

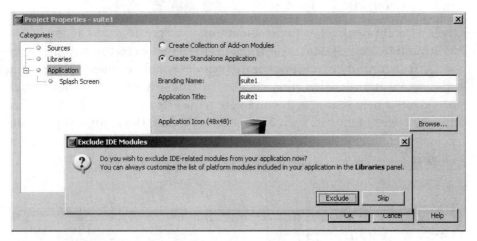

Figure 1.4: Excluding the IDE's modules

In the **Application** panel, you can also set the application's title and splash screen. If you set the application title to "TestApp" and then run the application without the IDE's modules, you will see Figure 1.5.

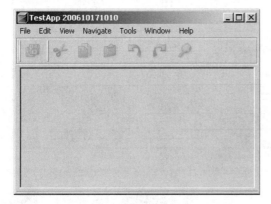

Figure 1.5: A bare NetBeans Platform application

This is your starting point when you create applications on top of the NetBeans Platform.

1.2.3   Using File Templates

Often we will instruct you to do something like "create a new action." The NetBeans IDE uses a system of *file templates* to facilitate creating new files with specific structures. The **New File** wizard includes panels to collect information and generate more detailed initial code for specific sorts of files. So the instruction "create a new action" tells you to go to the **File** menu, choose **New File**, and then select a template such as **NetBeans Module Development | Action**. The complete list of templates for NetBeans module development is shown in Figure 1.6.

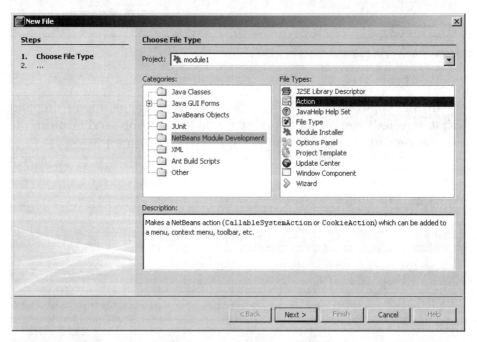

Figure 1.6: The **New File** wizard

1.2.4 Declaring Dependencies

Most chapters will begin with an instruction to declare one or more dependencies on NetBeans modules. The NetBeans modules provide the functionality and the APIs that you will work with throughout this book. For example, when you want to create a component palette for your application, your module will need to specify that it depends on the Component Palette API. So when you are told to "declare a dependency," just right-click the module project, choose **Properties**, and then set a dependency in the **Libraries** panel in the **Project Properties** dialog box, as shown in Figure 1.7. (You can also accomplish this by right-clicking the project's **Libraries** node and choosing **Add Dependency**.)

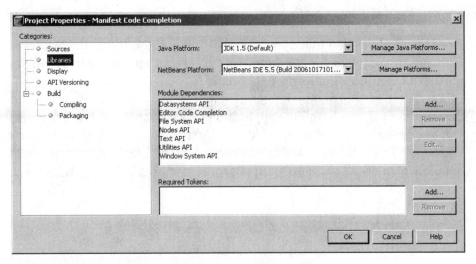

Figure 1.7: **Libraries** panel

When you click **Add** next to the **Module Dependencies** list in Figure 1.7, you will be able to search and select the NetBeans modules that you need. After you click **OK**, the dependency is declared in the module project's `nbproject/project.xml` file. For details, see Chapter 2.

1.2.5   Running a Module

Running a module means right-clicking the module project's node in the **Projects** window of the IDE and choosing the **Run** or **Install/Reload in Target Platform** menu item. This is the equivalent of invoking the run target in the module's Ant build file.

When you choose **Install/Reload in Target Platform**, a new instance of the NetBeans Platform application for which the module is registered starts up (if it was not already running). If the module was previously installed, it is uninstalled. Then, the module that you want to run is installed. If you choose **Install/Reload in Development IDE**, no new application is started up. Instead, the module is installed in the NetBeans IDE that you are currently using.

1.2.6   Branding an Application

Once the modules that make up an application built on top of the NetBeans Platform are complete, the appearance of the application still closely resembles the default NetBeans Platform. You can use the IDE to personalize the application. This procedure is also known as *branding*. In particular, you can brand the launcher's name, brand the application's splash screen, define a progress bar, and brand the application's title bar. Right-click a module suite project's node in the **Projects** window, choose **Properties**, and use the **Application** and **Splash Screen** panels to brand the application, as shown in Figures 1.8 and 1.9.

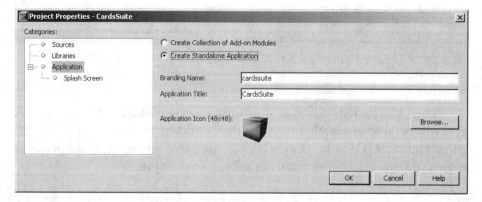

Figure 1.8: The **Application** branding panel

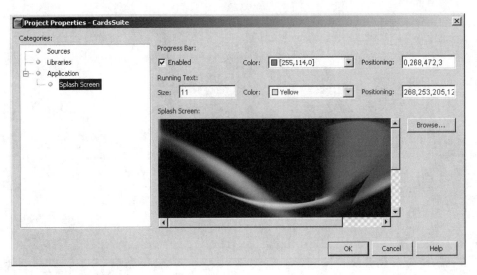

Figure 1.9: The **Splash Screen** branding panel

1.2.7   Distributing an Application

Once your application is complete, one way to distribute it is via a ZIP file. The IDE can create the ZIP file for you, containing the application's source structure and a launcher. Alternatively, you can use the IDE to generate a Java Network Launch Protocol (JNLP) application, also known as "Web startable" application, for you. You can create either a ZIP file or a JNLP application by right-clicking a module suite project's node and choosing **Build ZIP Distribution** or **Build JNLP Application**.

CHAPTER TWO

The Benefits of Modular Programming

2.1 Distributed Development

Nobody writes software entirely in-house anymore. Outside the world of embedded systems, almost everyone relies upon libraries and frameworks written by someone else. By using them, it is possible to concentrate on the actual logic of the application while reusing the infrastructure, frameworks, and libraries written and provided by others. Doing so shortens the time needed to develop software.

The rise of open source software over the past decade makes library reuse doubly compelling. For many kinds of programs there are existing solutions for various problems, and those solutions are available at zero monetary cost. The set of open source offerings starts with UNIX kernels, base C libraries, command-line utilities, and continues over Web servers and Web browsers to Java utilities such as Ant, Tomcat, JUnit, Javacc—ad infinitum. Writing modern software is as much a process of assembly as it is creation. Picking available pieces and composing them together is a large part of modern application development. Instead of writing everything from scratch, people who need an HTTP server for their application select Apache or Tomcat. Those who need a database could choose MySQL or PostgreSQL. The application glues these pieces together and adds its own logic. The result is a fully functional, performant application developed in remarkably little time.

Consider how Linux distributions work. RedHat's Fedora, Mandriva, SUSE, and Debian all contain largely the same applications, written by the same people. The distributor simply packages them and provides the "glue" to install them together. Distribution vendors often write only central management and installation software and provide some quality assurance to make sure all the selected components work well together. This process works well enough that Linux has grown considerably in popularity. As evidence of the meaningfulness of such a model, consider that Mac OS X is in fact a FreeBSD UNIX with a bunch of add-ons from Apple. The key thing to note is that the software in question is created through a *distributed development model*. The developers and distributors of the software may not even know or communicate with each other, and are usually not even in the same place geographically.

Such distributed development has specific characteristics. The first thing to notice is that the source code for the application (or operating system) is no longer under a developer's complete control. It is spread all over the world. Building such software is unquestionably different from building an application whose source code is entirely in your in-house repository.

The other thing to realize is that no one fully controls the schedule of the whole product. Not only the source code, but also the developers are spread all over the world and are working on their own schedules. Such a situation is not actually as unusual or dangerous as it sounds. Anyone who has tried to schedule a project with a team of more than fifty people knows that the idea of ever having "full control" over the process is at best a comforting illusion. You always have to be prepared to drop a feature or release an older version of one or another component. The same model works with distributed development.

The basic right everyone has is the freedom to use a newer or older version of a library.

The ability to use external libraries and compose applications out of them results in an ability to create more complex software with less time and work. The trade-off is the need to manage those libraries and ensure their compatibility. That is not a simple task. But there is no other practical, cost-efficient way to assemble systems of today's complexity.

2.2   Modular Applications

The technological solution to the challenges of distributed development is modularization. A modular application, in contrast to one monolithic chunk of tightly coupled code in which every unit may interface directly with any other, is composed of smaller, separated chunks of code that are well isolated. Those chunks can then be developed by separate teams with their own life cycles and their own schedules. The results can then be assembled together by a separate entity—the distributor.

It has long been possible to put a bunch of libraries on the Java classpath and run an application. The NetBeans Platform takes the management of libraries further—by actively taking part in the loading of libraries and enforcing that the minimum version of a library that another library uses is adequate. Such libraries are what we call *modules*. The NetBeans *Module System* is a *runtime container* that ensures the integrity of the system at runtime.

2.2.1   Versioning

Breaking an application into distinct libraries creates a new challenge—one needs to ensure that those independent parts really work together. There are many possible ways to do so. The most popular is *versioning*. Each piece of a modular application has a version number—usually a set of numbers in Dewey decimal format, such as `1.34.8`. When a new version is released, it has an increased version number, for example `1.34.10`, `1.35.1`, or `2.0`. If you think about it, the idea that an incremented version number can encode the difference between two versions of a complex piece of software is patently absurd. But it is simple to explain, and it works well enough that the practice is popular.

The other parts of a modular system can then declare their external dependencies. Most components will have some external requirements. For example, a component in a modular system might rely on an XML parser being present, or on some database driver being installed, or on a text editor or Web browser being present. For each of these, another module can request a specific minimum version of their interfaces. Even if the dependencies on external libraries are minimized, every program in Java depends on a version of Java itself. A true modular system should make it possible to specify the desired minimum

JDK version. A module could require `JDK >= 1.5`, `xmlparser >= 3.0`, and `webbrowser >= 1.5`. At runtime, the code responsible for starting the application must ensure that the requested dependencies are satisfied—that the XML parser is available in a version 3.0 or newer, the Web browser is in version 1.5 or higher, and so forth. The NetBeans Module System does that.

Using such dependency schemas to maintain dependencies between components in a modular system can work only if certain rules are obeyed. The first rule is *backward compatibility*—that if a new version is released, all contracts that worked in the previous version will work with the new one as well. This is easier to say than to achieve. Rule number two is that components of the system need to accurately say what they need. When a module's set of dependencies changes, it needs to say so, so that the system can accurately determine if they are satisfied. So if a piece of a modular system starts to rely on new functionality, such as an HTML editor, it needs to add a new dependency (e.g., `htmleditor >= 1.0`). And if you start to use a new interface to the HTML editor component—one which was only added in version 1.7 of the component—the dependency needs to be updated to require `htmleditor >= 1.7`. The NetBeans Module System makes this second part relatively simple in practice, since a module's compile-time classpath will only include modules it declares a dependency on. So unless the module's list of dependencies is updated, it will not compile.

2.2.2   Secondary Versioning Information

The versioning scheme just discussed refers to the *specification version* of a library. It describes a specific snapshot of the public APIs in that library.

It is a fact of life that some versions of libraries can contain bugs which must be worked around. For this reason, a secondary version identifier—an *implementation version*—should be associated with a component. In contrast to the specification version, this is usually a string like "Build20050611" which can only be tested for equality. This provides a secondary identifier that can be used to determine if a specific piece of code to work around a given bug is needed. The fact that a bug is present in (specification) version 3.1 does not mean it will also be in version 3.2 or even in a different build of 3.1. So, for reasons of bugfixing or special treatment of certain versions, associating an implementation version with a library can be useful.

2.2.3   Dependency Management

The system of versions and dependencies needs a manager that makes sure all requirements of every piece in the system are satisfied. Such a manager can check at each piece's install time that everything in the system remains consistent—this is how RPMs or Debian packages work in Linux distributions. Metadata about such dependencies is also useful at runtime. Such metadata makes it possible for an application to dynamically update its libraries without shutting down. It can also determine if the dependencies of a module it is asked to dynamically load can be satisfied—and if not, it can describe the problem to the user.

NetBeans IDE is a modular application. Its modules—its constituent libraries—are discovered and loaded at runtime. They can install various bits of functionality, such as components, menu items, or services; or they can run code during startup to initialize programmatically; or they can take advantage of declarative registration mechanisms that various parts of the platform and IDE offer to register services and initialize them on demand. The NetBeans Module System uses the declared dependencies of the installed components to set up the parent classloaders for each module's own classloader, determining what JARs will be searched when a module tries to load a class. This ensures that any one module's classpath excludes any module JARs which are not above it in its dependency tree and enforces the declared dependencies of each component—a module cannot call code in a foreign module unless it declares a dependency on that foreign module, so it will not be loaded at all if some of its dependencies cannot be satisfied.

2.3   A Modular Programming Manifesto

No one is surprised anymore that operating systems and distributions are designed in a modular way. The final product is assembled from independently developed components. Modularity is a mechanism to coordinate the work of many people around the world, manage interdependencies between their parts of the project, and assemble very complex systems in a reasonably reliable way.

The value of this approach is finally filtering down to the level of individual applications. Applications are getting more and more complicated, and they are increasingly assembled from pieces developed independently. But they still need to be reliable. Modular coding enables you to achieve and manage that complexity. Since applications are growing in size and functionality, it is necessary to separate them into individual pieces (whether you call them "components," "modules," or "plugins"). Each such separated piece then becomes one element of the modular architecture. Each piece should be isolated and should export and import well-defined interfaces.

Splitting an application into modules has benefits for software quality. It is not surprising that a monolithic piece of code, where every line in any source file can access any other source file, may become increasingly interconnected, unreadable, and ultimately unreliable. If you have worked in software for a few years, you have probably been on a project where there was some piece of code which everyone on the team was afraid to touch—where fixing one bug always seemed to create two new bugs. That is the entropy of software development. There is economic pressure to fix problems in the most expedient way possible—but the most expedient way is not necessarily in the long-term interest of the codebase. Modular software limits the risk of creeping coupledness by requiring that different components of the system interoperate through well-defined API contracts. It's not a silver bullet, but it makes it considerably harder to have the sort of decay that eventually dooms many complex pieces of software.

Comparing modular design and traditional object-oriented design is a lot like the comparisons of *structure programming* with *spaghetti code* from the 1960s. Spaghetti code was the name given to Fortran or BASIC programs where every line of code could use a GOTO statement to transfer execution to another place in the program. Such code tended to be written in such a chaotic way that often only the author of a program could understand the program's logic. Structured programming tried to reduce this disorder by introducing blocks of code: for loops, while loops, if statements, procedures, and calls to procedures. Indeed, this improved the situation and the readability and maintainability of applications increased. If nothing else, one could be sure that a call to a method will return only once.[1]

The classic object-oriented style of programming in some ways resembles the situation before structured programming arrived. With the term "classic object-oriented style," we are referring to the style of programming typically taught today. It is also the sort of code you get from using UML tools: heavy use of inheritance, and almost everything overridable and public. In such an application, any method in any class may potentially call almost any method of any other class. Indeed there are `public`, `private`, and `protected` access modifiers, but the granularity of access permissions is done on the level of a single class or class member. That is far too low-level to serve as a basic building block of application design. Modularity is about the interaction between systems, rather than between small parts of subsystems.

Modular applications are composed of modules. One module is a collection of Java classes in Java packages. Some of these packages are public, and public classes in them serve as an exported API that other modules can call. Other classes are private and cannot be accessed from outside. Moreover, to be a module, a library must list its dependencies on its surrounding environment—other modules, the Java runtime, etc.

Inside a module, one can still apply bad coding practices, but the architecture of an application can be observed by checking the dependencies among all its modules. If one module does not have a dependency on another, then its classes cannot directly access the other module's classes. This keeps the architecture clean by preventing GOTO-like coding constructs that could otherwise couple completely unrelated parts of the codebase.

Sometimes people say that their application is too small for modular architecture to be applicable. It may indeed be so. But if it is beyond the level of a student project, then it is likely to evolve over time. As it evolves, it is likely to grow. And as it grows, it is very likely to face the "entropy of software" problem.

---

1. Except for boundary conditions where it may never return, throw an exception, etc.

The initial step in designing a complex application is to design its architecture. For this, it is necessary to define and understand the dependencies between parts of the application. It is much easier to do this in case of modular applications.

Thus it is always wise to start designing any application in a modular way. Doing so creates an infrastructure that will let you build more robust applications and avoid a great deal of manual bookkeeping. Rewriting messy, interconnected traditional object-oriented applications to give them a good modular design is a hard task. And it is not often that a project can afford the time it takes to be rewritten or rearchitected. Often, programmers have to live with old, monolithic code with ever-increasing maintenance costs—because the code is known to work.

Modular design starts you out in an environment where the architecture cannot slowly decay into unmaintainability without anyone noticing. If you create a new dependency between two parts of a modular application, you need to do some explicit gestures to set up that dependency. It cannot happen by accident. While that is not a cure for messy designs, it is an environment that encourages well-thought-out ones.

Modularity gives systems clearer design and control of module interdependencies; it also gives developers more flexibility in maintenance. Consider that when starting any new project—regardless of the project's initial scope. Modular design will have large benefits for the architecture of the entire application as it grows from its infancy. The real benefits of modular programming might not be apparent in the first version of an application. But they will become obvious later with the reduced cost of creating the 2.0 and 3.0 versions. Since modular programming does not add significant cost to creating the 1.0 version of an application, there is little reason not to use this approach on all projects. Many programmers are surprised (even sometimes horrified) to find something they wrote fifteen years ago still in use. Since we cannot predict the future of our code, we might as well architect it to last from the start.

2.4   Using NetBeans to Do Modular Programming

Creating a skeleton for a new NetBeans module is as easy as creating a plain old Java application project in the IDE. Just start NetBeans IDE, select **File | New Project**, and choose **NetBeans Plug-in Modules | Module Project**. Give the module a name and a location and you will end up with a brand-new project opened in the **Project** window. Create a Java class in the package that has been precreated for you. Then, in the IDE's Source Editor, use any the features of the JDK platform that you are running against. All the classes from the JDK are accessible and can be used without any special setup.

A slight difference compared to plain Java coding is the way one uses additional libraries. Instead of directly choosing a JAR file, one creates a *module dependency* on another module. To do this, open the **Libraries** subnode of your project and invoke the **Add Module Dependency** dialog. NetBeans contains a lot of modules and you can choose which ones to add as libraries. There are also many *library wrapper modules*, each presenting a third-party library as a standard NetBeans module. For example, there is Apache.org's Commons Logging library—just type `common`, select the library, and click **OK** (Figure 2.1). Now the editor knows how to use logging classes so you can safely type, for example, `org.apache.commons.logging.LogFactory.getLog("name.of.your.log")` and the result will be compilable. This may not look like a huge advantage over selecting the JAR file directly; however, notice that it was enough to specify just the identifying name of the module and the **Library Manager** dialog located it for us. Adding explicit dependencies to a module project is quite simple.

It appears that creating a single module and reusing existing resources is fairly easy. However, the power of modular applications is in having multiple modules with dependencies, so the question is, how to create such modular application inside NetBeans IDE? The answer is a *module suite*. A suite is a container for a set of modules which can see each other and communicate among themselves (Figure 2.2). To create a suite, choose **NetBeans Plug-in**

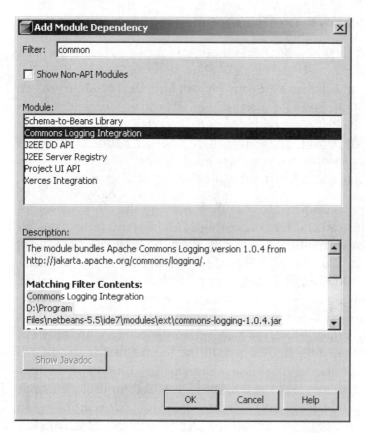

Figure 2.1: Adding a dependency on a module wrapping the Apache's Commons Logging library

Modules/Module Suite in the **New Project** wizard. Then follow the steps in the wizard. After clicking **OK**, a new project be visible in the **Projects** window. In contrast to the regular project, a suite does not have its own sources. It is merely a project to bind together other, interdependent NetBeans module projects. So, choose **Suite/Modules**, invoke a popup menu on that node, and, using the **Add Existing** menu item, add the previously created module into the suite.

A suite can contain more than one module. To demonstrate that, we can convert an existing library into a module in the suite. Choose **New Project**

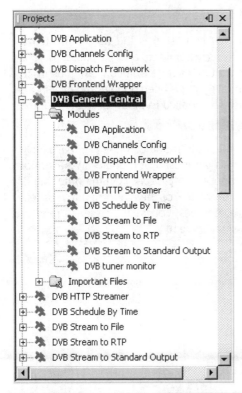

Figure 2.2: A suite can contain many modules

again and select **NetBeans Plug-in Modules/Library Wrapper Module Project**, choose some plain existing Java JAR file, such as an Apache library, and follow the steps to create its wrapper and make it part of the suite we just created. When done, the suite will show the two modules under the **Modules** node and it will be possible to create a dependency between them. Select the first module again, right-click it, and choose **Properties** from the popup menu. In the **Properties** dialog, click the **Libraries** category to show the UI for setting up dependencies. Add a dependency on the just added library wrapper module. When done, classes in the first module will be able to use classes from the library.

Modules vs. Plugins

One point of potential terminology confusion is the use of the terms "plugin" and "module." For most practical intents and purposes, there is no difference. A module is simply a unit of code that you can "plug in" to the platform or the IDE. The term "plugin" has been popularized by various other environments and can easily be applied to modules created for the NetBeans Platform as well.

Traditionally, we have used the term "module" in the NetBeans environment, since the platform itself is composed of modules. (You cannot say that the core platform is composed of "plugins.") On the other hand, if you are creating new features for the IDE or the platform but your feature set is composed of multiple modules, you might prefer to refer to those modules collectively as a single plugin.

CHAPTER THREE

Modular Architecture

The previous chapter focused on the need for modular applications. This chapter describes some of the best practices we have learned while developing NetBeans IDE in a modular way for the past eight years. In addition, this chapter describes the basic terminology used when working with modules in the NetBeans Module System and gives examples of the common ways to use the NetBeans runtime container.

3.1 Modules—The Assembly Units of a Modular Application

By now it should be clear that a modern application is not written as one big chunk of code, but rather composed from a set of smaller pieces. In NetBeans terminology, those pieces are called *modules*. The person responsible for the final application can then select those modules that are most suitable for his or her needs. It is not always necessary to select the latest version of a module. The latest version might be too buggy or not cooperate well with the rest of the system. It may be better to select an older version of a module or even not include the given module in the final application at all.

Looking at the above description of how you might assemble modules together, we get a general picture of what the architecture of a modular application looks like. Much architectural information is contained in the dependency graph of its modules. The module should be a relatively encapsulated component that can be added to and upgraded inside of the application without having a negative impact on the other parts of the system. This is indeed a very broad definition that can cover many possible solutions. However, it clearly describes the priorities that we will use when judging whether a design of a modular application is correct or not.

3.2   Types of Modules

Modules can play various roles. Some modules add new user interface elements; others are just libraries with important backing functionality. Each module has different requirements for its own integration into the application. Because the assembler of the application and the actual creator of the module need not be the same person, there is a need for communication. A good container for the execution of modular applications is likely to provide some attributes that allow the module to be annotated with a description of its requirements that need to be fulfilled in order to include that module inside of an application. In an ideal state, these attributes are not only useful for a human being that assembles the application, but also for the container that does the execution. In such a situation, it can be ensured that if the final application is assembled consistently according to these attributes, it will also run. For this to work, you need an execution container with a relatively good means for expressing these restrictions. The NetBeans runtime container provides a huge variety of useful attributes, as will be explored in the following paragraphs.

Chapter 2 already concentrated on the need and the possible use of module versioning, its usefulness in contending with various versions of modules, and the way the runtime classpath for their execution is constructed. Let's move a step forward and look at modules from the point of view of the roles they can play.

3.2.1   End-User Interface Module

One of the simplest module examples is a module that contributes some end-user functionality, such as menu items, toolbar buttons, components, etc., but which does not expose any other functionality that could be programmatically used by other modules. Obviously, there is no reason for other modules to depend on such a module. As a result, such a module can and very likely will have some dependencies on other modules, but it will have no public packages and there will be no other modules in the system requesting a dependency on it. Moreover, in a componentized and dynamic application like NetBeans IDE, the module will very likely be under the control of the user. For example, in the **Module Manager** dialog, the user will be given a chance to disable or reenable the module. By doing this, the user can customize the working environment—hide or show some of the user interface (UI) elements such as menus, toolbars, etc. Such a module is an example of a *regular, end-user-oriented* module of the system. There is no other way to interact with it than through the exposed user interface elements and its lifecycle is fully under the control of the end user.

There is just one reason why someone would want to depend on such a *completely closed* module: The assembler of the final application might want to ensure that the UI provided by that module is always available in the final application, as the UI functionality provided by such a module is really essential. As an example, take the IDE's Favorites module. It provides an "explorer" window to browse local files. If an application needs such functionality, it can create an integration module that depends on the Favorites module. Thus it can be sure that the Favorites feature will always be available to the user.

3.2.2 Simple Library

A *simple library* is an easy to understand and common type of module widely used by people writing open source or otherwise reusable libraries for things such as Apache Commons Collections. A simple library is just a JAR file with some packages containing useful classes. Other modules can just depend on it, instantiate its classes, override its methods, etc. But there is no attempt to support multiple "vendors" (as described in Section 3.2.3 below) because it it assumed that any improvements to be made (e.g., optimizations) should be made in the main source base so that all clients benefit.

 Sometimes a multiple-vendors approach does not even make sense because the library provides controlled access to the functionality of some part of an application's UI, for example a scripting API for a word processor. Again, the module would have some public classes (plus a lot of private ones), but on a general level the physical packaging and usage is just like in the case of a *simple library*.

3.2.3   Multiple Vendor Support

Often, one goal of software programming is to avoid locking in users to an implementation of a feature as provided by a specific vendor. Making code usable by multiple vendors can be achieved in a variety of ways, not all of which are optimal from perspectives of reusability, compatibility, and scalability. In some cases, there might be a generally accepted specification that allows for multiple implementations. Often the "specification" is just a PDF file with descriptions, specifications, and code snippets. The vendors then have to create modules that contain not just the API's implementation, but also the API classes from the specification that people will then code to. Those "vendors" then distribute their own self-contained JARs or frameworks (containing both the interface *and* the implementation classes). The client code compiles and runs against one or more vendors' JARs. Presumably, client code compiled against one vendor's copy (e.g., the reference implementation) could then run against another vendor's copy, since the interface names and signatures should match. However, that leaves a lot to chance—it is usually much better for there to be a single canonical instance of the API classes. Duplicating these API classes violates the DRY principle.[1]

Such a system works, but it is a crude and nonmodular approach that can cause spectacular problems at times. The biggest problem here is that there cannot be multiple implementations of the same specification used simultaneously. Anyone who has dealt with the vagaries of various Java XML parsers[2] knows there may sometimes be very valid reasons to want two versions of the same thing loaded in the same VM. This is possible in a modular system, as long as it is not the same module trying to load both.

The specification is part of each vendor's JARs, but all such JARs may not contain the same version of the specification. The packages containing the specification are likely to overlap. They can either be loaded once into the VM or multiple times by different classloaders. Neither option will really work. If the classes are loaded just from one vendor's JAR and the other one is of a

---

1. The DRY Principle—"Don't Repeat Yourself"—is a general dictum in software design to keep only one copy of any given piece of data to avoid problems with keeping all copies up to date.

2. http://weblogs.java.net/blog/timboudreau/archive/2006/10/

different version, the two implementations may not link and can throw inscrutable exceptions because of missing methods or classes at runtime. On the other hand, if the classes are loaded twice, then every client needs to decide in advance which of the vendor's modules it is going to use; it cannot use both without using reflection. From a modular point of view, this is more of an anti-pattern than an example to follow. Generally, these situations are pure evil to debug, yet such a problem is easy to avoid in a system where dependencies are well-defined and explicit.

3.2.4   Modular Library

A viable improvement over the multiple-vendors scenario is a real *modular library*. It puts the specification and implementation into different modules and enforces their separation by the module boundary. There is one module which contains the specification—the actual interfaces, abstract classes, etc. mentioned in the specification. Then there may be one or more separate modules (possibly from other vendors) which implement that specification.

It is possible to find a lot of different ways to register an implementation in the JDK, as there was no clear standard for doing so in the early days. For example, `SecurityManager` has the setter `setSecurityManager()` which can be called just once; otherwise it throws an exception. `URLHandlerFactory` is a similar case: It has one setter method to register one factory class. This pattern allows registration of just one implementation for the given application. This may be fine in certain situations, but does not make much sense for other use cases. Actually both `SecurityManager` and `URLHandlerFactory` would benefit from multiple registrations. For example, NetBeans code needs multiple `SecurityManager`s, since the security concerns might need to be split among multiple modules. Indeed, we need multiple `URLHandlerFactory`s, since many modules want to provide their own URL schemas.

That is why it is better to allow multiple factory classes to be registered. For example, `JEditorPane.registerEditorKitForContentType()` allows you to register one kit per MIME type, as it has been anticipated that multiple modules would try to register their own kits.

A real modular architecture is likely to encourage the *modular library* design and use the *simple library* design where appropriate as well. Solving the multiple-vendors problem by duplicating classes is simply bad design in a modular world, because you duplicate the actual .class files of the specification across vendors. Besides causing a general mess, this can actually prevent modules from communicating. Imagine if two modules using DOM were trying to pass an org.w3c.dom.Document between themselves but org.w3c.dom.* was being loaded from two different vendors' implementations (Crimson and Xerces, say). You would get ClassCastExceptions or linkage errors, even though the interfaces are identical.

As a last dig at the entire idea of having multiple versions of a specification flying around inside of JARs that implement the specification, the copy-based approach does not permit easy publishing of a revision to the specification independently of updates to vendor implementations. One needs to use special semantics, such as "this JAR implements such-and-such specification version such-and-such," which the NetBeans Module System has to interpret somehow. It is difficult to believe this practice has been considered sane, much less desirable.

By contrast, a modular library is straightforward in a modular system, and you do not even need any special semantics for "specification" or "implementation." A "specification" is simply a module which exposes some packages with interfaces and a factory or two, and is accompanied by documentation explaining its permissible behavior and how to plug in an implementation. An "implementation" is simply a module without exposed packages which depends on the specification module and registers implementations of the factories using whatever service registration system the specification module documents. A "client" is a module which depends on the specification module and calls the factory methods.

There is a need for some sort of "functional dependency" declaration permitting either the client or the specification to request that at least one implementation be loaded before the specification can be used. The NetBeans Module System uses *provides/requires tokens* (similar to RPM require lists) for this purpose. In contrast to "classpath dependencies," which are specified by depending on some specification version of another module, "functional dependencies" just request a module providing the given functionality to be present. While a dependency on a specification version changes the classpath and directly influences the "linkage"—for example what methods can be called and what fields accessed—a "functional dependency" is much weaker. It does not care about linkage; it just requests a certain functionality to be "present." The meaning of "present" is a bit fuzzy, as there may be multiple ways that the requester of some functionality is really going to use that functionality. The requester might not even link to the functionality directly. We will look at a few techniques for handling dependencies in subsequent chapters.

3.3   Module Lifecycle

In Chapter 2, we saw a NetBeans module as being a JAR file with a slightly enhanced manifest. Indeed, just having a manifest would not be enough to make a useful module—some code is often needed as well. That is why, in order to perform more complex tasks, let us introduce certain classes from the NetBeans *Modules API*.

Dynamic systems built from components have to deal with the possibility of the components being started and shut down—loaded and unloaded—while the rest of the system is running. This is called the component *lifecycle*.

The easiest way to control module lifecycle in NetBeans is to implement a subclass of `org.openide.modules.ModuleInstall` and register it inside the module's manifest file. Or, more simply, just use the **New File** wizard and instantiate the **NetBeans Module Development | Module Installer**, which does everything automatically.

`ModuleInstall` is an abstract class that contains, among others, the following important methods:

`public void restored()`   Is called when an already-installed module is restored (during startup). Should perform whatever initializations are required.

Note that it is possible for module code to be run before this method is called, and that code must be ready nonetheless. For example, data loaders might be asked to recognize a file before the module is "restored." For this reason, but more importantly for general performance reasons, modules should avoid doing anything here that is not strictly necessary—often by moving initialization code into the place where the initialization is actually first required (if ever). This method should serve as a place for tasks that must be run once during every startup, and that cannot reasonably be put elsewhere.

Basic programmatic services are available to the module at this stage. For example, its classloader is ready for general use, any objects registered declaratively in the default lookup (described in Section 4.3) are ready to be queried, and so on.

`public boolean closing()`   Is called when NetBeans is about to exit. The default implementation returns `true`. The module may cancel the exit if it is not prepared to be shut down.

`public void close()`   Is called when all modules agreed with closing and NetBeans will be closed.

To continue with our discussion of coding in a modular way, let us assume that the goal is to create a modular application that handles the validation of various textual formats, for example manifest files. Other types can be validated as well, so the application should allow other modules to extend it with additional validation code. The core of the architecture is a module that allows any module to register its own *validator*. The module will also provide the means for invoking validation on the given source, etc. Then there will be at least one module that provides validation for one or more specific types of files.

The first step is to create a module `org.netbeans.examples.validate` that will contain the class to register and invoke validation programmatically:

```
public interface Validator {
  public boolean supportsMimeType(String mimeType);
  public void validate(InputStream is) throws IOException;
}

package org.netbeans.examples.validate.api;
public final class Validations {
  private Validations() {}
  private static List<Validator> validators =
    new ArrayList<Validator>();
  public static void registerValidator(Validator v) {
    validators.add(v);
  }
  public static void unregisterValidator(Validator v) {
    validators.remove(v);
  }
  public static void validate(String mimeType, InputStream is)
    throws IOException {
    Iterator<Validator> it = validators.iterator();
    while (it.hasNext()) {
      Validator v = it.next();
      if (v.supportsMimeType(mimeType)) {
        v.validate(is);
        return;
      }
    }
    throw new IOException(
              "No validator found for " + mimeType);
  }
}

public interface Validator {
  public boolean supportsMimeType(String mimeType);
  public void validate(InputStream is) throws IOException;
}
```

This is the public part of the *Validator API* module which should be in the public package of the module. Then there can be, for example, an action called when a textual file is selected which invokes its validation. Such action is likely to be in the `org.netbeans.examples.validate` package. This package is not visible externally and other modules cannot refer to it. The actual implementation of the action is not that important at this moment—just imagine that it is using the methods from the Validator API to invoke the validation on a given input stream:

```
public actionPerformed(ActionEvent ev) {

  FileObject fo = findFileObjectFromEvent(ev);
  InputStream is = fo.getInputStream();

  try {
    Validators.validate(fo.getMIMEType(), is);
  } catch (IOException ex) {
    // In 5.5 and older:
    ErrorManager.getDefault().notify(ex);
    // In 6.0 use:
    // org.openide.util.Exceptions.printStackTrace(ex);
  } finally {
    is.close();
  }
}
```

This is all one needs to do when designing an abstract API module that defines some functionality but does nothing without participation from other modules. Now, let's create a module that will plug into the application and validate manifest files. Create the new module `org.netbeans.examples.validate.manifest`. Create a new suite and add both modules to the suite. Then create a dependency on `org.netbeans.examples.validate` as described in Section 1.2.4 and create a new **Module Installer** using the **New File** wizard. This class allows the module to perform some code when the module is initializing as well when it is closing down. So, just write:

```
package org.netbeans.examples.manifestvalidator;

public final class ManifestValidatorInstall
    extends ModuleInstall {

  private static Validator INSTANCE = new ManifestValidator();

  public void restored() {
    Validations.registerValidator(INSTANCE);
  }

  public void close() {
    Validations.unregisterValidator(INSTANCE);
  }
}
```

```
final class ManifestValidator implements Validator {
  public boolean supportsMimeType(String mimeType) {
    return "text/x-manifest".equals(mimeType);
  }

  public void validate(InputStream is) throws IOException {
    // Just try to read the file as manifest:
    Manifest mf = new Manifest(is);
  }
}
```

The overall picture of the expected dependencies is shown in Figure 3.1. One module provides the APIs and other modules can implement them and register themselves as "validators."

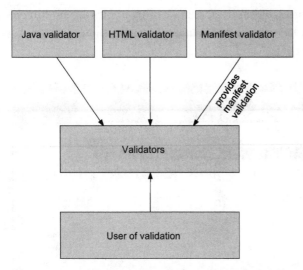

Figure 3.1: Architecture of Validator API and all the service providers that plug into that API

3.4   Groups of Modules

As can be seen from the `Validator` example, sometimes a module cannot operate alone, but rather needs to act in sync with other modules. When one module is activated, a set of modules is enabled. Similarly, when one is disabled, more than one can be disabled as well. In a sense, modules behave in *orchestration*—one guides the state of the others. This is a very important aspect of modules running inside a NetBeans-based application. The way a module is enabled and disabled is determined by the module's *activation type*.

There are three basic types of modules in the NetBeans runtime container—*regular*, *autoload*, and *eager*. Each of these is useful for different module roles. Basically, if a module represents important, user-visible functionality, then it should be a *regular module*. It will act as a *director* of the enablement state of other modules. Regular modules are listed in the platform's **Module Manager** as shown in Figure 3.2, where users can enable or disable them. As an example, start NetBeans IDE, choose **Tools | Module Manager**, and select a module that does not have many dependencies, such as **Data Files | Image**, and disable it. Now browse a `.jpeg`, `.gif`, or `.png` file in the **Projects** window. You will notice that these types of image files are no longer recognized as images and can only be opened as plain text files. Go back to

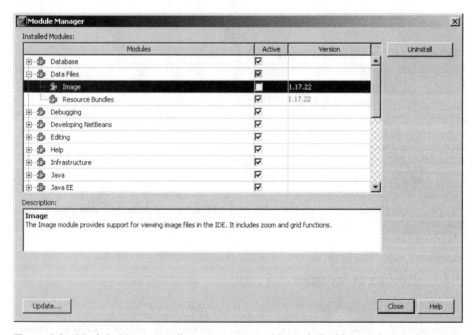

Figure 3.2: **Module Manager** allows users to enable and disable regular modules

Module Manager and reenable the **Image** module. Once again, you can browse image files as images rather than as text.

As a *regular* module, the **Image** module can be enabled or disabled by the user. On the other hand, certain modules should not be controlled by end users at all. For example, modules providing useful libraries should be enabled when some other module needs such a library. It should not be possible to disable a library module via an explicit user action. The *autoload* modules are listed under the node called **Libraries** in the NetBeans IDE 5.5. In some way they are like drums and bass in an orchestra—without them nothing works, but it usually makes little sense to have just drums and bass. For example, notice that in the IDE there is one node called **CVS Client Library**. If you invoke a **Properties** dialog from its popup menu, you can find out that it is used by another regular module called **CVS Versioning System**, as shown in Figure 3.3.

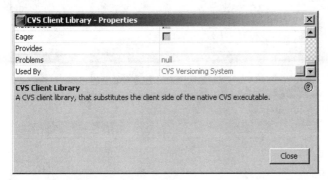

Figure 3.3: Properties of the **CVS Client Library** show that it is used by the **CVS Versioning System** regular module

Let's locate this module (it is under the **Version Control** category) and disable it. The regular module is disabled without any further questions, but that is not all—we can verify under the **Libraries** node that the **CVS Client Library** is now disabled as well. It is easy to verify that enabling the regular module influences the state of the autoload one. This type of module is useful for libraries that provide no user-visible functionality and are only used by other libraries that do.

However, autoload modules are not the only ones that are out of direct control of end users. There are also *eager* modules. In contrast to autoloads, eager modules are enabled as soon as possible—like an eager trumpet in an orchestra that just jumps into a song at the earliest opportunity. All such modules in NetBeans IDE 5.5 are grouped under the **Bridges** node in the **Module Manager**. Like autoload modules, eager modules cannot be disabled directly by the user. As the alternative name "bridges" suggests, this type of modules is often used to bridge functionality between two independent modules. For example the **Internationalization of Form** eager module depends on two regular ones—**Form** and **Internationalization**. If both of these modules are enabled, then it gets automatically enabled as well and connects them together, so that GUI forms can be internationalized. To see this in action, choose either the **Form** module or the **Tools | Internationalization** one

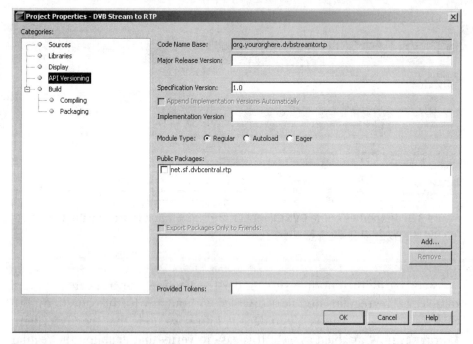

Figure 3.4: Enablement type of a module can be specified in the **Project Properties**

and disable it. Without any additional questions, the system also disables the **Internationalization of Form** bridge, as now its dependencies are not satisfied. As in the previous case, reenabling the disabled regular module also enables the **Internationalization of Form**.

When developing your own modules, you can assign the default activation type in the **Project Properties** dialog, as shown in Figure 3.4.

CHAPTER FOUR

Loosely Coupled Communication

4.1 Registration and Discovery

Chapter 3 included sample code showing you how to create the right architecture for validators. Despite the fact that the example correctly presents the use of various inter-module dependencies of the NetBeans runtime container, it contains a lot of boilerplate code that does nothing except ensure proper communication between the modules. Specifically:

- A significant amount of code in the `Validator` example registers all available validators. There is a hash map that holds all the validators and methods to allow dynamic additions and removals. The rest of the code—the actual code that does the work and looks up the right validator and performs the validation—is in fact in a minority.

- Every module providing the actual implementation of a validator that has to create and register its own subclass of the `ModuleInstall` class and inside its `restored()` and `closed()` methods calls the right registration and deregistration methods. Again, the amount of boilerplate code is large in comparison with the actual result. Moreover, this code has to execute on startup and has to execute always, regardless of whether the application ever searches for a validator or not.

If you study sources of a modular application, including NetBeans IDE, you will find out that this "registration pattern" is very common. Everyone needs to expose the registration mechanism, even code in the Java standard libraries themselves (URLStreamHandler and javax.xml.parsers.* are just two examples). As a result, one has to repeat and copy the similar code over and over again in every place that wants to allow modular registration and perform the lookup among registered objects. This is indeed suboptimal. NetBeans programmers realized this and created a general class that handles all the common actions of the "registration and discovery."

 There are many variants of the registration and discovery style. For example, the java.awt.Toolkit uses the property-based solution. The class Toolkit checks the value of java.awt.Toolkit to instantiate its implementation:

```
public Toolkit getDefaultToolkit() {
  java.awt.Toolkit t = null;
  String classname =
    System.getProperty("java.awt.Toolkit");
  if (classname != null) {
    try {
        Class c = Class.forName(classname);
        t = (java.awt.Toolkit) c.newInstance();
    } catch (Exception ex) {
        System.out.println
          ("Cannot initialize toolkit: " + classname);
        ex.printStackTrace();
    }
  }
  // Fallback
  if (t == null) {
    t = new GenericAWTToolkit();
  }
}
```

This is a bit nicer as the API is not polluted with useless setter and registration methods. However, it needs to properly configure the Java Virtual Machine runtime. You need to initialize the properties at its start or early during execution of the program.

The support that is part of the NetBeans architecture aims at providing a general solution to fit almost everyone's needs. This solution is

- Built on top of existing standards and enhances those standards where necessary.

- Well suited to the dynamic modular environment provided by the NetBeans runtime container.

As a result, the solution is uniformly suitable for registration and discovery of any kind of interface or class. It supports listeners that allow everyone to observe changes in the registered objects—for example, when a module is enabled or disabled. Without additional delay, let's introduce *lookup*.

4.2   MetaInf Services

In version 1.3, the JDK started to use a concept called *service providers*. This concept introduces a completely declarative style of registration, which in fact is based on just the current classpath of a Java virtual machine and nothing else. Since this registration style uses the Java classpath to define those objects that are registered, it is very easy to use. In order to change the set of registered providers, just pick up a JAR file that offers such a provider and include it in your application's classpath. The provider will be immediately accessible to any code that searches for it.

The basic idea is that each JAR file (in NetBeans terminology, each module) that wishes to provide an implementation of some interface, for example `javax.xml.parsers.DocumentBuilderFactory`, can create its own implementation of the interface, say `org.saxon.MyFactory`, and expose it to the system as a *service* by creating a `META-INF/services/javax.xml.parsers.DocumentBuilderFactory` file inside its own JAR file. The file then contains names of the implementation classes, one per line. In this example it would contain one line registering the `saxon` factory: `org.saxon.MyFactory`.

The `DocumentBuilderFactory.newInstance()` method then searches for all `META-INF/services/javax.xml.parsers.DocumentBuilder-Factory` files by using `ClassLoader.getResources("META-INF/services/javax.xml.parsers.DocumentBuilderFactory")`, reads their content, and instantiates the class(es) found there by calling their default constructors. The first implementation of the `DocumentBuilderFactory` is then returned from the `newInstance()` method.

As already mentioned, this style has been in place since JDK 1.3 and is a standard way to deal with service providers. Not only has NetBeans adopted this style, it is also gaining in popularity among other Java developers. As a result, JDK 1.6 has introduced the new utility class `java.util.ServiceLoader`. Using its methods (as shown below), you can easily look up all registered services without writing the "search, read, and instantiate" algorithm described above by hand.

`Iterator<S> iterator()`   Lazily loads the available providers of this loader's service.

`static   <S>   ServiceLoader<S>   load(Class<S>   service, ClassLoader loader)`   Creates a new service loader for the given service type and classloader.

Therefore, in order to implement the `DocumentBuilderFactory.newInstance()` method, you can (beginning with JDK 1.6) simply write:

```
return ServiceLoader.load(DocumentBuilderFactory.class,
                someClassLoader).iterator().next();
```

Using the "service providers" registration pattern is a nice way to achieve *dependency injection* without having to fuss with additional configuration files. The configuration is the classpath!

Some people have complained about the fact that we call the "service providers" pattern a *dependency injection*, because it does not follow the "Hollywood principle"—that is, "don't call us, we'll call you." Yes, it is true that one needs to do an action to obtain the injected resource—for example, call `ServiceLoader.load(...).iterator().next()`. However, the call to `ServiceLoader.load(...)` can also be seen as creating a "slot" that then gets "injected." This is in fact similar to creating a setter or a field and annotating it as a "slot" that should be injected.

As a result, we have decided to call this pattern *dependency injection*, despite its deviation from some strict definitions of the term.

4.3   The Global `Lookup`

`org.openide.util.Lookup` is one of the most fundamental classes in the NetBeans APIs. Given all the fame of the *service provider* pattern and the `java.util.ServiceLoader` class, you might ask why a NetBeans project would want to advertise some other way of doing things. Here are a few reasons why:

- `Lookup` is available in versions for older JDKs, so you can use it as a replacement for `ServiceLoader` when running on JDKs older than 1.6.

- `Lookup` is ready to work inside the NetBeans runtime container. It knows how to discover all the modules in the system, how to read their defined services, etc.

- `Lookup` supports listeners. Client code can attach a listener and observe changes in `Lookup` content. This is a necessary improvement to adapt to the dynamic environment created by the NetBeans runtime container, where modules can be enabled or disabled at runtime, which in turn can affect the set of registered service providers.

- `Lookup` is extensible and replaceable. While the `ServiceLoader` class in JDK 1.6 is a final class with hard-coded behavior, the NetBeans `Lookup` is an extensible class that allows various implementations. This can be useful while writing unit tests. Or, you can write an enhanced version of `Lookup` that not only reads `META-INF/services` but, for example, finds the requested service providers through some other mechanism.

- `Lookup` is a general-purpose abstraction. There can be one instance of the JDK's `ServiceLoader` per classloader. There can be thousands independent `Lookup` instances, each representing a single place to discover and query services and interfaces. In fact, this is exactly the way `Lookup` is used in NetBeans—it represents the "context" of each dialog, window element, node in a tree, etc. However, that is out of the scope of this chapter; this is explained in more detail in Chapter 5.

Just this short list indicates that there is a lot of functionality in the NetBeans `Lookup` implementation that makes it worth using. You do not even need to build for the NetBeans runtime container to take advantage of it. The functionality is available in a standalone JAR file and can be reused in any Java application. Just add the `org-openide-util.jar` file as a library in your application. In release 5.5, the location of the JAR file is `platform6/lib/org-openide-util.jar`. The location in release 6.0 is likely to be similar.

Note that some "syntactic sugar" has been added to `Lookup` in NetBeans 6.0—the NetBeans project has started to use Java generics. As with many other NetBeans APIs, the 6.0 version of the Lookup API is generified and, therefore, is much easier to use than the 5.x version, which required far more class-casts.

Although most of this book is about 5.5, in this "lookup" example, let's use the generic version as it is shorter. Just remember that when the code does the following:

```
URLStreamHandlerFactory found = Lookup.getDefault().
   lookup(URLStreamHandlerFactory.class);
```

in release 5.5, one has to add one more cast to make things work:

```
URLStreamHandlerFactory found =
   (URLStreamHandlerFactory)Lookup.getDefault().
   lookup(URLStreamHandlerFactory.class);
```

Otherwise the code in 5.5 and 6.0 is semantically the same.

Here is a list of important methods in the `Lookup` class in both release 5.5 (without generics) and release 6.0 (with generic interfaces):

`static Lookup getDefault()` Static method to obtain the global `Lookup` in the whole system. This is the `Lookup` instance that knows about all installed modules and their services exported through `META-INF/services` registration. The content of this `Lookup` is updated when new modules are added and when existing ones are disabled or removed.

`<T> T lookup(Class<T> clazz)` The simplest method to look up an instance of a given class. Useful when you need just one instance (e.g., the first one) and do not care about the others. For example, the already mentioned implementation of the `newInstance()` method of `DocumentBuilderFactory` could be rewritten to use this method:

```
return Lookup.getDefault().lookup
       (DocumentBuilderFactory.class);
```

`<T> Lookup.Result<T> lookup(Lookup.Template<T> template)`
> Advanced query method that takes a query template and returns a *result* that can be further queried for `allInstances()` returning an unmodifiable `Collection` containing objects of type `T`. The `Result` also allows you to attach and detach a `LookupListener` and thus observe changes in the value returned from `allInstances()`.

As you can see, `Lookup` offers a rich and user-friendly interface for the JDK's standard `META-INF/services` registration pattern, which works in almost any JDK version. It works well inside NetBeans-based applications, but also can be used as a standalone library for anyone who wants "drag-and-drop into classpath" dependency injection capabilities.

 There are other useful and handy methods in the `Lookup` class. NetBeans 6.0 APIs not only generified the interface, but also added more methods. However, to make the code easily usable with 5.5, we will stick with the methods listed here.

There is a default instance of `Lookup` available from `Lookup.getDefault()`. The default `Lookup` will return objects registered on the classpath in the `META-INF/services` folders of the JARs on the classpath. It offers a few extensions to the standard registration mechanism. It allows natural ordering of multiple registered services (by use of `#position=<natural number;>` as a line immediately following the registered class name) and hiding services provided by other modules (by using `#-<classname_to_hide>`). These defaults provide reasonably powerful behavior to handle all sorts of situations. For more intricate usages, there is a way to replace the default `Lookup` by setting a system property early during startup. there is always a way to use a custom `Lookup` implementation instead of the default one.

4.4   Writing an Extension Point

Now that we have discussed the motivations for an all-purpose registration and lookup pattern, let's now rewrite the Validator example described in the previous chapter:

```
package org.netbeans.examples.validate.api;
import org.openide.util.Lookup;

public final class Validations {
  private Validations() {}

  private static Lookup.Result<Validator> validators =
    Lookup.getDefault().lookup(
      new Lookup.Template<Validator>(Validator.class)
    );
  // Or in 6.0 version just:
  // Lookup.Result<Validator> validators =
  // Lookup.getDefault().lookupResult(Validator.class);

  public static void validate(String mimeType, InputStream is)
  throws IOException {
    for (Validator v : validators.allInstances()) {
      if (v.supportsMimeType(mimeType)) {
        v.validate(is);
        return;
      }
    }
    throw new IOException("No validator found for " + mimeType);
  }
}

public interface Validator {
  public boolean supportsMimeType(String mimeType);
  public void validate(InputStream is) throws IOException;
}
```

Instead of having the homegrown hash map and registerValidator() and unregisterValidator() methods, this example relies on the implementation of Lookup.getDefault() and its means for registration. Since that follows the JDK's declarative standard for the registration of service providers, the public interface of the Validations class is limited to just the validate() method. That is a great simplification for all the providers of the various Validator implementations.

When writing the "manifest validator," for example, you no longer need to know anything about `ModuleInstall` or call methods during initialization and deinitialization of the module. Instead, you just need to declare that the `ManifestValidator` provides an implementation of the `Validator` interface:

```
package org.netbeans.examples.manifestvalidator;
public final class ManifestValidator implements Validator {
  public boolean supportsMimeType(String mimeType) {
    return "text/x-manifest".equals(mimeType);
  }

  public void validate(InputStream is) throws IOException {
    // Just try to read the file as manifest:
    Manifest mf = new Manifest(is);
  }
}
```

As you can see, the code for the `ManifestValidator` is exactly the same as in the previous version of the example. The only additional thing to do is to create `META-INF/services/org.netbeans.examples.validate.api.Validator` and add to it the following line:

```
org.netbeans.examples.manifestvalidator.ManifestValidator
```

With a module (or even a plain JAR file, if executed outside of the NetBeans runtime container) containing just the `Validator` implementation and its declarative registration, you can fully rely on the behavior of `Lookup.getDefault()` and be assured that the validator is automatically registered when the module is enabled (or when the JAR is put on the application classpath). Now, isn't that a nice simplification?

CHAPTER FIVE

Lookup

The `Lookup` class, which we introduced in Chapter 4, is used for much more than just dependency injection. In NetBeans-based applications, it is used for other purposes as well. All of these involve *decoupling*. This chapter will introduce some of the other ways `Lookup` is used in the NetBeans APIs.

The basic usage pattern remains the same for any `Lookup` instance, as shown in Example 5.1.

Example 5.1: Using `Lookup`

```
Foo foo = someLookup.lookup ( Foo.class );
```

The code in Example 5.1 asks a `Lookup` for an instance of `Foo`. If there is at least one `Foo` in the `Lookup`, it will be returned; otherwise `null` will be returned.

`Lookup` is used pervasively in NetBeans. One way to think of a `Lookup` is as a `Map` where the keys are `Class` objects and the value for each key is an instance of that class. `Lookup` is a typesafe way of asking for an instance of some known interface. It is used for a number of things in NetBeans:

Expressing an object's capabilities One way of doing decoupling is to get an object that another module's code created and try to cast it to a specific type. A common pattern in NetBeans, instead, is to have the object the other module created implement `Lookup.Provider` (an interface with a single method, `public Lookup getLookup()`) and ask that `Lookup` for objects your code wants to work with. Your code asks the object if it has an instance of some known interface. This approach turns *is-a* relationships into *has-a* relationships. If you want to save an object representing a file, you do not test if that object implements a `Saveable` interface; rather, you ask if it *has* an instance of `SaveCookie` (which has one method, `save()`). This approach is much more flexible than trying to implement all the capabilities of an object by having it implement additional interfaces. In particular, the capabilities of an object may change over time, but its Java type cannot. So, instead of having, for example, a `canSave()` method, when a file does not need saving, it simply does not have a `SaveCookie` available.

Dependency injection and decoupling   One module defines some interfaces. Another one implements them. The first module can use `Lookup.getDefault()`—the global lookup—to find the implementation(s) of an interface it defines, as described in Chapter 4.

Dynamic service discovery   The *default lookup* is a place where modules can very simply inject objects that should be global services or pseudosingletons, as described in Section 4.3.

Singletons

The *singleton pattern* is a design pattern for creating an object of which there should always be only one instance. There are many ways to do this in Java, the simplest being to have a factory method and a private constructor, and to cache the singleton instance and return it from all calls to the factory method.

The singleton pattern has a number of uses in NetBeans programming. Typically, it is used for *global services* which would make no sense as multiple instances. For example, there is an interface called `StatusDisplayer` which lets any module set the text on the statusbar in the main window of the application. There is only one statusbar, so it makes sense that there is only one instance of `StatusDisplayer`. The implementation of the Window System's APIs which you do not call directly—the module `org.netbeans.core.windows`, hereafter

> referred to as `core/windows` (its path in CVS)—injects its imple-
> mentation of `StatusDisplayer` by placing it in the default lookup.
> The code that wants to write to the statusbar simply calls
> `StatusDisplayer.getDefault().setStatusText("Something")`.
>
> The downside to using a factory method and caching a singleton in-
> stance of a service in a static field is that the instance of the singleton may
> remain unused for a long time—but it will be permanently retained in
> memory. There are various strategies to work around this problem using
> `WeakReference`, `SoftReference`, and so forth, all of which mean
> writing more code. Using the default lookup, it is easy to create a global
> singleton which can nonetheless be garbage-collected and reconstituted
> on demand. If a previously created instance is garbage-collected and later
> a new one is created on demand, then, if the objects are identical, they
> might as well be the same object.

Two other common uses of the Lookup API are important to know
(Example 5.2).[1]

Example 5.2: Finding multiple objects of the same type in a `Lookup`

```
Lookup.Template template = new Lookup.Template (Foo.class);
Lookup.Result foos = someLookup.lookup (template);
Collection c = foos.allInstances();
```

In Example 5.2 it is clear that there can be more than one instance of a
given type in a `Lookup`, and it is possible to get a collection of those objects.

The third usage pattern is one of the most important. A `Lookup` is not a
static thing—its contents can change over time. So, there is another thing we
can do with this code, as shown in Example 5.3 (when developing for
NetBeans 5.x, you will need to remove the generic types and add casts where
appropriate).

---

1. Some convenience methods have been added to `Lookup` in NetBeans 6. There, this
code can be written much more simply as `Collection <? extends Foo> c =
someLookup.lookupAll (Foo.class)`. Also, in NetBeans 6, `Lookup.Template`,
`Lookup.Result`, and `Lookup.Result.allInstances()` all have generic types, so
the code for using them becomes much simpler.

Example 5.3: Listening for changes in a `Lookup`

```
class RegistryOfFoos {
  private final Lookup.Result <? extends Foo> foos;
  private final MyLookupListener listener;
  RegistryOfFoos(Lookup someLookup) {
    Lookup.Template <Foo> template =
      new Lookup.Template ( Foo.class );
    foos = someLookup.lookup ( template );
    listener = new MyLookupListener();
    foos.addLookupListener ( listener );
    foos.allItems(); // Needs to be called once to activate the
                     // Lookup.Result
  }

  private static class MyLookupListener
                      implements LookupListener {
    public void resultChanged (LookupEvent e) {
      Collection <? extends Foo> c = foos.allInstances();
      // Do something with it here
    }
  }
}
```

`allItems()` **or** `allInstances()`

You might have noticed that Example 5.3 refers to `Lookup.Result.allItems()` while other places refer to `Lookup.Result.allInstances()`. What is the difference?

`allInstances()` forces instantiation of all objects that match the query that produced the `Lookup.Result`. In some cases, it is enough to know how many matches there are to a query, or if there are any at all. For example, to decide whether an action should be enabled, the objects that are the result of the query may not be needed immediately (they will be needed if the action is *invoked*.

There are ways of registering objects in a `Lookup` declaratively—for example, `.settings` files (as discussed in Section 6.6.3) which provide enough information that a `Lookup` over such files can know if it has an object of a particular type without actually having to create the object.

> Use `Lookup.Result.allItems()` when you just need to know if there are any matches to a query of a `Lookup`; use `allInstances()` when you will actually need to call the objects returned by the query.

There are two things to note in Example 5.3. First, a strong reference to the result object is kept. A common mistake is to create and add the listener but keep no reference to the `Lookup.Result`. A `Lookup` does not keep a reference to `Lookup.Result` objects it creates—so if your code does not keep a reference to it either, the object will be garbage-collected immediately and no events will ever be fired. Second, note the call to `allItems()`. A `Lookup.Result` will not fire changes until it has been asked at least once for its contents.

5.1   Objects That Own Lookups

There are a number of classes in NetBeans' more basic APIs which have a method `getLookup()` (they implement `Lookup.Provider`). Three prominent ones are:

`Project`   From the Projects API. A project is little more than an object which ties together a directory and a `Lookup`. The Projects API defines some classes that may optionally be in a the `Lookup` of an instance of `Project`. Various modules implement `Project` and provide their implementations of these interfaces. Other APIs can define other classes that may also appear there. For example, the Java Projects API defines an interface called `ClassPathProvider`, which can be found in the `Lookup` of Java source projects—yet the general contract of the Projects API is in no way tied to Java-language projects. The entirety of the `Project` class is:

```
public interface Project extends Lookup.Provider {
  FileObject getProjectDirectory();
  Lookup getLookup();
}
```

Various interfaces that can be requested from a `Project`'s `Lookup` are defined in the Projects API. For example, `ProjectInformation` is an object that can provide basic information such as the display name of the `Project`. Other APIs, such as the Java Projects API, define additional interfaces. So, module code interacts with `Projects` by requesting various objects from the `Project`'s `Lookup`.

The result of this indirection is that the Projects API is clean and small; it defines what a project *is* without having to define every possible thing that implementations of `Project` will ever need.

`TopComponent`   A `TopComponent` is a GUI panel with hooks to allow the NetBeans Window System to manage it. Someone who implements a `TopComponent` subclass can provide objects to the rest of the system to indicate selection in the component via the `Lookup` returned by `TopComponent.getLookup()`.

`Node`   `Node`s are generic tree-node-like objects that represent an underlying data model. For example, the trees of files and folders in the **Projects** and **Files** windows of the IDE are trees of `Node`s. `org.openide.nodes.Node` also has a `getLookup()` method.

Objects that own a `Lookup` typically use it to expose *capabilities*. A more naive approach to publishing objects' capabilities for other code to invoke would use the Java type system directly—for example, to save a file you would do something like:

```
public void actionPerformed (ActionEvent e) {
  Object o = something.getSelection();
  if (o instanceof Saveable && ((Saveable) o).canSave()) {
    ((Saveable) o).save();
  }
}
```

However, this approach is far less powerful. Java objects cannot change their type on the fly—but it is perfectly reasonable for the set of capabilities of an object representing, say, a file on disk to change on the fly. For example, there are some things you can do to a Java class file that you cannot do only with the source. But a source does not always have a corresponding class file. The fact that a `Lookup`'s contents can change means that an object representing a Java source's corresponding class file can be made available when the class file is created by running the compiler, and thrown away if the class file is deleted. So our pseudocode above would look like this, using the `Lookup` approach:

```
public void actionPerformed (ActionEvent e) {
  Lookup lkp = Utilities.actionsGlobalContext();
  SaveCookie save = lkp.lookup (SaveCookie.class);
  if (save != null) {
    save.save();
  }
}
```

What is actually happening when a file is being edited and saved in Net-Beans is this: A `SaveCookie` appears in the `Lookup` of the `Node` for that file. The code that would save the file does not need to know what the call to its `save()` method will do. It only needs to know that a `SaveCookie` is present.

5.2   Lookup **as a Communication Mechanism**

The example of the Projects API in the previous section is particularly interesting. It is a case of a provider API, also known as a *Service Provider Interface* (SPI). Different modules plug in different *project types* by installing instances of `ProjectFactory` in the default lookup. You can see these in the different choices offered by the **New Project** wizard in the IDE. So there are many implementations of the `Project` class in the IDE.

Any situation where you are plugging in an implementation of some functionality is where private contracts can be useful. Some implementations of the functionality may offer features that other implementations do not. Clients of the API (for example, imagine an `Action` that can operate on a Java project) will want to take advantage of functionality only offered by Java projects. A project's `Lookup` is a clean way for some project implementations to provide their own functionality and capabilities without the `Project` class having to have methods that would be meaningless for some kinds of projects.[2]

Imagine we are writing an image editor similar to Photoshop or Gimp. We would have an interface for the individually editable layers that are stacked together to make up the image being edited. We would also have an interface

---

2. For example, this book is being written using a module that provides support for DocBook XML projects. It would be annoying and wrong if such a project had to have a `getClassPath()` method, since classpaths are meaningless for a project whose goal is to create a book, not write Java software.

for tools that operate on the image's layers to draw lines or shapes. We would want the implementation of layers to be pluggable, so it's possible to have raster (bitmap) layers, vector layers, text layers, etc. Thus, new modules can provide new kinds of layers without requiring a rewrite of existing modules. It is nearly guaranteed that some tools will only be able to do something useful to some kinds of layers. If our layer interface includes a `getLookup()` method, it is no problem for tools to query a given layer object and decide if they should be enabled or not. If some interfaces available from tools turn out to be consistently useful, they can eventually be added into the official API. So in this way, not only do we have a clean way to have private contracts between components of the system, but we have an API which is designed with room to grow. The API can be evolved to add functionality without breaking backward compatibility.

Example 5.4 sketches some interfaces that our hypothetical paint program would use to allow a drawing tool to draw in an image. There would probably be a factory for `Layer` objects that will allow modules to plug in their own implementations of `Layer` by providing their own `LayerFactory`. However, as currently written, they make some assumptions that are not necessarily true. One of them is that all possible implementations of `Layer` will provide a `Graphics2D` object to draw into. A `Layer` implementation that, say, allows for text input might simply save the text, font, colors, and position of the text it should draw. There would not be a backing pixel bitmap. But right now, our API assumes there always is one.

Example 5.4: Minimal painting tool interface

```
/** Minimal painting tool interface. One can imagine a Tool might
 * implement MouseListener or MouseMotionListener to paint.
 */
public interface Tool {
  public boolean canAttach (Layer layer);
  public void attach (Layer layer);
  ...
}
public interface Layer {
  public java.awt.Graphics2D getGraphics();
  ...
}
```

A bit of refactoring allows us to improve these interfaces, as seen in Example 5.5.

Example 5.5: Improved painting tool interface

```
/** Minimal painting tool interface.
 *  One can imagine a Tool that implements
 *  MouseListener or MouseMotionListener to paint.
 */

public interface Tool {
  public boolean canAttach (Layer layer);
  public void attach (Layer layer);
  ...

}

public interface Layer extends Lookup.Provider {
  /** Some implementations will contain an instance
   *  of RasterSurface
   */
  public Lookup getLookup(); // Actually specified in
                             // Lookup.Provider
  ...

}

public interface RasterSurface {
  // Some layer types may include a RasterSurface object
  // in their Lookup

  public Graphics2D getGraphics();
}
```

What we have done here is factored out the assumption that there will be a Graphics2D object into a separate interface. That interface may or may not really be provided by a Layer object. A Tool that could be used against a raster layer (one with an underlying buffer of pixel data, for example, a BufferedImage), such as a tool for drawing lines or rectangles, can implement canAttach(), as shown in Example 5.6.

Example 5.6: Using `Lookup` to decouple implementation and API

```
public class MyTool implements Tool, MouseListener,
                                  MouseMotionListener {
  public boolean canAttach (Layer layer) {
    return layer.getLookup().lookup
      (RasterSurface.class) != null;
  }
  ...
}
```

Most importantly, we've coded this API in such a way that it has room to grow *without breaking backward compatibility*. As new kinds of layers are added, tools that work with them can also be added, yet they are not required to be so tightly coupled that you can only write a new `Tool` if you're also implementing the `Layer` it applies to.

Of course it is necessary to keep a sense of proportion in using `Lookup` for this sort of thing. A `Lookup` is a bit like a "magic bag of stuff." If all APIs were magic bags of stuff containing other magic bags of stuff, the result would be hard to understand and use. `Lookup` should be used to keep APIs clear and focused on solving a single problem. As a case in point, our Layer API example does not need to "save the world" anymore. It does not need to cover every possible thing that every `Layer` implementation will ever want to do.[3]

5.3   Lookup**s and Proxying**

Part of the power of `Lookup` comes from its available implementations—simply being able to pass a class and get an object is not too exciting in itself. For example, `ProxyLookup` allows you to merge two lookups into one and even change, on the fly, which underlying `Lookups` it is proxying. The code in Example 5.7 illustrates the simplest possible example of proxying.

---

3. Readers interested in further exploring this approach to decoupled design in practice, as applied to image editors, may find the Imagine project (`http://imagine.dev.java.net`) of interest.

Example 5.7: Using `ProxyLookup` to merge two `Lookups`

```
Lookup first = Lookups.singleton ("hello");
Lookup second = Lookups.singleton (new Integer(1));
ProxyLookup merge = new ProxyLookup (first, second);

// Note: In NB 6 this can be written simply as
// merge.lookupAll (Integer.class)
Collection <Integer> ints = merge.lookup(new
  Lookup.Template(Integer.class)).allInstances();
assert ints.contains (new Integer (1));

Collection <String> strings = merge.lookup(new
  Lookup.Template(String.class)).allInstances();
assert strings.contains ("hello");
```

So, composing additional objects into a `Lookup`, alongside objects from another `Lookup`, is easy:

```
public FooNode(Node original, APIObject ob) {
  super (original, Children.LEAF, new ProxyLookup(
    original.getLookup(), Lookups.singleton(ob)));
}
```

For a practical example of using this approach, see Section 15.5.1.

A more ambitious example would be to combine an existing `Lookup` and another one which can be dynamically altered. For this, an implementation of `Lookup` from the NetBeans APIs, `AbstractLookup`, is useful (despite its name, it is not an abstract class). An `AbstractLookup` is a `Lookup` whose contents you can change. Its constructor takes an `InstanceContent`. `InstanceContent` is similar to a `Collection`. It represents the content of an `AbstractLookup`. You can call `add()`, `set()`, and other collection-like methods on the `InstanceContent` and the contents of the `Lookup` will change (in a thread-safe, reentrancy-safe way). As Example 5.8 shows, compositing an existing `Lookup` with the one you control is easy.

Example 5.8: `ProxyLookup`s propagate changes from the `Lookup`s they proxy

```
class L implements LookupListener {
  boolean changed = false;
  public void resultChanged(LookupEvent e) {
    changed = true;
  }
};

Lookup one = Lookups.fixed ("some", "random", "stuff");

InstanceContent dynamicContent = new InstanceContent();

Lookup two = new AbstractLookup (dynamicContent);

ProxyLookup master = new ProxyLookup (one, two);

L listener = new L();
Lookup.Result <String> res =
  master.lookup (new Lookup.Template(String.class));
res.addLookupListener(listener);
res.allInstances();

dynamicContent.add("A new string");

// The following assertions will be true

assert listener.changed;
assert result.allInstances().contains ("A new string");
```

Example 5.9 shows a `Node` subclass which proxies another `Node` and adds an additional object into its own `Lookup`.

Finally, on occasion it is useful to have a `Lookup` which proxies another `Lookup` and can change what `Lookup` it is proxying on the fly, as Example 5.10 shows.

Example 5.9: Using `ProxyLookup` in `Node` subclasses

```
public class FooNode extends FilterNode {
  private final InstanceContent content;
  public FooNode (Node original, APIObject ob) {
    this (original, ob, new InstanceContent);
  }

  public FooNode(Node original,
                APIObject ob, InstanceContent content) {
    super (original, Children.LEAF,
          new ProxyLookup(original.getLookup(),
    new AbstractLookup (content));
    this.content = content;
    content.set (Collections.singleton (ob));
  }
}
```

Example 5.10: Changing the set of proxied `Lookup`s on the fly

```
public class TestIt {
  public static void main (String[] ignored) {
    class L implements LookupListener {
      boolean changed = false;
      public void resultChanged(LookupEvent e) {
        changed = true;
      }
    };

    Lookup first = Lookups.fixed ("some", "random", "stuff");

    MyProxyLookup master = new MyProxyLookup (first);

    L listener = new L();
    Lookup.Result <String> res =
      master.lookup (new Lookup.Template(String.class));
    res.addLookupListener(listener);
    res.allInstances();
    Lookup second = Lookups.fixed ("more", "things");

    master.setOtherLookup (second);
    assert listener.changed;
  }
```

```
private static class MyProxyLookup extends ProxyLookup {
  MyProxyLookup (Lookup first) {
    super (first);
  }
  void setOtherLookup (Lookup other) {
    assert other != this;
    setLookups (other);
  }
}
}
```

5.4   Lookup **and Selection**

The mechanisms just discussed are part of how selection works in NetBeans. We've mentioned that TopComponent is a panel component which can be managed by the NetBeans Window System. Every component you see in a tab in the main window is an instance of TopComponent. A TopComponent panel is created and opened in a particular area of the in the main window, such as the editor area or the output window area. Its open() method will cause it to become visible in a tab in the main window.

TopComponent also has a getLookup() method. TopComponent implements Lookup.Provider. You have probably noticed that toolbar buttons in the IDE enable and disable themselves depending on what component has focus or what is selected in a tree view. Lookup is one of the things that makes this possible. There is a Lookup available from the static utility method Utilities.actionsGlobalContext(). It proxies the Lookup of whatever TopComponent has keyboard focus. Code such as an Action which should be conditionally enabled can simply listen for whatever object it is interested in by getting a Lookup.Result from Utilities.actionsGlobalContext() and listening to that. Such code does not have to keep track of which tabs are open and which one has focus—it does not have to care that there even is such a thing as a windowing system. It can simply pay attention to the contents of Utilities.actionsGlobalContext(). As the user changes keyboard focus between components in the main window, it will fire the appropriate events, and the action can enable or disable itself as needed.

When invoked, it can get the objects it needs to operate on from the
`Utilities.actionsGlobalContext()` Lookup.

5.5   Writing Lookup-Sensitive Actions

`Utilities.actionsGlobalContext()` enables us to write context-sensitive
actions very easily—they do not even need to be in the same module as the
thing they will operate on. Example 5.11 is a simple action that will save
the current file if it needs saving.[4]

Example 5.11: Saving the current file

```
public class SimpleSaveAction extends AbstractAction implements
    ContextAwareAction, LookupListener  {
  private final Lookup lkp;
  private final Lookup.Result <SaveCookie> result;
  public SimpleSaveAction() {
    this (Utilities.actionsGlobalContext());
  }

  private SimpleSaveAction (Lookup lkp) {
    this.lkp = lkp;
    result = lkp.lookup(new Lookup.Template(SaveCookie.class));
    result.addLookupListener(this);
    resultChanged (null);
  }

  public void actionPerformed(ActionEvent e) {
    for (SaveCookie ck : result.allInstances()) {
      try {
          ck.save();
      } catch (IOException ex) {
          java.util.logging.ErrorManager.getDefault().notify(ex);
      }
    }
  }
}
```

---

4. Note that the Action template in NetBeans 5.5 will produce somewhat different code,
based on the older `CookieAction` base class. The effect is the same and implementing
`ContextAwareAction` is a more current approach.

```
public Action createContextAwareInstance(Lookup lkp) {
  return new SimpleSaveAction (lkp);
}
public void resultChanged(LookupEvent e) {
  super.setEnabled(result.allInstances().size() > 0);
}
}
```

The key here is the method `createContextAwareInstance()`. This enables the system that actually creates the popup menu you see on the screen to create an instance of the action that is specifically tied to the object that was right-clicked (i.e., if focus or selection changes without the popup menu being closed, it would not be good for the menu to operate on the wrong object).

5.6   Tracking the Global Selection

Seeing the global selection `Lookup` in action helps to clarify what is really happening. In this example, we will create a simple NetBeans module which just tracks the changes in the global selection and writes the result to the console.

Create a new standalone NetBeans module. Right-click the generated package and choose **New | File/Folder**. Under the **NetBeans Module Development** category, choose **Module Installer** and complete the wizard. This will generate a class with some code that will run during startup. Implement that class as follows:

```
public class Installer extends
    ModuleInstall implements LookupListener {
  private Lookup.Result <Object> result = null;
  public void restored() {
    EventQueue.invokeLater (this);
  }

  public void run() {
    result = Utilities.actionsGlobalContext().lookup(
      new Lookup.Template(Object.class));
    result.addLookupListener(this);
    result.allInstances();
  }
```

```
public void resultChanged(LookupEvent e) {
  Lookup.Result result = (Lookup.Result) e.getSource();
  System.out.println
    ("\n------------------------------------------------");
  System.out.println(result.allInstances());
  }
}
```

Note that it is quite unusual to query a `Lookup` with `Object.class`. One of the purposes of `Lookup` is to defer loading and object creation until a particular type is really requested. Passing `Object.class` will force the instantiation of everything that could possibly be in the `Lookup`. But it does make a clear example of how `Utilities.actionsGlobalContext()` works.

Run the newly created module, so another copy of NetBeans IDE starts and loads it. Text will appear in the **Output** window of the initial instance of the IDE, when you move keyboard focus between tabs in the main window of the second one. In the case of tree or list controls such as the **Runtime** or **Project** tabs, you will also see text output when you change the selection in the tree. In that case, the `TopComponent` that shows the tree of `Nodes` is alternately proxying the `Lookup` of whichever `Node` is selected. Try switching to the **Runtime** tab, and notice the list of objects possessed by different nodes there. Also note that if you open a Java file, the selection is actually changing when you move the caret into the text of a different method.

5.7   Legacy Variants of the Lookup Pattern in NetBeans APIs

There have been variants of the lookup pattern (pass a class object, get back one or more instances of that class) in NetBeans APIs for years, so you may encounter it outside of the context of `Lookup` per se. Two of these are worth mentioning:

`Node.getCookie(Class)` **and** `DataObject.getCookie(Class)`   This is the immediate precursor to `Lookup`. The main difference is that anything returned by it must implement the marker interface `Node.Cookie`. `Node` has a `getCookie()` method, as does `DataObject`. Where possible, use `Node.getLookup().lookup()` instead of `Node.getCookie()`—it will return the same objects, with the exception that `getCookie()` cannot return things that are not instances of `Node.Cookie`.

In NetBeans 5.5, there is no equivalent `getLookup()` method on `DataObject`, so one must either use `DataObject.getCookie()` or `DataObject.getNodeDelegate().getLookup().lookup()`, the latter being a bit verbose. In NetBeans 6 and up, there exists `DataObject.getLookup()` which should be preferred.

`SystemAction.get (Class c)`   This is an older example of the singleton pattern in NetBeans APIs, as applied to `Action` objects.

5.8   Common Lookup Patterns

To summarize, below are a number of common patterns for using `Lookup` in NetBeans. You will encounter them when writing modules:

Subclassing `Node` **or** `DataNode`   This is done to implement support for viewing or editing a new file type. Probably you will want to provide some object that represents the file's contents and can be manipulated programmatically. For example, if you are providing support for reading and editing `.properties` files, you might put an actual `java.util.Properties` object into the `Lookup` belonging to the `Node` that represents that file. Other modules or parts of the UI can simply query for instances of `Properties` and do something if one is found. Thus, your `.properties` support module could be replaced with a completely different implementation and any actions or UI components that were written to work with `Properties` objects in the current selection will continue to work unchanged.

Asking a `Project` **for objects from its** `Lookup`   `Projects` typically have instances of a number of common API classes in their `Lookups`. For example, `ProjectInformation` is a class which can provide the icon and display name of that `Project`.

Extending `TopComponent`   Sometimes you may need to compose objects, such as a `SaveCookie` or a `Node` selected from a tree component, into your `TopComponent`'s `Lookup`, so that standard actions like **Save** will work when your component has focus.

Writing any sort of master/detail view   The Nodes and Explorer APIs make it very convenient to write master/detail views, with one component showing a list or a tree of objects and another showing the details of the selected one. A natural and convenient way to implement such things is by using the Nodes API and the global selection. So, the detail view typically listens for changes in the presence or absence of the type of object it edits, while the master view controls the selection. For an example of this, see Section 9.2.3.

CHAPTER SIX

Filesystems

From deep in the mists of time, up through NetBeans 3.6, the NetBeans IDE had a way of assembling the classpath for your project by *mounting filesystems* (think UNIX mount points). You assembled your classpath by aggregating together a pile of directories (see Figure 6.1).

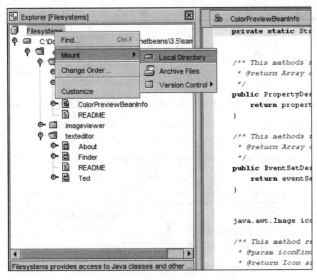

Figure 6.1: Mounting filesystems in NetBeans 3.5.1

That style of UI was changed in 4.0, but the *Filesystems API* which made it possible is still used considerably under the hood. The Filesystems API allows NetBeans code to treat things that are not files in the `java.io.File` sense (such as entries in a JAR or ZIP file) as files, so the same code can work with resources stored in any kind of file-like storage.

6.1   `FileSystem`s and `FileObject`s

A `FileSystem` is a hierarchy of folders and files, much like the filesystems on the disk in your computer. A `FileSystem` has a *root folder* which may contain files and folders, those folders may contain other folders, and so forth (Figure 6.2). The Filesystems API defines NetBeans filesystems.

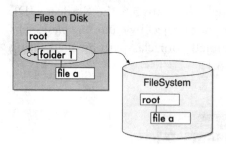

Figure 6.2: A filesystem

You may be wondering why NetBeans would need its own conception of files—isn't `java.io.File` good enough? NetBeans `Filesystems` are *virtual* filesystems. They can, but do not have to, represent files on disk. `Filesystems` are the reason you can, in the NetBeans IDE, expand a JAR file and open files within that JAR file just as if they were plain files on disk. There is a `JARFilesystem` that handles things inside JAR files. So if you're working with NetBeans `Filesystems`, your code simply deals with `org.openide.filesystems.FileObjects` (NetBeans equivalent to `java.io.File`). It is completely transparent to your code whether the file is on the local disk, in a JAR or a database, or on an FTP server somewhere—or perhaps not existing as a file anywhere at all: A "file" could be (and often will be) an element in an XML file somewhere.

`FileObjects` in NetBeans are rather like `java.io.Files`. Here are the ways in which they differ:

1. You get `FileObjects` from a `FileSystem`, you don't construct them. A `FileObject` should always really exist on disk or in whatever backing storage its `FileSystem` uses. The one exception is if you have a `FileObject` which has just been deleted (you can check this with `FileObject.isValid()`). You will never have a not-yet-created `FileObject` as you can with `new File ("foo/bar")`.

2. `FileObjects` have MIME types. The content type of a `FileObject` is knowable from the `FileObject` itself.

3. `FileObjects` have *attributes*. Attributes are ad-hoc key/value pairs. The keys are strings, the values can be any Java type. These are useful for associating additional metadata with a `FileObject`—for example, the path to the icon that should be used to represent it, so the file does not need to be read in order to show it in some piece of UI.[1]

4. `FileObjects` have their own input and output streams—you do not create an input stream for a `FileObject`; it is provided via the `getInputStream()` method of `FileObject`.

5. You can listen for changes on a `FileObject`. Those changes include deletion, modification, and creation or deletion of child files of a folder.

6.2 What Kinds of `FileSystem`s Will I Be Dealing With?

What kinds of `FileSystem`s are you likely to encounter while writing NetBeans modules? The first answer is, *it doesn't matter*. Typically there are only two kinds of `FileSystem`s you will deal with: The *System Filesystem*, which

---

1. Since NetBeans 4.0, adding or using `FileObject` attributes on `FileObjects` representing actual files on the user's disk is discouraged for performance reasons. But they are still quite useful in the configuration data declared in XML layer files as part of the *System Filesystem*.

we will discuss in a moment . . . and everything else—that is, you are dealing with the users' files on disk, which might be in JARs, or raw files on disk, or whatever. Your code will care about the content and meaning of the files, not how or where they are stored.

Something that occasionally confuses people is the fact that FileSystems are used for two distinct purposes in NetBeans: configuration data (the System Filesystem) and the user's data on disk. While that notion may take a moment to digest, the result is quite powerful: The same code that would display in the UI, say, a tree of files on the user's hard drive, can also be used to display a tree of configuration files, where the "files" in this case represent objects provided by your module that the user should select from or interact with in some way.

6.3   Layering

It is a predictable bit of engineering cleverness that once you have an interface representing some named data store:

```
public interface RegistryOfThings {
  public Thing getThing (String name);
}
```

someone will come along and create an implementation of that store which merges together a group of other stores:

```
public final class MetaRegistryOfThings {
  private final RegistryOfThings[] toProxy;
  public MetaRegistryOfThings (RegistryOfThings[] toProxy) {
    this.toProxy = toProxy;
  }

  public Thing getThing(String name) {
    for (int i=0; i < toProxy.length; i++) {
      Thing thing = toProxy[i].getThing ( name );
      if (thing != null) return thing;
    }
    return null;
  }
}
```

So it is with `FileSystems` as well. Though you will probably never use it directly, there is a class called `MultiFileSystem` that allows an individual `FileSystem` to act as a proxy for a multitude of other `FileSystems` (Figure 6.3).

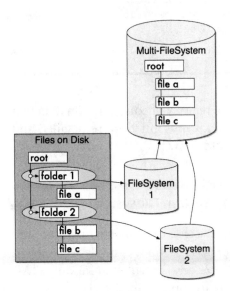

Figure 6.3: Layered filesystems

This and one other piece fit together to make up that registry of configuration data we have mentioned once already, the System Filesystem.

6.4 XML Filesystems

The NetBeans Platform also contains an implementation of the `FileSystem` interface over an XML file. The notation is about what one would expect, given the requirements of filesystems listed above, as shown in Example 6.1.

XML filesystems in and of themselves are not too exciting, and you will probably never touch the `XMLFileSystem` class directly in your code. But a combination of `MultiFileSystem` and `XMLFileSystem` is what makes up

Example 6.1: XML filesystems

```
<filesystem>
  <folder name="SomeFolder>
    <file name="SomeTextFile.txt"
          url="file:///path/to/file/on/disk.txt">
      <attr name="SomeKey" stringvalue="SomeValue"/>
    </file>
  </folder>
</filesystem>
```

the System Filesystem, which is the general registry of configuration data that allows modules to declaratively install things in a much more detailed and nuanced way than the default Lookup could allow.

6.5   Declarative Registration II: The System Filesystem

In Section 4.3 we discussed the declarative registration mechanism that the default Lookup provides. The default Lookup is useful for simple registration of objects—you put some files in META-INF/services in your module's JAR file, and the default Lookup can instantiate the objects they declare.

However, such simple registration is not always enough. Sometimes you will want to associate additional metadata with an object, such as what it is used for, or to be able to show some objects in a UI without necessarily instantiating them until some method on the object needs to be invoked. If you have an icon and a localized display name for an object—and these can be specified as file attributes—you can show it in a tree or a list, even if the actual object has not been instantiated.

Also, sometimes what you want to register is just some textual data, which doesn't really map to a particular Java type. While you could put an instance of java.lang.String in the default Lookup, so could anyone else, and you'd still have the problem of sifting through the Strings you found there to do anything useful. The metaphor of a hierarchy of folders and files on disk is a much more appropriate form of storage for such data since different places (folders) can be created for different types of things.

The System Filesystem provides a more advanced mechanism than the default `Lookup` for registering any kind of data. As you will see, it can still be a registry of Java objects if Java objects are what you need; but it does not have to be. Folders in the System Filesystem are extension points which modules can define and document; other modules can then add content to them. As you will see in Chapter 7, the path to various files can have semantic meaning to code that is looking for objects other modules have installed in the System Filesystem.

6.5.1   How the System Filesystem Works

Each module that wants to contribute some files or objects to the System Filesystem may do so very simply. The module should define an *XML layer*—a file containing an XML fragment like the one in Example 6.1. Also, the module should provide a pointer to that file in its JAR manifest:

```
OpenIDE-Module-Layer: com/foo/path/to/layer.xml
```

If you create your modules from the **Module Project** template in NetBeans IDE, the module's XML layer file is automatically created for you—in the base package of the module there will be a file called `layer.xml`. Many of the template wizards that create `Actions` and other NetBeans-specific classes will modify the layer file to include registration information for the thing the wizard creates.

What is happening at runtime is this: The system merges all the layer files from all the modules in the system that provide them, building a big merged filesystem out of the little XML filesystem files. Modules can create and add to whatever folders they want. They can also actually *remove* things from the System Filesystem by using this syntax:

```
<filesystem>
  <folder name="Menu">
    <folder name="Help_hidden"/>
  </folder>
</filesystem>
```

The above code will remove the **Help** menu from the menu bar in the main window.

6.5.2   The System Filesystem Is Read/Write

If the System Filesystem were nothing more than the merge of a bunch of XML files from modules, it would still be useful as a static registry of information, but it would not be a terribly powerful one. A great deal of the value of the System Filesystem comes from the fact that it is *read/write*. Clearly it is not modifying the XML files in the module JAR files they come from, when someone writes or deletes a file from the System Filesystem. So how is this accomplished?

We mentioned that the System Filesystem was a merge of XML layer files from various modules. If we are merging together a bunch of XML filesystems, all we need to do to make it writable is to merge in one writable, non-XML filesystem—an actual filesystem rooted in a directory on disk. Figure 6.4 illustrates how such merging works.

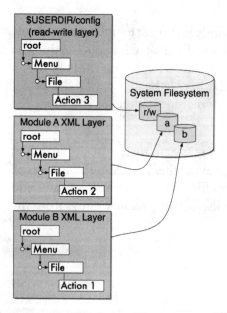

Figure 6.4: The System Filesystem

That is exactly what the System Filesystem does. The top layer of the stack of filesystems that make up the System Filesystem is a real directory on the user's hard disk. It is a subdirectory of the *userdir*—a directory under the user's home directory on their computer, where NetBeans and NetBeans- based applications store data that should be persisted across runs of the application. The userdir is the reason why, when you restart the NetBeans IDE, the same files and projects are opened as when you last shut down. To be precise, the writable root of the userdir for the NetBeans IDE is `$HOME/.netbeans/config/` (it can be changed by altering the launch script or passing `--userdir /path/to/dir` on the command line at startup).

6.5.3   Using `FileChangeEvent`s from the System Filesystem

Since the System Filesystem is read/write and `FileObjects` can fire events, it follows that folders in the System Filesystem can be listened to and fire events when their children change. This is, in fact, exactly how many things in the UI, such as menus, react to changes in the set of loaded modules. If you install a module at runtime, and that module adds a new menu to the main menu, the Window System's infrastructure that composes the main menu from files and folders in the System Filesystem will notice that a new folder has been created, and create a corresponding new menu. If that module is later uninstalled, and it is the last module using or defining that folder, then the menu will disappear.

So a common pattern in many pieces of NetBeans UI is this:

1. One module defines some component that can be opened. That component shows a tree or list view of the contents of some folder in the System Filesystem. The contents might be files representing Java objects from some SPI that that module defines, or anything else that, per the module's documentation, other modules should put there. Examples are template files, navigator panels, palette items, or basically anything you can imagine that a module might make pluggable.

2. Other modules contribute objects to this folder, in accordance with the rules the first module describes in its documentation—that is, what kind of files are allowed, what their contents (if any) should be, or, if the files represent instances of Java objects, what Java classes are allowed.

3. The first module listens for changes in the content of the folder its API defines as the place to put things and updates the UI as the contents change. The contents might change because of some user action, such as adding a folder to the **Favorites** window, or because a module has been installed which adds to, or removes from, the folder.

A simple example of this is the **Favorites** window in the IDE, accessible from **Window | Favorites**. It defines a folder in the System Filesystem where *shadow files* can be put. A shadow file is the equivalent of a UNIX symbolic link—it is a pointer to another file somewhere else, which behaves as if it were the same file as the original.

If you right-click in the **Favorites** tab and choose **Add to Favorites**, you get a file chooser that lets you choose a file. That file then appears as an item in the tree in the **Favorites** window. What is happening behind the scenes is this: The **Favorites** window shows a view of one folder in the System Filesystem (the actual folder is $HOME/config/Favorites). The **Add to Favorites** action simply creates a new .shadow file that links to the file or folder, somewhere on the user's hard drive, that you chose in the file chooser. A .shadow file behaves exactly as if it were the file it points to.

Here's another illustration of the power of using the same infrastructure to visualize both the user's files on disk and configuration data—creating a tree over a folder full of files in NetBeans is quite easy (for an example of how to do that, see Section 9.5). So, the amount of code such a module needs is actually quite small, even though it is providing substantial and useful functionality.

6.5.4   Exploring the System Filesystem—Menus

The way the main menu is composed via the System Filesystem makes a good demonstration of how the System Filesystem is used. The implementation of the Window System APIs (the core/windows module) defines the Menu folder which is the root folder for the main menu bar in the System Filesystem. Other modules can define subfolders of it. Each subfolder corresponds to a menu visible in the main menu bar. So, a module can define the following in its layer.xml file:

```
<filesystem>
  <folder name="Menu">
    <folder name="File">
      <file name="com-foo-module-OpenFileAction.instance"/>
    </folder>
  </folder>
</filesystem>
```

and another module can have this:

```
<filesystem>
  <folder name="Menu">
    <folder name="File">
      <file name="com-foo-othermodule-ExitAction.instance"/>
    </folder>
  </folder>
</filesystem>
```

The result will be a **File** menu with two items on it—**Open File** (assuming that's what the above action sets its name to) and **Exit**.

In practice, you do not need to define your own open file and exit actions—these already exist in the NetBeans APIs and the module Core—UI defines standard menus most applications will want, such as **File**, **Edit**, and **Help**.

6.5.4.1   Ordering Attributes

Now, one problem with the XML fragments above is that we don't know what order the actions will appear in, and having the **Exit** menu item as the first item on the **File** menu would be a bit weird. The System Filesystem (really the Datasystems API which will be discussed in Chapter 10) allows for *ordering attributes* which will let you define the order in which items will appear in a menu. So, if we want the **Exit** item to always appear after the **Open File** menu item, we can do it as shown in Example 6.2.

What has been added is one *file attribute*. Note that it is an attribute of the *folder* representing the menu itself. The attribute's name is what tells the system how to order the items—it lists the two filenames of the menu actions, separated by a / character. That tells the system that the first one should always be ordered earlier than the second one. The value `boolvalue="true"` simply indicates that the system should pay attention to this ordering attribute. If

Example 6.2: Using ordering attributes to specify file order

```
<filesystem>
  <folder name="Menu">
    <folder name="File">
      <file name="com-foo-othermodule-ExitAction.instance"/>
      <attr name="com-foo-module-OpenFileAction.instance/⏎
com-foo-othermodule-ExitAction.instance"
        boolvalue="true"/>
    </folder>
  </folder>
```

another module wants to provide its own different ordering of menu content, it could simply duplicate this attribute, with a value of `false` to turn it off.

In the above example, there are only two menu items, so only one ordering attribute is needed. If you have more than two, you will need at least two ordering attributes per file to guarantee its relative location, one specifying what should come before and the other specifying what should come after.

6.5.4.2   *Manipulating Menus Programmatically and through the UI*

A picture being worth a thousand words, what we will do now is demonstrate some minimal manipulation of the System Filesystem to get a more visceral sense of how it works.

If you have a copy of NetBeans IDE, you already have a copy of the NetBeans Platform. What we will do is start the bare NetBeans Platform and manipulate the menus in it. We will do this the old-fashioned way, in a command shell.

1. Open a command shell, and `cd` to the directory where you have NetBeans installed. Then navigate to the `lib/` subdirectory containing the platform cluster. If you are using a Macintosh, this will be `NetBeans.app/ Contents/Resources/NetBeans/platform6/lib`, otherwise it will be `$NB_HOME/platform6`.

2. Run the following command (substituting some unimportant directory on your hard drive for `tmp` and using `\` as the directory separator on Windows and `/` on other platforms, see Figure 6.5):

```
nbexec --userdir /tmp/userdir
```

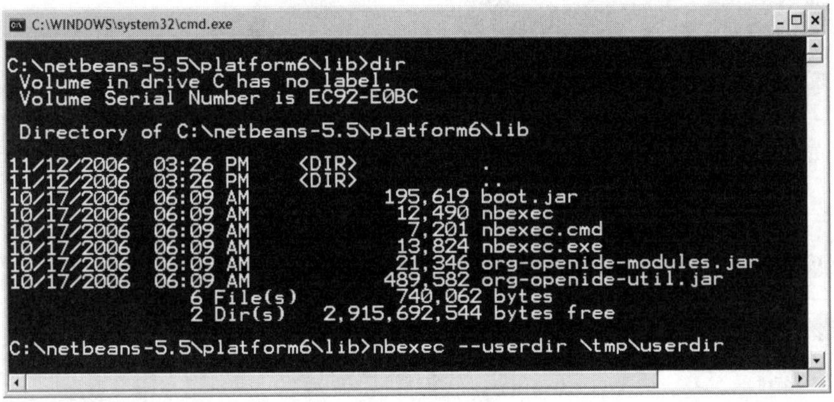

Figure 6.5: Running the bare NetBeans Platform

This will start a copy of NetBeans with only the modules from the platform cluster installed.

Figure 6.6 shows the bare NetBeans Platform running with no additional modules installed. Note that more modules can still be removed and all of the menus, toolbars, menu items, and toolbar buttons can be removed or replaced by your modules as well.

3. Click the **Tools | Options** menu item to open the **Options** dialog. Expand the nodes as shown in Figure 6.7, right-click the node for the **View** menu and choose **Delete** from the popup menu. Notice that when you do this, the actual **View** menu disappears.

4. Shut down this copy of the platform. In the text shell, navigate to the directory you passed on the command line as the userdir. List the subfolder `config/Menu`. Notice that there is a file called `View_hidden` (Figure 6.8). This file was created by our deleting the **View** menu in the UI.

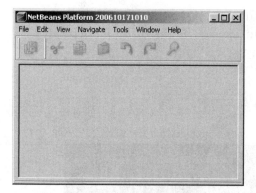

Figure 6.6: The bare NetBeans Platform

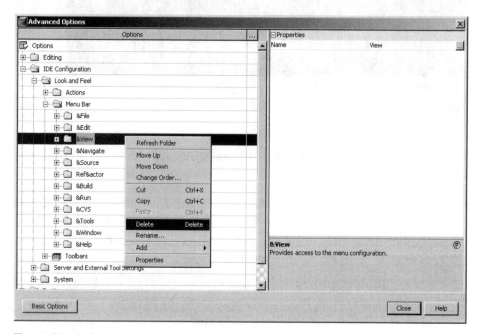

Figure 6.7: Deleting a menu in the UI

Figure 6.8: File hiding in the System Filesystem

5. To prove that there is no magic here, let's try manually removing another menu. `cd` into `config/Menu` and run the following command:

```
echo > Help_hidden
```

Restart the platform and you will find that the **Help** menu is now also gone.

So, in fact, there is quite a bit of power at our fingertips to affect NetBeans configuration, simply by making changes in the System Filesystem. The next step is to do the same thing programmatically.

1. Create a new module as described in Section 1.2.1. As mentioned above, the new module will automatically have an XML layer—the file called `layer.xml`—in it.

2. Edit the new module's `layer.xml` file, adding one line between the `<filesystem>` tags, so it looks as follows:

```
<filesystem>
  <file name="Help_hidden"/>
</filesystem>
```

Hiding Files and Dependencies

Note that if you want to hide a menu item, a file, or a folder in the System Filesystem, the module that does this needs to depend on the module that defines the thing you want to hide. Otherwise, that module may be higher in the stack of layers in the System Filesystem, in which case the module that actually defines the file is overriding *your* module that hides it. If you do not want to have, just to hide items in the System Filesystem, a module depending on classes it does not call, consider creating an empty module with nothing but a layer file that is installed with your real modules, and make that module depend on these other things and hide them.

Also note that the standard menus and toolbars are defined in the module Core–UI. You can disable this module in your platform-based application and that will get rid of almost all of the standard menus and toolbars.

3. Run the new module and notice that, indeed, when NetBeans starts up, the **Help** menu is absent from the main menu.

For that matter, one could write code to do the same thing—simply find the Menu/Help folder's FileObject and call its delete() method, though in practice this is not a common thing to do.

Adding Actions to Menus.   We've shown how to delete menus and items from menus—but how do you add items? NetBeans module-building support makes this quite simple. There is a template visible in the **NetBeans Module Development** category in the **New File** wizard which does this quite handily. What it really does is add an *instance file*—a file representing an instance of an object—to a folder representing a menu.

To try this out, perform the following steps:

1. Once again, create a new module as described in Section 1.2.1. As mentioned above, the new module will automatically have an XML layer—the file called layer.xml—in it.

2. Select the package created from the code name of the module, right-click it, and choose the **New Action** wizard from it (Figure 6.9).

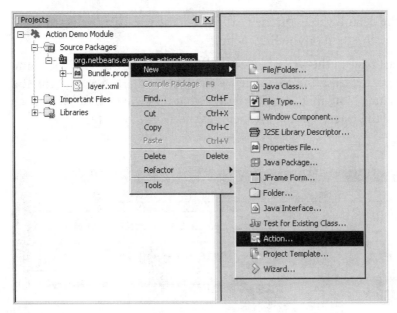

Figure 6.9: Selecting the **New Action** wizard

3. Accept the values on the first page of the wizard—we are creating an **Always Enabled** action (Figure 6.10).

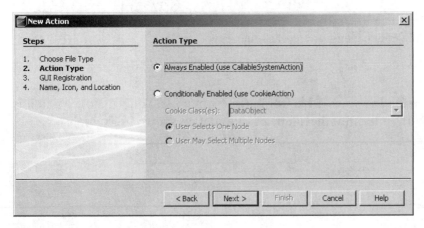

Figure 6.10: **New Action** wizard, page one

4. Accept the default values on the next page of the wizard as well—this will give us a menu item on the **File** menu.

5. On the last page of the wizard, use the classname `MyAction` for the name of the `Action` class the template will create, and `My Action` for the display name. Note that the wizard says what files will be modified at the bottom of this page, and the list includes the `layer.xml` file.

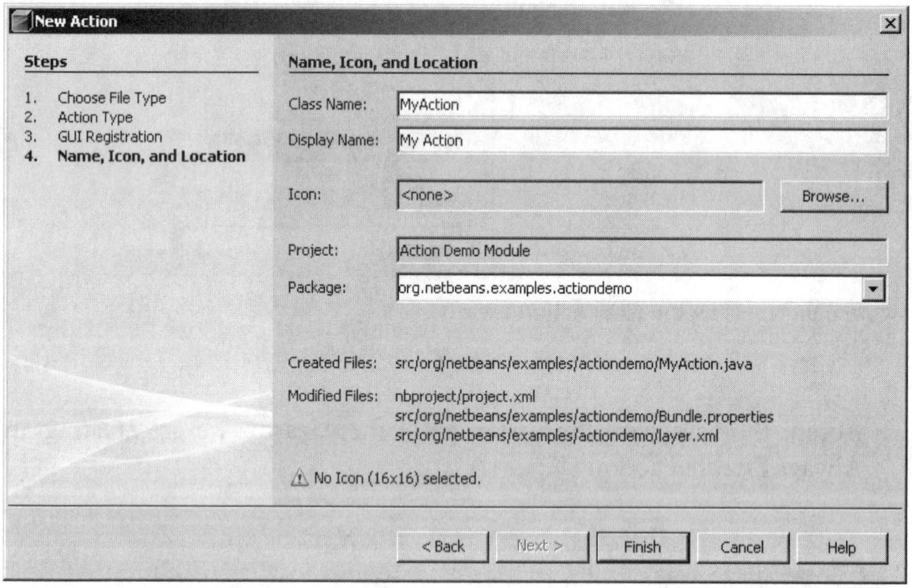

Figure 6.11: Entering an `Action` class name

Open the `layer.xml` file from the new module. You will notice that it is contributing a file into the `Menu/File` folder, as shown in Example 6.3.

Example 6.3: Specifying an `Action` on the **File** menu in XML

```
<filesystem>
  <folder name="Actions">
    <folder name="Build">
      <file name="org-netbeans-examples-actiondemo-MyAction.↲
instance"/>
    </folder>
  </folder>
  <folder name="Menu">
    <folder name="File">
      <file
        name="org-netbeans-examples-actiondemo-MyAction.shadow">
        <attr name="originalFile"
          stringvalue="Actions/Build/org-netbeans-examples-↲
actiondemo-MyAction.instance"/>
      </file>
      <attr name="org-netbeans-examples-actiondemo-MyAction.↲
shadow/org-netbeans-modules-project-ui-NewProject.shadow"
        boolvalue="true"/>
    </folder>
  </folder>
</filesystem>
```

What Is the `Actions` **Folder?**

You will notice that the **New Action** wizard in NetBeans always creates an action in some subfolder of `Actions/` and then creates shadow files that link to it for menu items, toolbar buttons, and keybindings.

The `Actions/` folder exists to provide a home for all `Actions` that modules have registered. That way, a user can delete a menu item from the UI, but still have a way to copy/paste that item back into the menu from which it was deleted. Without it, if you delete, for example, the **New Project** action, there would be no way to get it back. The `Actions/` folder can be viewed in the **Advanced Options** dialog under **IDE Configuration | Look And Feel**.

It is also probably fairly evident what this code does. We mentioned earlier that `.shadow` files operate as links to make one file act as if it were another file in a different place. The generated code uses this mechanism to ensure that only one instance of `MyAction` is ever created, even though it might be used from a menu item as well as from a toolbar button or a keyboard shortcut. So, in the `Actions/Build` folder, we have the canonical instance of `MyAction`. In `Menu/File` there is a `.shadow` file that points to the original in `Actions/Build`. It is probably clear from the (admittedly somewhat clunky) name of the `.instance` file what it is—its name is a munged form of the fully qualified classname `org.netbeans.examples.actiondemo.MyAction`. Effectively, by its filename, the file instructs the system that it represents an instance of that class.

Editing the System Filesystem the Easy Way.   The module development support in NetBeans 5.5 and later adds a very easy way to edit the System Filesystem without having to hand-edit XML files (Figure 6.12). Under your module project's node in the **Projects** window, expand the subnode **Important Files**. Then expand the node **XML Layer** underneath that. Beneath it there are two nodes, labeled <**this layer**> and <**this layer in context**>. The latter shows the entire contents of the System Filesystem as it will be when your module is run. You can open and edit files in it, and if you modify a file, a copy will be saved into your module and your module's XML layer will provide your version of that file. You can move, delete, and rearrange files using the nodes under <**this layer in context**> to make changes to the System Filesystem as you desire, and the layer file in your own module will be updated to reflect the changes you are making.

6.6   Getting from `FileObjects` to Java Objects

In Section 6.5.4.2, we ended up with the **New Action** wizard, creating a `.instance` file in the System Filesystem, as a way of telling the system to instantiate an object whose Java type was based on the file's name. The `.instance` files are the simplest and most common method of object registration in the System Filesystem. You can either use the fully qualified name of the class, with "`-`" characters substituted for "`.`" characters as shown in Example 6.4, or you can use a shorter filename and use a file attribute to provide the information as shown in Example 6.5.

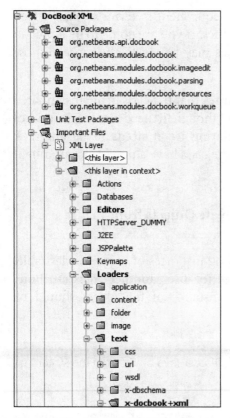

Figure 6.12: Using the GUI to edit a module layer

Example 6.4: Declaring a Java object—filename specifies the type

```
<file name="com-foo-mymodule-Foo.instance">
```

Example 6.5: Declaring a Java object—file attribute specifies the type

```
<file name="A.instance">
  <attr name="instanceClass" stringvalue="com.foo.mymodule.Foo"/>
</file>
```

Examples 6.4 and 6.5 are completely equivalent in terms of their effect; the choice is really one of style and aesthetics. If you are going to be typing in lots of ordering attributes, shorter names may be worth the more verbose syntax of having one attribute per file.

Either of the above mechanisms requires that the class being instantiated via a .instance file be a public class (though it need not be in one of the *public packages* of the module declaring it—it needs to be an API); and the above mechanisms require that the class have a public, no-argument constructor.

6.6.1   Using Factory Methods to Create Objects from `.instance` Files

Sometimes a little more nuance in creating instances of objects is desirable. For this reason, it is also possible to use another file attribute, `instanceCreate`, to specify how the instance of the object should be obtained, as shown in Example 6.6.

Example 6.6: Using a factory method to instantiate a Java object from the System Filesystem

```
<file name="A.instance">
  <attr name="instanceClass" stringvalue="com.foo.mymodule.Foo"/>
  <attr name="instanceCreate"
    methodvalue="com.foo.mymodule.FooFactory.createFoo"/>
</file>
```

The code in Example 6.6 specifies a factory method which should be called to create the actual object instance. The `instanceCreate` attribute tells the system to look for a static method on the class `FooFactory` called `createFoo()`. That method may either

- take no arguments, *or*

- take an argument of `FileObject`, in which case it will be passed the `A.instance FileObject`, *or*

- take an argument of `java.util.Map` (since 6.0), in which case the passed map will provide access to `A.instance FileObject`'s `getAttribute()` method without requiring direct linkage dependency on filesystems.

The latter form, which takes a `FileObject`, is the more useful of the two—that way you can create multiple instances of a class.

The `methodValue` Attribute

This attribute can be useful in quite a number of situations, and not only in `.instance` files. For example, imagine you have a `.shadow` file that should point to a different file depending on what OS the user is running. You could do that as follows:

```
<file name="foo.shadow">
  <attr name="originalFile"
    methodvalue="com.foo.SomeClass.someStaticMethod"/>
</file>
```

Then you would simply implement `com.foo.SomeClass.someStaticMethod()`:

```
public static FileObject someStaticMethod() {
  if (Utilities.getOperatingSystem()
              == Utilities.OS_MAC) {
    // Return one FileObject
  } else {
    // Return some other FileObject
  }
}
```

6.6.1.1 POJO Programming with NetBeans

The paradigm of using "Plain Old Java Objects" when working with frameworks—that is, enabling frameworks to work with *your* objects without you having to implement special interfaces—has gotten a lot of play recently. The ability of NetBeans to represent any object in the System Filesystem makes such an approach easy.

For example, suppose we wanted to provide a folder full of URLs. We need a module that displays them to the user somehow and allows the user to access the corresponding Web pages. We could simply allow those who want to contribute URLs to this folder to add an attribute to the `FileObjects` they define, which is the URL that should be used. Our factory method will receive the `FileObject`, get the `URL` attribute, and create the URL, as shown in Example 6.7.

Example 6.7: Creating a factory method to instantiate Java objects from `FileObjects`

```
package org.netbeans.examples.urls.api;
// Imports omitted...
public class URLFactory {
  public static URL createURL (FileObject file) {
    try {
        String urlString = (String) file.getAttribute("target");
        return new URL(urlString);
    } catch (MalformedURLException ex) {
        ErrorManager.getDefault().notify(ex);
        return null;
    }
  }
}
```

For this to work, other modules would add entries in their `layer.xml` files, as shown in Example 6.8.

Example 6.8: Registering a file that will be processed by the factory method

```
<folder name="urls">
  <file name="NetBeansPlatformWebSite.instance">
    <attr name="instanceClass" stringvalue="java.net.URL"/>
    <attr name="instanceCreate"
      methodvalue="org.netbeans.examples.urls.api.URLFactory.⏎
createURL"/>
    <attr name="target"
      stringvalue="http://platform.netbeans.org"/>
  </file>
</folder>
```

The full source to this example is included on the accompanying CD.

6.6.2   Programmatic Access to the System Filesystem

We've been talking quite a bit about the System Filesystem. How do you get access to it in the first place? The code to do so in NetBeans 5.x is a little verbose,[2] but straightforward enough:

```
Repository.getDefault().getDefaultFileSystem();
```

Typically you will want access to some folder and its contents, which is quite simple:

```
Repository.getDefault().getDefaultFileSystem().
                    getRoot().getFileObject("someFolder");
```

All of the things you can do to files on disk you can also do to files in the System Filesystem, including deleting, copying, and renaming. The utility class `FileUtil` has a number of very useful methods for manipulating `FileObjects` and is worth remembering.

6.6.2.1   Getting Instances of Objects from `FileObjects`

Depending on what you need to do, there are several ways you can take a file in the System Filesystem (or any filesystem) and access the Java object it represents (as in the case of `.instance` files, `.settings` files, or any other file type whose `DataObject` provides an `InstanceCookie`). For a single file, you can do it as shown in Example 6.9.

Example 6.9: Getting the Java object a `FileObject` represents

```
DataObject ob = DataObject.find (theFileObject);
InstanceCookie ck = (InstanceCookie) ob.getCookie (
  InstanceCookie.class);
// NetBeans 6 Code:
// InstanceCookie ck =
//   ob.getLookup().lookup (InstanceCookie.class);
if (ck != null) {
  Object theObject = ck.instanceCreate();
}
```

---

2. There is a proposal to provide a simpler method, but it is not yet known if it will be implemented for NetBeans 6.

This is very low-level approach; more often you will have a folder full of objects and will want all objects of a particular Java type. But it is illustrative of one thing: It is the file identification machinery of the *Datasystems API* (covered in detail in Chapter 10) that is doing the work of turning the file into a URL. This is the same machinery that identifies a `.java` file as a Java source file on the user's hard disk. `InstanceCookie` is a bit of indirection which any `DataObject` can provide.

What is `InstanceCookie`?

A `DataObject` is a wrapper for a `FileObject`. The type of `DataObject` created for a given file is determined by its MIME type. Any `DataObject` implementation that wants to represent a POJO can provide[3] an `InstanceCookie`, and the various parts of NetBeans that transform files into objects will be able to work with it. So, the `DataObject` that is created for the `FileObject` of a `.instance` file provides an `InstanceCookie` that takes the filename or attributes and uses them to create an *instance* of an object. For a full explanation of how all of this works, see Chapter 10.

For getting all of the objects of a given type from a folder, there is a convenient class, `FolderLookup`, which is part of the Datasystems API. Using our Example 6.7, the way one would get all the URL objects represented by files in a given folder is as shown in Example 6.10.

6.6.3   Using `.settings` Files

The `.settings` files are similar to the `.instance` files—both are ways to denote that a `FileObject` represents an instance of a Java object. Wherever you can use a `.instance` file, you can use a `.settings` file as well.

The main difference between the two is that `.settings` files are XML files that actually need to be read in order to create an object—this means that initial object creation may be slower than with a `.instance` file. However, the `.settings` file can list all of the supertypes of the Java object it represents, as well as all of the interfaces. So in cases where the object is expensive to create

---

3. "Plain Old Java Object," has recently become a term favored by those advocating simplicity for programmers in using various Web frameworks.

Example 6.10: Getting all objects of a given type from a folder

```
FileObject root =
  Repository.getDefault().getDefaultFileSystem().getRoot();
FileObject urlsFolder =
  root.getFileObject(URLS_FOLDER_IN_SYSTEM_FILESYSTEM);
DataFolder dataFolder = DataFolder.findFolder (urlsFolder);

// Note if we were really going to display folder contents
// in a UI, we would listen for changes on the Lookup.Result
FolderLookup fl = new FolderLookup (dataFolder);

// NetBeans 5.x and earlier:
Lookup.Template template = new Lookup.Template (URL.class);
Lookup.Result result = fl.getLookup().lookup(template);
Collection urls = result.allInstances();

// NetBeans 6 code:
// Collection <? extends URL> urls
//                   = lkp.getLookup().lookupAll(URL.class);
```

and you may only be testing whether one is present or not, it is possible for a
FolderLookup or similar class to answer that question without having to
actually create the object. Example 6.11 shows a sample .settings file created
by the **New Window Component** wizard.

Example 6.11: Using .settings files

```
<settings version="1.0">
  <module name="org.netbeans.examples.urls" spec="1.0"/>
  <instanceof class="org.openide.windows.TopComponent"/>
  <instanceof
    class="org.netbeans.examples.urls.UrlsTopComponent"/>
  <instance class="org.netbeans.examples.urls.UrlsTopComponent"
          method="getDefault"/>
</settings>
```

6.7   Browsing the System Filesystem

To get a better idea of what the System Filesystem is, simply browse it, look around, and see what sorts of folders are there and what kind of contents resides in them. Section 9.5 lists the source of a System Filesystem browser which can be found on the accompanying CD. You may want to run that module now.

6.8   Conclusions

The System Filesystem is a powerful read-write registry for any sort of configuration data, especially that which may change at runtime. The System Filesystem can contain ordinary file formats, such as .java files, as well—in fact, when you edit a template using **Tools | Template Manager**, you are editing a file in the System Filesystem.

Any module can create or add to a folder in the System Filesystem. In adding content to a folder, it should do so in accordance with the documentation of the module that created it. Table 6.1 is a reference for some of the file types commonly used with the System Filesystem.

Section 6.8.1 lists some of the more commonly used folders in the System Filesystem. Remember that for each folder, there is some module which defines it, and if you put things in that folder, you should probably have a dependency on that module.

Some folders use a convention of having subfolders that correspond to different MIME types in order to have separate registries of objects that apply to different types of files. For an example of this, see Chapter 7.

6.8.1   Commonly Used Folders in the System Filesystem

What follows is a reference to a subset of all the folders in the System Filesystem which may be of interest to module authors. Note that a folder's *display name* may be different than the folder's *actual name*. As shown in Example 6.12, it is possible for a folder's definition in an XML layer file to specify the SystemFilesystem.localizingBundle attribute indicating that the String value of that attribute is a pointer to a Bundle.properties file that

Table 6.1: Useful file types in the System Filesystem

File Extension	Description
`.instance`	Represents an instance of a Java object. The Java type is either encoded into the name of the file, as in `com-foo-MyClass.instance`, or specified by the `String` value of the attribute `instanceClass`.
`.settings`	Similar to `.instance` files, a `.settings` file also represents an instance of a Java object. A `.settings` file is an XML file that can list some or all of the classes and interfaces its object represents, so more queries can be done against a `.settings` file, without the need to instantiate the object it represents, to test whether or not it is an instance of some class.
`.ser`	A serialized binary Java object.
`.shadow`	These are similar to UNIX symbolic links—a `.shadow` file points to another file somewhere else and behaves as if it were that other file.

contains an entry for the path to the file. So a folder may be defined as shown in Example 6.12.

Example 6.12: Localizing names of files

```
<filesystem>
  <folder name="Menu">
    <folder name="MyMenu">
      <attr name="SystemFilesystem.localizingBundle"
        stringvalue="com.foo.mymodule.Bundle"/>
    </folder>
  </folder>
</filesystem>
```

The `SystemFilesystem.localizingBundle` indicates that there is a `.properties` file that can be found on the classpath at `com/foo/mymodule/Bundle.properties`, and that it will have an entry as shown in Example 6.13.

Example 6.13: Providing the localized name of a file in a resource bundle

`Menu/MyMenu=My Menu`

For example, the display name for the `Menu/` folder is "Menu Bar"; but modules that want to contribute items to a menu will get nowhere putting things in subfolders of `Menu Bar/`, since that is the display name, not the actual name of the folder.

Table 6.2 shows the filename of the folders in question, not their localized names as they might appear in the System Filesystem browser described in Section 9.5.

Table 6.2: Commonly used folders in the System Filesystem

Path	*What module defines it*	*What kinds of files belong there*	*MIME sub-folders?*
`Menu/`	Core–Windows	Subfolders are menus and submenus; in them, folder objects which resolve to a `JMenu`, `JMenuItem`, `JSeparator`, or `Action` are allowed, as well as any object implementing the `Presenter.Menu` interface.	No
`Keymaps/`	Core–Windows	Contains subfolders which correspond to sets of keybindings. An application built on the NetBeans Platform can contain more than one set of keybindings, so that different applications can have switchable sets of keybindings and thus emulate other applications that users may be familiar with. For example, the NetBeans IDE contains keybinding sets to emulate Emacs or Eclipse in addition to the default NetBeans keybindings. Subfolders contain specially named `.instance` (or similar) files for `Actions` whose filenames describe the key to which the action is bound. The file naming convention is described more fully in Section 9.3.3.	No

Table 6.2 *(Continued)*

Path	What module defines it	What kinds of files belong there	MIME sub-folders?
Shortcuts/	Core	A folder with keybindings that map actions to keystrokes, using the same naming convention as that used by subfolders of the Keymaps/ folder, but differing in that keybindings in Shortcuts/ are not specific to a particular key mapping theme such as Emacs or Eclipse.	No
Templates/	Data-systems API	Subfolders of this folder appear in the **New File** wizard. Of particular interest may be the folder Templates/Privileged, which defines those templates that should appear in the New subfolder displayed when you right-click a folder.	No
Toolbars/	Core—Windows	Subfolders of this folder indicate toolbars that are visible in the main window, and contain .instance files or similar which define Actions visible in those toolbars.	No
Options-Dialog/	**Options** dialog and SPI	Modules that want to register panels to be displayed in the **Options** dialog can add .instance files or similar to this folder or its subfolder Advanced/. For further details, see Chapter 18.	No
Loaders/	Data-systems API	Contains subfolders allowing modules to add actions to the Nodes for files of different types—so, for example, it is possible to write a new Action which should operate on Java source files, register it in the folder Loaders/text/x-java/Actions and have it appear in the popup menu for Java files when they are right-clicked in the **Projects** or **Files** windows of the IDE.	Yes
Projects-Tab-Actions/	Project UI API	Allows modules to register actions that appear in the IDE when you right-click in a whitespace area of the **Projects** window (an area that does not contain any node in the tree view).	No

Table 6.2 *(Continued)*

Path	What module defines it	What kinds of files belong there	MIME sub-folders?
`Favorites/`	Favorites	Contains `.shadow` files that are pointers to files on the users' disk. Anything linked here appears in the **Favorites** window that can be shown by invoking **Window | Favorites**.	No
`Editors/`	Editor MIME Lookup API	Contains subfolders defined by various modules that use the MIME Lookup API (described in Chapter 7, which adds a subfolder of its own). Subfolders map to MIME types. Underneath a subfolder such as `Editors/text/x-java`, you will find a number of subfolders that are registries of different types of objects that represent aspects of the presentation of files of that MIME type (in this case, `text/x-java`) in the editor and elsewhere. See Table 6.3 for a list of commonly used subfolders.	Yes
`Services/`	Core	An alternate way of registering objects in the default `Lookup` is to put `.instance` files or similar in this folder.	No
`UI/ Runtime/`	Core	Objects registered here will be shown in the **Runtime** window in the IDE. Commonly used for things which may need some configuration at runtime, such as databases or application servers.	No
`UI/ Options/`	Core	A registry of folders and files that appear in the **Advanced Options** dialog.	No
`Projects/ Actions/`	Project UI API	Registry of `Actions` which should be available on all projects in the **Projects** window of the IDE. For example, if you install the NetBeans Profiler, it adds a **Profile Project** action to all projects.	No
`Navigator/ Panels/`	Core–Navigator	A registry of objects providing GUI panels that can appear in the **Navigator** component in the main window of the IDE.	Yes

Table 6.3: Commonly used subfolders of `Editors/mime/path/`

Path	What kinds of files belong there
`Popup/`	Contains actions that should appear on the popup menu when the user right-clicks in the editor when editing a file of the given MIME type.
`CompletionProviders/`	This is a registry of objects that provide code completion for a given file type. For further details, see Chapter 14.
`HyperlinkProviders/`	A registry of objects that can make individual words or lines in the editor function as *hyperlinks* which, when clicked, invoke some code. For further details, see Chapter 16.
`Sidebar/`	A registry of objects which want to provide some component to appear on the left side of the editor, such as the code folding sidebar that appears in the editor and allows users to collapse sections of a document.
`GlyphGutterActions/`	A registry of `Action`s that should appear on the popup when the user right-clicks in the left edge of the editor (in the area where line numbers appear when line numbering is turned on).

The System Filesystem contains many other folders. The fact that a folder exists does not necessarily mean that the module that defines it is expecting other modules to put things there. In particular, it is common for modules to use System Filesystem folder-based registries in anticipation of creating a stable API in the future, while that API is not yet finalized. If you think you see a folder to which your module can usefully add something, take the time to find out what the API of the module defining the folder is and read its Javadoc documentation to find out how to properly use the folder in question.

CHAPTER SEVEN

Threading, Listener Patterns, and MIME Lookup

At this point we are going to take a break from reviewing APIs per se and write our first bit of IDE-like functionality. The "Pseudo Navigator" we will build in this chapter is quite like the actual **Navigator** component in the NetBeans IDE, but with a much simpler UI. It will demonstrate creating a modular API.

There are two significant differences between the way this is implemented and the way one would practically implement such functionality for use in the IDE: It does not use the Nodes API and makes minimal use of the Datasystems API. Both would be quite helpful. Their absence in this example should help to make clear what role they play.

In the process, we will introduce the *Editor MIME Lookup API*.[1] This module can be quite useful if you need to create registries of objects that other modules can contribute to in such a way that there is one registry of objects per MIME type.

In this example we will create the *Pseudo Navigator*. It will be a module that provides an SPI (Service Provider Interface). The SPI will consist of one

---

1. In NetBeans 6 you will find it referred to as the *MIME Lookup API*.

Java interface—a factory interface which can create a Swing `ListModel`[2] for
a file. Other modules can implement our factory interface and register their
implementation in the System Filesystem. The Pseudo Navigator component
will track the selected file. When the selected file changes, it will find out the
file's MIME type and look for a factory whose module has registered against
that MIME type. If it finds one, it will ask it to create a `ListModel` and it will
display that model.

Unlike the real **Navigator** component, our Pseudo Navigator component
will only use a `JList`. It will have no popup menus, no capability to show
trees instead of lists, and no way to have more than one type of model
selectable from it.

So, the first thing we are creating is a module that does not know anything
about any particular file type. The Pseudo Navigator module will be an empty
shell that can be populated by a `ListModel`. It has a way of finding the right
`ListModel` for different file types, tracks what file is selected in the NetBeans
UI, and tries to find a model to display for any file that is selected or being
edited.

7.1   Creating the Modules and SPI

To get started, create a new module suite called `PseudoNavigator` and
populate it with the single initial module called `pseudonavigator`. In
that module, create a new Java package called `org.netbeans.api.`
`pseudonavigator`. In that package, create a new Java file named
`ListModelProvider`.

Right-click the API module and choose **Properties** from the popup menu.
On the **API Versioning** panel, check the checkbox to make that package
"public." This will allow other modules which depend on our module to see
and use the classes in the `org.netbeans.api.pseudonavigator` package
(but not in any other packages in our module unless we explicitly make them

---

2. `javax.swing.ListModel` is the model class from the Swing API which represents
the contents of a `javax.swing.JList`. `JLists` are components that show
`ListModels`—they are a Swing list-box component.

public in the same way). The UI you will use to mark this package as public is shown in Figure 7.1.

While you have the **Project Properties** dialog open, set the **Source Level** to 1.5 as shown in Figure 7.2. The source code in this example takes advantage

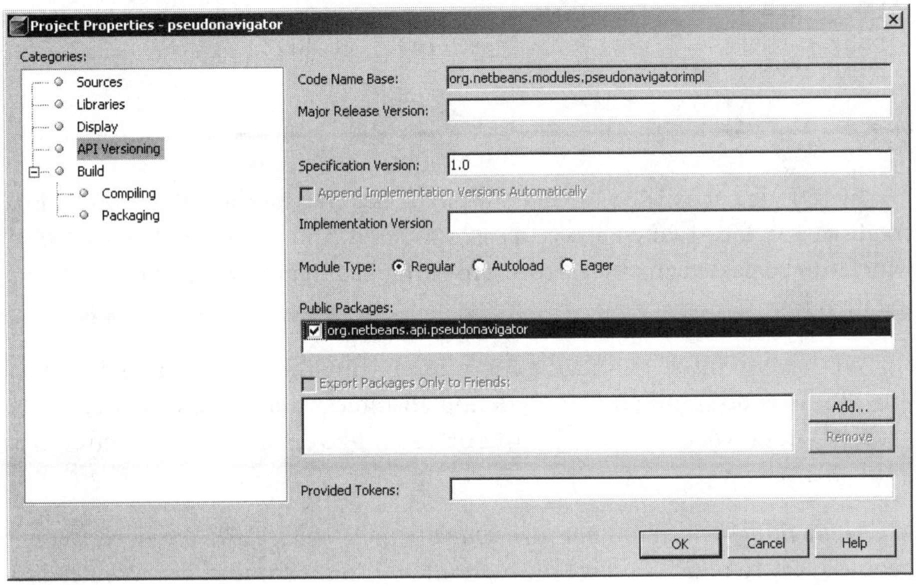

Figure 7.1: Marking an API package as public

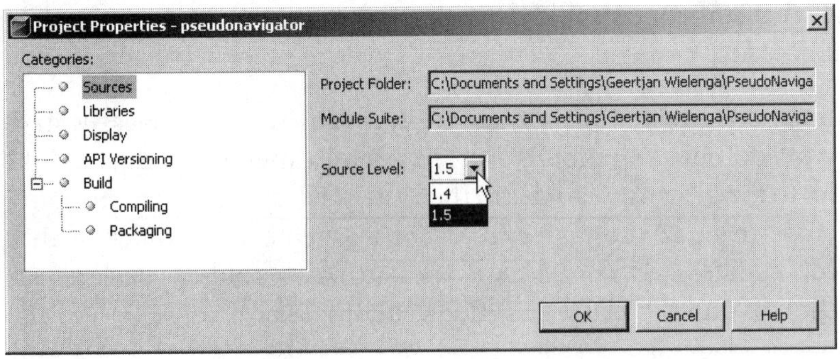

Figure 7.2: Setting a project's source level

of Java generics; however, the default source level for newly created module projects in NetBeans 5.5 is JDK 1.4 which predates generics.

Implement `ListModelProvider` as shown in Example 7.1.

Example 7.1: The `ListModelProvider` **interface**

```
public interface ListModelProvider <T extends Object> {
  public ListModel getListModel(FileObject file);
  public void selected (T t);
}
```

`ListModelProvider` is very simple. It has one method that is called to create a `ListModel` when passed a `FileObject`. And it has a callback method which can be passed an object from a model it has created when the user clicks the item in a `JList`.

We have defined `ListModelProvider`. But there is another piece to this SPI. It is not enough just to define an interface and a component. We need to define what to do with a `ListModelProvider` once someone has implemented it.

Many things which are not Java code are nonetheless API. We need to give people a way to register their `ListModelProviders` somewhere. We need to define a place where our code will look for `ListModelProvider`, so other people know how to register their custom `ListModelProviders` against specific file types. So, the second part of our SPI is not Java code at all. It is a definition of what someone should do with `ListModelProvider` once they have implemented it.

The Javadoc documentation for `ListModelProvider` will clearly state that the way to add new `ListModelProviders` for different types is to add subdirectories to the `Editors/` folder in the System Filesystem corresponding to a MIME type (e.g., `Editors/text/x-java`), create a subfolder of that folder called `ListModelProvider/`, and in that folder, declare an implementation of our API class, `ListModelProvider`.

7.2   Implementing `ListModelProvider`

Now that we have a general SPI for creating list models for different file types, we will create another module which will implement `ListModelProvider` so that the first module will have something to display. This will be an implementation that finds things that appear to be XML tags in a file. We will register it to be used on XML and HTML files.

So, let's add another module to our suite. Create that module by expanding the suite so the `Modules` subnode is visible and right-clicking it so the **Add New** menu item is visible. This is one way to create a new module and automatically add it to the suite (Figure 7.3).

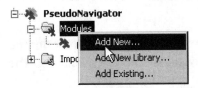

Figure 7.3: Adding a module to a suite

Call the module "XML Pseudo Navigator". Once it is created, create a Java class in it called `XmlListModelProvider`. The sample code uses the package name `org.netbeans.examples.xmlpseudonavigator`. It may be useful to use the same package name to simplify following our exercises.

7.2.1   Setting Up Dependencies

As we mentioned in the introductory chapters, if a NetBeans module wants to use a class from another NetBeans module, two things need to happen.

1. If module B wants to use classes from module A, it must explicitly say it needs Module A. Otherwise, it cannot see any classes from A—which means it won't compile, and even if some tricks are used to make it compile, it would just throw an exception at runtime the moment B tries to touch a class from A. The NetBeans Module System *really* does not allow unrestricted access between modules. This means a little more work

up-front: A module must say what it needs in order to function, and if those things are not there, it cannot be loaded. On the other hand, that potentially saves years of work trying to keep future versions of the program functioning on customer systems with wildly different versions of libraries. It makes something predictable that traditionally—in Java or in any other language—has not been: With the NetBeans Module System an application gets a guarantee that it will really be able to satisfy its dependencies.

2. If module A wants to let other modules use some of its classes (i.e., import them, call them, or refer to them in some way), then module A needs to say that it allows it. By default, a module is completely private. Even public classes in a module are public only within the module's JAR, and both the build process and the Module System's classloaders at runtime will block access to those classes.

We solved this problem when we checked the checkbox in the **Properties** dialog of the Pseudo Navigator module, making the `org.netbeans.api.pseudonavigator` package public, as shown in Figure 7.1. If our new module declares a dependency on that module, it will be able to see the interface `ListModelProvider` and will be allowed to implement it (Figure 7.4).

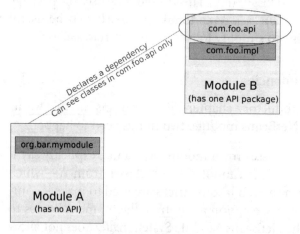

Figure 7.4: API partitioning

So, for the XML Pseudo Navigator module to actually implement `ListModelProvider`, our new module must depend on the Pseudo Navigator module which defines `ListModelProvider`. Right-click the new module's node in the **Projects** window and choose **Properties**. Select the **Libraries** panel in the dialog that appears and click the **Add Dependency** button. The dialog that appears is quite convenient: Even if we did not write the module that defines `ListModelProvider` ourselves—even if we did not know the name of that module—all we need to do is know the name of the class we want to use. The IDE will take care of finding the right module and adding the dependency correctly for us. Just type `ListModelProvider` into the text field at the top of the **Add Module Dependency** dialog, as shown in Figure 7.5.

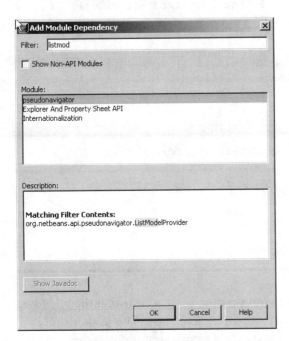

Figure 7.5: Adding a dependency

7.2.2 Creating `XmlListModelProvider`

Populate `XmlListModelProvider` as shown in Example 7.2. It is going to implement the interface we defined earlier, `ListModelProvider`.

Example 7.2: `XmlListModelProvider`–Implementing `ListModelProvider`

```
public class XmlListModelProvider
    implements ListModelProvider <XmlListModelItem> {

  private Reference<XmlFileListModel> last;
  public ListModel getListModel(FileObject file) {
    XmlFileListModel result = null;

    // First, check if this is the same file we set
    // the last time we had a nonnull result,
    // and if it has not been garbage-collected

    XmlFileListModel current = last == null ? null : last.get();
    if (current != null && file.equals(current.getFile())) {
      result = current;
    }
    if (result == null) {
      result = new XmlFileListModel (file);
      last = new WeakReference <XmlFileListModel> (result);
    }
    return result;
  }

  public void selected(XmlListModelItem item) {
    try {
        item.selected();
    } catch (IOException ex) {
        ErrorManager.getDefault().notify (ex);
    }
  }
}
```

The code in Example 7.2 does not do much—it is clear that the real logic
lives in `XmlFileListModel` and `XmlListModelItem`. This code simply receives a file and returns the same instance it created last if it gets the same file
(with a little bookkeeping to avoid memory leaks), or creates a new one and
remembers it with a `WeakReference`.

Weak References

A `java.lang.ref.WeakReference` keeps a *weak reference* to an object. This means that you can call `WeakReference.get()` and get the object that the `WeakReference` is a holder for, but the object can be garbage-collected (in which case `get()` returns `null`) if no other object in the VM holds a *strong reference* to it (i.e., no other object has assigned it to a field, or stored it in a `Collection` it owns, or similar).

Next, we will implement the objects that will be in our model—`XmlListModelItem` (Example 7.3). `XmlListModelItem` represents one XML tag that has been found in a file, storing the text of it and its position in the file. The only interesting logic in this class lives in the `select()` method. That method ensures the file is open and moves the caret to the position of the XML tag. An `XmlListModelItem` is just an object with a field for the text it represents and an integer for the location in the file.

Example 7.3: `XmlListModelItem`

```
final class XmlListModelItem {

  private final XmlFileListModel model;
  private final int position;
  private final String text;

  public XmlListModelItem(XmlFileListModel model,
                          String text, int position) {
    this.model = model;
    this.text = text;
    this.position = position;
  }

  public String toString() {
    return text;
  }

  public int getPosition() {
    return position;
  }
```

```
public void selected() throws IOException {
  if (this.model.file.isValid()) {
    DataObject ob = DataObject.find (model.getFile());
    // Make sure the file is open
    if (!openFileInEditor(ob)) {
      return;
    }
    // In NB 6 no cast needed from Lookup
    // EditorCookie ed = ob.getLookup().lookup(
    //    EditorCookie.class);
    EditorCookie ed = (EditorCookie) ob.getCookie(
                EditorCookie.class);

    if (ed != null) {
      ed.openDocument();
      JEditorPane pane = ed.getOpenedPanes()[0];
      pane.setSelectionStart(position);
      pane.setSelectionEnd(position);
      TopComponent tc = (TopComponent)
        SwingUtilities.getAncestorOfClass(TopComponent.class,
                                          pane);
      if (tc != null) { // It won't be
        tc.requestActive();
      }
    }
  }
}


private boolean openFileInEditor(DataObject ob) {
  EditCookie ck = (EditCookie) ob.getCookie(EditCookie.class);
  if (ck != null) {
    ck.edit();
    return true;
  }
  OpenCookie oc = (OpenCookie) ob.getCookie(OpenCookie.class);
  if (oc != null) {
    oc.open();
    return true;
  }
  return false;
}
}
```

This code makes use of a few classes from the NetBeans APIs which we haven't covered yet. Briefly, what they are and do is shown in Table 7.1.

Table 7.1: API Classes used in `XmlListModelItem`

Name	Description
DataObject	The call to `DataObject.find()` gets a `DataObject` to represent the file. These are covered in detail in Chapter 10. We can ask it for objects related to editing, such as the classes listed below.
EditCookie	The default **Open** action on some files is to open a graphical editor, not a text editor. This pattern is used for files associated with a graphical editor to also make available a text editor via the standard **Edit** action. We check for `EditCookie` first; usually it will be `null` and we will then check for `OpenCookie`, and if found, use that. For more information about actions such as **Open** and **Edit**, see Section 9.3.2.
OpenCookie	This is an object which can open a file in some sort of editor. It has one method, `open()`.
EditorCookie	If there is an open text editor window for a file, it will provide an `EditorCookie`. This class has methods for getting the Swing `Document` that editor is showing, and for getting the text editor control itself.
TopComponent	This is a GUI panel in the Window System—any component you see in a tabbed container in the NetBeans IDE's main window is a `TopComponent`. They are covered in depth in Chapter 8.

The other interesting code is going to be in `XmlFileListModel`. It will read a file, apply a regular expression to find XML tags in that file, and create `XmlListModelItems` which will be the model's contents.

Create the class `XmlFileListModel` in the XML Pseudo Navigator module and implement it as shown in Example 7.4. It will use a simple regular expression `<(\w\w\w.*?)>.*?\n` that will match nonclosing XML tags of at least three characters in length, one per line. It constructs one `XmlListModelItem` for each match the regular expression finds.

Example 7.4: Creating a Swing `ListModel` for XML files

```
public class XmlFileListModel extends FileChangeAdapter
        implements ListModel, Runnable, FileChangeListener {
  // The fileobject whose content we are modelling
  final FileObject file;

  // Our listener list
  private final List <ListDataListener> listeners =
    Collections.synchronizedList(new LinkedList
                                      <ListDataListener> ());

  // Flag indicating there is a pending job to do a parse
  private volatile boolean enqueued = false;

  // Regexp we'll use to match things - it will skip
  // very short tags and only id the first tag on a line
  private static Pattern pattern =
    Pattern.compile ("<(\\w\\w\\w.*?)>.*?\n");

  // Our model content list, which will only be accessed
  // on the event thread
  private final List <XmlListModelItem> contents =
    new ArrayList <XmlListModelItem> (20);

  // A list we'll use to populate content,
  // doing our I/O outside the event thread
  private List <XmlListModelItem> pendingContent = null;

  public XmlFileListModel(FileObject file) {
    this.file = file;
    file.addFileChangeListener(
        FileUtil.weakFileChangeListener(this, file));
    enqueue();
  }

  FileObject getFile() {
    return file;
  }

  public int getSize() {
    return contents.size();
  }
```

```
public Object getElementAt(int index) {
  return contents.get (index);
}

public void addListDataListener(ListDataListener l) {
  listeners.add (l);
}

public void removeListDataListener(ListDataListener l) {
  listeners.remove (l);
}

private void enqueue () {
  if (!enqueued) {
    RequestProcessor.getDefault().post (this);
  }
}

// From FileChangeListener - will be called
// if the file is saved
public void fileChanged(FileEvent evt) {
  enqueue();
}

// From FileChangeListener - will be called
// if the file is deleted
public void fileDeleted(FileEvent evt) {
  enqueue();
}

public void run() {
  // We run first off the event thread, and then
  // invoke ourselves to call this method again
  // from the event thread once we are done
  if (!EventQueue.isDispatchThread()) {
    try {
      // Make the list of our content
      // on the background thread
      pendingContent = parseFileAndCreateItems();
    } finally {
      EventQueue.invokeLater(this);
    }
  } else {
    // Second invocation, we are on the event queue now -
    // copy the list over
```

```java
        try {
            int sz = Math.max (pendingContent.size(),
                               contents.size());

            // Empty the backing storage.  We're running on
            // the event thread now, so nobody should be calling
            // ListModel methods while we do this
            contents.clear();
            // Replace the former contents with
            // the new list of items
            contents.addAll(pendingContent);

            ListDataListener[] l =
              listeners.toArray(new ListDataListener[0]);

            ListDataEvent e = new ListDataEvent (this,
              ListDataEvent.CONTENTS_CHANGED, 0, sz);

            for (int i = 0; i < l.length; i++) {
              l[i].contentsChanged(e);
            }
        } finally {
            pendingContent = null;
            enqueued = false;
        }
    }
}

private List parseFileAndCreateItems() {
  List <XmlListModelItem> result =
        new LinkedList <XmlListModelItem> ();
  if (file.isValid() && file.getSize() < Integer.MAX_VALUE) {
    try {
        String content = readFile();
        Matcher matcher = pattern.matcher(content);
        while (matcher.find()) {
          result.add (new XmlListModelItem (this,
                      matcher.group(1), matcher.start())));
        }
    } catch (IOException ex) {
        ErrorManager.getDefault().notify (ex);
    }
  }
  return result;
}
```

```java
private String readFile() throws IOException {
    InputStream in = file.getInputStream();
    ByteArrayOutputStream bytes =
        new ByteArrayOutputStream ((int) file.getSize());
    try {
        FileUtil.copy(in, bytes);
        byte[] arr = bytes.toByteArray();
        String s = new String (arr, 0, arr.length,
                               Charset.defaultCharset());

        String lineSep = System.getProperty ("line.separator");
        // We are computing offsets into a Swing document,
        // where the line separator will always be \n
        // no matter what the OS does
        if (lineSep.length() > 1) {
            s = s.replace(lineSep, "\n");
        }
        return s;
    } finally {
        in.close();
    }
}
}
```

7.2.2.1   Threading and XmlFileListModel

In code that reads and writes files in a GUI application, one unavoidable fact of life is threading. The Swing UI toolkit is *single-threaded*, meaning that, with a handful of documented exceptions, the only thread where calls to methods on Swing components should happen is the *AWT event thread*. This includes firing events, since firing an event from a model *will* call code in Swing components.

It is *possible* to do I/O on the AWT event thread, but doing so is a very bad idea. Even if you are reading a tiny file, there is no guarantee that the disk isn't failing or some other program isn't keeping the disk busy. Anything imaginable can go wrong with disk access. If you do I/O in the AWT event thread, you cannot guarantee that the application won't stall for some horrible length of time, blocking painting of its window completely while the I/O happens. File I/O is almost always something that should be done on a background thread, so it can't block the UI of the application.

Other than reading the file, all of the logic involved in Example 7.4 is bookkeeping to keep I/O operations off the AWT event thread. One new class from the NetBeans APIs that it touches is `org.openide.util.RequestProcessor` which is a NetBeans-specific thread-pool (one might just as easily use the newer thread-pool classes in `java.util.concurrent`). The point is to avoid doing file I/O and parsing in the AWT event thread.

So what does the code shown in Example 7.4 do? First, it implements `ListModel`. Its `getSize()`, `getElementAt()`, `addListDataListener()`, and `removeListDataListener()` are all methods from `javax.swing.ListModel`, and they are implemented very simply, calling a `java.util.List` named `contents` that `XmlFileListModel` uses internally to keep its data.

We could have used a convenience implementation from the JDK, such as `DefaultListModel`. In our case, the threading aspects of the code become clearer when we implement the model directly. We use a background thread to do our I/O, using a `volatile boolean` (thread-safe) flag to make sure that the I/O routine (the first half of the `run()` method) cannot be entered until a previous batch of I/O on the same file has completed and the `XmlListModelItems` that were created have been saved into the `contents` list.

An `XmlFileListModel` receives a file in its constructor. That file is stored in a `final` field in the model's constructor. So, any thread can access the `file` field without any worries—it cannot change: Final fields are thread-safe.

The model immediately begins listening to the file for changes. It enqueues itself to run on a background thread—this is why it implements `Runnable`—where the work of reading the file and constructing items will happen. The `run()` method uses a simple and useful pattern of checking which thread it is on, doing one batch of work in the background, and then reinvoking itself to run on the event thread to finish its work, as shown in Example 7.5.

Example 7.5: One `Runnable`, two threads

```
public void run() {
  if (!EventQueue.isDispatchThread()) {
      try {
          // Do the work you want to do in background
      } finally {
          EventQueue.invokeLater (this);
      }
  } else {
      try {
          // Fire events, modify things that should only be
          // touched in the event queue
      } finally {
          enqueued = false;
      }
  }
}
```

Locking Models

What `XmlFileListModel` is doing is *coarse-grained locking*. We could have used `Collections.synchronizedList()` without worrying about threading so much, because every method of a `List` produced by `Collections.synchronizedList()` will be protected by the `synchronized` keyword—meaning that if one thread is in a method of a synchronized list, any other thread that tries to call a method on the same synchronized list will have to stop and wait until the first thread exits, whatever the method *it* was in. This is *fine-grained locking*—we have a resource (our `List`), and all access to it is synchronized to guarantee that two threads will not modify it at the same time.

So why not do that, or use `DefaultListModel`, which, more or less, does the same thing? The short answer is, *synchronization makes your programs slower*. There is a cost to synchronization: You can stop other threads from running while you're doing something briefly, those other threads can stop you, and the CPUs have to coordinate among themselves to make sure the synchronization rules are not being violated.

In Example 7.5, we are using a `volatile boolean` flag—we actually avoid using the `synchronized` keyword entirely. The `volatile` keyword guarantees the value will always be read from main memory, not from a processor's memory cache (two processors' caches might not be up to date with each other). Our de-facto lock is the fact that only one thread at any given time will return `true` from `EventQueue.isDispatchThread()`—we are trusting that Swing and NetBeans will play by the rules and never call methods on our model from some random thread. As long as that holds true, we know that at the time we are copying data from the `pendingContents` field into the `contents` field, it is impossible for some other thread to be calling methods on the model (and possibly seeing the `List` that is the `contents` field when only half the data has been copied), because the code that does the copying owns the event thread.

When you do need synchronization to make some piece of code thread-safe, consider whether you are writing code that enters and exits synchronized blocks or methods in a loop. It is usually preferable to lock a *system*, do what you need to do, and release it, rather than doing many small calls each of which will lock and unlock.

What happens when `enqueue()` is called is this, step by step:

1. A `Runnable`, in this case the `XmlFileListModel` itself, is enqueued to be run in a different thread at some later (but not much later) time. The `enqueued` boolean flag is set to `true`. If anything else calls `enqueue()` while it is `true`, `enqueue()` will do nothing.

2. The `run()` method gets called on the background thread. It creates a new `List`, called `pendingContent`, reads the file, and fills `pendingContent` with `XmlListModelItems`.

3. Still on the background thread, after the file has been read, the model calls `EventQueue.invokeLater()`, passing itself. So at some later (but not much later) time, `run()` will be called again, this time from the AWT event thread.

4. `run()` is called again on the AWT event thread. It clears the `contents` list, fills it with all the items in `pendingContent`, fires events to notify the `JList` that the contents have changed, and sets the `enqueued` flag to `false`.

It's also worth noting that dispatching work to a background thread, when we are notified of file changes, has an added benefit—when your code is called by some object it is listening for changes on, you do not know what synchronization locks are currently being held. This can make it easier to *deadlock*.[3] Since we dispatch the work to our own thread, via `RequestProcessor`, we are always in control of what locks are held when we do our I/O. Since we never do work when being called by foreign code, we just enqueue work to be done on a thread we *do* control, and we do not need to worry about any of our model code deadlocking.

7.2.2.2   Weak Listeners

Another aspect that is useful to understand is the call to `FileUtil.weakFileChangeListener()` in the constructor. One of the most potent sources of memory leaks in Swing applications is forgetting to remove listeners. So, a general ethic guideline in NetBeans coding is that *whenever you are adding a listener that you never explicitly remove, you should use a weak listener.*

What is a weak listener? It is actually two objects. The first one is your listener; the second is a sort of a stub object that implements the same listener interface and will call the first object. For example, if you were to write it out in Java code (you won't need to), a weak property change listener could look like in Example 7.6.

You could then use `WeakPCL` wherever you would use a `PropertyChangeListener` and not fear creating a memory leak— just implement `PropertyChangeListener` and call, for example, `someObject.addPropertyChangeListener(new WeakPCL(this))`.

There is, of course, a dark side to weak listeners: If you want to use them, it's up to your code to remember the real listener object as long as it needs to be listening. If, using the code from Example 7.6, you wrote

---

3. A deadlock is a state where one thread requests a nonsharable resource while holding some other resource. Another thread, conversely, requests the resource held by the first thread and holds the resource requested by it. The execution is locked forever—locked to death.

Example 7.6: A weak listener

```
class WeakPCL implements PropertyChangeListener {
  private final Reference <PropertyChangeListener> real;
  WeakPCL (PropertyChangeListener theRealListener) {
    real = new WeakReference <PropertyChangeListener>
                              ( theRealListener );
  }

  public void propertyChange (PropertyChangeEvent pce) {
    PropertyChangeListener theListener = real.get();
    if (theListener != null) {
      theListener.propertyChange (pce);
    }
  }
}
```

```
someObject.addPropertyChangeListener(
          new WeakPCL(new MyListener()));
```

what would happen is, a new `MyListener` instance would be created. The only thing that knows about it is the `WeakPCL` which does not hold any strong reference to the object. The result is that the `MyListener` object would be garbage-collected within milliseconds of being created—it's instant garbage. If you've written code that should be listening for changes but it is not being notified, look for a pattern like this.

The `org.openide.util.WeakListeners` utility class can construct weak listeners for any `EventListener` using Java dynamic proxies and provides simple methods for creating weak listeners for many of the standard Swing listener classes. Other utility classes in other APIs do the same thing for listener interfaces those APIs define, as is the case with `FileUtil.weakFileChangeListener()`, and you can always use `WeakListeners.create()` to create a weak listener for any listener interface.

So what the code in `XmlFileListModel` is doing is adding itself as a listener to the file it represents, but doing so in a way that the file won't keep the `XmlFileListModel` in memory permanently. As long as the model is being used by a `JList`, it is being strongly referenced, so it will keep receiving file change events. Once the UI forgets about the model, nothing else will be strongly referencing it, and it can be garbage-collected. While it is alive, our model can find out when the file has been changed and update its contents.

7.2.3   Registering `XmlListModelProvider`

The last thing we need to do is make the XML Pseudo Navigator module register `XmlListModelProvider` so that the Pseudo Navigator can find it. As mentioned earlier, we will be using the Editor MIME Lookup API. We will need to register `XmlListModelProvider` for two MIME types: `text/xml` and `text/html`. Modify the `layer.xml` file in the XML Pseudo Navigator to look like the following:

```
<filesystem>
  <folder name="Editors">
    <folder name="text">
      <folder name="html">
        <folder name="ListModelProvider">
          <file name="org-netbeans-examples-xmlpseudonavigator-↲
XmlListModelProvider.instance"/>
        </folder>
      </folder>
      <folder name="xml">
        <folder name="ListModelProvider">
          <file name="org-netbeans-examples-xmlpseudonavigator-↲
XmlListModelProvider.instance"/>
        </folder>
      </folder>
    </folder>
  </folder>
</filesystem>
```

7.3   Providing a UI Component

The final step is to provide a window that can be opened to display `ListModels`. It will be part of the Pseudo Navigator module. It will need to be able to find `ListModelProviders` that other modules have contributed. `FileObjects` have a `getMIMEType()` method. So we can get a file and find out its MIME type. Then we need a way to look up the `ListModelProvider` registered to handle that MIME type (if one is registered at all).

Pleasingly, we don't have to write a huge amount of infrastructure to be able to track down the available `ListModelProviders` for a given MIME type. There is a module with its own API and SPI for creating just such registries, ready for us to use.

7.3.1   The MIME Lookup SPI and API

To solve the problem of registration, we need a way to associate specific `ListModelProvider` subclasses with specific file types. We need to create a place in which `ListModelProviders` can be registered by any module that wants to register one, and we need to tie somehow these `ListModelProviders` to a MIME type.

Fortunately, the NetBeans Platform comes with a handy module that makes this easy. It is the Editor MIME Lookup API.[4] MIME types are hierarchical. A MIME type such as `text/x-java` is not so different structurally or semantically from a file path. The API we will use takes advantage of this to map MIME types directly as paths in the System Filesystem. The MIME Lookup API maps MIME types to folders under the `Editors/` folder of the System Filesystem. We define the name of a subdirectory of any MIME type folder. As can be seen in Section 7.2.3, the folder name will be `ListModelProvider`. So if a module wants to register a `ListModelProvider` for `text/x-java`, it will create a file in the System Filesystem, for example `Editors/text/x-java/ListModelProvider/MyJavaProvider.instance`.[5]

7.3.1.1   Registering with the MIME Lookup Module

In order to handle various modules registries of different sorts of objects associated with MIME types efficiently, the Editor MIME Lookup module requires that we register our registry—we must tell it about the folder we want other modules to put things into. To do that we need to implement an interface

---

4. Don't be fooled by the word "editor" in the name. This API originated as part of the editor, and its sources still live as a subproject of the Editor project in NetBeans sources. However, it is not tied to the NetBeans Editor in any particular way.

5. The Editor MIME Lookup API also allows you to define folders to be used only when one MIME type is embedded in a file of another MIME type, such as a Java scriptlet inside a JSP page.

in the Editor MIME Lookup module's SPI, `org.netbeans.spi.editor.`
`mimelookup.Class2LayerFolder`. This interface simply associates a particular subfolder of each MIME type's folder under `Editors/` in the System
Filesystem with the type of object we expect to look up in it, and provides
the name of the folder. So we will add one class to the Pseudo Navigator
module. Create a new class, `org.netbeans.examples.pseudonavigator.`
`FolderMapper`. Implement it as follows in Example 7.7:

Example 7.7: Implementing MIME Lookup's SPI

```
public class FolderMapper implements Class2LayerFolder {
  public FolderMapper() {
  }
  public Class getClazz() {
      return ListModelProvider.class;
  }
  public String getLayerFolderName() {
      return "ListModelProvider";
  }
  public InstanceProvider getInstanceProvider() {
      return null;
  }
}
```

Now we need to register this class in the `META-INF/services` lookup,
so that the Editor MIME Lookup module's infrastructure will recognize our
our folder and objects. To do this, simply create a new file in the Pseudo
Navigator module, `META-INF/services/org.netbeans.spi.editor.`
`mimelookup.Class2LayerFolder`. Add to it one line of text to register our
implementation of that interface:

`org.netbeans.examples.pseudonavigator.FolderMapper`

7.3.2   Providing a Window Component to Show List Models

As yet there is no "Pseudo Navigator"—there is only an API that lets us create
`ListModelProviders`. There is nothing that will actually use them or
show them.

To create a component that will display the list models for which we have created a way to register, we will be using the **Window Component** wizard. It creates a UI component—a subclass of `org.openide.windows.` `TopComponent` that can be opened in the NetBeans main window. In Chapter 8 we will cover `TopComponent`s in depth. For now, it is enough to know that we can treat it as a standard Swing container such as a `JPanel`. The `TopComponent` will contain one child component, a `javax.swing.JList`, which can show a `ListModel`.

Right-click the `pseudonavigator` package and choose **New | Window Component** to bring up the template wizard that will create a new `TopComponent` subclass. Enter `PseudoNavigator` for the class name prefix in the third step of the wizard. We will do specific edits to turn it into the component we need. What do we know about the requirements so far?

- It will need to know when the selected file changes. The selected file is the file being edited in the editor, if an editor component has keyboard focus (in other words, if it is the active `TopComponent` in the Window System at the time). If focus is in a tree control, such as the **Projects** window, it should be notified when the selection in that tree changes and be able to find out what the selected file is.

- It must find out what is the MIME type of the selected file.

- It must find out if there is a `ListModelProvider` registered for that MIME type. If there is one, it must be able to get and call that `ListModelProvider`.

- If it indeed finds a `ListModelProvider`, it must ask it to generate a `javax.swing.ListModel` for the file that is selected and show that model in some component, presumably a `JList`.

- If it is showing a model and the user selects an item in the list, it must call the `selected()` method in the `ListModelProvider`, passing to it the item in the model that was selected. What happens when `selected()` is called is up to the `ListModelProvider` implementation. Presumably it will do something such as changing the caret position in the editor and sending keyboard focus back to it.

The first thing we need to do is add an `implements` clause to the class declaration of `PseudoNavigatorTopComponent`. Add the following to the class declaration:

```
implements ListSelectionListener, LookupListener
```

Clearly, if we are implementing `ListSelectionListener`, somewhere there is going to be a `JList`, so we can create a final field for that at the top of the class definition:

```
private final JList list = new JList();
```

Press Alt-Shift-F to invoke **Fix Imports**. Then move the caret into the class signature line, press Alt-Enter, and accept the hint **Implement All Abstract Methods**. This will generate stubs for the methods of `LookupListener` and `ListSelectionListener`.

In the constructor we will add some code to wire up the `JList` to our listener implementation and add it to the container:

```
add (list, BorderLayout.CENTER);
list.addListSelectionListener(this);
```

Note that above, we are referring to `java.awt.BorderLayout`. That is not the default layout manager, so we will need to change it in the GUI editor. Click the **Design** button in the editor toolbar and switch to the form editor view of the class. You are now using the GUI Builder, code-named "Project Matisse," which is described in Chapter 11. On the bottom left of the main window, the **Inspector** window should be visible (see Figure 7.6). Right-click the node for the form (the `TopComponent`) itself and, from the **Set Layout** menu, choose `BorderLayout`. The default layout, `GroupLayout`, could certainly work for our purposes, but we are creating a layout which contains a single component. The simplicity of `BorderLayout` is designed for this sort of situation.

As we mentioned above, our component will need to track the selected file, in order to display a `ListModel` in its `JList` whenever there is a provider that knows about the type of file that is selected in a tree view or is being edited in the editor. So the next step is to add some bookkeeping. Our component certainly does not need to be listening all the time—it may exist while not being on screen at all. But when it is visible to the user, it should be

Figure 7.6: Setting the layout to `BorderLayout`

tracking the selected file and trying to display it to the user. So the next step is to override the two notification methods that will be called when our component becomes visible and when it becomes hidden in the main window. We can start and stop listening to the global selection and looking for things to display in these methods, as shown in Example 7.8.

The call to `Utilities.actionsGlobalContext()` returns a `Lookup` that proxies the `Lookup` of whatever tab in the main window has focus and is described in detail in Section 5.4.

As described in Chapter 5, we are listening on the global selection context—the `Lookup` that is returned by the static method `Utilities.actionsGlobalContext()`. We are asking it to tell us about any instances of the class `DataObject` (which will be covered in depth in Chapter 10). For now it is enough to know that a `DataObject` is a wrapper for a file—the file provided by a module that implements editing for that file type.

Example 7.8: Listening to the global selection

```
private Lookup.Result <DataObject> lookupResult;
public void componentShowing() {
  lookupResult = Utilities.actionsGlobalContext().
                        lookupResult (DataObject.class);
  lookupResult.addLookupListener (this);
  resultChanged (null);
}

public void componentHidden() {
  lookupResult.removeLookupListener(this);
  lookupResult = null;
  setActivatedNodes(new Node[0]);
}
```

The code in Example 7.8 listens for changes in the selected `DataObject`. If the user selects a different file in the **Projects** or **Files** windows, or sends focus to the editor, the selected `DataObject` will change and our code will be notified and can look up a `ListModelProvider` (if there is one) for the newly selected file. The code that will do that lives in our implementation of the one method of `LookupListener`, `resultChanged()`.

For clarity, we implement `resultChanged()` adding in two utility methods, as shown in Example 7.9.

Example 7.9: Responding to selection changes

```
public void resultChanged(LookupEvent evt) {
  // The next line will generate a warning about unchecked
  // conversion in NetBeans 5.x, but is fine in 6
  Collection <? extends DataObject> objs =
                        lookupResult.allInstances();
  DataObject dob =
    objs.isEmpty() ? null : objs.iterator().next();
  setDataObject (dob);
  // We're ignoring multiselection here
  setActivatedNodes(dob == null ? new Node[0] :
    new Node[] {dob.getNodeDelegate()});
}
```

```
private void setDataObject (DataObject obj) {
  System.err.println("GOT " + obj);
  if (obj != null) System.err.println("MIME TYPE " +
                           obj.getPrimaryFile().getMIMEType());
  ListModelProvider provider = null;
  FileObject file = null;
  if (obj != null) {
    file = obj.getPrimaryFile();
    String mime = file.getMIMEType();

    Lookup lkp = MimeLookup.getMimeLookup(mime);

//------------- NetBeans 6 Version - much shorter:
//    Lookup lkp = MimeLookup.getLookup (MimePath.get(mime));
//    Collection <? extends ListModelProvider> providers =
//      lkp.lookupAll(ListModelProvider.class);
//    provider = providers.isEmpty() ? null :
//               providers.iterator().next();

    Lookup.Template template = new Lookup.Template (
          ListModelProvider.class);
    Lookup.Result result = lkp.lookup(template);
    Collection providers = result.allInstances();
    provider = providers.isEmpty() ? null :
      (ListModelProvider) providers.iterator().next();
  }
  setProvider (provider, file);
}

private ListModelProvider provider;
private void setProvider (ListModelProvider provider,
                          FileObject file) {
  this.provider = provider;
  if (provider == null) {
    DefaultListModel mdl = new DefaultListModel();
    mdl.addElement(NbBundle.getMessage(
      PseudoNavigatorTopComponent.class, "LBL_EMPTY"));

    list.setModel(mdl);
    list.setEnabled (false);
  } else {
    list.setEnabled (true);
    list.setModel (provider.getListModel(file));
  }
}
```

This code will be notified whenever the `DataObject` that is selected changes. When that happens, it will call `setDataObject()` with either `null` or a `DataObject`. `setDataObject()` gets the `FileObject` from the `DataObject` and asks it for the MIME type. From there, it uses the Editor MIME Lookup API to try get a `Lookup` containing any `ListModelProviders` that are registered against that MIME type. If it finds one, it will pass it to `setProvider()`, which will ask it for a a `ListModel` for the current file. Then it will pass that `ListModel` to the `setModel()` method of the `JList`.

The next step is to have our component handle the selection portion of the contract that the `ListModelProvider` interface defines. It has another method that should be called whenever an item in the list is selected. We are already implementing `ListSelectionListener` directly on `PseudoNavigatorTopComponent`, and the `valueChanged()` method of `ListSelectionListener` should already be present. Implement it as shown in Example 7.10.

This code will call back to the current `ListSelectionModel` when an item is clicked.[6]

Example 7.10: Implementing `ListSelectionListener`

```
public void valueChanged(ListSelectionEvent evt) {
  if (provider != null) {
    int index = list.getSelectionModel().getLeadSelectionIndex();
    if (index != -1) {
      Object obj = list.getModel().getElementAt(index);
      provider.selected(obj);
    }
  }
}
```

---

6. Note that the code in Example 7.10 will generate a compiler warning about not using generics. Unfortunately `javax.swing.ListModel` is not yet genericized in JDK 1.6. Nonetheless, we can give users of *our* API the convenience of using generics, even if `ListModel` does not yet support them.

7.4   Using the Pseudo Navigator

Now all that is left is to run our module and try out its functionality. Right-click the module suite and choose **Run** from the popup menu. Another copy of the NetBeans IDE will start, with the Pseudo Navigator and the XML Pseudo Navigator installed (Figure 7.7).

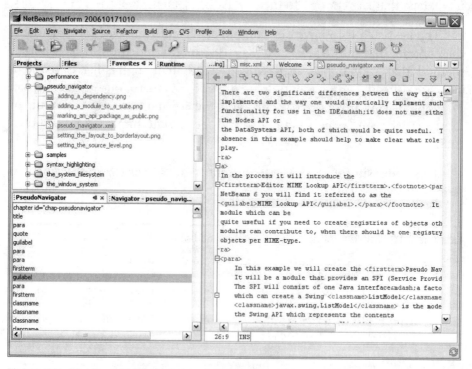

Figure 7.7: The Pseudo Navigator in action, editing this chapter

7.5   Conclusion: `PseudoNavigator`—What's Wrong with This Picture?

In this example, we have successfully created a component that shows a structured view of the contents of a file and allows users to navigate in the editor with that file loaded. What we have done is a perfectly legitimate way to do this sort of thing. It is also an example that should highlight the need for some of the APIs that will be covered in the coming chapters.

But there are some downsides to the approach: We are doing the parsing of a file. Imagine what would happen if every module wanting to do something with an `.xml` file had to parse it—so that, if an `Action` wants to make some change in the file it would need its own parsing code. This would quickly get wasteful, with lots of different pieces of code all doing the same work—parsing the file—over and over.

In Chapter 10, we will show how this is not necessary. In that chapter we will show how to create `DataObjects` for individual files, which can provide objects that let you programmatically validate or modify a file. A `DataObject` does the parsing; things such as **Navigator** views ask the `DataObject` for, say, a `Properties` object to represent a `.properties` file and manipulate that object instead of parsing the file themselves.

Additionally, what we wrote is closely tied to the `JList` class. If we decide that a `JTree` was a better choice, or want to offer the option of using both, it would result in quite a bit of recoding (`JTrees` and `JLists` do not use the same kinds of models, nor fire the same events). As you will see in Chapter 9, with the Nodes API and the Explorer API, changing from using a list to using a tree is a one-line change.

CHAPTER EIGHT

The Window System

One of the most basic things any GUI application needs is the ability to display windows on the screen. Swing provides for this with classes such as JFrame. But this hardly solves the entire problem of windowing for Swing applications. In a reasonably complex, modern application, quite a bit of plumbing is needed beyond the simple ability to put a window on the screen. An application window will typically contain menus, toolbars, and other common components. Many applications have a concept of *selection* or *context sensitivity*—certain actions that are represented in menus and toolbars can only be enabled when certain types of things are "selected." For example, a **Copy** menu item should only be enabled when there is something to copy.

Neither the code wiring up Actions to toolbar buttons and menu items, nor that which enables and disables actions depending on the state of components in the application's user interface is too much fun to write and debug. Moreover, it is not the business logic of the application—it's just plumbing code needed to give the user access to the business logic of the application. It is not the best use of an application developer's time to reinvent such logic for every application they write. It would be preferable to have a standard way of doing this sort of thing which can be reused across all applications.

Complex applications tend to have more than one *logical window*—master and detail views, lists of files, editors, palettes, property sheets, and other controls are common. Very often such controls are instantiated on the fly in an application, in response to a user's actions—the designer of the application may not know all of the possible combinations of UI controls that may appear on-screen in a given user session. So there is a need for organizing and managing of these controls—both programmatically, so your code can affect what controls are open, what have focus, and so forth; and manually, for users to be able to open and close controls and arrange them to suit their tastes and the task at hand.

The NetBeans Platform solves this conglomeration of UI problems with the *Window System API*. The classes in this API are in the package `org.openide.windows`—but much of the Window System API is a variety of XML file formats. The actual implementation of the Window System API lives in the module *Core—Windows*. So, following a pattern that will become familiar, the Window System comes in two pieces—one module which provides some APIs which you will call or subclass, and another module which provides the implementation of those APIs but does not contain classes that your code will directly call.

The Window System implementation takes care of selection management and logical window management. In fact, the implementation supports both an MDI[1] (multiple document interface) mode and an SDI[2] (single document interface) mode in which each tabbed container is in a separate top-level window.

One of the benefits of the Window System API is that application code is completely independent of how its components are realized on-screen. So, one could radically change the appearance and behavior of an application by changing the Window System implementation. If 3D user interfaces become

---

1. MDI is a bit of a misnomer, but is used for historical reasons to describe the default UI of the NetBeans IDE. MDI stands for *multiple document interface*, which traditionally means that an application provides its own desktop container window showing draggable, resizable windows inside it. You can create this kind of UI in plain Swing code using `JDesktopPane` and `JInternalFrame`. The term TDI, or *tabbed docking interface*, would better describe the current "MDI" mode of the NetBeans Window System. Until NetBeans 3.6, the MDI mode for NetBeans user interface was traditional MDI with inner floating frames.

2. SDI mode may be removed or become unsupported in future versions of NetBeans.

mainstream, all a NetBeans-based application will need to do is drop in a 3D replacement for the standard Window System implementation. If someone wants to write a Macintosh-oriented implementation that uses some of the different frame peers available on the Macintosh platform to create a more native-feeling, super-Mac-friendly UI, a NetBeans-based application would merely need to replace the JAR containing the Window System with that Mac-specific implementation's JAR to take advantage of it. The application's code need not change at all.

The Window System is *component-oriented*. Most of the time your code will deal with components you have created; the work of adding them to a GUI container in the main window is taken care of by the Window System. So the Window System API lets you concentrate on the business logic of the application—getting the right controls on-screen for the user to interact with, instead of spending your precious time on the plumbing code necessary to realize the components on-screen and to make menu items act on the active component.

8.1 What the Window System Does

The Window System handles a variety of aspects of user interface state.

Logical window management   In the NetBeans Window System, application code is concerned with *components* rather than windows per se. The Window System implementation takes care of creating the main application window (or windows). Application code uses a `JPanel` subclass that is part of the Window System API—`org.openide.windows.TopComponent`. So you write components which are subclasses of `TopComponent`, define which tabbed container they should be opened in, and then give those components to the Window System implementation to manage.

Such components are logically separate application windows—and for simplicity, documentation will often refer to "the Projects Window" when the window in question is actually a component in a tab control.

Window state   Components in the user interface may be in a combination of states: open, selected, and activated. At any given time, in the entire user interface of an instance of NetBeans, only one `TopComponent` is *activated*, meaning that it or its child control has input focus. Within a tabbed container in the NetBeans UI, only one of all the components in the container is selected. And all components which are open have visible tabs in that tabbed container.[3] So a `TopComponent` can exist without being opened; if it is open it may be selected (its tab is the selected one in the tabbed container it lives in); and it may be active (it or its subcomponent has keyboard focus).

Selection management   Each `TopComponent` has two forms of selection:

- Its *Lookup*—a sort of bag-of-stuff which can contain whatever the author of the component wants to put there. There are some standard API classes that can be put there, such as `SaveCookie`, or it can contain a component that the author provided, say, to get a `java.util.jar.Manifest` object when writing an editor for manifest files.

- Its *activated Nodes*—an array of zero or more `Node` objects. `Nodes` themselves implement `Lookup.Provider` (meaning they have a `getLookup()` method, as does `TopComponent`). The Explorer API contains components that can show `Nodes` and conveniently hook those components up to the `Lookup` of a `TopComponent`, as described in Chapter 9.

    As their name suggests, `Nodes` are hierarchical, tree-node-like objects. The *Explorer API* provides a number of UI components which can display `Nodes` to the user in trees, lists, tree-tables, etc. So, a common pattern is to have a child component inside a `TopComponent` container, which allows the user to select `Nodes`; the "activated `Nodes`" property of the `TopComponent` will track the GUI selection in the child component, firing changes in its activated nodes property when the selection changes. The `Lookup` obtained

---

3. If you do not want any tabs at all in your application, you can supply a different UI delegate for tabbed containers, as Geertjan describes in his blog (`http://blogs.sun.com/geertjan/entry/farewell_to_space_consuming_weird`).

from the `TopComponent`'s `getLookup()` method, in turn, will be one which proxies the `Lookups` of whatever `Nodes` are currently selected. `Nodes` will be more thoroughly discussed in Chapter 9.

8.2   Classes in the Window System API

As already mentioned, much of the Window System API consists of XML file formats that the default Window System implementation understands. As of NetBeans 5.5, it is rarely necessary to edit such files directly—more often they will be created by various wizards and templates. The surface area of the programmatic API of the Window System is relatively small. Most applications will not touch any classes but `TopComponent`.

Some classes you may encounter are:

`TopComponent`   A `TopComponent` is just a `JPanel` with some additional methods that allow it to be managed by, and interact with, the Window System. Methods that are likely to be useful for controlling `TopComponents`' lifecycle in the UI are shown in Table 8.1.

Table 8.1: Commonly used lifecycle methods of `TopComponent`

Name	*Description*
`open()`	Causes the component to appear in a tab in a tabbed container in the UI.
`requestVisible()`	Asks the Window System to make this component selected in the tabbed container it lives in.
`requestActive()`	Asks the Window System to transfer keyboard focus to this component, making it the one which owns UI-wide selection.
`close()`	Asks the Window System to close the component, removing it from the UI.

For each of the lifecycle methods from Table 8.1, there is a corresponding notification method which you can override to do some work when the component is opened, selected, activated, etc.: `componentOpened()`, `componentShown()`, `component-Activated()`, `componentDeactivated()`, `componentHidden()`, and `componentClosed()`.

The final stage of the lifecycle is persisting state information across sessions. For this, `TopComponent` implements `java.io.Externalizable`. It is much like serialization except that what you save is a *proxy* object for the object you want to save. That proxy object knows how to recreate the original object. In other words, if you want to remember that a component of a certain type was open and editing a certain file type, what you probably want to save is the path to the file that was being edited and recreate a component on restart making it open the same file in the same kind of editor—as opposed to serializing and writing out to disk all of the component's fields and state and every listener that might be attached to it. `Externalizable` enables you to save a proxy object for the component that you want to save, with enough data to recreate it on restart.

Note that you typically do not need to implement the methods of `java.io.Externalizable` (`writeExternal()` and `readExternal()`) directly; rather, you simply override the `writeReplace()` method to return a serializable object that is serialized in place of the component.

Mode   The name of this class is somewhat unfortunate, but cannot be changed for backward compatibility reasons. The concept here is *docking mode*—a way in which a component can be docked into a window. For practical purposes, a `Mode` is a tabbed container you see in the main window.[4] It is relatively rare to need to programmatically interact with `Mode`s. `Mode`s are created declaratively using XML, as described in Section 8.7.

WindowManager   `WindowManager` is the overall manager for the state of the application's user interface. It is relatively rare to write code that

---

4. Though it should be noted that `Mode` is not a UI component per se. It is the model for the content of a tabbed container.

touches this class—most often, you simply fetch a reference to the main window that you need for some reason (for example, `WindowManager.getDefault().getMainWindow()`).

`TopComponentGroup` A `TopComponentGroup` is a handle that allows activating one `TopComponent` to cause other `TopComponents` to change state. This is how the IDE's Form Editor (aka Matisse) causes activating the form editor component to trigger opening and selecting the component palette and the property sheet.

8.3 Using `TopComponent`

The simplest use of the Window System is creating a component and showing it in the main window, which we will do now. We will create a simple "scratchpad" component. In the real world, a scratchpad is a pad of paper for writing down temporarily useful, but ultimately disposable information. Our **Scratchpad** window will simply contain a text area where text can be pasted and copied back.

1. Create a new empty module, using **New Project** (Figure 8.1).

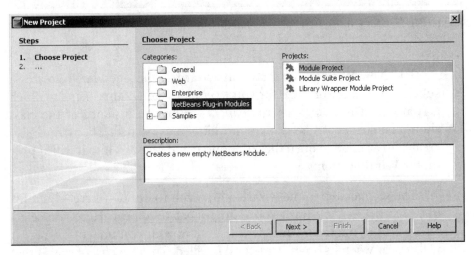

Figure 8.1: Creating a new module

2. Use the **New Window Component** wizard to create a new `TopComponent` subclass (Figure 8.2).

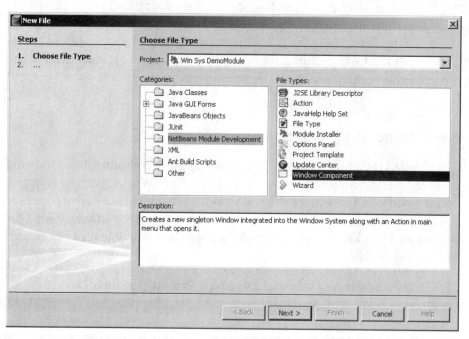

Figure 8.2: Creating a `TopComponent` subclass

The **New Window Component** wizard is the one which creates a subclass of `TopComponent` for you to edit and add components to. Such a component is a *singleton component*—only one instance of the class should be created, to be shown and hidden as needed. The wizard also creates an `Action` to open the component and registers it so it will appear on the **Window** menu.

The second step in the wizard allows you to decide where—literally, in which `Mode`—you want your component to appear. Here you select which area of the main window will contain your component—where it will appear when its `open()` method is called. The exact list of `Modes` that will appear depends on what modules are installed in the copy of NetBeans you are developing against. As mentioned in Section 8.2, Modes are created declaratively via XML files. So what you are seeing in the combo box in Figure 8.3 is the list of all such XML files in all of the modules in the copy of the NetBeans Platform you are building against.[5]

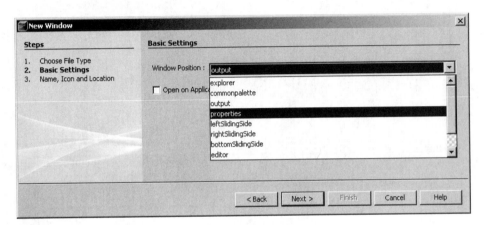

Figure 8.3: Selecting a mode

Use Demo for the class name prefix on the third page of the wizard. This will result in the generated TopComponent subclass having the class name DemoTopComponent.

3. Switch to the form editor view of DemoTopComponent.

4. Add a JTextArea to DemoTopComponent (Figure 8.4).

---

5. You can control what copy of NetBeans you are building against using **Tools | NetBeans Platform Manager**. By default you are building against the copy of NetBeans you are using; you can also get a standalone platform-only distribution and use that, or create your own stripped-down copy of NetBeans to work against, which contains only those things you need.

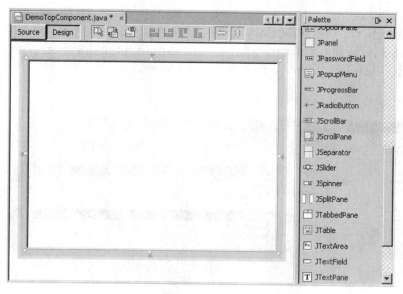

Figure 8.4: Adding a `JTextArea`

At this point, without editing any code, we have the basics of our Scratchpad module. There is enough to run NetBeans with the module installed, which you can do by pressing F6 or right-clicking the module project and choosing **Run Project** from its popup menu (Figure 8.5).

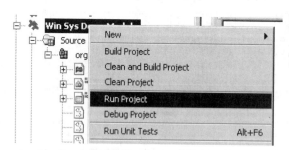

Figure 8.5: Running a module project

8.4   Persisting State across Sessions

One of the useful features of `TopComponent` is the ability to persist state across sessions. This means that if the user shuts down the application while a given `TopComponent` is open, on restart, that same `TopComponent` will be reopened in more-or-less[6] the same state it was in on shutdown.

As mentioned in Section 8.2, this is done using `java.io.Externalizable`. The wizard, by default, generates skeleton code for this, which just looks up the default instance of the component and returns that.[7] We will add a bit of data to this object so that the text in our scratchpad persists across restarts.

The default persistence code which was generated is shown in Example 8.1.

`PREFERRED_ID` is a unique string ID for the component. This is the name the component would *like* to be saved with (in case of a duplicate, the Window System may provide a modified version of the name), and it is used to look up our singleton component instance. `getPersistenceType()` returns a constant that indicates that the component indeed wants to be saved at shutdown. `writeReplace()` returns the object that will be serialized in place of serializing the whole `TopComponent`. The `ResolvableHelper` class is what will be serialized. This is where we will save our data. Since we're using Java serialization, we don't need to do anything special beyond creating fields for the data we want to save and populating them with data. Modify the code as shown in Example 8.2.

---

6. Exactly how much state is preserved across restarts is up to the author of the `TopComponent`—for example, remembering what file was being edited and reopening that file in an editor is important, but persisting the exact caret position and what characters are selected usually is not.

7. "Looking up the default instance" means calling a static method, `findDefault()`, which was generated by the wizard. What this really does is ask the Window Manager to deserialize the persisted version of our component and return that instance of it. It might seem that there is a chicken-and-egg problem here—if the module is newly installed, is there any persisted version of the component to restore? In fact, the answer is yes. The XML files the wizard generated *are* a persisted instance of our component. The way a module adds a window to the overall configuration is by adding a persisted instance of it to the overall configuration of NetBeans.

Example 8.1: The default persistence code

```
protected String preferredID() {
  return PREFERRED_ID;
}

public int getPersistenceType() {
  return TopComponent.PERSISTENCE_ALWAYS;
}

/** replaces this in object stream */
public Object writeReplace() {
  return new ResolvableHelper();
}

final static class ResolvableHelper implements Serializable {
  private static final long serialVersionUID = 1L;
  public Object readResolve() {
    return DemoTopComponent.getDefault();
  }
}
```

Example 8.2: Modifying the default persistence code

```
public Object writeReplace() {
  return new ResolvableHelper(jTextArea1.getText());
}

final static class ResolvableHelper implements Serializable {
  private static final long serialVersionUID = 1L;
  private final String text;
  ResolvableHelper (String text) {
    this.text = text;
  }

  public Object readResolve() {
    DemoTopComponent result = DemoTopComponent.getDefault();
    result.jTextArea1.setText(text);
    return result;
  }
}
```

Try running the module again. Type some text into the text field and shut down NetBeans. Run the module yet again. You will note that the text you entered during the previous session has been preserved.

8.4.1   Window System Persistence Modes

There are three persistence modes a `TopComponent` can have: `PERSISTENCE_ALWAYS`, meaning that the component's state should always be saved on shutdown and restored to its current state (which may be closed) on restart; `PERSISTENCE_NEVER` which means that the component will never be persisted on shutdown; and `PERSISTENCE_ONLY_OPENED`, which is appropriate for file editors—if the component is open, it will be persisted; otherwise it will not.

The default persistence mode of a `TopComponent` is `PERSISTENCE_ALWAYS`. To change it, override `getPersistenceType()` in your `TopComponent` subclass.

8.5   Window System Persistence Data

Let's have a look at the files that were generated when we used the **New Window Component** wizard to create `DemoTopComponent`.

`Bundle.properties`   This file was created when we created the project. It contains the localized display name and description of the module. It was modified, when the **New Window Component** wizard ran, to also contain localized names for our Scratchpad component and the action that displays it.

`DemoAction.java`   This is an action class which looks up the default instance of our component and calls `open()` and then `requestActive()` on it.

`DemoTopComponent.form`   This is the form file metadata which is used by the Swing GUI editor—it will be omitted from the module JAR by the build script, since it is not needed at runtime; it is only used by the GUI designer in NetBeans during development.

`DemoTopComponent.java`   This is the Java source for our `TopComponent` subclass.

`DemoTopComponentSettings.xml`   This is one of a pair of files that defines the persisted default instance of `DemoTopComponent`. Settings files are a NetBeans file type to represent a persisted instance of some object. They are somewhat like a file containing a serialized object, but are in XML, and do not necessarily contain any serialized data—by default a settings file can simply specify what class to instantiate and the system will try to do so via `Class.newInstance()`.

```
<?xml version="1.0" encoding="UTF-8"?>
<!DOCTYPE settings
   PUBLIC "-//NetBeans//DTD Session settings 1.0//EN"
   "http://www.netbeans.org/dtds/sessionsettings-1_0.dtd">
<settings version="1.0">
   <module name="org.netbeans.modules.winsysdemo"
           spec="1.0"/>
   <instanceof class="org.openide.windows.TopComponent"/>
   <instanceof class="org.netbeans.modules.winsysdemo.↵
DemoTopComponent"/>
   <instance class="org.netbeans.modules.winsysdemo.↵
DemoTopComponent" method="getDefault"/>
</settings>
```

A slightly more common idiom in NetBeans is `.instance` files, which you will learn about in Chapter 10. Their principal difference from settings files is that by specifying all of the classes and interfaces an object implements, it is possible for the system to answer questions about the type of a stored object without instantiating it to know what class it really is.

Suffice it to say that this file instructs to create an instance of `DemoTopComponent` when one is needed, and to do so by calling the static `getDefault()` method that the wizard put in `DemoTopComponent`.

`DemoTopComponentWstcref.xml`   This is a class which ties the settings file described above to a particular declaratively-defined `Mode`.

```
<?xml version="1.0" encoding="UTF-8"?>
<!DOCTYPE tc-ref PUBLIC "-//NetBeans//⏎
DTD Top Component in Mode Properties 2.0//EN"
"http://www.netbeans.org/dtds/tc-ref2_0.dtd">
<tc-ref version="2.0" >
  <module name="org.netbeans.modules.winsysdemo"
          spec="1.0"/>
  <tc-id id="DemoTopComponent"/>
  <state opened="false"/>
</tc-ref>
```

The next file, `layer.xml`, contains the code that will actually install these XML files into NetBeans runtime configuration. Note that the ID string in this file is the same as that returned by `DemoTopComponent.preferredID()`.

`layer.xml`   This is the configuration file that defines what our module installs—much of the declarative runtime configuration of NetBeans is defined in such layer files, provided by modules that want to contribute some classes or objects to the runtime configuration of the application. For a more complete discussion of the System Filesystem, see Section 6.5. If you open the JAR manifest for our demo module, you will find a line in it that points to this layer file:

```
OpenIDE-Module-Layer: org/netbeans/modules/winsysdemo/⏎
layer.xml
```

So, clearly, there is no magic happening here. On startup, the manifest for our module is read. The line above is parsed, and then other parts of the system cause the contents of our layer file to be merged into the overall configuration of the application. Our layer file contains the following contents:

```xml
<?xml version="1.0" encoding="UTF-8"?>
<!DOCTYPE filesystem
  PUBLIC "-//NetBeans//DTD Filesystem 1.1//EN"
  "http://www.netbeans.org/dtds/filesystem-1_1.dtd">
<filesystem>
  <folder name="Actions">
    <folder name="Window">
      <file name="org-netbeans-modules-winsysdemo-↵
DemoAction.instance"/>
    </folder>
  </folder>
  <folder name="Menu">
    <folder name="Window">
      <file name="DemoAction.shadow">
        <attr name="originalFile"
          stringvalue="Actions/Window/org-netbeans-↵
modules-winsysdemo-DemoAction.instance"/>
      </file>
    </folder>
  </folder>
  <folder name="Windows2">
    <folder name="Components">
      <file name="DemoTopComponent.settings"
            url="DemoTopComponentSettings.xml"/>
    </folder>
    <folder name="Modes">
      <folder name="properties">
        <file name="DemoTopComponent.wstcref"
              url="DemoTopComponentWstcref.xml"/>
      </folder>
    </folder>
  </folder>
</filesystem>
```

The full scope of XML filesystems is covered in Chapter 6. Modules can create folders and define their own contents for folders in the System Filesystem. They can also add contents to existing folders. Some of what this file does should be self-evident—our DemoAction is being installed into a folder called Menu/Window and, when we run the module, indeed the action to display our component is on the **Window** menu.

Slightly less obvious is what the Windows2 "folder" and its contents do. The Window System API defines the folder Windows2 and its subdirectories `Modes` and `Components`. The `Components` folder is where instances of singleton components live—our settings file is put there. The second file, `DemoTopComponent.wstcref`,[8] is like a symbolic link or a pointer to the first: Subfolders of the `Windows2/Modes` folder correspond to declaratively created `Modes` representing tabbed containers that appear in the main window. So we are defining the component we are adding to the system, and then providing a pointer that indicates where it should be displayed.

To recap, in the configuration of the Window System, docking areas (`Modes`) are folders under `Windows2/Modes`. The Window System configuration also contains a folder where each `TopComponent` registered by a module puts a file that describes how to instantiate that component and what its unique ID is. The subfolders of `Windows2/Modes` each identify one tabbed docking area in the main window, and in turn contain files that each identify the unique ID of one component that wants to be opened in that particular docking area when its `open()` is called (see Figure 8.6).

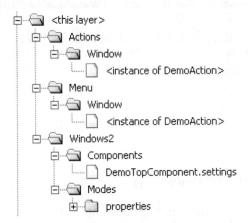

Figure 8.6: System Filesystem contents provided by the Window System demo module

---

8. The somewhat unwieldy file extension `wstcref` stands for "Window System TopComponent reference."

So what we are really providing with our module is a set of canned data about an *already persisted* component—essentially our module fools the Window System into thinking there was already a copy of our component opened that it had saved during a previous run. The action that opens the component looks up the fake-persisted instance of the component and opens and displays it. If the user manipulates the component, opening, closing it, or dragging it to a different location, versions of the files we have created reflecting those changes will be saved at shutdown, in the user's settings directory. And it will be those files, not our originals, that will be used to decide what to do with our component on subsequent restarts. Thus the state of the Window System is preserved across restarts.

To get a sense of this in action, try the following. Run the Window System demo module. Open our Scratchpad component. Drag it to another location in the main window—for example, the top right corner of the main window. Shut down and run the module again. Note that the system has remembered where our component should be—it remains where we left it on the previous run. Now run **Clean** on the module and run it again. Note that the information about our repositioning of the component has been forgotten— when you perform the **Run**, the user settings directory is set to `[$YOUR-MODULE'S-PROJECT-ROOT-FOLDER]/build/testuserdir`. The **Clean** action deletes this data. If you are interested in exactly what data is being stored, perform the above exercise of opening, dragging the window, and shutting down again. Then examine the files in `[$YOUR-MODULE'S-PROJECT-ROOT-FOLDER]/build/testuserdir/config/Windows2Local`. There you will find files a lot like the ones we have created, but modified and moved around to reflect the new location of the Scratchpad component.

8.6   Creating Editor-Style (Nondeclarative) `TopComponent`s

So far, we have only defined a palette-style, singleton `TopComponent`. Creating `TopComponent`s of which there can be multiple instances is even easier. To do this, you simply create a subclass of `TopComponent`. Then just create a new instance of that component and call `open()` and `requestActive()` on it. Newly created, nondeclaratively defined `TopComponent`s will always open in the "editor area" in the center of the main window.

8.6.1   Opening Your Component Somewhere Else

As mentioned, by default, newly created `TopComponents` open in the editor area in the middle of the main window. If you want to have a programmatically created `TopComponent` in some other location, the code to do so is quite straightforward (and it is likely the only time application code will need to directly reference the `Mode` at all). In this case, we look up a `Mode` object by its ID and dock our `TopComponent` into it (if it indeed exists):

```
public void open() {
  Mode mode = WindowManager.getDefault().findMode ("properties");
  if (mode != null) mode.dockInto (this);
  super.open();
}
```

8.7   Advanced Window System Configuration: Defining Your Own Modes

Now that we have our component, one thing we might possibly want to do is to give it its own location on screen, rather than reusing an existing location. This means we need to define our own `Mode`. As of NetBeans 5.5, there is no special support for doing this via wizards and templates, so we will be doing this the old-fashioned way—by hand-editing XML files.

Fortunately, we can cheat a bit: The data a module would install to create a new `Mode` is a fake-persisted instance of a `Mode`. In other words, if we start up the IDE, open the Scratchpad component, drag it to a new location in the main window, and shut down, a new `Mode` will be created automatically for us when we drop the component, and *the files by which we would need to declare that `Mode` in our own module* will be saved to disk. We just need to copy that data to the layer file for our module and we have our custom `Mode`.

Run the Scratchpad module, open the **Scratchpad** window from the **Window** menu. When it appears, drag its tab upward, dropping it so it is positioned as shown in Figure 8.7.

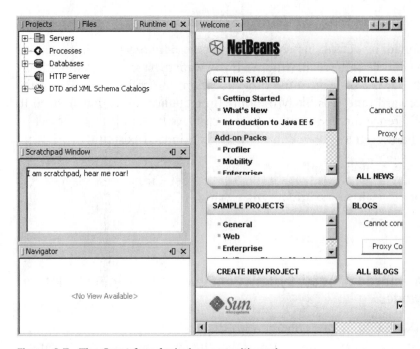

Figure 8.7: The **Scratchpad** window repositioned

Shut down the copy of the IDE with the Scratchpad module installed. When you run a NetBeans module the way we just did, a userdir is created for test runs, `build/testuserdir`. As described in Section 6.5.2, the place where changes made at runtime to the contents of the System Filesystem are saved is the `config/` subdirectory of the userdir. Switching to the **Files** window, we can browse to this directory. Expand the `Windows2Local` subdirectory—this is where Window System data is saved (see Figure 8.8).

You can see a file called `anonymousMode_1.wsmode`. That is the XML persistence data for the `Mode` that was created when you dragged the **Scratchpad** component to a new location. Its content is listed in Example 8.3.

The data here is not much different from what might be passed to a `GridBagLayout` for weighted component layout.

Figure 8.8: Userdir contents on disk after running the Scratchpad module

Example 8.3: The XML persistence data for the `Mode`

```xml
<mode version="2.1">
  <name unique="anonymousMode_1" />
  <kind type="view" />
  <state type="joined" />
  <constraints>
    <path orientation="vertical" number="20" weight="0.7"/>
    <path orientation="horizontal" number="20" weight="0.32"/>
    <path orientation="vertical" number="21" weight="0.25"/>
  </constraints>
  <bounds x="0" y="0" width="0" height="0" />
  <frame state="0"/>
  <active-tc id="ScratchpadTopComponent"/>
  <empty-behavior permanent="false"/>
</mode>
```

Why `Windows2` **and** `Windows2Local`**?**

These two directories amount to the same thing. The numeral 2 comes from the fact that there was an earlier form of windows persistence data up through NetBeans 3.5, and that format is still at least somewhat supported (at any rate, it has a claim on the `Windows` folder).

On first start, the Window System implementation copies all of the data it finds in `Windows2/` in the System Filesystem over to `Windows2Local`. At runtime, the configuration data lives in the `Windows2Local` directory, but layer files that want to modify the Window System should place their files in `Windows2/` in the System Filesystem.

The truly clever thing we can do is just painlessly copy these files into the Scratchpad module by taking advantage of the **XML Layer** node underneath the project in the **Projects** window. Right-click the `anonymousMode_1.wsmode` file and choose **Copy** from the popup window.

Switch to the **Projects** window. Expand the **Scratchpad** project and, underneath it, the nodes **Important Files | XML Layer | <this layer in context>**; find the `Windows2` folder underneath it, and the `Modes` folder underneath `Windows2`—as shown in Figure 8.9. Right-click the `Modes` folder and choose **Paste** from the popup menu.

The metadata for a `Mode` is a file/folder pair with the same name. As can be seen in Figure 8.8, there is also a subdirectory of `build/testuserdir/config/Windows2Local/Modes` named `anonymousMode_1`. Go back to the **Files** window, copy that directory, and paste it too into the `Windows2Local/Modes` folder of the XML layer node. The folder for the `Mode` contains `.wstcref` files described in Section 8.5. By copying the `anonymousMode_1` directory, we have also copied a `.wstcref` file that points to the Scratchpad component.

Next we need to delete the original `.wstcref` file that the **New Window Component** wizard generated (the Scratchpad component cannot be in two places at once). Do so as shown in Figure 8.10.

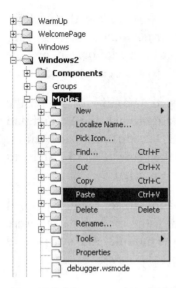

Figure 8.9: The `Windows2` folder

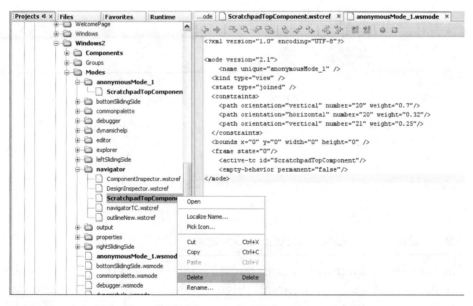

Figure 8.10: Deleting the original `.wstcref` file

We need to make a minor change to the `.wsmode` file that defines `anonymousMode_1`. Double-click *the node for that file underneath the XML layer node*, in `Windows2Local/Modes`, to open it in the editor. Change the line `<empty-behavior permanent="false"/>` to say `true` instead.

Now we need to get rid of the existing persisted data, in order to try the module on a fresh userdir and see if it works. Right-click the **Scratchpad** project and choose **Clean**. This will delete the `build/` directory, and with it the test userdir from the previous run. Then run the project. The **Scratchpad** component will appear in exactly the same place it was left.

Going back to the **Projects** window, it is possible to see what happened when we pasted files under the **XML Layer** node—the files we pasted were copied into the same directory as the layer file in the module, and entries were added to the layer file for those files (see Figure 8.11).

Figure 8.11: Files added to the project by pasting into a layer file

8.8   Using `TopComponent` **Groups**

The last topic to cover with regards to the Window System is `TopComponent` *groups*. Sometimes it is desirable to have the opening of a particular `TopComponent` trigger the opening of other related `TopComponents`. For example, when the GUI Builder is opened/activated, the **Palette** window, **Property Sheet**, and **Inspector** also appear. Wherever you have a

TopComponent which should be surrounded by several other palette-like
windows, TopComponent groups can be used to make one component's
activation trigger the opening and/or selection of others.

Like the .wsmode files defined in Section 8.7, a TopComponent group is
defined in a folder under Windows2/ in the System Filesystem. Also, like
Modes, it is defined as a file/folder pair. An XML file defines the group; a
folder with the same name as the XML file contains files, one for each
TopComponent that is part of the group. Contents of the Groups/ folder are
shown in Figure 8.12.

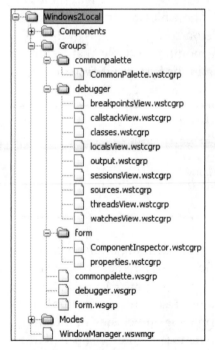

Figure 8.12: The Window System Groups folder

As can be seen in Figure 8.12, there are two file extensions involved—two
XML formats. The first, wsgrp, stands for "Window System Group." It defines
the group for the Window System, so that the implementation knows to look

for a matching folder, and defines whether or not the group is open on startup, as shown in Example 8.4.

Example 8.4: Window System Group

```
<group version="2.0">
  <module name="org.netbeans.spi.palette/0" spec="1.0" />
  <name unique="commonpalette" />
  <state opened="false" />
</group>
```

The other file extension shown in Figure 8.12 is `wstcgrp`. This stands for "Window System `TopComponent` Group." These files are very much like the `wstcref` files for `Modes`. They identify singleton `TopComponents` by their IDs. Similarly to `wstcref` files, each one is a pointer to a file that defines a `TopComponent` in `Windows2/Components` in the System Filesystem.

Example 8.5: Window System `TopComponent` Group

```
<tc-group version="2.0">
  <tc-id id="properties"/>
  <open-close-behavior open="true" close="true"
                       was-opened="false"/>
</tc-group>
```

The file listed in Example 8.5 is an example defining a reference to the standard **Properties** window. It identifies the singleton `properties` window by its `TopComponent` unique ID. The line `<open-close-behavior open="true" close="true" was-opened="false"/>` defines the behavior of this component with respect to the opening and closing of the group. If `open` is set to `true` then the component referenced should be opened when the group is opened; if not, it should not be opened. If `close` is set to `true`, then the component should be closed when the group is closed; if not, it should be opened by the group, but remain open after the group is closed. The `was-opened` attribute is added by the Window System when it saves the example file, indicating whether the component was opened independently by the user or not—in other words, whether the user had already opened the

Property Sheet using **Window | Properties**, before the group was opened. In that case it would be wrong for the system to close it simply because the group was closed. This metadata preserves that information.

As should be apparent from the fact that the contents of a group are defined as a folder, a module can contribute its own `TopComponent`s to an existing group. So if you wanted to have your `TopComponent` always be opened when the **Form Editor** is opened, your module should simply add the appropriate `wstcgrp` file into the `Windows2/Groups/form` and the system will take care of the rest.

8.8.1 Opening a Component Group Programmatically

There are many actions that could be useful triggers for showing a `TopComponent` group. So there is no declarative mechanism for defining a trigger to open a group. The Window System API contains a class `TopComponentGroup`. To open or close a group, simply ask the `WindowManager` for the `TopComponentGroup` object by its ID (the ID is defined in the group's `wsgrp` file, as shown in Example 8.4). A code for opening a `TopComponent` group can be found in Example 8.6.

Example 8.6: Opening a `TopComponent` group

```
TopComponentGroup group =
  WindowManager.getDefault().findTopComponentGroup("MyGroup");
if (group != null) {
  group.close();
}
```

CHAPTER NINE

Nodes, Explorer Views, Actions, and Presenters

Most applications have one or more data models they need to present to the user. There are common controls in all UI toolkits to display data structures to the user. In the case of Swing, `JLists` and `JTrees` are two such controls. Yet working with these can be somewhat tiresome—there are a lot of low-level details, such as cell renderers, to master. Moreover, switching from using a list to using a tree involves a lot of rewriting. In a plain Swing application, different data models with different kinds of objects in them will each need their own code to handle selection changes, double-clicking, showing popup menus, etc. So, in plain Swing, for each tree or list you want to use, there is quite a bit of tedious plumbing code to write.

In a NetBeans-based application, there are also matters that need to be handled, such as the global selection context determining which menu items and toolbar buttons are enabled and what they will do when invoked. Controls need to be wired up to the global selection.

The *Nodes API* handles all of these concerns. It makes it easy to create a tree-like model. The *Explorer API* provides a variety of UI components which can render that model. You can take an `org.openide.nodes.Node` and create any of a variety of UI components—lists, trees, tree-tables, combo boxes, etc.—which will display the `Node` and its children, with built-in popup menus for the `Actions` a `Node` provides from its `getActions()` method. Explorer views provide a rich and consistent UI for displaying data models.

`Nodes` provide a presentation layer that can adapt any data model into an explorer view.

The Explorer API components are easy to wire up to the global selection so that toolbar buttons and menu items enable and disable as they should. Context views such as the **Property Sheet** or **Navigator** can display information about the selected `Node`.

The combination of these two APIs makes it very easy to create rich user interfaces with remarkably little code.

9.1   The Nodes API

A `Node` is an object that presents some underlying object to the user in the UI. `Nodes` are not a data model per se—rather, they are a *presentation layer*. A `Node` makes an underlying model object human-friendly by providing the attributes needed to present that object in a user interface. A `Node` has

- *A display name* that is human-readable and can be localized into different human languages.
- *A description* that can appear in a tooltip.
- *An icon* that can appear beside the `Node`'s display name in a list or tree.
- *Actions* that can appear on a popup menu.
- *Children*. Each `Node` has an `org.openide.nodes.Children` object that can create child nodes.
- *Properties* that are named getters and setters. These can be modified by the user on the **Property Sheet**, a UI component that is part of the Explorer API and can be used to display properties of any object.

`Nodes` are not used as a data model. Rather, they are a layer of indirection between a data model (which might be files on disk or anything that is usefully shown to the user in a list or tree—anything you can put in a `Collection`) and the user.

All, or nearly all, of the list and tree components you see in the NetBeans IDE are explorer views of `Nodes`. In the **Files** window you have `Nodes` representing folders on disk; in the **Projects** window you have different Nodes providing a different, logical view of those same folders. Many other pieces of UI in NetBeans are also views of folders on disk or in the System Filesystem. The first page of the **New Project** wizard is really a master/detail view of a list of folders in the System Filesystem on the left and the contents of those folders on the right (Figure 9.1).

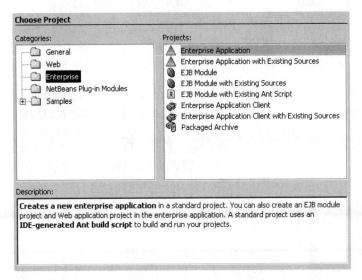

Figure 9.1: The **New Project** dialog is a master/detail view with folders on the left and the files in the selected folder on the right

As we will demonstrate in Chapter 10, getting a Node for any folder on the user's disk or in the System Filesystem is quite simple. Once you have a FileObject, you can call

```
DataObject.find(theFileObject).getNodeDelegate()
```

to get a Node you can use in a UI component to display that folder or file in some way. If you want to provide a custom icon or display name or actions for a Node representing a folder, you can create a FilterNode which wraps the original Node and lets you override any attributes of its presentation.

The following classes and constants are those you are likely to encounter and use when developing user interfaces for NetBeans-based applications:

`AbstractNode`   Despite its name, `AbstractNode` is *not* an `abstract` class. It is a convenience base class which you will commonly use if you are creating `Nodes` that do not represent files. For example, in a subclass of `Children.Keys` you might do something like this:

```
AbstractNode result = new AbstractNode (Children.LEAF);
result.setDisplayName ("Please wait...");
```

Often you will not subclass `AbstractNode`, but rather, use it as is and create a custom `Children` object to provide child `Nodes`.

`BeanNode`   This useful class allows you to take any Java object and make a `Node` from it. `BeanNode` will, via introspection, find all of the JavaBean properties of the object and expose them as `Node` properties that can be shown in the **Property Sheet**. If a `BeanInfo` class is available from `java.beans.Introspector.getBeanInfo()`, then it will be used to provide an icon, a localized display name, and property editors. This makes it possible to create a `Node` for any object that already follows the JavaBeans specification simply by calling `new BeanNode (theObject)`.

`Children.Keys`   An `org.openide.nodes.Children` object needs to be passed to the constructor of an `AbstractNode`. The `Children` object will create child nodes on demand (for example, when the user expands a tree node in the UI). There are several other base classes in the Nodes API for creating `Children` objects, but in almost all cases, `Children.Keys` should be used (with the exception of `FilterNode.Children`).

`Children.LEAF`   This is a singleton `Children` object which you can use if your `Node` has no `Children`. A `Node` that has `Children.LEAF` as its children object will not have an expansion handle when shown in a tree view.

`FilterNode`   This is a `Node` which takes another `Node` and acts as a clone of it, with the same child nodes, actions, etc. You can use or subclass

`FilterNode` to give it different `Children`, icons, display name, properties, or other attributes.

`Node.Property`   This is a named, typed value that can be shown in the **Property Sheet** UI component. `Propertys` have `javax.beans.PropertyEditors` which validate user-entered values.

`PropertySet`   A `Node` has one or more `PropertySets` which contain their properties.

`Sheet` **and** `Sheet.Set`   These are convenience classes that make it easy to create the **Property Sheet** content for a `Node`. Just override `createSheet()` in a `Node` subclass, call `super` to get the `Sheet` object, and add `PropertySets` to it. `Sheet` can create instances of the subclass `Sheet.Set` for you, which you can add individual `Property` objects to.

9.1.1   Using the Nodes API

As mentioned, `Nodes` are a *presentation layer*. They *are not* data, they *represent* data. So we need a data model to represent with `Nodes`. For this example we have prepared a data model—a model for any card game with decks of cards and piles of cards between which cards can be moved. You can find it in the sources on the accompanying CD in the module called "Cards." We will use that library as a model for a collection of cards. While the result of this exercise won't replace your favorite solitaire game any time soon, it should work to make the concepts clear.

The Cards Library

The Cards library is quite straightforward. There is an object called a `Deck` that owns a collection of `Cards`; cards are things that aggregate a `Suit` and a `Rank` such as "Ace," "Two," "Queen," or "King." Suits and ranks are specified as Java 1.5 enums. It has a class called `Pile`, and any `Card` can be in only one `Pile` at a time. A `Pile` has an `AddPolicy` which determines when it is legal to add a card, and a `VisibilityPolicy` which determines which cards you can know the identity and suit of, and which are "face-down." Most card games amount to an assortment of piles of cards with different policies for visibility and legality of adding a card. If a `Card` object is asked for its identity or suit when it is not visible in a pile, it will throw an exception; `Card.isFaceDown()` can be used to determine if the suit and identity of a card can be known. A `Card` can provide an image of itself which will be either a card back or the face of the card, depending on its state.[1]

The library was written rather quickly, for the purposes of illustration in this book. It is intended to provide a convenient and familiar data model, rather than be the end-all and be-all of such libraries, of which there were probably too many in the world before we wrote ours (but it was fun!).

The first step is to create a module suite. It will hold the Cards library and allow our `Node`-based UI to use classes from it. Name it "CardSuite." When you have created the suite, right-click the **Modules** subnode of the project, choose **Add Existing** and add the `Cards` module from wherever you have it unpacked on your disk.

The next step will be to set the **Source Level** of the project to Java 1.5. By default, in NetBeans 5.5, module projects use a source level of 1.4. The Cards library uses Java generics, and we can take advantage of them in our own code as well if we set the source level to 1.5, as shown in Figure 9.2.

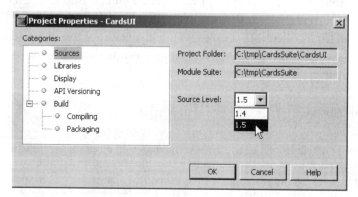

Figure 9.2: Setting the **Source Level**

---

1. For the card images in this library we are indebted to David Bellot, Jesse Fuchs, and Tom Hart, who provide them under the Creative Commons license at `www.eludication.org/playingcards.html`.

Now we are ready to write our first Node. We will create a UI that shows several "hands" of cards in a JTree using Nodes. Add a new module to the suite. Call it "CardsUI." To save time, add dependencies on Cards, Explorer and Property Sheet API, Nodes API, Utilities API, and Window System API—we will need all of these for the module (Figure 9.3).

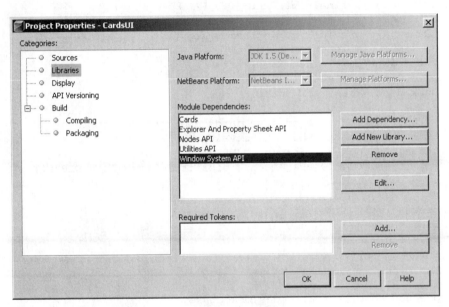

Figure 9.3: Initial dependencies for the CardsUI module

In fact, our very first Node won't involve subclassing Node at all. We will simply create an AbstractNode which we can use directly. This will be the root of the tree we show, and the only interesting thing about it is its child Nodes that represent individual cards. Create a new class called GameChildren and assign it to the subclass Children.Keys. Implement it as shown in Example 9.1. To create the root node for our tree of cards, we will simply call new AbstractNode (new GameChildren()).

Example 9.1: GameChildren–providing a node's children

```java
public class GameChildren extends Children.Keys {
  private final List <Pile> hands = new ArrayList <Pile> ();
  private final Pile undealt;
  private static final int NUMBER_OF_JOKERS = 2;
  private static final int NUMBER_OF_HANDS = 3;
  private static final int CARDS_PER_HAND = 5;

  // Game just provides string names for piles of cards -
  // a simple implementation below
  private Game game = new GameImpl();
  public GameChildren() {
    Deck deck = new Deck (game);

    // Deal three hands of five cards and get the remainder
    // of the deck as the return value
    undealt = deck.deal(hands, NUMBER_OF_HANDS,
              CARDS_PER_HAND, VisibilityPolicy.ALL_VISIBLE);
  }

  protected void addNotify() {
    List <Pile> keys = new ArrayList <Pile> (hands);
    keys.add (undealt);
    setKeys (keys);
  }

  protected Node[] createNodes(Object key) {
    Pile pile = (Pile) key;
    PileNode result = new PileNode (pile);
    result.setDisplayName (game.nameOf(pile));
    return new Node[] { result };
  }

  private final class GameImpl implements Game {
    public String nameOf(Pile pile) {
      if (undealt == pile) {
        return NbBundle.getMessage(GameImpl.class,
                            "LBL_REMAINDER");
      } else {
        int ix = hands.indexOf (pile);
        return NbBundle.getMessage (GameImpl.class,
                       "LBL_HAND", new Integer (ix));
      }
    }
  }
```

```
    public int getJokerCount() {
      return NUMBER_OF_JOKERS;
    }
  }
}
```

The constructor's code should be relatively self-evident. We create a new deck of cards, and ask it to deal three hands of five cards each. We pass to it a `List` we have already constructed, for it to put the hands into. And we are returned another `Pile` of cards which contains all the cards that were not dealt out. There is an implementation of the `Game` interface from the Cards library—all this does is provide string names for piles of cards and specify how many Joker cards should be in the deck of cards used.

The next bit of code is *the* critical method in any implementation of `Children.Keys`. The idea behind `Children.Keys` is that you have some array or collection of objects which this `Children` object will create `Nodes` for. The `addNotify()` method is called the first time someone clicks the expansion handle and the UI actually asks for the child nodes of the `Node` that owns the `Children` object. When it is called, we should compute the collection of keys that are the data model that determines the `Nodes` substructure.

`NbBundle` and Localized Strings

The one other interesting thing in `addNotify()` in Example 9.1 is the use of the class `NbBundle`. This is a utility class from the NetBeans Utilities API which is used in place of `java.util.ResourceBundle` for loading localized strings. It is able to work with *branding*, so that an application that wants to reuse a module can replace some of the localized strings in that module. It also has more efficient caching than the standard JDK `ResourceBundle` offers, and is less verbose to invoke—you simply pass it a `Class` object and it will automatically look for a `.properties` file called `Bundle.properties` in the same package as the `Class` object you passed. Additionally, you can format a string with substitutions, as we do for specifying hand numbers. So the value of `LBL_HAND` in `org/netbeans/examples/cardsui/Bundle.properties` is Hand `{0}`, and `{0}` will automatically be replaced by the third argument to `getMessage()`.

The next method, createNodes(), is the method that actually creates the Nodes. It will be called once for each object in the collection we passed to setKeys(). It can return one or more Nodes for each key (the return value is an array of Nodes, though typically there will be a 1:1 mapping between keys and Nodes).

We have yet to create PileNode. It will be a Node with children that represent the cards in one Pile. Create this class now, as shown in Example 9.2.

Example 9.2: PileNode—creating a node to represent a collection of objects

```
public class PileNode extends AbstractNode {
  public PileNode(Pile pile) {
    super (new PileChildren (pile), Lookups.singleton(pile));
  }

  private Pile getPile() {
    return (Pile) getLookup().lookup (Pile.class);
  }

  private static class PileChildren extends
      Children.Keys implements ChangeListener {
    private Pile pile;
    public PileChildren (Pile pile) {
      this.pile = pile;
      pile.addChangeListener (WeakListeners.change (this, pile));
    }

    protected void addNotify() {
      setKeys (pile.getCards());
    }

    public Node[] createNodes(Object key) {
      Card card = (Card) key;
      return new Node[] { new CardNode (card) };
    }

    public void stateChanged (ChangeEvent e) {
      setKeys (pile.getCards());
    }
  }
}
```

The `Children` implementation is similar to the implementation of `GameChildren`. We have a model object that is giving us a `Collection` of some sort. We use that `Collection` as the model for our `Children` object and provide one `Node` per key. We are passing a `Lookup` instance to the super-class constructor of `AbstractNode`. Its content will be returned from our `Node`'s `getLookup()` method. The result is that the `Pile` object will be available in the global selection whenever the user selects a `PileNode`. This means we can write actions, **Navigator** views, and so forth that will simply look for a `Pile` object in the global selection, and have no knowledge of our UI implementation. Other modules could write code that operates on `Pile` or (later) `Card` objects, and our module could be replaced by a different module implementing a different game—and those modules will work just as nicely with it as with the UI we are creating now. Whenever a `PileNode` is selected, a `Pile` object will be available from the `Lookup` returned by `Utilities.actionsGlobalContext()`. Other modules can simply listen for a `Pile` object in that global context and be notified that a `Pile` object has appeared in the global selection whenever the user selects a `PileNode` in the UI.

Next we need to create `CardNode` which was mentioned in the source in Example 9.2 but was not yet defined. It will be similar to `PileNode` in that it provides a `Card` object in its `Lookup`. Create another new class in the CardsUI module and implement as shown in Example 9.3.

Example 9.3: `CardNode`—creating a node to represent an object in a data model

```
public class CardNode extends AbstractNode {
  // We want no icon at all, so just use a transparent image
  static final BufferedImage ICON =
    new BufferedImage (1, 1, BufferedImage.TYPE_INT_ARGB);
  static {
    Color c = new Color (255, 255, 255, 255);
    Graphics2D g = ICON.createGraphics();
    g.fillRect (0, 0, 1, 1);
    g.dispose();
  }

  public CardNode(Card card) {
    super (Children.LEAF, Lookups.singleton(card));
  }
```

```
private Card getCard() {
  return (Card) getLookup().lookup (Card.class);
}

public Image getIcon (int type) {
  return ICON;
}

public String getDisplayName() {
  Card c = getCard();
  Suits s = c.getSuit();
  if (s != null) { // Will be for Joker cards
      return s.getUnicodeChar() + " " + c.getName();
  } else {
      return c.getName();
  }
}

public String getHtmlDisplayName() {
  Card c = getCard();
  String result = null;
  if (!c.isFaceDown()) {
    Suits s = c.getSuit();
    Color color = null;
    if (s != null) {
      color = s.getColor();
      if (Color.RED.equals(color)) {
        result = "<font color=#FF0000>" + getDisplayName();
      }
    }
  }
  return result;
}
}
```

Once again we are putting the object the Node represents into its Lookup in the constructor—and components or actions sensitive to Card objects will be notified when a Card object is selected by the user selecting a CardNode.

Note that in getDisplayName() we fetch the Unicode character for the card suit (♠, ♣, ♥, or ♦) and prepend it to the name of the card that we return.

HTML display names

One interesting piece of code is `getHtmlDisplayName()`. This is an important method. A `Node` can provide an HTML version of its display name, as long as it adheres to a limited subset of the HTML spec. Font color and style are supported, so `<b>`, `<i>`, `<u>`, and `<s>` tags are supported, along with `<font color='somecolor'>` tags. A slight extension to the HTML spec is supported in color tags—you can specify a `UIManager` color key by prepending a `!` character to the color definition, for example `<font color='!textText'>`. The actual color will be resolved by calling `UIManager.getColor("textText")`. The result is that you can use HTML code to colorize the display name of any `Node` and do that in a way which, if you use `UIManager` keys, will work in any Swing look-and-feel (if you hardcode colors, you can end up in a situation where you are displaying black text on a black background, so this is quite useful).

There is no separate property for firing changes in the HTML display name of a node—simply fire a regular name change. By default, `getHtmlDisplayName()` returns `null`; if you are not actually using HTML markup, simply use the normal `getDisplayName()` method. Strings from `getHtmlDisplayName()` are assumed to be HTML—you do not need to prepend `<html>` to such strings.

In our case, we are not being so graceful: We are hard-coding the red color (of course, people who run their applications with all-red UIs are a minority; besides, two of the four standard playing card suits *have* a color and that color is red). The point is that a `Node`'s display name can be marked up with HTML to communicate information not only by its text but also by its format and color.

9.1.1.1   *Creating a* `Node` *with a* `Lookup` *Whose Contents Can Change*

We have `PileNode` implemented to provide `Nodes` for all the cards in a pile. In many card games, the top card in a pile is visible. So, there is a method, `Pile.peekTopCard()` that will let us get it, and a `ChangeListener` may be attached to an instance of `Pile` to track changes in the list of cards in a `Pile`. We are using the factory method `Lookups.fixed()` to get us an instance of `Lookup` which never changes and includes the `Pile` object. We need a `Lookup` which can change as the content of the `Pile` changes.

The Utilities API offers us two classes which can help with that, AbstractLookup and InstanceContent. Contrary to its name, AbstractLookup is *not* an abstract class. InstanceContent is an object similar to a Collection which holds the content of a Lookup. It gives the creator of the AbstractLookup access to privileged operation. The owner that holds InstanceContent may simply call InstanceContent.set (someCollection) to change the contents of the lookup.

Modify the head of PileNode.java as shown in Example 9.4.

Example 9.4: Creating a node whose Lookup can change

```
public class PileNode extends AbstractNode
                      implements ChangeListener {
  private final InstanceContent content;
  public PileNode (Pile pile) {
    this (pile, new InstanceContent());
  }

  private PileNode(Pile pile, InstanceContent content) {
    super (new PileChildren (pile), new AbstractLookup(content));
    content.set (Arrays.asList (pile,
                                pile.peekTopCard(), this), null);
    this.content = content;
    pile.addChangeListener(WeakListeners.change (this, pile));
  }

  public void stateChanged(ChangeEvent e) {
    Set newContent = new HashSet();
    newContent.add (getPile());
    Card card = getPile().peekTopCard();
    if (card != null) { // the pile could be empty
      newContent.add (card);
    }
    content.set (newContent, null);
  }
```

This way, our detail view that shows the selected card will show the top card in a Pile when a PileNode is selected, and whatever the selected Card is when a CardNode is selected.

9.2   The Explorer API

Now that we have Nodes to represent our data model, we need a way to show them on-screen. For this we will use the *Explorer API*. The Explorer API consists of a set of components that can render Nodes. They make it very easy to construct a UI once you have a data model.

9.2.1   Types of Explorer View Components

All of the explorer view components are managed by an ExplorerManager object. It controls the selection. View components will automatically find their manager when they are added to a java.awt.Container subclass as a TopComponent. Explorer views are JavaBeans components with a default constructor which can be used in the NetBeans GUI Builder.

When they are added to a container, explorer views will search through their parent containers until they find one that implements ExplorerManager.Provider and then start listening to and using the ExplorerManager returned by that component's getExplorerManager() method. Other than a bit of plumbing code, using explorer view components is as easy as adding a JLabel to a JPanel. All of these controls—lists, trees, combo boxes, etc.—have some concept of *selection*. If you want to write code for tracking what is selected, rather than listening to the view component, you can simply listen for property changes in the ExplorerManager that is managing selection. Any code that is using one kind of explorer view can easily swap it for another kind. Compare this to the amount of rewriting you would need in plain Swing to change code that used a JTree to use a JList or vice versa.

In simple cases, if you want to track the selection in the explorer views in your component, you can simply listen on the content of the Lookup of your TopComponent. As long as you include a small amount of plumbing code, shown in Example 9.5, in your TopComponent's constructor, you can simply listen for changes in the Lookup. Typically a TopComponent which contains an explorer view will wire up its Lookup and *activated node* properties to the ExplorerManager that is managing the component. So what will happen is that the Lookup of the TopComponent will automatically proxy the Lookup(s) of the selected Node(s) in the explorer view components. The majority of this wiring-up is done with a single line in the constructor of a TopComponent:

```
associateLookup (ExplorerUtils.createLookup(manager,
                                    getActionMap()));
```

Here is a partial list of the UI components available in the Explorer API. A few classes have been omitted for components that are not generally used in NetBeans and may be less well maintained (e.g., IconView or ListTableView).

BeanTreeView   This is the class you will use most often when you want to display Nodes in a JTree.

ListView   This displays all the children of a root Node in a JList. It can be configured to show varying depths of children and will indent them—so it can be used for showing tree-like data, but is not itself a tree control.

ChoiceView   This displays all the children of a root Node in a JComboBox.

TreeTableView   This is a combination of a tree and a table—a table with expandable and collapsable cells *plus* columns that contain additional data about the Node shown in the Tree column.

When a TreeTableView is constructed, it is passed an array of *prototype* Node.Property objects. If the Node in a row has a property with the same *name* (as returned by Property.getName()), then that property will be shown in the appropriate column (Figure 9.4).

PropertySheetView   This is an Explorer UI component which shows a **Property Sheet**. The **Property Sheet** shows the *properties* of the selected Node and provides a UI for editing them (Figure 9.5).

Once the card game module is completed, you can start experimenting with the different explorer view components available, simply by replacing the new BeanTreeView() call with any of the other components in org.openide.explorer.view.

Installed Modules:

Modules	Active	Version
⊟ Database	☑	
Database APIs	☑	1.2.21.4
Database Core	☑	1.3.21
Database Explorer	☑	1.19.21.4
Database Schema (JDBC Implementati	☑	1.8.21.3.4
Java DB Database Support	☑	1.7.22
SQL Editor	☑	1.3.21.4
⊞ Data Files	☑	

Figure 9.4: The **Module Manager** dialog uses a `TreeTableView`

Figure 9.5: The **Property Sheet** component

9.2.2 Creating a `TopComponent` to Display Nodes

The next step is to create a `TopComponent` that can show our nodes in a window in the application. This will be an editor-style window that shows a tree of `Nodes` representing the hands in one instance of our pseudo card game. Do not use the **New Window Component** wizard in this case. Just create a new empty Java class that does two specific things. First, it implements `ExplorerManager.Provider`. That means it will have a `getExplorerManager()` method (Example 9.5).

Example 9.5: A `TopComponent` to display nodes

```
public class CardGameTopComponent extends TopComponent
                implements ExplorerManager.Provider {
  private final ExplorerManager manager = new ExplorerManager();
  public CardGameTopComponent() {
    ActionMap map = this.getActionMap ();
    map.put(DefaultEditorKit.copyAction,
            ExplorerUtils.actionCopy(manager));
    map.put(DefaultEditorKit.cutAction,
            ExplorerUtils.actionCut(manager));
    map.put(DefaultEditorKit.pasteAction,
            ExplorerUtils.actionPaste(manager));

    associateLookup (ExplorerUtils.createLookup (manager, map));

    setLayout (new BorderLayout());
    BeanTreeView view = new BeanTreeView();
    view.setRootVisible(false);
    manager.setRootContext(new AbstractNode
                              (new GameChildren()));
    add (view, BorderLayout.CENTER);
    if ((Utilities.getOperatingSystem()
          & Utilities.OS_WINDOWS_MASK) != 0) {
      view.getViewport().getView().setFont
        (new Font ("SansSerif", Font.PLAIN, 12));
    }
  }

  protected void componentActivated() {
    ExplorerUtils.activateActions(manager, true);
  }

  protected void componentDeactivated() {
    ExplorerUtils.activateActions(manager, false);
  }

  public ExplorerManager getExplorerManager() {
    return manager;
  }
}
```

The initial lines of code in this constructor, up to and including the line beginning with `associateLookup(...`, are boilerplate for wiring up an `ExplorerManager` to the rest of the NetBeans Window System, so that selection changes inside our component will affect the global selection (and toolbar buttons and menu items will be enabled and disabled correctly). The implementation of `componentActivated()` and `componentDeactivated()` is more of the same. You can copy this code into almost any `TopComponent` you are writing if it needs to contain an explorer view.

The remainder of the constructor code is fairly straightforward Swing code. We instantiate a component, `BeanTreeView`, from the Explorer API. It will automatically find our `ExplorerManager` and be managed by it when it is added to `CardTopComponent`.[2]

The final method in Example 9.5 is the implementation of `ExplorerManager.Provider`. After that, there are only two methods left to implement, as shown below. We will implement `getPersistenceType()` so that it returns `TopComponent.PERSISTENCE_NEVER`, to indicate to the Window System that it should not try to save any in-progress card game on shutdown.

```
static int games = 0;
  public int getPersistenceType() {
    return PERSISTENCE_NEVER;
  }
  protected void componentOpened() {
    if ("".equals(getDisplayName()) || getDisplayName() == null)
    {
      Integer gameNumber = new Integer (games++);
      String displayName = NbBundle.getMessage
        (CardGameTopComponent.class, "LBL_GAME", gameNumber);
      setDisplayName(displayName);
    }
  }
}
```

2. The final lines of the constructor in Example 9.5 are a small concession to the vagaries of cross-platform UI difficulties. The Unicode characters such as ♥ are not available in all fonts. In fact, they are missing from the Tahoma font that the Windows platform uses by default. So we are explicitly setting the font to one of those shipping with Java that has a more complete Unicode character support.

9.2.3   Adding a Detail View

As mentioned, the Cards library comes with a lovely set of images of playing cards that we can use. You will note that we are not using them from the `getIcon()` method of our `Nodes`. The images are nice, but they do not scale down to a 16×16 icon too well. So we make a choice, as seen at the top of `CardNode`, to not try to use images of playing cards as icons. It is easy to do this with minimal modifications to the example source code, but part of developing software is recognizing where an adornment such as an image does or does not add value. A part of a card's image usually displays that card's value represented as a series of small icons—for example, the 7 of hearts card shows seven small heart glyphs to indicate its suit and number. In a 16×16 icon, these end up being less than one pixel in size. So, let's forget about using card images as icons, and instead do what we do in `getDisplayName()`—display the suit and name as clearly as possible.

We *will* use the card images—that is the next step in our example. And the example points out the value of using `Lookup`. The code that will find and show the image of a card will not need to have any particular knowledge of cards. It only needs to find a `Card` object and call its method to get an image of the card.

The next step is to create a component to display the image. This will involve a bit of simple Java2D code, as shown in Example 9.6. The component knows about a card and asks it for an image to paint, which it then draws on itself in its `paintComponent()` method.

Example 9.6: A Swing component to display cards

```
public class CardComponent extends JComponent
                          implements LookupListener {
  private Card card;
  public CardComponent() {
  }

  private void setCard (Card card) {
    setToolTipText(card == null ? null : card.getName());
    this.card = card;
    repaint();
  }
```

```
private Lookup.Result selectedCards;
public void addNotify() {
  super.addNotify();
  Lookup.Provider provider = (Lookup.Provider)
    SwingUtilities.getAncestorOfClass(Lookup.Provider.class,
                                 this);
  if (provider != null) {
    selectedCards = provider.getLookup().
                   lookup(new Lookup.Template(Card.class));
    selectedCards.addLookupListener(this);
    Collection <? extends Card> cards =
                             selectedCards.allInstances();
    setCard (cards.isEmpty() ? null : cards.iterator().next());
  }
}
public void removeNotify() {
  if (selectedCards != null) {
    selectedCards.removeLookupListener(this);
    selectedCards = null;
  }
  super.removeNotify();
}
public void paintComponent(Graphics g) {
  if (card == null) {
      super.paintComponent(g);
  } else {
      Graphics2D g2d = (Graphics2D) g;
      BufferedImage img = card.getImage (getSize());
      g2d.drawRenderedImage(
        img, AffineTransform.getTranslateInstance(0D, 0D));
  }
}
public Dimension getPreferredSize () {
  return new Dimension (150, 215);
}
public Card getCard() {
  return card;
}
public void resultChanged(LookupEvent lookupEvent) {
  Collection <? extends Card> cards =
                             selectedCards.allInstances();
  setCard (cards.isEmpty() ? null : cards.iterator().next());
}
}
```

The result is a component that does something very similar to what `BeanTreeView` does. Just as any explorer view locates its `ExplorerManager` by searching the component hierarchy for a parent container that implements `ExplorerManager.Provider`, `CardComponent`'s `addNotify()` method searches for a `Lookup.Provider`. As `TopComponent` implements `Lookup.Provider`, it will find the instance of `CardTopComponent` that we will place it in.

Note that if we wanted to make this component a standalone view that could be put in any `TopComponent`, all we would need to do is change the code from finding the `Lookup` of a parent `TopComponent` to getting its `Lookup.Result` from `Utilities.actionsGlobalContext().lookup()`.

To use this component, we will modify the second half of the constructor of `CardTopComponent` slightly, to create a `JSplitPane` with the tree on one side and the detail view on the other:

```
setLayout (new BorderLayout());
BeanTreeView view = new BeanTreeView();
view.setRootVisible(false);
manager.setRootContext(new AbstractNode (new GameChildren()));
CardComponent comp = new CardComponent();
JSplitPane split = new JSplitPane(JSplitPane.HORIZONTAL_SPLIT,
                                  view, comp);
add (split, BorderLayout.CENTER);
```

The end result will look as shown in Figure 9.6.

9.2.4   Adding Another Detail View Using the Explorer API

The detail view we just created which shows an image of the selected card simply used the Lookup API to track the selection. We can also do that using the Explorer API, to create explorer views that show a subtree of the `Nodes` in a master view.

In this case we will add yet another component to our game window. This one will show the children of whatever `Node` is selected in the tree. And to introduce `FilterNode`, it will show those cards with a different icon, as Figure 9.7 demonstrates.

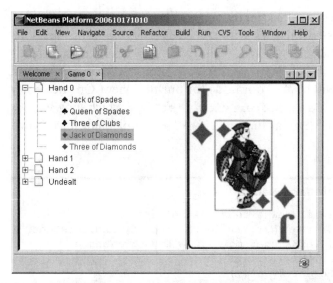

Figure 9.6: `CardTopComponent` in action

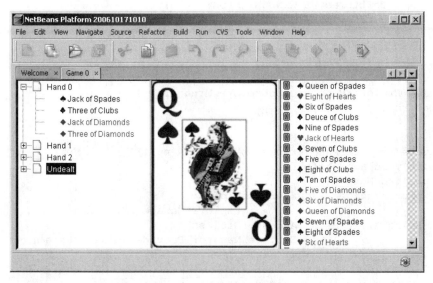

Figure 9.7: Card window with an additional detail view using `ListView`

Create a new Java class called `CardsDetailView`. Its goal is very simple. It is a `JPanel` subclass, which, as with `CardTopComponent`, implements `ExplorerManager.Provider`. We will wire up this component's `ExplorerManager` to the one in `CardTopComponent` so that the selected node in the tree view will be the root node for our new view. Our new view will be using `org.openide.explorer.view.ListView`, which shows `Nodes` in a `JList` instead of a `JTree` as in `BeanTreeView`. Implement it as shown in Example 9.7.

Example 9.7: Implementing `CardsDetailView`

```
public class CardsDetailView extends JPanel
    implements ExplorerManager.Provider, PropertyChangeListener {
  private final ExplorerManager mgr = new ExplorerManager();
  public CardsDetailView() {
    setLayout (new BorderLayout());
    ListView view = new ListView();
    add (view, BorderLayout.CENTER);
    if ((Utilities.getOperatingSystem() &
          Utilities.OS_WINDOWS_MASK) != 0) {
      view.getViewport().getView().setFont (new Font
                          ("SansSerif", Font.PLAIN, 12));
    }
  }

  public ExplorerManager getExplorerManager() {
    return mgr;
  }

  private ExplorerManager parentManager = null;
  public void addNotify() {
    super.addNotify();
    ExplorerManager.Provider provider =
                            (ExplorerManager.Provider)
      SwingUtilities.getAncestorOfClass
                      (ExplorerManager.Provider.class, this);

    if (provider != null) {
      parentManager = provider.getExplorerManager();
      parentManager.addPropertyChangeListener (this);
      updateRootNode();
    }
  }
```

```
public void removeNotify() {
  if (parentManager != null) {
    parentManager.removePropertyChangeListener (this);
  }
}

private void updateRootNode() {
  Node[] n = parentManager.getSelectedNodes();
  if (n.length == 0) {
    mgr.setRootContext(new AbstractNode (Children.LEAF));
  } else {
    // don't worry about multiple selection
    Node selectionInParent = n[0];

    mgr.setRootContext ( selectionInParent );
  }
}

public void propertyChange(PropertyChangeEvent e) {
  if (ExplorerManager.PROP_SELECTED_NODES.equals
      (e.getPropertyName())) {
    updateRootNode();
  }
}
}
```

The code in Example 9.7 is quite straightforward. When our `JPanel` subclass is added to a container, it will search the hierarchy of parent containers looking for an `ExplorerManager.Provider`. This is exactly what `BeanTreeView` and `ListView` and the other explorer view components do. When it finds one, it will get the `ExplorerManager` in question and begin listening for property changes. Whenever `ExplorerManager.PROP_SELECTED_NODES` is fired, it knows that the parent `ExplorerManager`'s selection has changed and updates its own `ExplorerManager`. The parent `ExplorerManager` is the one that belongs to `CardTopComponent`. When it changes, it gets the new selection from that `ExplorerManager` and sets its own `ExplorerManager`'s root context to the selection from the parent. In Example 9.7, if there is nothing selected, we simply create an empty dummy node by calling `new AbstractNode (Children.LEAF)` and set that as the root context. Since it will have no children, the list view will be empty if nothing is selected.

Modify `CardTopComponent` to include an instance of `CardsDetailView` by rewriting the relevant section of its constructor as shown in Example 9.8.

Example 9.8: Using `CardsDetailView` in a window component

```
setLayout (new BorderLayout());
BeanTreeView view = new BeanTreeView();
view.setRootVisible(false);
manager.setRootContext(new AbstractNode (new GameChildren()));
CardComponent comp = new CardComponent();
JSplitPane split =
  new JSplitPane(JSplitPane.HORIZONTAL_SPLIT, view, comp);

JSplitPane split2 = new JSplitPane (
  JSplitPane.HORIZONTAL_SPLIT, split, new CardsDetailView());

add (split2, BorderLayout.CENTER);
```

9.2.4.1   Using `FilterNode` to Change the Icon

We mentioned above that we would like to have a different icon for the `Nodes` that appear in our list view in the new detail component. `org.openide.nodes.FilterNode` makes that easy. By default you can create a new `FilterNode` for any `Node` and it will appear and behave exactly as the original. Simply call `new FilterNode (someNode)` to clone an existing `Node`. You can then set the display name or description to be something different. Or, you can provide a different `Children` and/or `Lookup` for the clone. Or, you can subclass `FilterNode` to provide a different icon, actions, or whatever else you would like, as we are about to do.

First, we will modify the `updateRootNode()` method to use the classes we are about to create, as shown in Example 9.9.

Now we are ready to extend `FilterNode` to return a different icon. For the icon file you can use any 16×16 GIF or PNG image; the one shown in screen shots here is available on the accompanying CD. Add two nested classes of `CardsDetailView`, as shown in Example 9.10.

Example 9.9: Handling selection changes from `ExplorerManager`

```
private void updateRootNode() {
  Node[] n = parentManager.getSelectedNodes();
  if (n.length == 0) {
     mgr.setRootContext(new AbstractNode (Children.LEAF));
  } else {
     // don't worry about multiple selection
     Node node = n[0];
     Node iconFilterNode = new FilterNode (node,
                                    new IconFilterChildren(node));

     mgr.setRootContext(iconFilterNode);
  }
}
```

Example 9.10: Using `FilterNode` to provide an alternate icon for an existing node

```
private static class IconFilterChildren extends
                                        FilterNode.Children {
  public IconFilterChildren (Node original) {
    super (original);
  }

  protected Node[] createNodes(Object childNodeFromOrig) {
    Node toClone = (Node) childNodeFromOrig;
    Node result = new IconFilterNode (toClone);
    return new Node[] { result };
  }
}

private static final String ALTERNATE_ICON_PATH =
    "org/netbeans/examples/cardsui/alternateIcon.png";
private static final class IconFilterNode extends FilterNode {
  IconFilterNode (Node orig) {
    super (orig);
  }

  public Image getIcon (int beanInfoIconType) {
    return Utilities.loadImage (ALTERNATE_ICON_PATH);
  }
}
```

`IconFilterChildren` is a factory for `IconFilterNodes`; `IconFilterNode` is a clone of whatever `Node` is passed to its constructor, with the exception that we override `getIcon()` to always return a different image than the empty one returned by `CardNode`. Run the module now, with the code from Example 9.10, and you will find that when you select one of the hands of cards, the list of cards in that hand appears in the new detail view.

9.3   Actions

Actions are user-visible, invokable objects represented in a menu, a popup menu, a toolbar button, or bound to a keystroke. The concept of, and classes for, actions come from the Swing UI toolkit itself—`javax.swing.Action` and the convenience base class `javax.swing.AbstractAction`.

NetBeans includes a number of `Action` subclasses that are useful in various contexts; for simple things, using `AbstractAction` is enough. `AbstractAction` only requires that we override its `actionPerformed()` method to do whatever work should be done when the user invokes the action and, if the action is to be displayed in a menu, provide a localized string name for the action using `putValue (Action.Name, theLocalizedString)`.

What we now need is an `Action` which will create an instance of `CardTopComponent` and open it. For this, we can take the simplest approach possible and just use the `AbstractAction`. The **New Action** wizard used elsewhere in this book will create a subclass of `org.openide.util.CallableSystemAction` (which in turn is an indirect subclass of `AbstractAction`); the principal difference between this and `AbstractAction` is that `SystemAction` allows you to associate a help ID with an action, so that you can provide specific context-sensitive help associated with a menu item or toolbar button. In this case, we are not providing a help ID, and `AbstractAction` does everything we need.

Create a new Java class named `CardGameAction` as shown in Example 9.11.

Example 9.11: Creating `CardGameAction`

```
public class CardGameAction extends AbstractAction {
  public CardGameAction() {
    putValue (NAME, NbBundle.getMessage (CardGameAction.class,
           "LBL_CARD_GAME_ACTION"));
  }

  public void actionPerformed(ActionEvent e) {
    TopComponent tc = new CardGameTopComponent();
    tc.open();
    tc.requestActive();
  }
}
```

Now we need to do only two more things to have a usable module that can show our CardsUI. First, in `org/netbeans/examples/cardsui/Bundle.properties`, add the line

```
LBL_CARD_GAME_ACTION=New Card Game
```

This will be the text that appears on the menu item for the action. Then we need to register it in the module's layer file. Edit `org/netbeans/examples/cardsui/layer.xml` as shown in Example 9.12.

Example 9.12: Adding items to the main menu via an XML layer

```
<filesystem>
  <folder name="Menu">
    <folder name="File">
      <file name="org-netbeans-examples-cardsui-CardGameAction.↵
instance"/>
    </folder>
  </folder>
</filesystem>
```

At this point we are ready to run the module for the first time. A new action should appear at the top of the **File** menu, **New Card Game**. Select it and a card game window will open.

9.3.1   Presenters

Actions are useful, but what if you need a submenu? An `Action` is not a GUI component. `Presenters` come to the rescue. There are three subinterfaces of `Presenter`: `Presenter.Menu`, `Presenter.Toolbar`, and `Presenter.Popup`. An action may implement any or all of the above to change the way that action is presented in the UI. If you want to show, say, a `JComboBox` in a toolbar, simply write an `Action` that implements `Presenter.Toolbar` and returns the `JComboBox` as the *toolbar presenter* of the `Action`.

So, in our poor-man's card game, it might be nice if card nodes had an action that would let the user move a card to a different pile. Currently `CardNode` has no actions, so if you right-click it, no popup menu appears. We need to override `CardNode.getActions()` to return an action, as shown in Example 9.13.

Example 9.13: Overriding `CardNode.getActions()`

```
public Action[] getActions (boolean popup) {
  return new Action[] {
    new MoveToPileAction (getCard()),
  };
}
```

Next, we need to implement `MoveToPileAction`. This will be an `Action` which implements `Presenter.Popup` and returns a `JMenu` for the *popup presenter* of the action, rather than the usual `JMenuItem`. The `JMenu` will have menu items for all of the piles available, as shown in Example 9.14.

Run the module again, expand the nodes for the piles of cards, right-click a card, and move it to a different pile with the action (Figure 9.8). Note also how the UI automatically updates itself, so the `Node` for a `Card` that has moved automatically disappears and a `Node` for it automatically appears under the pile it was moved to. This is accomplished by our code in `PileChildren` that adds a `ChangeListener` to the `Pile` it represents, and the `stateChanged()` method then calls `setKeys()` again with the updated list of `Card`s in the pile when an event is fired. `Children.Keys` takes care of computing the difference

Example 9.14: Providing a custom submenu from a node's action

```
private static final class MoveToPileAction
    extends AbstractAction implements Presenter.Popup {
  private final Card card;
  private static final String PROP_PILE = "pile";
  MoveToPileAction (Card card) {
    this.card = card;
  }

  public JMenuItem getPopupPresenter() {
    JMenu result = new JMenu();
    result.setText(NbBundle.getMessage (MoveToPileAction.class,
                                 "LBL_MOVE_TO_PILE"));

    // Get the list of all the Piles that have at least one card
    // in them from the Deck
    List <Pile> piles = card.getDeck().allPiles();

    // Get the Game object (see GameChildren) that can supply
    // a String name for each pile
    Game game = card.getDeck().getGame();
    for (Pile pile : piles) {
      JMenuItem item = new JMenuItem ();
      item.setText(game.nameOf(pile));
      // Store the Pile object this menu item represents,
      // so we can fetch it in actionPerformed()
      item.putClientProperty (PROP_PILE, pile);
      if (pile == card.getPile() || !pile.canAdd(card)) {
        item.setEnabled (false);
      }
      item.addActionListener (this);
      result.add (item);
    }
    return result;
  }

  public void actionPerformed (ActionEvent ae) {
    JMenuItem item = (JMenuItem) ae.getSource();
    Pile pile = (Pile) item.getClientProperty (PROP_PILE);
    pile.add (card);
  }
}
```

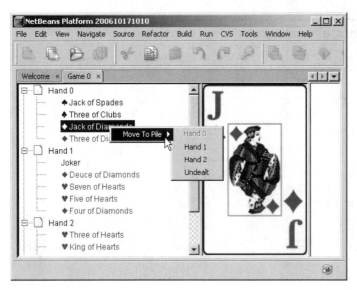

Figure 9.8: `CardNode` with `MoveToPileAction`

between the old and new sets of keys, preserving the `Nodes` for keys that are still there, removing `Nodes` for keys that are gone, and adding `Nodes` for newly added keys.

So while a card game with a `JTree` as its UI is not likely to take the world by storm, it does demonstrate how simply one can build a remarkably sophisticated UI on top of an existing data model.

Also, note that when you right-click a card node in `CardsDetailView`, you see a popup menu with `MoveToPileAction` just as you do in the tree control. We have implemented this logic in one place, and any view that shows our `Nodes` will automatically provide the appropriate popup menu (Figure 9.9).

As an exercise for the reader, the next steps in improving this UI would be to eliminate the card `Nodes` from the tree view. There are two ways to

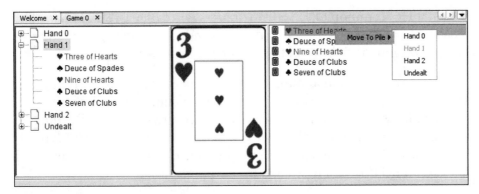

Figure 9.9: `Node` actions in the detail view

approach that problem. The first would be to replace the `BeanTreeView` with a `ListView`; the second would be to use a `FilterNode` that wraps `PileNode` and uses `Children.LEAF` as its children object.

9.3.2   The Actions API and Standard NetBeans Actions

The Actions API in NetBeans provides a number of standard actions that you can reuse in your own code. These will be subclasses of `SystemAction`. There is a static method, `SystemAction.get()`, to which you can pass a `Class` object in order to fetch an instance of the action in question. So, for example, a `Node` representing a file that needs saving can simply get the standard `SaveAction` from NetBeans APIs to achieve that (Example 9.15). As long as that `Node` also provides an instance of `SaveCookie` in its `Lookup`, that action will work against it.

Example 9.15: Using the standard `SaveAction`

```
public Action[] getActions (boolean popup) {
   return new Action[] { SystemAction.get (SaveAction.class) };
}
```

Another common `Action` to reuse is `OpenAction` which, like `SaveAction`, depends on `SaveCookie` and looks for an instance of `OpenCookie` in the `Lookup` of the `Node` it is invoked against.

There are a substantial number of `Actions` which do useful things and are defined in the Actions API—any common functionality, such as cut, copy, paste, find, goto, next error, etc., is likely to be covered and reusable from the Actions API. Enumerating that API's contents is out of scope for this book, but the Javadoc documentation is quite complete and the commonly useful ones are straightforward to work with.

9.3.3   Installing Global Actions in Menus, Toolbars, and Keyboard Shortcuts

There are two main uses for actions—providing a list of actions dynamically in the popup menu for a `Node` and providing always-visible actions that are part of the main menu or toolbars or keybindings.

In Example 9.12, we showed how to install an action in a menu by putting a `.instance` file for it into a subdirectory of `Menu` in the System Filesystem. Doing so for toolbars is similarly straightforward—each subfolder of the `Toolbars` folder of the System Filesystem maps to a toolbar in the main window.

Binding global keyboard shortcuts uses a similar model, except that it uses the filename to define what key is being bound. There is an Emacs-like syntax which such filenames use, with some wildcard characters that will map to Ctrl on PC and the Command key on Macintosh—for the gory details of it, see the Javadoc documentation for `Utilities.stringToKey()`.[3] Essentially, you create a file with a name such as `C-6` and that means you are binding an action to `CTRL-6` which should be invoked whenever the user presses that key combination. Using `D` instead of `C` in the above gets a similar keybinding but uses the Command key on Macintosh systems and thus is more Mac-friendly. Declaring an action binding will look similar to Example 9.16.

---

3. www.netbeans.org/project/www/download/dev/javadoc/org-openide-util/org/openide/util/Utilities.html#stringToKey(java.lang.String)

Example 9.16: Creating a global keybinding for an action

```
<filesystem>
  <folder name="Shortcuts">
    <file name="D-6.instance">
      <attr name="instanceClass" stringvalue="com.foo.MyAction"/>
    </file>
  </folder>
</filesystem>
```

9.3.4   Context-Aware Actions

Some actions are context-aware—they need an object to operate on. If actions are declaratively installed, there needs to be a way for them to get hold of the context in which they are called, find the object they need to operate on, and do something with it. There are two major classes in NetBeans APIs that enable doing this. The older one is called CookieAction—it is what the **New Action** wizard generates sources for. A CookieAction is enabled whenever there is an instance of some class available from the getCookie() method of the selected Node(s) (this means it is also available from the Lookup of the Node, getCookie() is simply the older idiom for the same thing).

The other class relating to custom actions is ContextAwareAction which is an interface and is Lookup-based. In both cases, the class is sensitive to some object type being available or not for whatever is globally selected. As a case in point, we will recycle an example from Chapter 5—creating a custom **Save** action which can save a file if it needs saving. In Example 5.11 in that chapter we showed how to create such an action using ContextAwareAction, which is the more modern approach but not yet in general use. It is currently simpler, code-wise, to use CookieAction for this purpose, as much of the code can be generated by the **New Action** wizard.

The general rule for which one to use is, whichever involves writing less code. The other distinction is that CookieAction requires that the object it operates on implements the Node.Cookie marker interface. So if you want to write an action that is sensitive to objects from a library you do not control, use ContextAwareAction; otherwise you will need to create an object that *does* implement Node.Cookie and has a method that lets you get the object from the library. While such indirection is not hard, it is messy and adds complexity. Example 5.11 demonstrates using `ContextAwareAction`. For an example of creating a class that provides an object from another API, see the `ManifestProvider` in Section 10.2.2.

9.3.4.1   Creating a Custom Save Action with `CookieAction`

To create our custom **Save** action using `CookieAction`, simply start with the **New Action** wizard. Check the radio button for creating a **Conditionally Enabled Action** and enter `SaveCookie` in the combo box that asks what Java type the action should be sensitive to (Figure 9.10).

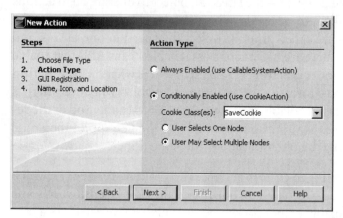

Figure 9.10: Creating a new `CookieAction` subclass

In the next steps, add a menu item to the **File** menu and, if you have a 16×16 GIF or PNG icon handy, a toolbar button. Name the class `CustomSaveAction`.

The only step left is to implement the `performAction()` method of `CookieAction`. It will be passed the array of `Nodes` that were selected when it was invoked. Simply implement the method as shown in Example 9.17.

The code in Example 9.17 is all that's necessary to do—run the module, modify a file or several files, and use the custom **Save** action to save them.

Example 9.17: Using `CookieAction`

```
protected void performAction(Node[] activatedNodes) {
  for (int i=0; i < selection.length; i++) {
    SaveCookie c =
      (SaveCookie) selection[0].getCookie(SaveCookie.class);
    if (c != null) {
      try {
          c.save();
      } catch (IOException ex) {
          ErrorManager.getDefault().notify (ex);
      }
    }
  }
}
```

9.4   Node **Properties**

Another attribute of `Nodes` is that they have *properties*. These are name/value pairs which can be shown and edited in a **Property Sheet**. Properties are represented in NetBeans by the class `Node.Property`. A `Node.Property` has a value type, a `String` name, a display name and description, and methods for setting and getting the value of the property.

There are two ways to create properties in NetBeans. One is by explicitly creating `Node.Property` objects. You override `Node.createSheet()` and add the property objects you want there. The other is by using the JavaBeans specification. The JavaBeans specification says that for any Java type there may be a `BeanInfo` subclass providing things like localized names for properties and `PropertyEditors` for them.

The choice of which to use depends on what you are doing and which approach is likely to be simpler. If you are dealing with an existing class that already has `BeanInfo` then it is quite straightforward to use `BeanNode` as the superclass for something like `CardNode`, and all the necessary information will be found by the system using `java.beans.Introspector` (Figure 9.11). The NetBeans IDE does contain an editor for `BeanInfo` classes that makes it considerably easier to create them, but nonetheless, `BeanInfos` are not exactly for the faint of heart (Figure 9.12).

We have included `BeanInfo` classes for the `Card` class in the Cards library, and the code to use a `BeanNode` as an alternate superclass for `CardNode` can

Figure 9.11: Creating a `BeanInfo` for an existing Java class

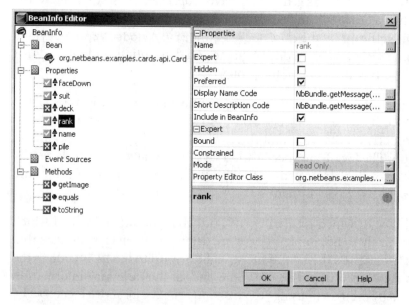

Figure 9.12: Editing `BeanInfo`

be found in comments in the sources on the accompanying CD. A few other changes will be necessary, since the way to get the object represented by a BeanNode is via InstanceCookie—the Card object is not directly in the Lookup of a BeanNode. So, getCard() in CardNode needs to be changed as shown in Example 9.18.

Example 9.18: Using InstanceCookie

```
public Card getCard() {
  InstanceCookie ck =
    (InstanceCookie) getCookie (InstanceCookie.class);
  Card card = (Card) ck.instanceCreate();
  return card;
}
```

If you only need to add a few properties, it may be simpler just to override createSheet() in CardNode to provide properties from it. For creating actual property objects, there are two Nodes API classes that can help.

PropertySupport.ReadOnly   Makes it easy to write a Node.Property by overriding a few methods, such as providing a PropertyEditor and a localized display name for the property.

PropertySupport.ReadWrite   Makes it easy to create read-write properties.

Example 9.19 is the code needed to add Rank and Suit properties to CardNode.

Example 9.19: Adding properties to CardNode

```
protected Sheet createSheet() {
  Sheet result = super.createSheet();
  Sheet.Set set = result.createPropertiesSet();
  set.put (new SuitProperty (getCard().getSuit()));
  set.put (new RankProperty (getCard().getRank()));
  result.put(set);
  return result;
}
```

```
private static final class SuitProperty
          extends PropertySupport.ReadOnly {
  private final Suits suit;
  SuitProperty (Suits suit) {
    // id name, value type, display name, description
    super ("suit",
            Suits.class, NbBundle.getMessage(SuitProperty.class,
            "LBL_SUIT"), NbBundle.getMessage(SuitProperty.class,
            "DESC_SUIT"));
    this.suit = suit;
  }

  public Object getValue() throws IllegalAccessException,
                               InvocationTargetException {
    return suit;
  }

  public PropertyEditor getPropertyEditor() {
    return new SuitPropertyEditor();
  }
}

private static final
    class RankProperty extends PropertySupport.ReadOnly {
  private final Rank rank;
  RankProperty (Rank rank) {
    super ("rank",
            String.class, NbBundle.getMessage(SuitProperty.class,
            "LBL_RANK"), NbBundle.getMessage(SuitProperty.class,
            "DESC_RANK"));
    this.rank = rank;
  }

  public Object getValue() throws IllegalAccessException,
                               InvocationTargetException {
    return rank.toString();
  }
}
```

What we are doing is creating two subclasses of `PropertySupport.ReadOnly`. They are added to the default property set in `createSheet()`. That method uses two convenience classes—`Sheet` is a container for `PropertySets` (of which `Sheet.Set` is a subclass) and a factory for them;

you can get a new `Sheet.Set` from the `Sheet` object and add properties to it, set its display name and other properties (Figure 9.13).

Figure 9.13: Properties of a card in the **Property Sheet** using `BeanNode`

9.5 `Nodes` and `DataObjects`: Creating a System Filesystem Browser

Much of the power of the NetBeans Platform comes from the ability to reuse infrastructure for showing `Nodes` and, moreover, from being able to create registries of objects merely by adding a folder in the System Filesystem and providing a view of that.

In this example we will create a simple viewer for the System Filesystem. The code we write here could easily be used in your own module to provide a view of some parts of the System Filesystem—for example, a folder or a registry of objects that you have created and want to show to the user. The only change that would be needed is to show some folder other than the root folder of the System Filesystem.

Create a new module named `sfsviewer`. Add a dependency on the Filesystems API and Datasystems API—we will need them to get `Nodes` for the `FileObjects` in the System Filesystem. Also, add a dependency on the Explorer and Property Sheet APIs, so we can use `BeanTreeView`, and on the Nodes API.

Use the **New Window Component** wizard to create a new `TopComponent` subclass. In the GUI editor, set its layout to `BorderLayout` as shown in Figure 7.6. In its constructor, create a new `BeanTreeView` and add it with the constraint `BorderLayout.CENTER` just as we did for `CardsTopComponent`. Have it implement `ExplorerManager.Provider` in the same way as `CardsTopComponent`—create an instance of `ExplorerManager` and return it from `getExplorerManager()`.

In the skeleton `TopComponent` created by the wizard, there are two empty methods, `componentOpened()` and `componentClosed()`. Override them as shown in Example 9.20.

Example 9.20: Managing component lifecycle

```
public void componentOpened() {
  FileSystem sfs =
    Repository.getDefault().getDefaultFileSystem();
  FileObject root = sfs.getRoot();
  try {
      DataObject dataObject = DataObject.find(root);
      Node rootNode = dataObject.getNodeDelegate();
      mgr.setRootContext(rootNode);
  } catch (DataObjectNotFoundException ex) {
      Logger.getLogger ("global").log(Level.SEVERE,
                                      ex.getMessage(), ex);
  }
}

public void componentClosed() {
  // No reason to let the UI hold onto all the objects
  // it's showing if nobody is looking at them
  mgr.setRootContext (new AbstractNode(Children.LEAF));
}
```

When you run this module, it will give you a live view of the contents of the System Filesystem. It can be worthwhile to poke around and get to know some of its contents—this can help you get an intuitive sense of how things are likely to be implemented and thus ideas on how you might implement your own modules. The same infrastructure that lets the IDE show the user's files on disk is being harnessed here to browse the configuration data of the copy of NetBeans you are running (Figure 9.14).

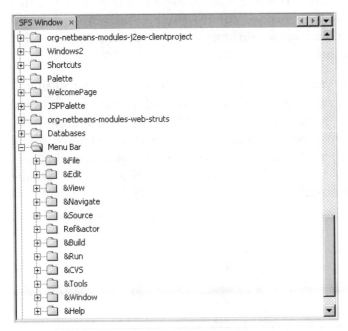

Figure 9.14: Browsing the System Filesystem

9.6   Epilogue: Of Nodes, Property Sheets, and User Interface Design

The main example in this chapter is that of a (half-finished) card game. As you can imagine, playing cards through an interface of tree controls, popup menus, and property sheets would provide a user experience worthy of headline news in the next "UI Bloopers" book. And that is one of the reasons we chose it.

Tree controls and the like can afford the programmer great convenience. Sometimes too much convenience. Real-world usability studies show that non-programmer-users find property-sheet-based UIs baffling. An early design mistake in NetBeans was the original **Options** dialog (you can still see it if you go to **Tools | Options** and click the **Advanced Options** button, but it now has much less content than it used to). It was possible to simply drop a JavaBean object in a folder in the System Filesystem and, magically, it would appear in the **Options** dialog. This led to an incredible proliferation of settings objects, and as a result it was nearly impossible to find things that many people wanted to change—such as editor fonts and colors—amid all the settings for how many pixels the editor scrollbar should jump when you click somewhere other than on the scrollbar thumb.

That is not to say you should not use property sheets—but you should know your audience, and you should *design* your UI. Libraries such as the Node and Explorer APIs can speed up creating a UI immensely. But good user experience comes from good UI design. There are many good books on UI design out there.[4] Where it would be possible to rely solely on `Nodes` and `PropertySheets` and create an adequate UI, we strongly suggest you take the time to build an extraordinary one.

---

4. Among the best is Joel Spolsky's *UI Design for Programmers*, ISBN 1893115941.

CHAPTER TEN

DataObjects and DataLoaders

In Chapter 6 we covered the *Filesystems API*. That API duplicates some part of the capabilities of `java.io.File`. `FileObjects` represent files on disk and provide input and output streams from them. The Filesystems API extends the concept of "files" by not requiring the things it considers to be "files" to be files on disk—they may be entries in a JAR file, or files on an FTP server, or any other kind of hierarchical, data-bearing storage someone might choose to create. Figure 10.1 shows the role of `FileObjects` in NetBeans' overall internal model of files and their contents.

We have extended the concept of "files" to mean anything that is hierarchical and has named data. There is still a need to turn `FileObjects` into something that can be accessed programmatically, beyond parsing the file. As we noted in Section 7.5, no one wanting to do something to a `.java` file or a `.properties` file or any other data format should be forced to write a parser or read an input stream.

The Datasystems API is a layer on top of the Filesystems API, which enables *programmatic* access to the contents of files. A module will define a `DataLoader` that can read files of a particular MIME type (it typically also provides a MIME resolver that allows the system to identify files with a certain extension or contents as being of that MIME type). That `DataLoader` will construct `DataObjects` for individual files. A code that wants to interact with the content of a file can then ask the `DataObject` for instances of interfaces

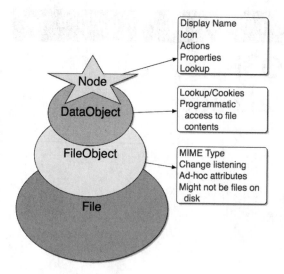

Figure 10.1: The roles of `FileObjects`, `DataObjects`, and `Nodes`

it knows about. That is, you might ask a `DataObject` for a `.properties` file to give you a `java.util.Properties` object representing its content (or for some object that can, in turn, make a `Properties` object for it). Or you might ask a `DataObject` for a JAR manifest (`.mf`) file to give you a `java.util.jar.Manifest` to represent it. You might ask the `DataObject` for a `.java` file to give you an abstract syntax tree of the structure of that file.

Your code would then interact with the `Manifest` or `Properties` object or the syntax tree object, instead of directly reading and writing the contents of the file. And the whole system is more efficient since it is the job of the `DataObject` to parse the file—it is no longer everyone's problem, as it was in Chapter 7. A `DataObject` represents a file; it provides the objects that let other classes and modules programmatically manipulate the file's content.

You can get a `DataObject` for any `FileObject` easily. Call `DataObject.find( theFileObject )`. The exact type of the `DataObject` is not interesting because of the *lookup pattern*. What is interesting about a `DataObject` is not what type of `DataObject` it *is*, but what objects it *has*. A naive design would have you get a `DataObject` and then cast it to various types and try to call methods of those types. There is a much more elegant way to do such tests. It uses the lookup pattern (as described in Chapter 5). The lookup pattern allows us to turn *is-a* relationships into *has-a* relationships. When you get a `DataObject` that represents some file on disk, you do not try to cast it as a particular interface or `DataObject` subclass. Rather, you *ask* it if it *has* an instance of an interface that both you and, presumably, the `DataObject` know.

Where Is `DataObject.getLookup()`**?**

Usage of `Lookup` has been unified in NetBeans 6 and up. In NetBeans 6 you simply call `someDataObject.getLookup().lookup(SomeClass.class)`. In NetBeans 5.x and earlier, the code pattern is a little more convoluted—either `someDataObject.getCookie(SomeCookie.class)` if you know that the object you are asking for implements the empty marker interface `Node.Cookie`, or `someDataObject.getNodeDelegate().getLookup().lookup(SomeClass.class)` if it does not.

All of these code patterns add up to the same thing: You are asking an object that represents a file to give you an instance of some class or interface that both you and the `DataObject` representing the file know about. This is the lookup pattern. If two objects know about a common interface, one object may ask another if it has an instance of that interface. As described in Section 5.2, this results in a remarkably clean way to couple the things that know about each other—those can be very specific to a particular file type or a set of file types.

Yet at the same time, the thing actually processing the content of the file can be replaced. If you write something that is sensitive to `Properties` objects,[1] that code doesn't need to care what is providing the `Properties` object, or whether there is a file with the extension `.properties` underlying the object, or where the `Properties` object is coming from at all. It makes that code more reusable.

So, handlers for other kinds of files that map keys and values can be installed in the application, and as long as they make a `Properties` object

---

1. Note that `java.util.Properties` objects have nothing to do with `Node.Property` objects or the *properties* of a `Node`.

available, the code that handles `Properties` objects will work flawlessly. At the same time, you can have much more general interfaces, such as `SaveCookie` which anything that can be *saved* may provide, as discussed in Chapter 5. Thus, the ability to query a `DataObject` for known interfaces makes a varying level of coupledness possible. And the fact that you ask a `DataObject` *for* things provides mutability—a file that does not need to be saved does not provide a `SaveCookie` and one that does need saving does provide one. You can detect changes in the available objects from a `DataObject` by listening for changes in `DataObject.PROP_COOKIE`, or you can do the same on its `Node` by listening on the `Lookup` of its `Node` for appearing or disappearing of particular Java types.

10.1   DataObjects: Where Do They Come From?

As a case in point, what is happening when you, say, expand a `Node` for a folder in the **Files** window of the IDE, as shown in Figure 10.2?

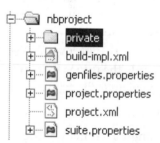

Figure 10.2: Expanding a folder that contains a variety of files

What has been expanded is a `Node` (as covered in Chapter 9)—a `Node` representing the folder on disk. That `Node` has a `Children` object that can manufacture child `Nodes`. The `Children` object is going to ask the folder on disk for its child files and folders. These will be `FileObjects`. It takes those and, for each one, calls `DataObject.find()` to get a `DataObject` for each file. For each of those, it calls `DataObject.getNodeDelegate()` to get the `Node` for that file.

The interesting part happens when `DataObject.find()` is called. There will be a bunch of `DataLoaders` registered in the system; each one can make `DataObjects` for `FileObjects`. `DataObject.find()` identifies the MIME type of the file, locates the one that is registered for that MIME type, and asks it to create a `DataObject` for the files. So if there is a manifest file, and there is a module which registers support for manifest files (identifying them by the filename extension `mf`), it will find the `DataLoader` that module is providing and ask it to create a `DataObject` (Figure 10.3).

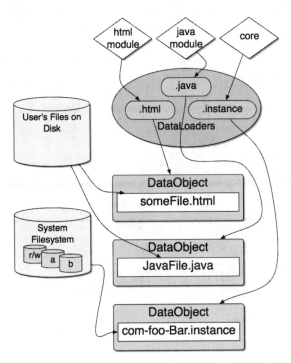

Figure 10.3: Under the hood—expanding a folder

The `DataObject` for a file gets to create the `Node` that renders it in the UI. So the `DataObject` is indirectly responsible for what icon the file appears with, what display name it shows, the actions available from its popup menu, etc.

10.2   Adding Support for a New File Type

NetBeans module writing support makes it easy to add support for a new file type. There is the **New File Type** wizard in the **NetBeans Module Development** category that generates all the necessary files, including skeleton `DataLoader` and `DataObject` classes.

10.2.1   Adding Support for Manifest Files to NetBeans

In this example—and throughout much of the rest of the book—we will be adding support for JAR manifest files to NetBeans. Manifest files are simple files that contain key/value pairs storing metadata about a Java library.

1. Create a module. Right-click its package and select the **New File Type** wizard, as shown in Figure 10.4.

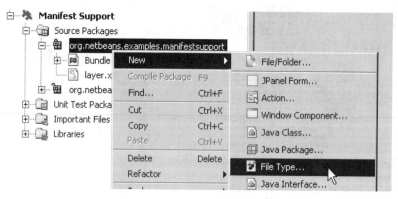

Figure 10.4: Using the **New File Type** wizard

2. In the **New File Type** wizard, fill in the first page of the wizard with the MIME type `text/x-manifest`. Notice that the other option on this page is **XML Root Element**—you can also register your own `DataLoader` for specific subtypes of XML files. In this case we will simply fill in `mf` as the filename extension, as manifest files are not XML (Figure 10.5).

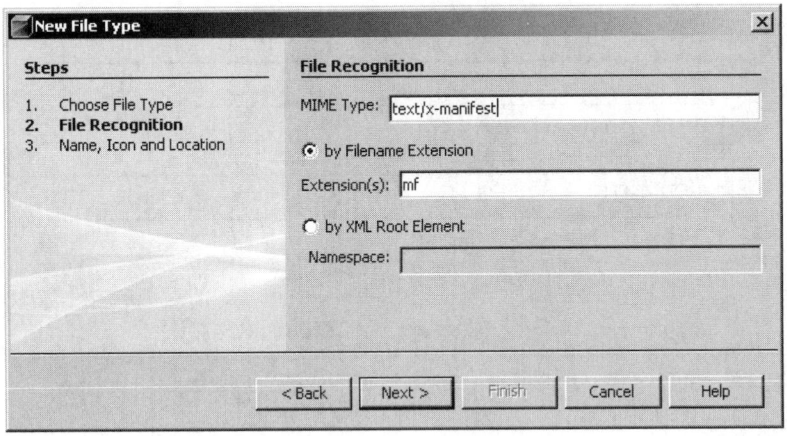

Figure 10.5: Filling in MIME type and filename extension

3. The next step of the wizard allows you to specify the **Class Name Prefix** (a word that will be prepended to the names of various files that will be created) for the `DataLoader` and `DataObject` classes that are being created. It also allows us to specify the icon to be used for `.mf` files, and gives us a last chance to change in which package the source files will be created. Enter `Manifest` for the class name prefix. Note the list of files and folders that will be created and modified by this wizard—it is generating quite a bit of code for us.

If you have a handy 16×16 image file that can be the icon for manifest files, you can optionally supply one in the **Icon** field (Figure 10.6). The **Browse** button allows you to locate an image file on your disk to have that file copied into your module. If not provided, you will get a default icon which you can change later. Press **Finish** to complete the wizard.

We now have skeleton support for manifest files. Let's take a look at what files were created (Figure 10.7).

`ManifestDataLoader.java`   This is the `DataLoader` that will be a factory for `DataObjects` representing manifest files.

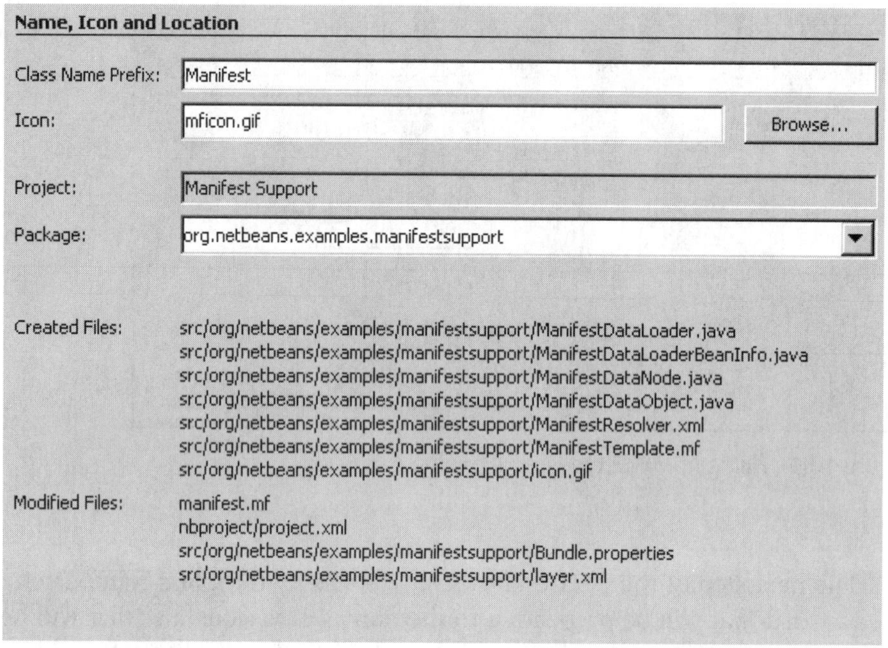

Name, Icon and Location

Class Name Prefix: Manifest

Icon: mficon.gif   Browse...

Project: Manifest Support

Package: org.netbeans.examples.manifestsupport   ▼

Created Files: src/org/netbeans/examples/manifestsupport/ManifestDataLoader.java
                     src/org/netbeans/examples/manifestsupport/ManifestDataLoaderBeanInfo.java
                     src/org/netbeans/examples/manifestsupport/ManifestDataNode.java
                     src/org/netbeans/examples/manifestsupport/ManifestDataObject.java
                     src/org/netbeans/examples/manifestsupport/ManifestResolver.xml
                     src/org/netbeans/examples/manifestsupport/ManifestTemplate.mf
                     src/org/netbeans/examples/manifestsupport/icon.gif

Modified Files: manifest.mf
                     nbproject/project.xml
                     src/org/netbeans/examples/manifestsupport/Bundle.properties
                     src/org/netbeans/examples/manifestsupport/layer.xml

Figure 10.6: Specifying name, icon, and class name for a data loader

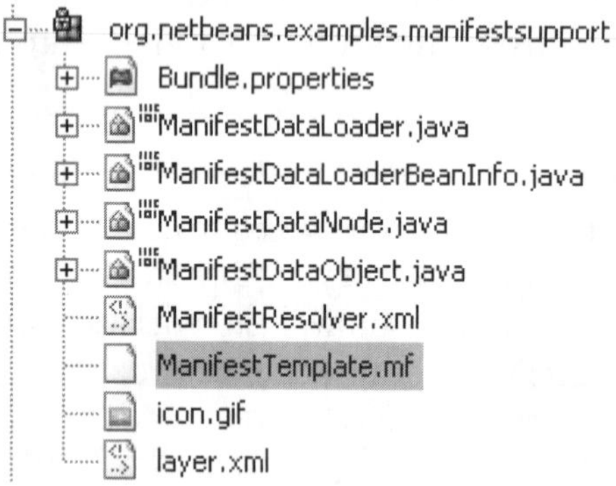

org.netbeans.examples.manifestsupport
  Bundle.properties
  ManifestDataLoader.java
  ManifestDataLoaderBeanInfo.java
  ManifestDataNode.java
  ManifestDataObject.java
  ManifestResolver.xml
  ManifestTemplate.mf
  icon.gif
  layer.xml

Figure 10.7: Files created by the **New File Type** wizard

`ManifestDataLoaderBeanInfo.java`   A `DataLoader` is a JavaBean object—it will be visible to users in the **Advanced Options** dialog where users can manually modify the list of filename extensions a `DataLoader` is associated with.

The `BeanInfo` class simply provides the properties, icon, and localized names for the `DataLoader` so that this part of the **Advanced Options** dialog has human-friendly, translatable names for `DataLoaders` (Figure 10.8).

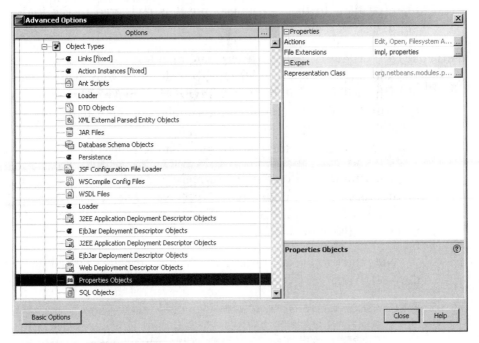

Figure 10.8: Viewing all data loaders in the **Advanced Options** dialog

`ManifestDataNode.java`   This is a `Node` subclass that will be what users see for manifest files in the **Files** or **Projects** windows of the IDE, or in any other UI that provides a view of a folder using `Nodes`, if that folder contains a manifest file.

The `Node` provides the user-visible attributes of manifest files by providing `Actions`, a display name, description, and optionally child nodes for manifest files.

`ManifestDataObject.java`   This is the file that defines our `DataObject` subclass. `ManifestDataObjects` will be created by our loader to represent the content of `.mf` files when the system finds one.

`ManifestResolver.xml`   This is an XML file that defines a MIME resolver—it is what maps the `.mf` extension to our `DataLoader` so that it will be the one asked to create `DataObjects` for manifest files. In the `layer.xml` file it is registered in the folder `Services/MimeResolver`.

`ManifestTemplate.mf`   This is a template manifest file. Typically when you add support for a new file type, you also want to provide a template that will appear in the **New File** wizard, to make it easy for users to create new files that contain some sample code they can modify. By default the **New File Type** wizard creates such a template—we can edit it to contain skeleton content for a manifest file later.

The sample manifest template is registered in the `layer.xml` file, in the `Templates/Other` folder. The **New File** wizard uses the `Templates` folder in the System Filesystem to supply the templates that are visible in the wizard.

Note the two file attributes used by our template's virtual file in the XML layer:

```
<file name="ManifestTemplate.mf"
      url="ManifestTemplate.mf">
  <attr name="SystemFileSystem.localizingBundle"
    stringvalue=
      "org.netbeans.examples.manifestsupport.Bundle"/>
  <attr name="template" boolvalue="true"/>
</file>
```

The `SystemFileSystem.localizingBundle` attribute is a pointer to the `Bundle.properties` file in our source code. The same is done for `ManifestResolver.xml`. In both cases, these are the files being registered in the System Filesystem, and these files will actually represent Java objects. This attribute can be used on files representing instances of objects to give them a localized display name. The properties file in question contains the path of the file in the System Filesystem as the key, and a localized display name as the value:

```
Services/MIMEResolver/ManifestResolver.xml=Manifest Files
Templates/Other/ManifestTemplate.mf=Empty Manifest file
```

`layer.xml`   This is the layer file our module uses to register items in the System Filesystem, as described in Section 6.5. The **New File Type** wizard added some content to it, so it now registers our MIME resolver and manifest template as noted above. It also contains a long list of actions registered in the folder `Loaders/text/x-manifest/Actions`. These are some standard actions, such as **Cut**, **Copy**, and **Paste**, all defined in NetBeans' APIs. The layer file contains `.shadow` files that point to where these standard actions are defined by the modules that implement them, in subfolders of the `Actions/` folder. Actions defined in this way will appear on the popup menu when you right-click a manifest file in the **Files** or **Projects** windows in the IDE.

Other modules that want to extend the functionality available on manifest files by adding actions to their popup menu can simply register their own actions into `Loaders/text/x-manifest/Actions`.

`mficon.png`   This is the image file shown in Figure 10.6. If you selected a different image file or no image at all, this file may have a different name.

One other file that was modified was the JAR manifest of our module. In NetBeans 5.5, `DataLoaders` are registered in a module's manifest.[2] The manifest for our module now looks like this:

---

2. It appears that in NetBeans 6 it will be possible to register `DataLoaders` in the default `Lookup` using `META-INF/services`. Manifest-based registration is the oldest model for declaratively registering objects in NetBeans, only used by very few things these days. But the above code will, for backward compatibility reasons, work for the foreseeable future.

```
Manifest-Version: 1.0
OpenIDE-Module: org.netbeans.examples.manifestsupport
OpenIDE-Module-Layer: org/netbeans/examples/manifestsupport/⏎
layer.xml
OpenIDE-Module-Localizing-Bundle: org/netbeans/examples/⏎
manifestsupport/Bundle.properties
OpenIDE-Module-Specification-Version: 1.0

Name: org/netbeans/examples/manifestsupport/⏎
ManifestDataLoader.class
OpenIDE-Module-Class: Loader
```

Manifest files can have *sections*, set off from the rest of the manifest by a blank line, that name a class and provide some metadata about it. The lines registering our `DataLoader` are such a section.

At this point we have a module we can run. Run the module and try creating a new JAR manifest by using our template that was added to the **New File** wizard. You will notice that it and the resulting file both have the correct icons.

10.2.2   Providing a Manifest Object from Manifest Files

`DataObjects` represent files, with an understanding of what that file is and how to interpret its contents. The next step is to provide a way to get some programmatic object from our `DataObject` that represents a manifest. The class from the JDK, `java.util.jar.Manifest`, will make a handy read-only representation of the contents of a manifest, and its constructor throws `java.io.IOException` so we have a way of finding out if a manifest is malformed.

However, creating a manifest involves reading the entire file. That is not something we ought to be doing in the constructor of our `DataObject` or its `DataNode`. So, we will add a small amount of indirection by creating our own class with a `getManifest()` method.

1. Create a new package in the module, `org.netbeans.examples.manifestsupport.api`.

2. In that package, create a new class, `ManifestProvider`. Implement it as an interface with a single method, `getManifest()`:

```
public interface ManifestProvider {
  public Manifest getManifest();
}
```

We now have an API that will allow other modules to get hold of a
`Manifest` object from a `DataObject` or `Node` representing a `.mf` file (or
any other file that implements this interface and provides it). So, we can
now write other modules that operate solely on this interface and do not
need to care what kind of `DataObject` is supplying it.

3. In order to make our API usable to other modules, add the package
   `org.netbeans.examples.manifestsupport.api` to the list of public
   packages on the **API Versioning** panel of the module's **Properties** dialog.

10.2.3 Providing `ManifestProvider` from `ManifestDataObject` and `ManifestDataNode`

Now that we have an API, something needs to implement it. There are two
ways we can do that. As mentioned in Section 5.7, while in NetBeans 6, a
`DataObject` can supply a `Lookup`, an older variant of the lookup pattern is
the most straightforward way to do it in NetBeans 5.x. There is a method on
`DataObject`, `getCookie(Class clazz)`. It is similar to `Lookup` in that you
pass a `Class` object and get an instance of that class back. The `getCookie()`
method returns objects that implement the marker interface `Node.Cookie`.[3]
In our first example of how to do this sort of thing, we will use the older
approach. So, first we must modify the `ManifestProvider` interface to
implement `Node.Cookie`:

```
public interface ManifestProvider extends Node.Cookie {
  public Manifest getManifest();
}
```

`ManifestDataObject`'s constructor is already adding to the set of
`Node.Cookie` objects available to it:

---

3. In fact, this is one of the main reasons for `getCookie()` being replaced by `Lookup`
and eventually deprecated—`getCookie()` requires that everything implements this
marker interface, which makes it impossible to return, say, standard JDK classes from it.

```
public ManifestDataObject(FileObject pf,
    ManifestDataLoader loader) throws
    DataObjectExistsException, IOException {
  super(pf, loader);
  CookieSet cookies = getCookieSet();
  cookies.add((Node.Cookie) DataEditorSupport.create(this,
                            getPrimaryEntry(), cookies));
}
```

To the constructor we will add the following line:

```
cookies.add (new ManifestProviderImpl());
```

In NetBeans 6.0, the `CookieSet` has been extended to work with any Java object, not just those that implement `Node.Cookie`. That is why in 6.0, the `ManifestProvider` would not need to implement that marker interface; it would be added to the `CookieSet` with the new method

```
cookies.assign(ManifestProvider.class,
               new ManifestProviderImpl());
```

Now we need to implement `ManifestProviderImpl`. Add an inner class to `ManifestDataObject` as shown in Example 10.1.

Example 10.1: Implementing `ManifestProvider`

```
private class ManifestProviderImpl implements ManifestProvider {
  public Manifest getManifest() {
    if (EventQueue.isDispatchThread()) {
        throw new IllegalStateException(
                  "Don't call on event thread");
    }
    try {
        FileObject file = getPrimaryFile();
        InputStream in = file.getInputStream();
        return new Manifest (in);
    } catch (IOException ioe) {
        // The manifest was malformed
        return null;
    }
  }
}
```

Note the thread test in Example 10.1. Calling `getManifest()` will do file I/O. Generally it is a bad idea to do I/O in the event thread. While manifest files are not likely to be large, I/O can be slow and, if done in the event thread, will block the entire application from repainting until it is done. It is a good idea to do any I/O on a background thread. Now that we have defined a threading model, we will enforce it by throwing an exception if the method is called on the event thread. Any class with a threading model should document what its threading model is, so a note about this should be added to the Javadoc for `ManifestProvider`.

We now have an implementation for `ManifestProvider`. Foreign code that knows about the `ManifestProvider` interface can get it in any of the three ways:

```
someManifestDataObject.getCookie(ManifestProvider.class)
someManifestDataNode.getCookie(ManifestProvider.class)
someManifestDataNode.getLookup().lookup(ManifestProvider.class)
```

When a manifest file is selected in the active `TopComponent` UI, any piece of code that knows about the `ManifestProvider` class (i.e., any piece of code that depends on our module) can call

```
Utilities.actionsGlobalContext().lookup(ManifestProvider.class)
```

to find out if the currently selected `Node` in the whole UI has a `ManifestProvider` and, if it does, call its `getManifest()` method.

10.2.3.1   *Using* `Lookup` *instead of* `Node.Cookie`

`Lookup` is the more modern variant of the pattern where you pass something a `Class` object and get back an instance of that class. Most actions in modern NetBeans code deal with `Nodes`, not `DataObjects`—or, more likely, do not even touch `Nodes` but rather use `Utilities.actionsGlobalContext()` to look up the current selection. So if we don't mind that `ManifestProvider` will not be available from `ManifestDataObject.getCookie()` (it will be indirectly available via `ManifestDataObject.getNodeDelegate().getLookup().lookup()`), we can simply provide a `Lookup` that contains a `ManifestProvider` from `ManifestDataNode`.

1. Edit the constructor of `ManifestDataNode` as follows:

```
public ManifestDataNode(ManifestDataObject obj) {
  super(obj, Children.LEAF, Lookups.fixed (new Object[] {
    obj, new ManifestProviderImpl (obj),
  }));
  setIconBaseWithExtension(IMAGE_ICON_BASE);
}
```

2. Create the class `ManifestProviderImpl` as a static *nested*[4] class of `ManifestDataNode`:

```
private static final class ManifestProviderImpl
                             implements ManifestProvider {
  private final DataObject obj;
  ManifestProviderImpl (DataObject obj) {
    this.obj = obj;
  }

  public Manifest getManifest() {
    if (EventQueue.isDispatchThread()) {
      throw new IllegalStateException(
                  "Don't call on event thread");
    }
    FileObject file = getPrimaryFile();
    try {
        InputStream in = file.getInputStream();
        try {
            return new Manifest (in);
        } finally {
            in.close();
        }
    } catch (IOException ioe) {
        // The manifest was malformed
    }
    return null;
  }
}
```

The two forms are basically equivalent. If you are developing for NetBeans 6 or later, the `Lookup` variant is probably the preferable

---

4. An *inner* class is a Java class defined inside the source for another Java class without using the keyword `static`. Instances of inner classes cannot exist except in the context of an instance of the outer class, which they retain a reference to. A *nested* class is one that does use the `static` keyword.

approach—`Node.getCookie()` and `DataObject.getCookie()` will eventually be deprecated.

10.2.4   Icon Badging

Now that we have `ManifestProvider`, we need a use for it. One use is determining if a manifest is valid. If the content of a manifest contains syntactical or other errors, the constructor for `Manifest` will throw an exception. NetBeans has a facility for *icon badging*—merging two images together. So `ManifestDataNode` could return an icon with a red "X" drawn on top of it if a manifest file does not represent a valid manifest.

As noted above, `ManifestProvider.getManifest()` should not be called in the AWT event thread—it does file I/O, and that should be done in the background. So this code will include a bit of threading complexity in order to dispatch a background task to check the validity of the manifest file.

1. The first order of business is to override `getIcon()` to provide our existing icon with a red "X" badge in the lower right corner when the contents of the manifest are invalid. You can get the error badge image from the accompanying CD or provide your own 11 by 11 image to be drawn over the icon for manifest files. Add a static field to the class with the path to the error badge image in the module's sources, for example

```
private static final String ERROR_BADGE_PATH
  = "org/netbeans/examples/" +
    "manifestsupport/errorbadge.png";
```

Then, in `ManifestDataNode.java`, override `Node.getIcon()` as follows:

```
public Image getIcon (int type) {
  Image original = super.getIcon (type);
  if (isValidManifest()) {
    return original;
  } else {
    Image errorBadge =
            Utilities.loadImage (ERROR_BADGE_PATH);
    return Utilities.mergeImages(original,
                              errorBadge, 5, 5);
  }
}
```

The `Utilities` class in question here is `org.openide.util.Utilities`. Its `loadImage()` method is the proper way in NetBeans to create image objects from image files, as it works with NetBeans module classloaders and supports the branding of images (in other words, another module or application can replace the icon we provide with its own to give the application a custom appearance).

2. Now we need a method called `isValidManifest()`. Here we begin to encounter threading code. We will use a `Boolean` object to keep track of whether the manifest is good or bad (shortly we will add code to listen for changes in the file so we can update the icon when the file is saved). If the `Boolean` is `null`, then we have not yet checked to see if the manifest is good or not; if it is `Boolean.FALSE`, we know the file's contents are bad; if it is `Boolean.TRUE`, we know that the file's contents are good. Since it will be accessed by multiple threads, we will always access it in a `synchronized` block:

```
private Boolean isValid = null;
private synchronized boolean isValidManifest() {
  if (isValid == null) {
    postValidityCheckInBackground();
  }
  return isValid == null ? true : isValid.booleanValue();
}
```

3. Now we need an implementation of `postValidityCheckIn-Background()`—this method will dispatch a `Runnable` that will check the validity of the manifest file on a background thread and set the value of `isValid`. This will use a NetBeans-specific thread-pool class called `RequestProcessor`. There is a default instance available from `RequestProcessor.getDefault()` which we can use to run work in the background. Since it is possible to get changes from the file twice in the time it takes for the background task to run, and we only want to check once, we will save the `RequestProcessor.Task` returned by `RequestProcessor.Post` and check if it is `null` before posting another task to check the manifest. So there will be a field called `validityCheckTask` of the type `RequestProcessor.Task`; that object, too, will be accessed by multiple threads, and therefore should only be read or assigned inside a `synchronized` block:

```
RequestProcessor.Task validityCheckTask = null;
private synchronized void
    postValidityCheckInBackground() {
  if (validityCheckTask == null) {
    validityCheckTask =
      RequestProcessor.getDefault().post (this);
  }
}
```

4. Next, we need a runnable. To save creating an extra class, simply change `ManifestDataNode` to implement `Runnable`. Then implement its `run()` method of `Runnable` and a method that will actually call `ManifestProvider.getManifest()` as follows:

```
public void run() {
  try {
      checkValidManifest();
  } finally {
      synchronized (this) {
        validityCheckTask = null;
      }
  }
}
```

```
private void checkValidManifest() {
  ManifestProvider provider = (ManifestProvider)
          getLookup().lookup(ManifestProvider.class);
  boolean iconChanged;
  synchronized (this) {
    boolean wasValid = isValidManifest();
    isValid = provider.getManifest() != null ? Boolean.TRUE :
              Boolean.FALSE;

    iconChanged = isValid.booleanValue() != wasValid;
  }
  // Fire the icon change outside the synchronized block
  if (iconChanged) {
    fireIconChange();
  }
}
```

5. Lastly, we need to actually listen for changes in the file. With somewhat different code, we could revalidate the manifest, as it is being edited, after every keystroke. In later chapters we will add error underlining and other features to cover this need. For now, we simply want the icon for a

manifest to show if the file is good or bad, and updating that on save is simple and good enough for us.

We will use a `FileChangeListener` to listen to the *primary file* of the `DataObject` for changes. There is a convenience class, `FileChangeAdapter`, in the Filesystems API, which we may subclass for this purpose. First, we will modify the constructor of `ManifestDataObject`:

```
private FileChangeListener fileListener =
                            new IconUpdateChecker();
public ManifestDataNode(ManifestDataObject obj) {
  super(obj, Children.LEAF);
  setIconBaseWithExtension(IMAGE_ICON_BASE);

  FileObject file = obj.getPrimaryFile();
  file.addFileChangeListener(
    FileUtil.weakFileChangeListener(fileListener, file));
}
```

Note that we are using `FileUtil.weakFileChangeListener()`. This is because we will never explicitly remove the listener from the file.

As you can probably guess, `IconUpdateChecker` will be an inner class extending `FileChangeAdapter`:

```
private class IconUpdateChecker extends FileChangeAdapter {
  public void fileChanged(FileEvent fe) {
    postValidityCheckInBackground();
  }
}
```

6. There is one easy-to-miss thing that we're not handling here, which is a potential bug: When a file is renamed, the `FileObject` underlying the `ManifestDataObject` will change. Right now, if the user edited a manifest file and renamed it, the old `FileObject` we were listening to is gone—we would never get notification that the file had been saved again.

We can solve this very simply. We will add a `PropertyChange-Listener` to the `ManifestDataObject` that our `Node` is representing and notice when the primary file property changes. First, modify the class declaration of `ManifestDataNode` to also implement `PropertyChangeListener`. Next, add this line to the constructor:

```
obj.addPropertyChangeListener(
    WeakListeners.propertyChange(this, obj));
```

Why Use a Weak Listener?

Note that we are using `org.openide.util.WeakListeners` to listen to the `DataObject`. What would happen if we simply call `obj.addPropertyChangeListener(this)`? It would be a memory leak—even if there were nothing displaying the `ManifestDataNode` for a `ManifestDataObject`, the list of property change listeners that the `ManifestDataObject` has would keep a strong reference to its node forever. So, even if it is no longer being used for anything, our `ManifestDataNode` could never be garbage-collected. Using `WeakListeners` solves this problem: The `DataObject` will only have a weak reference to the node. So the `Node` can be garbage-collected if nothing is using it, even if the `DataObject` that created it is still in use.

For more information about weak listeners, see Section 7.2.2.2.

Next, implement the `propertyChange()` method of `Property-ChangeListener` as follows:

```
public void propertyChange(PropertyChangeEvent evt) {
  if (DataObject.PROP_PRIMARY_FILE.equals (
      evt.getPropertyName())) {
    FileObject nue = (FileObject) evt.getNewValue();
    if (nue != null) {
      nue.addFileChangeListener(
        FileUtil.weakFileChangeListener(fileListener, nue));
    }
  }
}
```

To try this out, simply run the module, create a new manifest, and enter a few lines of garbage text in it. When you save, the file's icon will be badged with a red "X". If you then correct the content and save again, the badge will be cleared.

10.2.5 Testing `ManifestDataObject` with `JUnit`

Testing is an important part of development, and we would be remiss if we did not cover it in this book. The NetBeans IDE and module building environment make it easy to write unit tests for your code and run them. What we will do now is create a unit test for `ManifestDataObject` that will ensure that it obeys the contracts we have defined for `ManifestProvider` and is working correctly. To start, we need to create a unit test class. Since the ManifestSupport module was created using the module template in the IDE, there is already a `test/unit` subdirectory of the project waiting for unit test source code to be added to it. Simply right-click `ManifestDataObject.java` and choose **Tools | Create Unit Tests**, as shown in Figure 10.9.

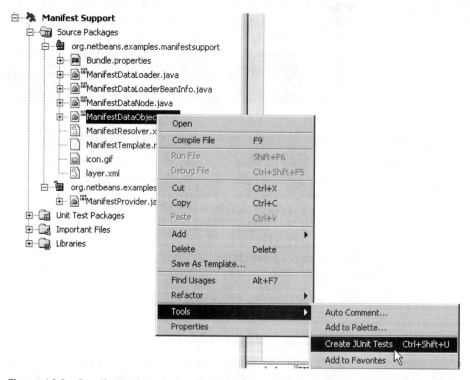

Figure 10.9: Creating unit tests for `ManifestDataObject`

Especially in the case of distributed development or open source development on the Internet, tests are a way to guarantee that one developer does not undo or break the work of another. If your development practice requires that programmers run tests before checking code into version control, it is much harder for one mistake to disrupt other people's work. It is also possible to set up a build server that will continuously build the software, run the tests, and, if they start to fail, email the people who have made changes since the last build that passed the tests.[5]

This will create an empty JUnit test case that we can fill with test methods (the **Create JUnit Tests** action may have generated some test methods by default—if so, delete these methods). First, in the setUp() method, we will need some manifest files to test against. We will create them in the system temporary directory and populate them with content. One will be a valid manifest and another will be invalid. Populate the top of the test class as follows (mainly, this code creates the files and makes a FileSystem so we can get FileObjects for the files).

```
private static final String BAD_MANIFEST_CONTENT =
   "Manifest-Version: 1.0\n" +
   "junk junk junk\n" +
   "some more junk\n";

private static final String GOOD_MANIFEST_CONTENT =
   "Manifest-Version: 1.0\n" +
   "Java-Bean: true\n" +
   "OpenIDE-Module-Name: com.foo.bar";

private FileObject bad;
private FileObject good;
protected void setUp() throws Exception {
   // Get the system temp dir
   File dir = new File (System.getProperty ("java.io.tmpdir"));
   File goodManifest = new File (dir, System.currentTimeMillis() +
                                 "good.mf");

   goodManifest.createNewFile();
   writeFile (GOOD_MANIFEST_CONTENT, goodManifest);
```

---

5. One excellent open source tool for setting this sort of thing up is Hudson (hudson.dev.java.net).

```
    File badManifest = new File (dir, System.currentTimeMillis() +
            "bad.mf");
    badManifest.createNewFile();
    writeFile (BAD_MANIFEST_CONTENT, badManifest);

    // Deprecated, but the only way to do it for tests without
    // loading all of core to get declarative MIME resolvers
    // loaded. This call just manually sets the MIME type to be
    // associated with the .mf extension
    FileUtil.setMIMEType("mf", "text/x-manifest");

    // Create a local filesystem so we can make FileObjects
    // from Files
    LocalFileSystem fs = new LocalFileSystem ();
    fs.setRootDirectory(dir);

    good = fs.getRoot().getFileObject(goodManifest.getName());
    bad = fs.getRoot().getFileObject(badManifest.getName());

    // Sanity check
    assertNotNull (good);
    assertNotNull (bad);
}

private void writeFile (String content, File file)
                                    throws Exception {
    Charset charset = Charset.forName ("UTF-8");
    ByteBuffer buf = charset.encode(content);
    FileOutputStream str = new FileOutputStream (file);
    FileChannel channel = str.getChannel();
    FileLock lock = channel.lock();
    try {
        channel.write (buf);
        channel.force(true);
    } finally {
        lock.release();
        channel.close();
    }
}

protected void tearDown() throws Exception {
    good.delete();
    bad.delete();
}
```

Now we are ready to add test methods. JUnit will treat any method whose name starts with "test" as a test method. It will call setUp(), then that method, then tearDown(), and report the results. The first test method will be a basic sanity check:

```
public void testManifestProviderPresent () throws Exception {
  System.out.println("testManifestProviderPresent");
  DataObject goodDob = DataObject.find (good);
  assertTrue (goodDob instanceof ManifestDataObject);
  assertNotNull (goodDob.getCookie(ManifestProvider.class));
}
```

If this test passes, then we know that, at least, all of the plumbing that creates DataObjects (including our DataLoader) is working.

An important thing is to test boundary conditions—to test that a system fails in the way it has been documented to. We documented that ManifestProvider will throw an exception if called in the AWT event thread. So, let's enforce that no one breaks this behavior in the future with a test:

```
public void
    testManifestProviderThrowsExceptionWhenCalledInEventThread()
    throws Exception {
  System.out.println("testManifestProviderPresent");
  DataObject goodDob = DataObject.find (good);
  final ManifestProvider provider = (ManifestProvider)
    goodDob.getCookie(ManifestProvider.class);
  class R implements Runnable {
    private Exception exception;
    public void run() {
      try {
          provider.getManifest();
      } catch (Exception e) {
          exception = e;
      }
    }
  };
  R r = new R();
  EventQueue.invokeAndWait (r);
  assertNotNull (r.exception);
}
```

Now we can test that our implementation of ManifestProvider behaves as it should:

```java
public void testDataObject() throws Exception {
  System.out.println("testDataObject");
  DataObject goodDob = DataObject.find (good);
  DataObject badDob = DataObject.find (bad);
  assertTrue (goodDob instanceof ManifestDataObject);
  assertTrue (badDob instanceof ManifestDataObject);
  ManifestProvider mp = (ManifestProvider)
    goodDob.getCookie (ManifestProvider.class);
  assertNotNull (mp);
  assertNotNull (mp.getManifest());
  // Prove that you can get the ManifestProvider in all the ways
  // you should be able to
  assertSame (mp, goodDob.getNodeDelegate().getCookie (
    ManifestProvider.class));

  assertSame (mp, goodDob.getNodeDelegate().getLookup().lookup (
    ManifestProvider.class));
}

public void testBadManifest() throws Exception {
  System.out.println("testBadManifest");
  DataObject badDob = DataObject.find (bad);
  ManifestProvider mp =
    (ManifestProvider) badDob.getCookie (ManifestProvider.class);
  assertNotNull (mp);
  assertNull (mp.getManifest());
}
```

More tests are possible and are included with the source code on the accompanying CD. At this point we'll move on to running the tests.

One last step is needed before we are ready to run: As we noted above, DataLoaders are registered in module manifests. But when we are running unit tests, we are not running the full IDE—the NetBeans Module System is not there to read and process those manifests. The solution for testing purposes is to put ManifestDataLoader in the default Lookup for tests only. Simply create a META-INF/services directory under **Unit Test Packages** in the project, as shown in Figure 10.10, and add the appropriate file to declare our DataLoader.[6]

---

6. If you are using NetBeans 6 or later, the **New File Type** wizard already created this file for you.

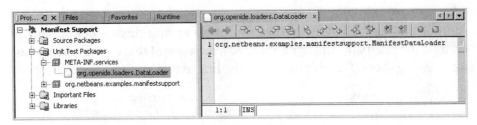

Figure 10.10: Including `ManifestDataLoader` in the default `Lookup` when unit tests are run

10.2.5.1   Running Unit Tests

To run the unit tests, simply right-click the project and choose **Run Unit Tests** from the popup menu. However, you will find there is a problem—the output you see will probably look like this:

```
Testcase: testBadManifest(org.netbeans.examples.manifestsupport⏎
.ManifestDataObjectTest):
Caused an ERROR
org/openide/NotifyDescriptor
java.lang.NoClassDefFoundError: org/openide/NotifyDescriptor
    at org.netbeans.examples.manifestsupport.ManifestDataObject⏎
.<init>(ManifestDataObject.java:21)
    at org.netbeans.examples.manifestsupport.ManifestDataLoader⏎
.createMultiObject(ManifestDataLoader.java:30)
    at org.openide.loaders.MultiFileLoader.handleFindDataObject⏎
(MultiFileLoader.java:120)
    at org.openide.loaders.DataObjectPool.handleFindDataObject⏎
(DataObjectPool.java:122)
    at org.openide.loaders.DataLoader.findDataObject(⏎
DataLoader.java:357)
    at org.openide.loaders.DataLoaderPool.findDataObject(⏎
DataLoaderPool.java:394)
    at org.openide.loaders.DataLoaderPool.findDataObject(⏎
DataLoaderPool.java:354)
    at org.openide.loaders.DataObject.find(DataObject.java:460)
    at org.netbeans.examples.manifestsupport.⏎
ManifestDataObjectTest.testBadManifest(ManifestDataObjectTest.⏎
java:157)
```

What is happening here is that we are missing some dependencies. When running unit tests, all of the NetBeans runtime environment is not present or even on the classpath, and our tests need a bit more of that environment than we're giving them. The culprit here is the line in `ManifestDataObject`:

```
cookies.add((Node.Cookie) DataEditorSupport.create(this,
                    getPrimaryEntry(), cookies));
```

`DataEditorSupport`, which creates the text editor for manifest files, has some dependencies that our module doesn't have. Since we are calling `DataEditorSupport` indirectly, from our test class, we need to satisfy its dependencies by putting the JARs for those modules on the test classpath. Fortunately, this is easy to do—there is an Ant property we can set to add additional JARs to the test classpath. On the **Files** window, open `nbproject/project.properties`. Add the following lines to the file:[7,8]

```
test.unit.cp.extra=${netbeans.dest.dir}/platform7/modules/org-\
   openide-dialogs.jar:${netbeans.dest.dir}/platform7/modules/\
   org-openide-awt.jar
```

What we are doing is adding the Dialogs API and the UI Utilities API to the test's classpath so that `DataEditorSupport` can load the classes that it needs. If you run the tests now, they will work correctly.

10.3   Using Custom File Types Internally

As mentioned earlier, the System Filesystem is just another filesystem. Sometimes it is useful to create a file type which users will never see. Perhaps you have some API where you define a folder in the System Filesystem and let

---

7. If you are using a version of NetBeans later than 5.5, the `platform7` directory—the platform cluster—may be named `platform8` or higher. It will typically be a subdirectory of your install of NetBeans—just see what the name of the subdirectory is and substitute that for `platform7` in the text above.

8. In NetBeans 6, this usage of `test.unit.cp.extra` is deprecated; there is a new `project.xml` schema that lets you express test dependencies more cleanly. This *may* be backported to an update of the module development tools for 5.5 but at the time of this writing it is not clear if that will happen.

other modules add files there—but the data you want them to save there is fairly complex. You could define a bunch of file attributes that should be set on each file, but that can get quite ugly and hard to debug. In such a case, it may be easier to define a custom filename extension and format and let modules add files in that format to the folder in question. For an example of this, see Chapter 15.

10.4 Serialized Objects and the System Filesystem

POJOs—"Plain Old Java Objects"—are all the rage in the server-side programming world. They allow programmers to write simple classes that do not depend on any particular framework. The System Filesystem can be used to read and write serialized objects as a means of storing objects across sessions. Simply create a new file with the extension .ser and write your object out to it:

```
public void save (String filename) throws IOException {

  FileObject folder = Repository.getDefault().
    getDefaultFileSystem().getRoot().getFileObject ("myfolder");
  FileObject writeTo = folder.getFileObject (filename, "ser");

  if (writeTo == null) {
    writeTo = folder.createData (filename, "ser");
  }

  ObjectOutputStream stream =
    new ObjectOutputStream (writeTo.getOutputStream());

  try {
      stream.writeObject (this);
  } finally {
      stream.close();
  }
}
```

Any code that converts files into objects represented by those files will be able to deal with .ser files just as well as with .instance files.

That being said, Java serialization is often not the best format for saving things. If the fields of your object change across releases, code written to deserialize the new version of your classes will not understand the serialization format of the older version. For this reason, using serialization for nontrivial objects is generally not recommended—creating a custom file format or using `.instance` or `.settings` files will be more robust across releases of your code.

CHAPTER ELEVEN

Graphical User Interfaces

11.1 Introduction

As we have already seen, the NetBeans Platform does much of the hard work of putting together a standalone application, providing everything from the windowing system to an extendable help system and options manipulation. But while you can save a great deal of work by extending these parts of the NetBeans Platform, you will inevitably have to code some graphic user interface (GUI) elements such as dialogs and wizard panels.

Creating GUIs has traditionally been more difficult than it needs to be. Standard layout managers such as BorderLayout aren't easy to work with. While GridBagLayout provides for easier manipulation of forms, the use of absolute pixels to position components often leads to problems when the program is run on different operating systems or the display text is translated into another language.

In the 5.0 release, NetBeans IDE revolutionized the approach to GUI layout management by introducing the NetBeans GUI Builder (previously known as project Matisse)—the combination of a new layout manager called GroupLayout and a visual interface for designing forms with this layout manager. The NetBeans GUI Builder approach arranges components using grouping and relative proximity rather than JPanels and absolute X and Y locations. Components are anchored to the sides of a container and to other components. For example, you can set two components to be aligned on their baselines or along their left or right edges. When the size of components changes as a result of the form being localized or resized by the user, all of the components remain aligned correctly.

One of the ways the NetBeans GUI Builder maintains correct alignment of forms is by letting the look and feel of the program dictate the default spacing between components, instead of defining the spacing in absolute pixels. This means that your form will always look like a native application on any operating system.

You can use the NetBeans GUI Builder to design any Swing-based form. In addition to creating new forms with Swing components, you can also use the GUI Builder to work with components defined in the NetBeans Platform, such as `TopComponent`.

NetBeans IDE comes with a number of tools for working with Java GUI forms. These tools include:

- **Form Editor** provides both **Design** and **Source** views for you to create visual components. The **Design** view is an area where you can drag, drop, and rearrange the visual components that make up the user interface of the client you are building. The **Source** view contains the generated source code for the class you are designing and allows you to enter your own code for the class.

- **Inspector** window provides a tree view of all of the components in the form, whether visual (such as menus, text fields, labels, and buttons) or nonvisual (such as button groups and data sources). This window appears in the same space as the **Navigator** window.

- **Palette** window. Provides a list of components that you can drag and drop onto your form. You can choose from Swing and AWT components or add your own custom beans.

- **Properties** window contains a list of editable properties for the selected component and access to special property editors for the more complex properties.

- **Connection** wizard helps you create event listener and event handler code that links two components.

- **Form Tester** quickly displays a runtime view of the form under construction, allowing checks of resizing and other behavior.

- **Palette Manager** enables you to add custom components to the **Palette** window. Choose **Tools | Palette Manager | Swing/AWT Components** to open this window.

The **Form Editor**, **Inspector** window, **Palette** window, and **Properties** window are shown in Figure 11.1. You can access the **Connection** wizard, **Form Tester**, and **Palette Manager** via buttons in the toolbar area of the **Form Editor**.

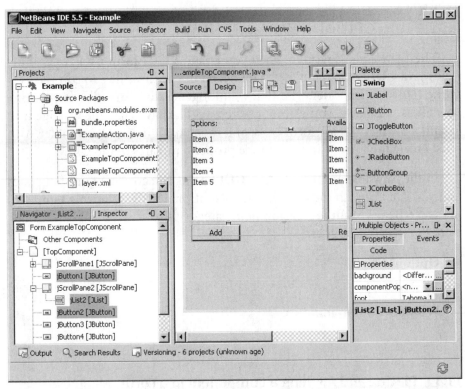

Figure 11.1: **Form Editor** windows, including the **Inspector**, **Form Editor** (**Design** view), **Palette** window, and **Properties** window

This section is not a complete guide to developing visual applications with Swing in NetBeans IDE; a whole book could be devoted to that. Instead, it focuses on a few of the unique but somewhat tricky features of Swing and the IDE that assist in the designing of visual applications.

11.2   Creating a New GUI Form

When you create a GUI form with the IDE's GUI Builder, the IDE creates two files:

- A Java file that contains the Java source code for the form.
- An XML `.form` file that contains information about the form's layout. The IDE's GUI Builder uses this file to edit the form.

The `.form` file is written when you create a GUI form using one of the IDE's Java GUI Form templates. You need both of these files to edit the GUI in the IDE's GUI Builder. The IDE will not generate `.form` files for existing Java GUIs. Similarly, you cannot create a regular Java class file, change it to extend a Swing or AWT form class, and then edit it in the GUI Builder. You must create the form using one of the proper templates in the IDE.

In the **New File** wizard, the **Java GUI Forms** category contains templates that you can use with the GUI Builder. Additionally, the following templates in the **NetBeans Module Development** category also create forms that can be edited in the GUI Builder:

- **Options Panel**
- **Wizard**
- **Window Component**

11.3   Placing and Aligning a Component in a Form

To design forms with the NetBeans GUI Builder, you drag components from the **Palette** into your form. As you drag the component close to other components or the container's edges, the component automatically snaps to align with other components.

To add a component to a form:

1. Click a component in the **Palette** to select it.

2. Move the cursor to the location in the form where you want to place the component. The IDE suggests alignment and anchoring as you come near other components.

3. Click to place the component. If you want to add multiple components, hold down the Shift key and click multiple times.

For instance, in Figure 11.2, the first `JLabel` is anchored to the top and left edges of the `JFrame`, with the default spacing defined by the look and feel.

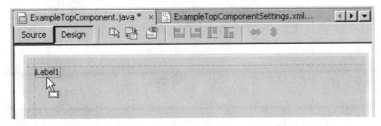

Figure 11.2: `JLabel` **snapped to the top right corner of a** `TopComponent`

In Figure 11.3, `JLabel2` is snapped to the baseline of the **Options** `JLabel`.

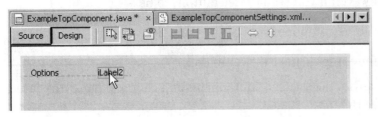

Figure 11.3: `JLabel` **snapped to the baseline of another** `JLabel`

After you've placed the components, you can select any component to see the components to which it is anchored, as shown in Figure 11.4. For example, the dark arrow on the left of the **Options** `JLabel` shows that that component is anchored to the left side of the `JPanel`.

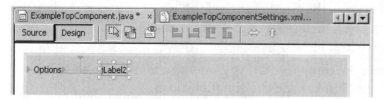

Figure 11.4: Guidelines showing the anchoring relationships of the two `JLabels`

 You can edit the display text of any `JLabel`, `JTextField`, or `JButton` by double-clicking it in the **Design** view.

11.4   Setting Component Size and Resizability

To change a component's size, grab one of its corners or edges and drag it to the desired size. Many components automatically expand in size to accommodate any text or icons inserted into them.

Another important function is forcing components to be the same size. For example, our form has the standard **OK**, **Cancel**, and **Help** buttons. By default, each button is only as wide as its display text. The form would look much better, however, if you set all three buttons to be the same width.

To force multiple components to be the same size:

1. Shift-click the components to select them.

2. Right-click any of the selected components and choose **Same Size | Same Width/Same Height**.

To set a component to automatically resize as its container resizes, do one of the following:

- Resize the form to snap to one of the edges of its container.
- Use the vertical and/or horizontal "same size" toolbar buttons.

Figure 11.5 shows all of these concepts at work together. The two `JLists` must have the same width and automatically resize both vertically and horizontally when you resize the dialog. To achieve this state, do the following:

1. Insert two `JLists`, each snapped to the left edge of the `JLabel` above them.
2. Expand the `JList` on the left to snap to the side of the `JList` on the right.
3. Expand the `JList` on the right to snap to the edge of the `JFrame`.
4. Select both `JLists` by Shift-clicking them.
5. Click the vertical and horizontal "same size" toolbar buttons to set the resizing behavior.
6. Right-click either of the `JLists` and choose **Same Size | Same Width**.

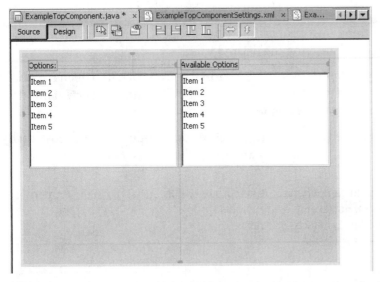

Figure 11.5: Two `JLists` set to be the same size and resize automatically

11.5   Specifying Component Behavior and Appearance

You can use the **Properties** window to set the behavior and appearance of components that you have added to a form. The **Properties** window displays the properties of the component selected in the **Inspector** or the **Form Editor**. The properties come in three categories:

- **Properties**. A configurable list of characteristics for the component. Technically speaking, these are the JavaBeans properties for the component.

- Events. A list of event listeners that you can attach to a component. You can specify event listeners here (or remove them here) or use the **Connection** wizard. See Section 11.6 later in this chapter.

- Code. Some NetBeans IDE-specific properties that you can use to customize the way the code is generated. See Section 11.7 later in this chapter.

To edit component properties:

1. Select the property category by clicking the appropriate button at the top of the **Properties** window (**Properties**, **Events**, or **Code**).

2. Edit the component's properties in the **Properties** window by selecting the property and entering the desired value.

3. If a property has an ellipsis (...) button, you can click it to open a special property editor that enables you to modify the property and the initialization code generated for it.

4. In the property editor, use the **Select Mode** combo box to choose each custom editor for the property and make the necessary changes.

 For some components, the key property is listed in bold in the **Properties** window. For example, the "model" property for the `JTable` and `JList` properties is marked in bold.

11.6   Generating Event Listening and Handling Methods

The IDE relieves you of the task of providing the infrastructure of event handling by generating the code to link the occurrence of each event with the invocation of a private method in the form class. For example, a `JButton` named `myBtn` might have the code

```
myBtn.addActionListener(new java.awt.event.ActionListener() {
  public void actionPerformed(java.awt.event.ActionEvent evt) {
  myBtnActionPerformed(evt);
}
```

added to its initialization, where the generated method `myBtnActionPerformed()` looks like this:

```
private void myBtnActionPerformed(
            java.awt.event.ActionEvent evt) {
  // TODO add your handling code here:
}
```

Within your Java code, comments—generated or otherwise—that start with `TODO` have special significance. To see a list of your `TODO` lines, display the **ToDo** window via **Window | ToDo** or press Ctrl-6. From the displayed window, you can navigate to the source line with the `TODO` by a double-click in the **ToDo** window.

Generating this event infrastructure code can be done in a couple of ways:

- By right-clicking the component and choosing the event to be handled from the **Events** menu.

    The IDE generates the event handler and positions the cursor to the appropriate `TODO` line in the generated private method. You then fill in the rest of the event handling code.

- By using the **Connection** wizard to generate code. Use this approach when an event on a component should result in the modification of another component.

    To use the **Connection** wizard:

1. Enter connection mode by clicking the **Connection Mode** icon in the **Form Editor**'s toolbar.

2. Open the **Connection** wizard by clicking successively on the two components—first the component that will fire the event and then the component upon which an operation is to be performed.

3. In the **Select Source Event** page of the wizard (shown in Figure 11.6), select the event to be fired.

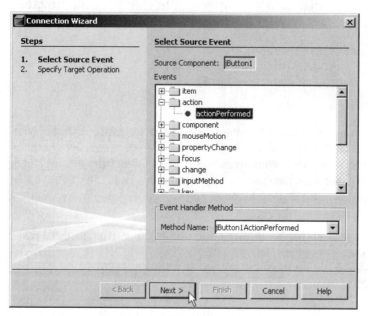

Figure 11.6: **Connection** wizard, **Select Source Event** page

4. In the **Specify Target Operation** page (shown in Figure 11.7), specify the operation to be performed on the target component. You can specify a property to set, call a method, or write your own custom code.

The **Connection** wizard approach is simply a "point and click" approach to the task. The code generated by the wizard is not guarded and can be modified in the editor after generation.

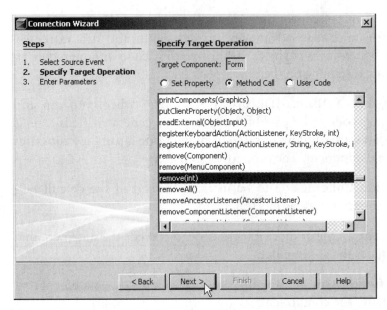

Figure 11.7: **Connection** wizard, **Specify Target Operation** page

11.7   Customizing Generated Code

NetBeans IDE dynamically generates the code for GUI construction. You can view this code in the **Source** view of the **Form Editor** (click the **Source** button in the **Form Editor**'s toolbar). In addition to the code generated within the class in its *class-name*.java file, the IDE maintains an XML file called *class-name*.form that details the structure of the form. Note that the source code control systems (such as CVS) supported by NetBeans ensure by default that the .form file is maintained in the repository as well as the .java file.

Within a .java source file, generated code is delimited by special comments (for example, //GEN-BEGIN:initComponents . . . //GEN-END:initComponents). The editor does not allow this code to be modified and indicates the unmodifiable code with a pale blue background. Although you could modify this code outside the IDE, it is not recommended, because those modifications would be lost if you reopen the form in the IDE. (The IDE regenerates the .java file of a form created in the IDE from the .form files each time you open the file in the IDE.)

Such locking of generated code prompted vigorous discussion in the NetBeans IDE team, but its advantages proved significant: It is extremely difficult to reliably "reverse-engineer" arbitrary Swing code without requiring restrictive coding discipline on the developer's part.

Instead of this, NetBeans IDE provides "hooks" where you can add (almost) arbitrary code to be part of the code to be generated. This code is added via a code-aware window accessed from the **Code** tab of the **Properties** window for the component. The properties used are:

Custom Creation Code   Code to be inserted instead of the default `new ComponentClassName();` statement.

Pre-creation Code   One or more lines of code to precede the statement that instantiates the component.

Post-creation Code   One or more lines of code to follow the statement that instantiates the component.

Pre-init Code   One or more lines of code to precede the first statement that initializes the properties of the component.

Post-init Code   One or more lines of code to follow the last statement that initializes the properties of the component.

In addition, the initial values of the various properties of components can be specified in various ways:

- A static value.
- A property from a component written to the JavaBeans architecture.
- A property of another component on the form.
- A call to a method of the form or one of its components. You can choose from a list of methods that return the appropriate data type.
- Any code you define, which will be included in the generated code.

11.8   Building an Explorer View Visually

As described in Chapter 9, the *Explorer API* provides specific UI components that you can use when building an explorer-type window component. When you create a window component using the GUI Builder, you have to change the creation code to use the appropriate UI component.

In the following example, we build a `TopComponent` containing a `BeanTreeView` component using the GUI Builder.

1. Create a new NetBeans module project called `TopComponentTest`. Set the project to be a standalone module.

2. Choose **File | New**, then select the **Window Component** template from the **NetBeans Module Development** category. Set the window component to open in the **Explorer** position and enter `ExplorerTest` as the **Class Name Prefix**.

3. Select `ExplorerTestTopComponent` in the Source Editor. Add a `JScrollPane` component to the form and expand it to lock to the four sides of the `TopComponent` form so that it automatically expands and contracts when the user resizes the window.

4. With the `JScrollPane` selected, click the **Code** button in the **Properties** window and enter the following in the **Custom Creation Code** property:

```
new BeanTreeView();
```

5. Switch to the **Source** view. Notice that the `JScrollPane` is initialized as follows:

```
jScrollPane1 = new BeanTreeView();
```

Since `BeanTreeView` comes from the Explorer API, we have to declare a dependency on the Explorer API module. Right-click the project's node and choose **Properties**. Click **Libraries** in the left of the dialog box, then use the **Add** button to add the Explorer and Property Sheet API module. Click **OK** to save changes and exit the **Project Properties** dialog box.

6. Install the module as described in Section 1.2.5 and run your application. You should see Figure 11.8.

Figure 11.8: The **ExplorerTest** window

11.9   Previewing a Form

You can quickly preview any form without having to compile and run your project. Just click the **Preview Form** button in the **Form Editor** toolbar. Although you can resize the form, type text into text fields, and otherwise manipulate the form, the form is not "live." You have to run the project to test any event handling code.

11.10 Using Custom Beans in the Form Editor

In addition to the standard Swing and AWT components available in the **Palette**, you can also build your own custom components and add them to the **Palette**.

To add a component to the **Palette**:

1. If you are developing the component in an IDE project, build the project.

2. Choose **Tools | Palette Manager | Swing/AWT Components**.

3. Click one of the following to specify the component location:

    Add from JAR   Choose this option if the component is in a built library. The component can be a compiled class (`.class` file) or a serialized prototype (`.ser` file).

    Add from Library   Choose this option if the component is in one of the libraries registered in the **Library Manager**.

    Add from Project   Choose this option if the form is in an IDE project. In this case, the IDE adds the project containing the component to the present project's classpath. Whenever you build your project, the component's project is built as well.

4. Click **Next**.

5. Select the component and click **Next**. The wizard displays all JavaBeans components in the specified location.

6. Specify the palette category for the component and click **Finish**.

 If the project containing the component is open in the IDE, you can right-click the component's node in the **Projects** window and choose **Tools | Add to Palette**.

11.11 Using Different Layout Managers

By default, NetBeans IDE uses the `GroupLayout` layout manager for any new forms that you create. The IDE also provides full support for the standard Swing layouts managers:

- `FlowLayout`
- `BorderLayout`
- `GridLayout`
- `GridBagLayout`

- CardLayout
- BoxLayout (note that the "struts" and "glue" normally used with BoxLayout are not provided as out-of-the-box components)

In addition, support for forms without a layout manager (NullLayout) and forms with absolutely positioned components (AbsoluteLayout) is provided. Neither of these is recommended for production use, as their behavior across platforms and their response to resizing are likely to be unacceptable.

To set the layout manager for a container:

1. Right-click a container in the **Inspector** window and choose the layout manager from the **Set Layout** menu.
2. To set the form to use a layout manager, choose the desired layout manager's name. To set the form to use GroupLayout, choose **Free Design**.

 To set the layout manager back to GroupLayout, choose **Set Layout | Free Design**.

CHAPTER TWELVE

Multiview Editors

12.1 Introduction

NetBeans includes support for *multiview editors*. A multiview editor is an editor component that contains a toolbar with buttons to switch between multiple *views* of a single file. If you have used the GUI Builder to edit Swing components in the NetBeans IDE, you have already seen a multiview editor in action. One view of the program is the Java source code for the file being edited; the other is the drag-and-drop editor that allows you to visually design the component. Both are editors working with the same file. When a file is modified in one view, the changes are immediately visible in the other. Multiview editors should be *bidirectional*, so that any change in one view of the file is seamlessly reflected in the others (there may be more than two views).

It is often desirable to present users with multiple ways to view and edit files. For example, you might want to provide a visual way to edit a file without taking away the possibility to directly view and modify the text of the file. Building on the previous chapter, where we show how to create simple support for handling a file type (including providing a basic text editor), we will now demonstrate how to use the NetBeans *MultiView Windows API* to create multiple views of a single file.

In Chapter 10, we show how to create a `DataLoader` for manifest files. Once you have created that `DataLoader`, the IDE recognizes manifest files as a distinct file type. You can then provide menu items and toolbar buttons specifically for working with that type. In addition, you have a very basic text editor for the object type. Subsequent chapters will demonstrate how you can enhance the text editor associated with a `DataLoader` to include features such as syntax highlighting and code completion.

Even if you go on to enhance the text editor, you might also want to provide a visual representation of the file to make editing easier, particularly for those who do not know the file type's syntax by heart. Apart from its being useful for new Java developers, a visual editor can also improve the efficiency of advanced users.

In this chapter, we will demonstrate how to add views for a file type by creating a *multiview editor* for manifest files. The text view will be the same as provided by default in the IDE, as shown in Figure 12.1.

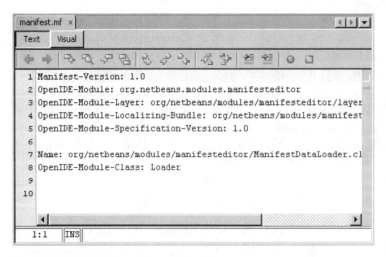

Figure 12.1: Text view of a manifest file

To that, we will add a "visual" view. Using the MultiView Windows API, we will create a toggle button for switching between the two views. In this case, the visual view will consist of a property sheet, as shown in Figure 12.2.

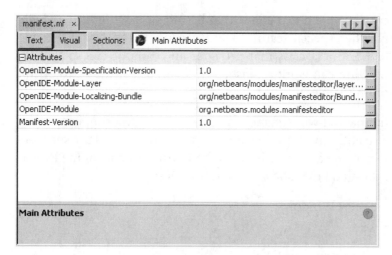

Figure 12.2: Visual view of a manifest file

When you make changes in one view, they will be reflected in the other view. This means that the multiview implementation must synchronize the two views. You could use one of several approaches for synchronizing the views. The focus of this chapter is on creating the views in the editor, not on synchronization between them. For one approach to synchronization between views, see the related sample on the accompanying CD.

12.2   Getting Started

We will base this chapter's example on the ManifestDataObject and associated classes created in Chapter 10. ManifestDataLoader is a factory for DataObjects for manifest files; those DataObjects are responsible for providing support for editing manifest files. The **New File Type** wizard has already generated basic editor support in the constructor of ManifestDataObject with the line shown in Example 12.1.

Example 12.1: Creating a plain text editor

```
cookies.add((Node.Cookie) DataEditorSupport.create(this,
                          getPrimaryEntry(), cookies));
```

That line creates a plain text editor that has no support for syntax highlighting or any other special features—but can open and edit a text file. `DataEditorSupport` is a class that provides an `OpenCookie` so that the standard **Open** action can work against a `ManifestDataObject` to open a plain text editor on the file.

For this example, we will enhance the existing manifest support project. The first step is to add some new dependencies to it, for we will use some additional APIs to provide a visual editor. In the **Libraries** panel of the **Project Properties** window, add the following dependencies:

- Core—MultiView Windows
- UI Utilities API
- Explorer and Property Sheet API

12.3   Understanding Multiview Editors

When working on this implementation of a multiview editor, the main NetBeans API classes we will use are `DataEditorSupport`, `CloneableEditor`, `MultiViewElement`, and `MultiViewDescription`. Here are brief descriptions of these classes:

`DataEditorSupport`   Provides the entry point for working with editors. Apart from providing the editor's plumbing, such as the connection between the editor and its `DataObject`, this is the class where the UI components that make up the multiview editor are registered and instantiated.

`CloneableEditor`   Provides the basics of a text editor. For example, this class handles the opening and closing of the editor, as well as typical editor functionality such as undo/redo management. Features such as syntax highlighting, code completion, and hyperlinks need to be implemented separately.

`MultiViewElement`   Provides the UI component for one view in the multiview editor, such as the standard text editor or the property-sheet-based editor we are creating.

`MultiViewDescription`   Describes the tabs in the multiview editor. This class provides a display name, an icon, and a help ID for one view. Most importantly, this class creates and returns its associated `MultiViewElement`.

12.4   Creating the Editor's Infrastructure

Before creating tabs in the multiview editor, we need to set up the surrounding editor infrastructure. We use `DataEditorSupport` to do this. It connects our multiview editor to our `DataObject`. Previously we used a utility method on `DataEditorSupport`, as shown in Example 12.1, to create a simple text editor. We will now, instead, *extend* `DataEditorSupport` so that we have more control over what kind of editor is created.

1. Create a class called `ManifestEditorSupport`. Let it extend `DataEditorSupport` and implement `OpenCookie` and `EditCookie` from the Nodes API, and `EditorCookie` from the Text API. These classes serve the following functions:

   `OpenCookie`   Permits an editor to be opened. `OpenCookie` works with the standard NetBeans `OpenAction`, which looks for an `OpenCookie` on the object it is invoked against and, if it finds one, calls `OpenCookie.open()` on it. What actually happens when `open()` is called is up to the implementor of `OpenCookie`.

   `EditorCookie`   Permits standard operations for text documents, such as opening, closing, and saving, and provides a way for outside code to access the Swing `Document` and editor pane for the text editor.

   `EditCookie`   `EditCookie` is just like `OpenCookie`, but works with the standard `EditAction`. It is useful when there is more than one kind of editor for a file. One type of editor can be invoked by the **Open** action and another by the **Edit** action.

   Right now, we will not add anything to the main body of the class except the constructor, which receives the `DataObject` and passes it to the superclass together with a custom editor environment. The editor

environment, which we will create in the next step, provides data to
`DataEditorSupport`, such as the input stream of the file that is the source
of the editor's contents. In the call to the superclass, the `DataObject` and
the editor's "environment" must be passed. The environment is a supple-
mentary object that provides a few methods to return the file being edited
(and, incidentally, allow it to be swapped with a different file if the file
being edited is renamed), do the actual work of saving the file, and so
forth. We will create the editor's environment in the next step.

```
public class ManifestEditorSupport extends DataEditorSupport
    implements OpenCookie, EditorCookie, EditCookie {

  private ManifestEditorSupport(ManifestDataObject obj) {
    super(obj, new ManifestEnv(obj));
  }
}
```

2. To create the environment, create an inner class called `ManifestEnv` that
   extends `DataEditorSupport.Env` and implements `SaveCookie`. Its
   abstract methods are outlined below:

`save()`   Invokes the save operation.

`getFile()`   Gets the file associated with the environment.

`takeLock()`   Locks the file.

   Implement the methods for the inner class of the manifest editor as
   follows:

```
public class ManifestEditorSupport extends DataEditorSupport
    implements OpenCookie, EditorCookie, EditCookie {

  private ManifestEditorSupport(ManifestDataObject obj) {
    super(obj, new ManifestEnv(obj));
  }

  private static final class ManifestEnv extends
    DataEditorSupport.Env implements SaveCookie {

    public ManifestEnv(ManifestDataObject obj) {
      super(obj);
    }
```

```
      public void save() throws IOException {
        ManifestEditorSupport ed = (ManifestEditorSupport)this.
                                     findCloneableOpenSupport();
          ed.saveDocument();
      }

      protected FileObject getFile() {
        return super.getDataObject().getPrimaryFile();
      }

      protected FileLock takeLock() throws IOException {
        return ((ManifestDataObject)super.getDataObject()).
                  getPrimaryEntry().takeLock();
      }

    }

  }
```

3. Our editor must be associated with the `DataObject`. To do this, we add the editor to the `DataObject`'s lookup. (`Lookup` is described in detail in Chapter 5. Specifically, read Section 5.7.) The `DataObject` should be rewritten as follows:

```
public class ManifestDataObject extends MultiDataObject
      implements Lookup.Provider {

    final InstanceContent ic;
    private AbstractLookup lookup;

    public ManifestDataObject(FileObject pf, ManifestDataLoader
          loader) throws DataObjectExistsException, IOException {
      super(pf, loader);

      // We use InstanceContent because we need a modifiable
      // Lookup; see step 5 for the reason behind our
      // modifications.

      ic = new InstanceContent();
      lookup = new AbstractLookup(ic);
      ic.add(ManifestEditorSupport.create(this));
      ic.add(this);
    }
```

```
protected Node createNodeDelegate() {
  DataNode n = new DataNode(this, Children.LEAF);
  n.setIconBaseWithExtension(
  "org/netbeans/modules/manifesteditorsupport/manifest.png"
  );
  return n;
}

public Lookup getLookup() {
  return lookup;
}

public Node.Cookie getCookie(Class type) {
  Object o = lookup.lookup(type);
  return o instanceof Node.Cookie ? (Node.Cookie)o : null;
}

}
```

4. In the `DataObject`'s constructor shown above, we make a call to `ManifestEditorSupport.create()`. Below is the definition of that method; add this definition to the main body of the `ManifestEditorSupport` class:

```
public static ManifestEditorSupport
    create(ManifestDataObject obj) {
  return new ManifestEditorSupport(obj);
}
```

5. Since our `ManifestEditorSupport` class extends `DataEditorSupport`, we have the methods provided by its superclass `CloneableEditorSupport` at our disposal. Here we override `notifyModified()` and `notifyUnmodified()`, which both belong to `CloneableEditorSupport`. These methods add and remove, respectively, the `SaveCookie` to and from the `Lookup` of the `ManifestDataObject`, managed by the `ManifestEditorSupport` class. When the editor is modified, a `SaveCookie` is added to the `Lookup`, allowing the editor's contents to be saved. When that happens, the `SaveCookie` is removed from the `Lookup`, so that it is not possible to save the editor. Add both methods below to `ManifestEditorSupport`. When a manifest file is

modified or unmodified, these methods will notify the `DataObject`'s lookup.

```
protected boolean notifyModified() {
  boolean retValue;
  retValue = super.notifyModified();
  if (retValue) {
    ManifestDataObject obj =
      (ManifestDataObject)getDataObject();
    obj.ic.add(env);
  }
  return retValue;
}

protected void notifyUnmodified() {
  super.notifyUnmodified();
  ManifestDataObject obj =
    (ManifestDataObject)getDataObject();
  obj.ic.remove(env);
}
```

We now have the basic infrastructure of our editor. In the next section, we will add the first tab used for editing the source code of manifest files.

12.5 Creating the Source View

The source view displays the text editor for manifest files. It will comprise one of the tabs of our multiview editor.

12.5.1 Describing a Source `MultiViewElement`

The `MultiViewDescription` class describes a single tab in a multiview editor. Its `createElement()` method returns one view of the file, which in our case is provided by a class that extends `CloneableEditor` and implements `MultiViewElement`. The implementation of the tab is described in the next section. In this section, we describe the tab by, for example, specifying an icon and a display name.

Why *Cloneable* **editor?**
Swing editors use the Model-View-Controller (MVC) architecture so that multiple editors can be created over one document. `CloneableEditor` extends that approach to NetBeans' text editor, so that it is possible to create multiple text editors over the same file, opened in different windows.

1. Create a class called `ManifestTextView`. Let it implement `MultiViewDescription`.

   The methods that `MultiViewDescription` requires you to implement are as follows:

   `createElement()`   Creates and returns its associated multiview element.

   `getDisplayName()`   Gets the localized display name of its multiview element.

   `getHelpCtx()`   Gets the help context of its multiview element.

   `getIcon()`   Gets the icon for its multiview element.

   `getPersistenceType()`   Gets the persistence type of its multiview element.

   `preferredID()`   A multiview description's unique id.

2. Implement the methods as follows:

```
public class ManifestTextView implements
    MultiViewDescription {

  private ManifestSourceEditor editor;
  private ManifestEditorSupport support;

  public ManifestTextView(ManifestEditorSupport
                          editorSupport) {
    this.support = editorSupport;
  }

  public int getPersistenceType() {
    return TopComponent.PERSISTENCE_ONLY_OPENED;
  }
```

```
    public String getDisplayName() {
      return "Text";
    }

    // We are not showing an icon:
    public Image getIcon() {
      return null;
    }

    public HelpCtx getHelpCtx() {
      return HelpCtx.DEFAULT_HELP;
    }

    public String preferredID() {
      return "text";
    }

    // Here we call a method returning
    // an editor, which we will create in
    // the next section:
    public MultiViewElement createElement() {
      return getEd();
    }

    private ManifestSourceEditor getEd() {
      assert EventQueue.isDispatchThread();
      if (editor == null) {
        editor = new ManifestSourceEditor(support);
      }
      return editor;
    }
  }
```

12.5.2   Creating a Source Editor

The MultiViewElement interface represents a single tab in a multiview editor. In this implementation of MultiViewElement, we extend CloneableEditor, which lets us implement several MultiViewElement methods by invoking the implementation of the superclass. For example, our implementation of componentOpened() is a call to the implementation of the same method defined on CloneableEditor.

1. Create a class called ManifestSourceEditor. Let it extend CloneableEditor and implement MultiViewElement and Runnable.

`MultiViewElement` requires you to implement the methods listed below. We use the `Runnable` interface to update the display name of the `TopComponent` that contains our element.

`canCloseElement()`   Determines whether the element can be closed.

`componentActivated()`   Is called when the multiview element is activated.

`componentClosed()`   Is called when the multiview element is closed.

`componentDeactivated()`   Is called when the multiview element is deactivated.

`componentHidden()`   Is called when the multiview element is hidden.

`componentOpened()`   Is called when the multiview element is opened.

`componentShowing()`   Is called when the multiview element is about to be shown.

`getLookup()`   Provides the `Lookup` for the multiview element.

`getVisualRepresentation()`   Provides the main visual presentation in the editor area of the multiview element.

`getToolbarRepresentation()`   Provides the toolbar for the multiview element.

`setMultiViewCallback()`   Makes use of a passed-in callback instance to manipulate the enclosing multiview element and keep the element alive during the lifecycle of the component.

2. Implement the methods as follows:

```
public class ManifestSourceEditor extends CloneableEditor
    implements MultiViewElement, Runnable {

  private JComponent toolbar;
  private MultiViewElementCallback callback;

  public ManifestSourceEditor() {
  }
```

```
ManifestSourceEditor(ManifestEditorSupport ed) {
  super(ed);
}

public JComponent getVisualRepresentation() {
  return this;
}

// Return the editor's custom toolbar,
// so our toggle button could integrate
// with it:
public JComponent getToolbarRepresentation() {
  if (toolbar == null) {
    JEditorPane pane = this.pane;
    if (pane != null) {
      Document doc = pane.getDocument();
      if (doc instanceof NbDocument.CustomToolbar) {
        toolbar = ((NbDocument.CustomToolbar)doc).
                                  createToolbar(pane);
      }
    }
    if (toolbar == null) {
      // attempt to create own toolbar?
      toolbar = new JPanel();
    }
  }
  return toolbar;
}

public void setMultiViewCallback(
            MultiViewElementCallback callback) {
  this.callback = callback;
  updateName();
}

public void componentOpened() {
  super.componentOpened();
}

public void componentClosed() {
  super.componentClosed();
}

public void componentShowing() {
  super.componentShowing();
}
```

```java
public void componentHidden() {
  super.componentHidden();
}

public void componentActivated() {
  super.componentActivated();
}

public void componentDeactivated() {
  super.componentDeactivated();
}

public CloseOperationState canCloseElement() {
  return CloseOperationState.STATE_OK;
}

public void updateName() {
  Mutex.EVENT.readAccess(this);
}

public void run() {
  MultiViewElementCallback c = callback;
  if (c == null) {
    return;
  }
  TopComponent tc = c.getTopComponent();
  if (tc == null) {
    return;
  }
  super.updateName();
  tc.setName(this.getName());
  tc.setDisplayName(this.getDisplayName());
  tc.setHtmlDisplayName(this.getHtmlDisplayName());
}

public Lookup getLookup() {
  return ((ManifestDataObject)(
    (ManifestEditorSupport)cloneableEditorSupport()).
    getDataObject()).getNodeDelegate().getLookup();
}
}
```

12.5.3   Adding the Source View to the Multiview Editor

In this section, we use `MultiViewFactory.createCloneableMultiView()`
to create panes in the multiview editor. Each pane must extend
`MultiViewElement`. So far, only our `ManifestTextView` class extends
`MultiViewElement`. In the `ManifestEditorSupport` class, the entry point
to our multiview editor, add the following code:

```
final MultiViewDescription[] descriptions = {
  new ManifestTextView(this),
};

protected CloneableEditorSupport.Pane createPane() {
  return (CloneableEditorSupport.Pane)MultiViewFactory.
    createCloneableMultiView(descriptions, descriptions[0]);
}
```

At this stage, when you build the project, your code should compile correctly. When you install the module and open a manifest file, you will see your
multiview editor, displaying one tab—the source view. A toggle button with
the label **Text** indicates that the manifest file is not open in the standard plain
text editor, but in your new multiview editor, as shown in Figure 12.3.

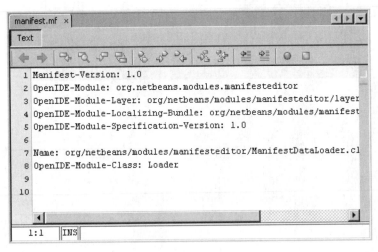

Figure 12.3: Single view in multiview editor

If we had not implemented `getToolbarRepresentation()`, the toggle button would not have been integrated into the editor's existing toolbar. Instead, if `null` had been returned, the toggle button would have appeared above the toolbar, as shown in Figure 12.4.

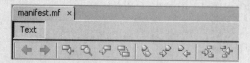

Figure 12.4: Wrong implementation of `getToolbarRepresentation()`

Secondly, if we had not returned our `CloneableEditor` in `getVisualRepresentation()`, but had returned `null` instead, we would have no visual component in the main part of our editor, as shown in Figure 12.5.

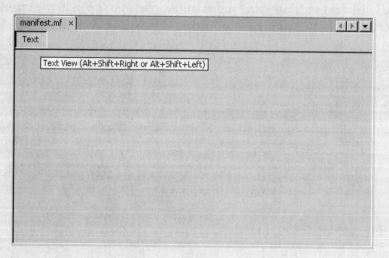

Figure 12.5: Wrong implementation of `getVisualRepresentation()`

12.6   Creating the Visual View

The visual view provides a visual representation of a file type. You can draw on a wide range of Swing and custom components to build your visual editor. However, for simplicity's sake, in this example we will implement the visual view as a property sheet.

12.6.1   Adding a Visual View to the Multiview Editor

For the source view, we implemented `MultiViewDescription` and `MultiViewElement` in separate classes, because we wanted to extend `CloneableEditor` in one of them. `CloneableEditor` has a number of its own methods that we need to implement; so, to make our code more manageable, we used two separate class files. For our visual view, we will extend `JPanel` that has no abstract methods of its own, so we will implement both `MultiViewDescription` and `MultiViewElement` within the same class file.

1. Create a class called `Visual`. Let it extend `JPanel` and implement `MultiViewDescription` and `MultiViewElement`.

2. Implement the methods as follows:

```
public class Visual extends JPanel implements
    MultiViewDescription, MultiViewElement {

  private ManifestEditorSupport support;
  private PropertySheet sheet;

  /** Creates a new instance of Visual */
  public Visual(ManifestEditorSupport ed) {
    support = ed;
  }
  public int getPersistenceType() {
    return TopComponent.PERSISTENCE_ONLY_OPENED;
  }
  public String getDisplayName() {
    return "Visual";
  }
  public Image getIcon() {
    return null;
  }
```

```java
public HelpCtx getHelpCtx() {
  return HelpCtx.DEFAULT_HELP;
}
public String preferredID() {
  return "visual";
}
public MultiViewElement createElement() {
  sheet = new PropertySheet();
  return this;
}
public JComponent getVisualRepresentation() {
  return sheet;
}
public JComponent getToolbarRepresentation() {
  return this;
}
public UndoRedo getUndoRedo() {
  return null;
}
public CloseOperationState canCloseElement() {
  return CloseOperationState.STATE_OK;
}
public Action[] getActions() {
  return support.getDataObject().
          getNodeDelegate().getActions(false);
}
public Lookup getLookup() {
  return ((ManifestDataObject)support.getDataObject()).
          getNodeDelegate().getLookup();
}

public void componentOpened() {}
public void componentClosed() {}
public void componentShowing() {}
public void componentHidden() {}
public void componentActivated() {}
public void componentDeactivated() {}
public void setMultiViewCallback(
  MultiViewElementCallback multiViewElementCallback) {}
}
```

3. Add the Visual class to the array of multiview descriptions that you defined in the ManifestEditorSupport class. Until now, you only had the ManifestTextView class listed. Now, include the Visual class too, as shown below:

```
final MultiViewDescription[] descriptions = {
  new ManifestTextView(this),
  new Visual(this),
};
```

4. Install the module again. Notice that you now have a new toggle button labeled **Visual**. When you click it, you see an empty property sheet in the **Visual** tab, as shown in Figure 12.6.

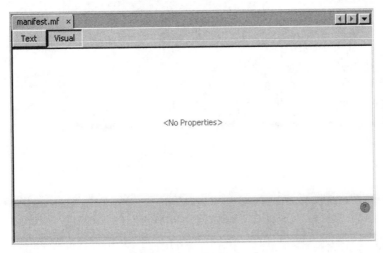

Figure 12.6: Empty property sheet in **Visual** view

12.7   Finishing the Sample

You now have a multiview editor that consists of two tabs, one for the source view and one for the visual view of manifest files. The source view is complete; however, we have only started implementing the visual view in this chapter. On the CD, you will find a sample that supplements the discussion in this chapter by implementing a property sheet for the **Visual** tab in your multiview editor.

CHAPTER THIRTEEN

Syntax Highlighting

13.1 Introduction

One of the central features of an editor is its ability to distinguish between different elements of a language. For example, by default the IDE displays all Java keywords in blue, while method names are shown in black. This enhances the readability of Java code by giving each element a distinct and consistent appearance. The NetBeans API that lets you build and maintain a list of *tokens* is `org.netbeans.api.lexer`. A token is a related sequence of characters. For example, one token may be a sequence of characters that makes up a Java keyword; another, a sequence of characters making up a method name.

Where Are the Lexer Modules?

The Lexer modules, which provide the functionality discussed in this chapter, are brand new at the time of writing. In NetBeans IDE 6.0, the modules are a standard part of the NetBeans distribution. However, in NetBeans IDE 5.5, you must install them from the NetBeans Update Center Beta. The required modules are: Lexer, Lexer to NetBeans Bridge, and Lexer to Editor Bridge. For more information, see the NetBeans Lexer Homepage.[1]

---

1. `http://lexer.netbeans.org`

To obtain tokens, you need to be able to scan a file. Such scanning is called *tokenizing*, because this process breaks the content of a file into tokens. When the user makes changes in the editor, the list of tokens needs to be updated to correspond to the current text of the document.

The algorithm that updates the token list incrementally is based on "General Incremental Lexical Analysis," a PhD thesis written by Tim A. Wagner and Susan L. Graham, from the University of California, Berkeley.

When you implement syntax highlighting support for a language, you first define tokens. Then you define a lexical analyzer that tokenizes files of a certain MIME type. You also need to create an XML file that contains the default colors for your tokens. (They are *default* colors because the user should be able to customize them in the **Options** window.) You register the XML file in the module layer file in the folder for the MIME type for which you want to provide syntax highlighting. You also use the layer file to declare the class that defines the tokens. By doing so, you bind the default colors to your tokens.

In this chapter, we will show how to create syntax highlighting for manifest files. At the end of this chapter, the "name," "colon," and "value" of manifest entries will have distinct colors, as illustrated in Figure 13.1.

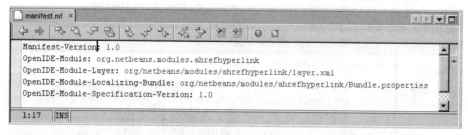

Figure 13.1: Manifest syntax highlighting example

13.2   Preparing to Create Syntax Highlighting

Before implementing syntax highlighting, you need to set up your module project. You also need to make sure that the application is able to recognize the type of file with which you want to work. Finally, you need a basic editor, on top of which you will add your syntax highlighting.

Create the following:

1. **A module project.** Use the **Module Project** wizard to define a new module project named `ManifestLexer` with `org.netbeans.modules.manifestlexer` as the code name base. When you complete the wizard, you have an empty module project. It contains a `Bundle.properties` file and the layer file, as described in Chapter 6.

2. **A file type containing the syntax you want to color.** As described in Chapter 10, you can use the **New File Type** wizard to create a data loader for the file type of your choice. Since this chapter focuses on manifest files, use the **New File Type** wizard to create a data loader for the MIME type `text/x-java-jar-manifest`. This MIME type will apply to files that have `mf` or `MF` as their filename extension.

   In the code listings that follow, you are assumed to have specified `Manifest` as the class name prefix in the **New File Type** wizard. As a result, you have files with names such as `ManifestDataObject` and `ManifestDataNode`. These are the files referenced in the code listings in the following sections.

3. **An editor infrastructure.** As described in Section 12.4, an editor's infrastructure consists of a class that extends `DataEditorSupport` and implements `OpenCookie`, `EditCookie`, and `EditorCookie`. You also need to add the editor to the data object's lookup, which is also described in that section.

   In the code listings that follow, you are assumed to have a class called `ManifestEditor`, which has been added to the lookup of `ManifestDataObject`.

13.3 Creating Token IDs

You need to identify the items in manifest files that you want the IDE to distinguish from each other—for example, a "name" and a "value." Each distinct

item is called a token. Each token has a token ID defined by the `TokenId`
interface.

Create a class called `ManifestTokenId`. This Java class specifies a token
ID for each item in a manifest file. Each distinct item is a token: "name,"
"colon," and "value." In addition, there is also a token for the end of the line
which determines where one name's value ends and the next name begins.

```
public enum ManifestTokenId implements TokenId {

  // The token IDs may be assigned to categories, and
  // the coloring information can then be assigned directly
  // to a tokenId.name(), for example "NAME", or to a token
  // category, for example "separator"
  NAME(null),
  COLON("separator"),
  VALUE(null),
  END_OF_LINE("whitespace");

  private String primaryCategory;

  private ManifestTokenId(String primaryCategory) {
    this.primaryCategory = primaryCategory;
  }

  public String primaryCategory() {
    return primaryCategory;
  }

  private static final Language<ManifestTokenId> language =
      new LanguageHierarchy<ManifestTokenId>() {

    // Specifies the association of the token IDs for
    // this language with the coloring information registered
    // in the layer file for the MIME type:
    @Override
    protected String mimeType() {
      return "text/x-java-jar-manifest";
    }

    // Creates the collection of all the token IDs
    // for this language:
    @Override
```

```
  protected Collection<ManifestTokenId> createTokenIds() {
    return EnumSet.allOf(ManifestTokenId.class);
  }

  // Creates extra token categories, for explicit association
  // of token IDs into categories:
  @Override
  protected Map<String,Collection<ManifestTokenId>>
                                  createTokenCategories() {
    return null;
  }

  // Provides information needed for restarting the Lexer:
  @Override
  protected Lexer<ManifestTokenId> createLexer(
          LexerRestartInfo<ManifestTokenId> info) {
    return new ManifestLexer(info);
  }

}.language();

public static Language<ManifestTokenId> language() {
  return language;
}

}
```

13.4   Creating a Lexical Analyzer

Create a class called ManifestLexer. This Java class tells the IDE which part
of the text is which token. This process, called *lexical analysis*, is usually mod-
eled by a set of states and transitions between them. The states represent information about the past. The analyzer is always in a single state. For example,
when the lexical analyzer is looking at a "value" part in a manifest entry, it is
able to tell that it is a "value" and not a "name" because it is in a state named
AFTER_COLON—that is, the analyzer has already seen a "name" part and a
"colon" part.

The analyzer starts in an initial state, which we will call INIT. In this state
it expects that the next input characters will be a name. It stays in this state
until it encounters a colon (which marks the end of the name). When a colon
is encountered, the analyzer returns a NAME token and enters the AFTER_NAME

state, meaning a name token has just been seen and we are now expecting a value. In this state, when a colon is encountered, we return a COLON token and enter the AFTER_COLON state. In this state we expect a value part, followed by the end of line. When we encounter an end of line character, we return a VALUE token and proceed to the INIT state again.

The analyzer must deal with the situation when a line does not contain a complete name/value pair but (for example) just the name part. This happens, for example, when the user creates a new, empty manifest file and starts typing in the editor. That is why in each state we expect that we could encounter a premature end of line and deal with this situation as well.

```java
public class ManifestLexer implements Lexer<ManifestTokenId> {

  private static final int EOF = LexerInput.EOF;

  // Lexer internal states - preferably small integers
  // for more compact token storage
  private static final int INIT = 0;
  private static final int AFTER_COLON = 1;
  private static final int AFTER_NAME = 2;

  private LexerInput input;

  private TokenFactory<ManifestTokenId> tokenFactory;

  private int state;

  public Object state() {
  // autoconversion uses Integer.valueOf() which caches
  // <-127,127>
    return state;
  }

  public ManifestLexer(LexerRestartInfo<ManifestTokenId> info) {
    this.input = info.input();
    this.tokenFactory = info.tokenFactory();
  this.state = (info.state() != null) ?
                (Integer)info.state() : INIT;
  }
```

```java
public Token<ManifestTokenId> nextToken() {
  int c = input.read();
  switch (state) {
    case INIT:
      return nextTokenInit(c);
    case AFTER_NAME:
      return nextTokenAfterName(c);
    case AFTER_COLON:
      return nextTokenAfterColon(c);
    default:
      throw new IllegalStateException();
  }
}
private Token<ManifestTokenId> nextTokenInit(int c) {
  switch (c) {
    case ':': // ":"
      state = AFTER_COLON;
      return token(ManifestTokenId.COLON);
    case '\r':
      input.consumeNewline(); // continue to '\n' handling
    case '\n':
      // state = INIT;
      return token(ManifestTokenId.END_OF_LINE);
    case EOF: // no chars -> finish lexing by returning null
      return null;
    default: // Name follows
      return finishName(c);
  }
}
private Token<ManifestTokenId> nextTokenAfterColon(int c) {
  switch (c) {
    case ':': // ":"
      state = AFTER_COLON;
      return token(ManifestTokenId.COLON);
    case '\r':
      input.consumeNewline(); // continue to '\n' handling
    case '\n':
      state = INIT;
      return token(ManifestTokenId.END_OF_LINE);
    case EOF: // no chars -> finish lexing by returning null
      return null;
    default:
      return finishValue(c);
  }
}
```

```java
private Token<ManifestTokenId> nextTokenAfterName(int c) {
  switch (c) {
    case ':': // ":"
      state = AFTER_COLON;
      return token(ManifestTokenId.COLON);
    case '\r':
      input.consumeNewline(); // continue to '\n' handling
    case '\n':
      state = INIT;
      return token(ManifestTokenId.END_OF_LINE);
    case EOF: // no chars -> finish lexing by returning null
      return null;
    default:
      throw new IllegalStateException();
  }
}

private Token<ManifestTokenId> finishName(int c) {
  while (true) {
    switch (c) {
      case ':':
      case '\r':
      case '\n':
      case EOF:
        input.backup(1);
        state = AFTER_NAME;
        return token(ManifestTokenId.NAME);
    }
    c = input.read();
  }
}

private Token<ManifestTokenId> finishValue(int c) {
  while (true) {
    switch (c) {
      case '\r':
      case '\n':
      case EOF:
        input.backup(1);
        state = INIT;
        return token(ManifestTokenId.VALUE);
    }
    c = input.read();
  }
}
```

```
private Token<ManifestTokenId> token(ManifestTokenId id) {
  Token<ManifestTokenId> t = tokenFactory.createToken(id);
  return t;
}

public void release() {
}

}
```

13.5   Extending the Options Window

Now that you have tokens and a lexical analyzer, you need to extend the **Options** window. As shown in Figure 13.2, you want the user to be able to change colors in the **Fonts and Colors** panel of the **Options** window. The illustration shows the following important fields:

Profile   Specifies a group of related fonts and colors. Only one profile can be selected at a time. You can create as many different profiles of fonts and colors as you like. In the IDE, the default NetBeans profile and the City Lights profile are provided. The City Lights profile provides a black background behind the text. For each profile, you must create an XML file conforming to the `http://www.netbeans.org/dtds/EditorFontsColors-1_1.dtd`. You must register the XML file in the layer file, within the folder of the relevant MIME type.

Language   Specifies a label for the syntax. You define the label in a localizing bundle.

Category   Lists the localized display names of the tokens. The tokens are defined in the class that implements `TokenID`. The class is declared in the layer file, within the MIME type's `language.instance` folder.

Font, Foreground, Background, Effects, Effect Color   Specify attributes of the selected token. The attributes are defined in the XML file that specifies the profile.

Preview   Specifies the content of the **Preview** box. The file that defines the preview text is declared in the `OptionsDialog/PreviewExamples` folder in the layer file.

Figure 13.2: **Fonts and Colors** panel of the **Options** window

Do the following to extend the **Options** window for your syntax:

1. In the `org.netbeans.modules.manifestlexer.syntax` package, create a `Bundle.properties` file with this content:

```
#Layer.xml entries for fonts & colors in Options window:
NAME=Name
VALUE=Value
COLON=Colon
separator=Separator
whitespace=Whitespace
```

2. Create a package called `org.netbeans.modules.manifestlexer.` `resources`. In this new package for resources, create the following files:

- `NetBeans-Manifest-fontsColors.xml`

- `CityLights-Properties-fontsColors.xml`

- `ManifestExample`

3. Define `NetBeans-Manifest-fontsColors.xml` as follows:

```
<?xml version="1.0" encoding="UTF-8"?>
<!DOCTYPE fontscolors PUBLIC
  "-//NetBeans//DTD Editor Fonts and Colors settings 1.1//EN"
  "http://www.netbeans.org/dtds/EditorFontsColors-1_1.dtd">

<fontscolors>
  <fontcolor name="NAME" foreColor="blue" default="default"/>
  <fontcolor name="VALUE" foreColor="magenta"
             default="default"/>
  <fontcolor name="separator" default="default"/>
  <fontcolor name="whitespace" default="whitespace"/>
</fontscolors>
```

4. Define `CityLights-Properties-fontsColors.xml` as follows:

```
<?xml version="1.0" encoding="UTF-8"?>
<!DOCTYPE fontscolors PUBLIC
  "-//NetBeans//DTD Editor Fonts and Colors settings 1.1//EN"
  "http://www.netbeans.org/dtds/EditorFontsColors-1_1.dtd">

<fontscolors>
  <fontcolor name="NAME" default="default"/>
  <fontcolor name="VALUE" default="default"/>
  <fontcolor name="separator" default="default"/>
  <fontcolor name="whitespace" default="whitespace"/>
</fontscolors>
```

5. Define `ManifestExample` as follows:

```
Manifest-Version: 1.0
```

The **Projects** window should now look as shown in Figure 13.3.

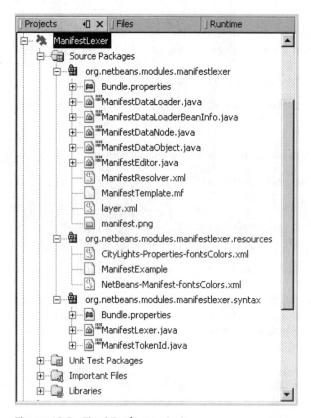

Figure 13.3: Final **Projects** window

13.6   Registering the Syntax Highlighting in the Layer File

As the final step of our Lexer implementation, we need to register the various items we created in the layer file. The following items need to be registered:

- The coloring XML files.

- The `ManifestTokenId` class. The Lexer API needs an association of a MIME type with a language description, so you need to register `ManifestTokenId.language()` in the layer file.

- The `LexerEditorKit` class. The `LexerEditorKit` is an implementation of the editor kit that is needed for Lexer-based syntax coloring. It adds the drawing layer that makes the syntax highlighting possible. This is needed in 5.5 and 6.0, but in future versions it should not be necessary because the editor kit will become an implementation class and we will register all functionality through the layer file.

- The preview file.

Register the above items as follows:

```
<folder name="Editors">
  <folder name="text">
    <folder name="x-java-jar-manifest">
      <attr name="SystemFileSystem.localizingBundle"
        stringvalue="org.netbeans.modules.manifestlexer.Bundle"/>
      <folder name="NetBeans">
        <folder name="Defaults">
          <file name="coloring.xml"
              url="resources/NetBeans-Manifest-fontsColors.xml">
            <attr name="SystemFileSystem.localizingBundle"
              stringvalue="org.netbeans.modules.manifestlexer.⏎
syntax.Bundle"/>
          </file>
        </folder>
      </folder>
      <folder name="CityLights">
        <folder name="Defaults">
          <file name="coloring.xml" url="resources/CityLights-⏎
Properties-fontsColors.xml">
            <attr name="SystemFileSystem.localizingBundle"
              stringvalue="org.netbeans.modules.manifestlexer.⏎
syntax.Bundle"/>
          </file>
        </folder>
      </folder>
      <file name="language.instance">
        <attr name="instanceCreate"
          methodvalue="org.netbeans.modules.manifestlexer.⏎
syntax.ManifestTokenId.language"/>
        <attr name="instanceOf"
          stringvalue="org.netbeans.api.lexer.Language"/>
      </file>
```

```
        <file name="EditorKit.instance">
          <attr name="instanceCreate"
            methodvalue="org.netbeans.modules.lexer.editorbridge.⏎
LexerEditorKit.create"/>
          <attr name="instanceClass"
            stringvalue="org.netbeans.modules.lexer.editorbridge.⏎
LexerEditorKit"/>
        </file>
      </folder>
  </folder>
</folder>

<folder name="OptionsDialog">
  <folder name="PreviewExamples">
      <folder name="text">
        <file name="x-java-jar-manifest"
              url="resources/ManifestExample"/>
      </folder>
  </folder>
</folder>
```

13.7   Finishing Up

Install the module and notice that your manifest files now have syntax
highlighting, as Figure 13.4 demonstrates.

Figure 13.4: Manifest syntax highlighting example

Use the **Options** window, as shown in Figure 13.2, to see how the colors
can be customized.

CHAPTER FOURTEEN

Code Completion

14.1 Introduction

When the user types in a *text-based editor*, you can enable the editor to show the *code completion box* suggesting ways of completing the text that the user is typing. The code completion box can provide documentation for each entry, giving the user detailed information about the suggestions it offers.

For example, while the user types in a Java file, a code completion box shown in Figure 14.1 pops up.

In this illustration, the code completion box lists suggestions below the word that is being typed in the editor. The letters typed before the cursor in the editor are "Uni"; therefore the code completion box provides entries that begin with those letters. Above the word, the user sees a documentation popup containing information on the current entry in the code completion box—in this example, a hyperlink to Javadoc for `SystemException` is shown. When the user clicks on the hyperlink, the upper part of the code completion box shows the Javadoc. In the documentation popup, the user can scroll backwards and forwards with the left and right arrow keys.

When the user presses the Enter key or clicks on the current entry in the code completion box, the word in the editor is completed with the selected entry. If all the entries in the code completion box begin with a number of common characters, those characters appears in the editor when the user

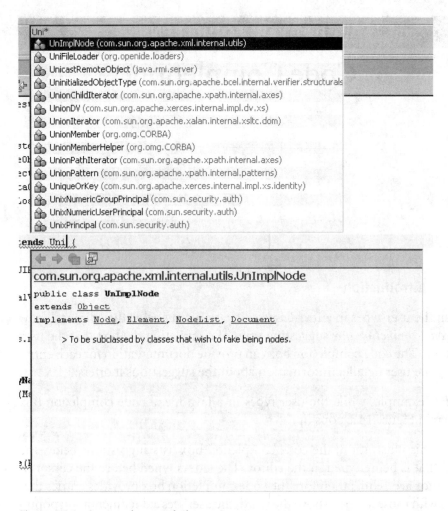

Figure 14.1: Java code completion

presses the Tab key. The code completion box remains open, so the user can select an entry to complete the word.

In this chapter, we will create a code completion box for manifest files. At the end of this chapter, the code completion box will look as shown in Figure 14.2.

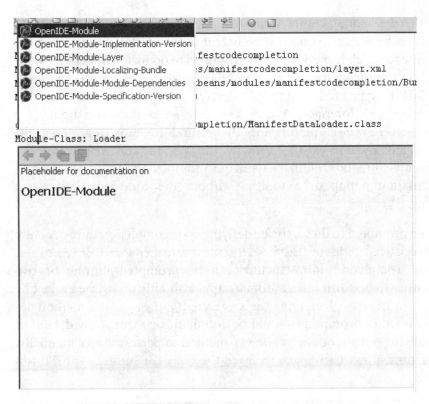

Figure 14.2: Manifest code completion

Notice that the code completion box in Figure 14.2 has two elements. First, the suggested entries are listed in the main part of the code completion box. Second, related documentation is found below the code completion box in the documentation popup. Finally, you can also let a tooltip appear right above the text, advising users what to do with the selected entry in the code completion box. Each of these elements will be discussed and implemented in this chapter.

14.2   Understanding Code Completion

A code completion box is provided by a service provider interface called `CompletionProvider`. The `CompletionProvider` interface is the entry point to the code completion feature. When you implement a `CompletionProvider`, you must register it in the module layer file for the MIME type to which it applies. When prompted to do so, the underlying code completion infrastructure asks all `CompletionProviders` registered for the given MIME type to create a `CompletionTask`, described by the `CompletionTask` interface. A `CompletionTask` is the main body of a `CompletionProvider`, performing the central function for which the `CompletionProvider` exists. Normally, the `CompletionTask` produces a code completion box. Other types of completion tasks produce a documentation popup or a tooltip, without the code completion box appearing.

When prompted to do so, the underlying code completion infrastructure asks the registered `CompletionProviders` to create their `CompletionTasks`. The code completion infrastructure can be prompted in one of two ways—either to perform tasks automatically or to only do it when asked by the user. The `CompletionProvider`'s `getAutoQueryTypes()` method determines whether prompting should be automatic or manual. By default, if you define the `getAutoQueryTypes()` method to perform tasks manually, the user must press Ctrl-Space to force the `CompletionProvider` to do its work.

Simple tasks can be performed in the AWT thread. For more complex tasks, you can use the API's support methods to reschedule the task to a separate thread so as not to block the AWT thread. In the example below, this is the approach taken. When the task completes, the result is passed back and presented to the user. For example, if the user types "OPE" and the task created a `CompletionItem` that works with manifest files, a list of keys beginning with "OPE" is returned in the code completion box.

Next, the user continues typing, while the task is refreshed. If the user presses Escape while the code completion box is open, the task is canceled. Afterwards, whenever the code completion box is prompted to appear again, the `CompletionProvider` is asked to create the task again.

14.3 Code Completion Query Types

Normally, when the user presses Ctrl-Space, the code completion box appears. It displays a list of entries that are defined as COMPLETION_QUERY_TYPE in the module's code completion implementation. However, you can provide additional types of queries listed in Table 14.1.

Table 14.1: Query types

Query Type	Description	Default Key Bindings
COMPLETION_QUERY_TYPE	Standard entries in the code completion box.	Ctrl-Space
DOCUMENTATION_QUERY_TYPE	Documentation, such as Javadoc, displayed in the documentation popup.	Ctrl-Shift-Space
TOOLTIP_QUERY_TYPE	Tooltip.	Alt-P

In this chapter, we will focus on the COMPLETION_QUERY_TYPE which is the most commonly used query type.

14.4 Preparing to Work with the CompletionProvider Interface

To implement a code completion feature, you need to create the following:

1. **A module project.** Use the **Module Project** wizard to define a new module project named ManifestCodeCompletion, with org.netbeans. modules.manifestcodecompletion as the code name base. When you complete the wizard, you have an empty module project. It contains a Bundle.properties file and a layer file, which is described in Chapter 6.

2. **A file type for which you want to create a code completion box.** As described in Chapter 10, you can use the **New File Type** wizard to create a data loader for the file type of your choice. Since this chapter focuses on

manifest files, use the **New File Type** wizard to create a data loader for the MIME type `text/x-java-jar-manifest`. This MIME type will apply to files that have `mf` or `MF` as their filename extension.

In the code listings that follow, it is assumed that you have specified `Manifest` as the class name prefix in the **New File Type** wizard. As a result, you have files with names such as `ManifestDataObject` and `ManifestDataNode`. These are the filenames referenced in the code listings in the following sections.

3. **Module dependencies.** The `CompletionProvider` interface belongs to the Editor Code Completion API. Before working with the interface, you need to declare a dependency on that API. Also, you need dependencies on the following modules:

   - Datasystems API

   - File System API

   - Nodes API

   - Text API

   - Utilities API

   - Window System API

4. **A `CompletionProvider` implementation class.** Create a class called `ManifestCompletionProvider`. Change its signature so that `CompletionProvider` is implemented. Implement the class as shown in Section 14.5.

5. **A `CompletionItem` implementation class.** Create a class called `ManifestCompletionItem`. Change its signature so that `CompletionItem` is implemented. Implement the class as shown in Section 14.6.

6. **A registration entry in the layer file.** `CompletionProviders` are registered in the layer file in the `Editors` folder, for the MIME type to which the provider applies. In this case, for manifest files, we register the `CompletionProvider` in the folder for the `text/x-java-jar-manifest` MIME type:

```
<folder name="Editors">
  <folder name="text">
    <folder name="x-java-jar-manifest">
      <folder name="CompletionProviders">
        <file name="org-netbeans-modules-manifestcode⌐
completion-ManifestCompletionProvider.instance"/>
      </folder>
    </folder>
  </folder>
</folder>
```

Make sure that the filename that you register in the layer file shows the correct package structure. For example, in the code above, the `CompletionProvider` is found in `org.netbeans.modules.manifestcodecompletion`.

You now have the start of your code completion support module. In the following sections, we will implement a code completion feature that helps users complete key/value pairs in manifest files.

14.5   Implementing a `CompletionProvider`

The `CompletionProvider` interface is the entry point to the code completion feature. You must register your implementation of this interface in the layer file, in the section of the corresponding MIME type, as described in Section 14.4.

The following methods are provided by this interface:

`getAutoQueryTypes()`   Checks whether a text just typed into a text component triggers an automatic query invocation. If a particular query type is returned, the `createTask(int, JTextComponent)` method is called. If no query type is returned, the user must manually invoke the code completion feature.

   Parameters:

   - `component` (the component in which the typing happened)
   - `typedText` (the text that the user typed)

Return type:

A   combination   of   the   `COMPLETION_QUERY_TYPE`,
`DOCUMENTATION_QUERY_TYPE`, and `TOOLTIP_QUERY_TYPE` values,
or `0` if no query should be automatically invoked.

`createTask()`   Creates a task that performs a query of the given type
on the given component. This method is invoked in the AWT
thread. The returned task may be either synchronous, if it isn't
complex, or asynchonous. In the latter case, you would use the
`AsyncCompletionTask` interface, as shown in the example below.
The task usually inspects the component's document, taking the text
up to the caret position, and returns the appropriate result.

Parameters:

- `queryType` (the type of query)
- `component` (the component on which the query is performed)

Return type:

`CompletionTask`

Listed below is a `CompletionProvider` for manifest files. When the task
is created, the query iterates through a list of keywords. The keywords
are added as items to a `CompletionResultSet` described by the
`CompletionResultSet` class. The `CompletionResultSet` is a listener interface for passing query results. The result set is used to create a new
`CompletionItem` described by the `CompletionItem` interface. A
`CompletionItem` represents a single result in the code completion box. For
example, all Java methods in the code completion box for Java files are
represented by a single `CompletionItem`, while all fields are represented by
another `CompletionItem`. The `CompletionItem` can provide features such
as an icon, a tooltip, and a default action for each `CompletionItem`. Below
is a very simple implementation of a `CompletionItem`; it does not narrow as
the user types but just provides all possible entries represented by the
`CompletionItem`. We will create a narrowing code completion box in
Section 14.7.

```
public class ManifestCompletionProvider implements
                                        CompletionProvider {

  public CompletionTask createTask(int queryType,
                  final JTextComponent component) {

    return new AsyncCompletionTask(new AsyncCompletionQuery() {

      protected void query(final CompletionResultSet resultSet,
                      Document doc, final int caretOffset) {

        final StyledDocument bDoc = (StyledDocument)doc;

        class Operation implements Runnable {

          int startOffset = caretOffset-1;

          public void run() {
            final Iterator it = keywords.iterator();
            while(it.hasNext()){
              final String entry = (String)it.next();
              resultSet.addItem(new ManifestCompletionItem(
                entry, startOffset, caretOffset));
            }
            resultSet.setAnchorOffset(caretOffset);
            resultSet.finish();
          }

        }

        Operation oper = new Operation();
        bDoc.render(oper);
      }

    }, component);

  }

  public int getAutoQueryTypes(JTextComponent component,
                              String typedText) {
    return 0;
  }
```

```
private final static List keywords = new ArrayList();
static{
  keywords.add("OpenIDE-Module");
  keywords.add("OpenIDE-Module-Module-Dependencies");
  keywords.add("OpenIDE-Module-Layer");
  keywords.add("OpenIDE-Module-Localizing-Bundle");
  keywords.add("OpenIDE-Module-Specification-Version");
  keywords.add("OpenIDE-Module-Implementation-Version");
}

}
```

14.6   Implementing a `CompletionItem`

The `CompletionItem` interface represents a single item of the result list that can be displayed in the code completion box.

The following methods are provided by this interface:

`defaultAction()`   Is invoked when the user presses the Enter key or double-clicks on this item with the mouse. This method is invoked from the AWT thread.

`processKeyEvent()`   Processes the key pressed when the `CompletionItem` is selected in the code completion box. This method is invoked from the AWT thread.

`getPreferredWidth()`   Returns the preferred visual width of the item. The visual height of the item is fixed at 16 pixels.

`render()`   Renders the item into the given graphics.

`createDocumentationTask()`   Returns a task used to obtain the documentation associated with the item, if any.

`createToolTipTask()`   Returns a task used to obtain the tooltip hint associated with the item, if any.

`instantSubstitution()`   When enabled for the item, the instant substitution should process the item in the same way as when the item is
selected and the Enter key is pressed by the user. Instant substitution
is invoked when there would be just a single item displayed in
the code completion box. The implementation can invoke the
`defaultAction(JTextComponent)` if necessary. This method is
invoked from the AWT thread.

`getSortPriority()`   Returns the item's priority. A lower value means a
lower index of the item in the completion result list.

`getSortText()`   Returns a text used to sort items alphabetically.

`getInsertPrefix()`   Returns a text used for finding the longest common
prefix when the Tab key is pressed or when the completion is opened
explicitly. The completion infrastructure evaluates the insert prefixes
of all the items present in the visible result and finds the longest common prefix. Generally the returned text does not need to contain all
the information that gets inserted when the item is selected. For example, in Java completion, a field name will be returned for fields,
a method name (but not parameters) for methods, and a nonfully
qualified name for classes.

   Listed below is a `CompletionItem`. It specifies what happens when an
entry is clicked in the code completion box. It also deals with the presentation
of the entries, including setting their icons and fonts.

```
public class ManifestCompletionItem implements CompletionItem {

    private static Color fieldColor = Color.decode("0x0000B2");

    private static ImageIcon fieldIcon = null;

    private ImageIcon _icon;
    private int _type;
    private int _carretOffset;
    private int _dotOffset;
    private String _text;
```

```java
public ManifestCompletionItem(String text, int dotOffset,
                              int carretOffset) {
  _text = text;
  _dotOffset = dotOffset;
  _carretOffset = carretOffset;

  if(fieldIcon == null){
    fieldIcon = new ImageIcon(Utilities.loadImage(
      "org/netbeans/modules/manifestcodecompletion/icon.png"));
  }

  _icon = fieldIcon;
}

private void doSubstitute(final JTextComponent component,
             final String toAdd, final int backOffset) {
  final StyledDocument doc =
        (StyledDocument)component.getDocument();

  class AtomicChange implements Runnable {
    public void run() {
      int caretOffset = component.getCaretPosition();
      String value = getText();

      if (toAdd != null) {
        value += toAdd;
      }
      try {
          doc.remove(_dotOffset+1, _carretOffset-_dotOffset-1);
          doc.insertString(_dotOffset+1, value + ": ", null);
          component.setCaretPosition(
            component.getCaretPosition() - backOffset);
      } catch (BadLocationException e) {
          ErrorManager.getDefault().notify(
            ErrorManager.INFORMATIONAL, e);
      }
    }
  }

  try {
      NbDocument.runAtomicAsUser(doc, new AtomicChange());
  } catch (BadLocationException ex) {
      ErrorManager.getDefault().notify(
                    ErrorManager.INFORMATIONAL, ex);
  }
}
```

```java
public void defaultAction(JTextComponent component) {
    doSubstitute(component, null, 0);
    Completion.get().hideAll();
}

public void processKeyEvent(KeyEvent evt) {
}

public int getPreferredWidth(Graphics g, Font defaultFont) {
    return CompletionUtilities.getPreferredWidth(
                            _text, null, g, defaultFont);
}

public void render(Graphics g, Font defaultFont,
                   Color defaultColor, Color backgroundColor,
                   int width, int height, boolean selected) {
    CompletionUtilities.renderHtml(_icon, _text, null, g,
        defaultFont, (selected ? Color.white : fieldColor), width,
        height, selected);
}

public CompletionTask createDocumentationTask() {
    return null;
}
public CompletionTask createToolTipTask() {
    return null;
}
public boolean instantSubstitution(JTextComponent component) {
    return true;
}
public int getSortPriority() {
    return 0;
}
public CharSequence getSortText() {
    return getText();
}
public CharSequence getInsertPrefix() {
    return getText();
}
public String getText() {
    return _text;
}
}
```

14.7   Adding a Filter to the `CompletionProvider`

After you follow the above steps and implement the NetBeans API interfaces, you will be able to compile and install the module. However, when you invoke the code completion box, the list of entries will not narrow as you type. For example, the code completion box in Figure 14.3 displays all available entries, unaware of the text that has been typed after it was opened. In the figure, the code completion box should only show the last item, because the cursor is right after `OpenIDE-Module-Sp` which can be completed only by that item.

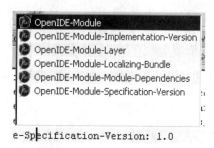

Figure 14.3: Code completion box that does not narrow

By adding a filter, you enable the code completion box to narrow while the user types. You need to specify where the items in the code completion box need to be compared afresh with the typed text. In the case of manifest files, only a space is significant. Whenever the user types a space, the code completion box needs to know that a new token is being started.

The filter needs to be defined within the `CompletionProvider`, because the `CompletionProvider` controls the `CompletionItems`. Once we have a filter, we need to test whether the filter exists and whether it is not `null`. If it is not `null`, the start of the typed token is compared with the entries in the code completion box, and only those that match are displayed. This happens at each keystroke, because after each keystroke the underlying code completion infrastructure asks all `CompletionProviders` registered for the MIME type to perform their tasks. This happens automatically if the `getAutoQueryTypes()` method is not set to zero, otherwise this only happens when the user invokes the keystroke calling up the query, such as Ctrl-Space for the standard query.

Below we define the filter that tests whether the start of a typed word matches the start of any of the words in the code completion box. Compared to our earlier implementation of this class, the `createTask()` method is significantly changed:

```java
public class ManifestCompletionProvider implements
                                        CompletionProvider {

    public CompletionTask createTask(int queryType,
                    final JTextComponent component) {

        return new AsyncCompletionTask(new AsyncCompletionQuery() {

            protected void query(final CompletionResultSet resultSet,
                            Document doc, final int caretOffset) {

                final StyledDocument bDoc = (StyledDocument)doc;

                class Operation implements Runnable {
                    String filter = null;
                    int startOffset = caretOffset-1;

                    public void run() {

                        // Here we create the filter:
                        try {
                            final int lineStartOffset =
                                Utilities.getRowFirstNonWhite(bDoc,
                                                    caretOffset);
                            if(lineStartOffset > -1 && caretOffset >
                                                    lineStartOffset) {
                                final char[] line = bDoc.getText(
                                    lineStartOffset,
                                    caretOffset-lineStartOffset).toCharArray();
                                final int whiteOffset =
                                    Utilities.indexOfWhite(line);
                                filter = new String(line, whiteOffset+1,
                                                line.length-whiteOffset-1);
                            }
                        } catch (BadLocationException ex) {
                            ErrorManager.getDefault().notify(ex);
                        }
```

```
                // Here we use the filter, if it's not null:
                if(filter != null){
                    final Iterator it = keywords.iterator();
                    while(it.hasNext()){
                      final String entry = (String)it.next();
                      if(entry.startsWith(filter)){
                        resultSet.addItem(new ManifestCompletionItem(
                          entry, startOffset, caretOffset));
                      }
                    }
                } else{
                    final Iterator it = keywords.iterator();
                    while(it.hasNext()){
                      final String entry = (String)it.next();
                      resultSet.addItem(new ManifestCompletionItem(
                        entry, startOffset, caretOffset));
                    }
                }
                resultSet.setAnchorOffset(caretOffset);
                resultSet.finish();

              }
            }


        Operation oper = new Operation();
        bDoc.render(oper);


      }
    }, component);
  }


  public int getAutoQueryTypes(JTextComponent component,
                              String typedText) {
    return 0;
  }


  private final static List keywords = new ArrayList();
  static{
    keywords.add("OpenIDE-Module");
    keywords.add("OpenIDE-Module-Module-Dependencies");
    keywords.add("OpenIDE-Module-Layer");
    keywords.add("OpenIDE-Module-Localizing-Bundle");
    keywords.add("OpenIDE-Module-Specification-Version");
    keywords.add("OpenIDE-Module-Implementation-Version");
  }
}
```

In a separate `Utilities` class, add the following two utility methods:

```
static int indexOfWhite(char[] line){
  int i = line.length;
  while(--i > -1){
    final char c = line[i];
    if(Character.isWhitespace(c)){
      return i;
    }
  }
  return -1;
}

static int getRowFirstNonWhite(StyledDocument doc, int offset)
    throws BadLocationException {
  Element lineElement = doc.getParagraphElement(offset);
  int start = lineElement.getStartOffset();
  while (start + 1 < lineElement.getEndOffset()) {
    try {
        if (doc.getText(start, 1).charAt(0) != ' ') {
            break;
        }
    } catch (BadLocationException ex) {
        throw (BadLocationException)new BadLocationException(
            "calling getText(" + start + ", " + (start + 1) +
            ") on doc of length: " + doc.getLength(), start
            ).initCause(ex);
    }
    start++;
  }
  return start;
}
```

When you install the module again, you will notice that the code completion box displays only those entries that can complete the typed text, as shown in Figure 14.4.

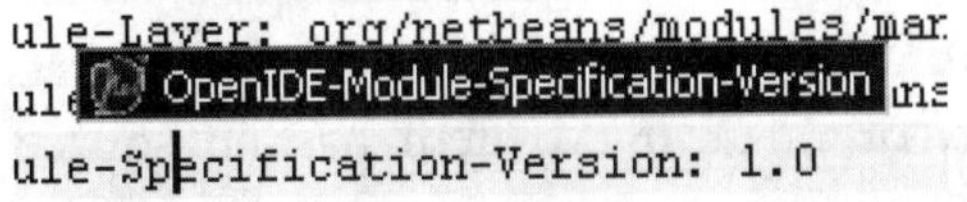

ule-Layer: org/netbeans/modules/man
ul OpenIDE-Module-Specification-Version ms
ule-Specification-Version: 1.0

Figure 14.4: Code completion box that narrows

14.8   Adding Documentation to the Code Completion Box

A CompletionItem's createDocumentationTask() method provides the documentation popup. If null is returned, the documentation section is not shown. However, by passing the CompletionItem to a class that implements CompletionDocumentation, you activate the documentation popup.

For example, here we create a new task that instantiates an implementation of CompletionDocumentation:

```
public CompletionTask createDocumentationTask() {
  return new AsyncCompletionTask( new AsyncCompletionQuery() {
    protected void query(CompletionResultSet completionResultSet,
                         Document document, int i) {
      completionResultSet.setDocumentation(
        new ManifestCompletionDocumentation(
          ManifestCompletionItem.this));
      completionResultSet.finish();
    }
  } );
}
```

The CompletionDocumentation interface contains the following methods:

getText()   Returns an HTML text displayed in the documentation popup of the code completion box.

getURL()   Returns a URL of the item's external representation that can be displayed in an external browser, or null if the item has no external representation. If non-null is returned, the third button in the code completion box is enabled and the user can click it to open a browser displaying the external representation.

resolveLink()   Returns a documentation item representing an object linked from the item's HTML text.

getGotoSourceAction()   Returns an action that opens the item's source representation in the editor, or null if the item has no source representation.

The following listing shows an implementation of Completion-Documentation:

```
public class ManifestCompletionDocumentation
            implements CompletionDocumentation {

  private ManifestCompletionItem item;

  public ManifestCompletionDocumentation(
      ManifestCompletionItem item) {
    item = item;
  }

  public String getText() {
     return "Placeholder for documentation on <h3>" +
            item.getText() + "</h3>";
  }

  public URL getURL() {
     return null;
  }

  public CompletionDocumentation resolveLink(String string) {
     return null;
  }

  public Action getGotoSourceAction() {
     return null;
  }

}
```

The above listing produces the documentation section shown in Figure 14.5.

14.9   Adding a Tooltip to the Code Completion Box

By default, nothing happens when the user presses Alt-P over an entry in the code completion box. However, if you implement CompletionItem. createToolTipTask(), you can let the IDE produce a tooltip for an entry when Alt-P is pressed. For example, the listing below will produce tooltips with the text "Press Enter to insert," followed by the selected entry:

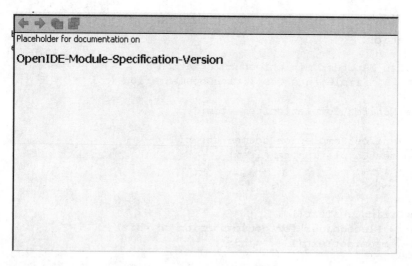

Figure 14.5: Documentation popup of manifest code completion

```
public CompletionTask createToolTipTask() {
  return new AsyncCompletionTask( new AsyncCompletionQuery() {
    protected void query(CompletionResultSet completionResultSet,
                         Document document, int i) {
      JToolTip toolTip = new JToolTip();
      toolTip.setTipText("Press Enter to insert \"" +
                         getText() + "\"");
      completionResultSet.setToolTip(toolTip);
      completionResultSet.finish();
    }
  } );
}
```

With this code, pressing Alt-P while the code completion box is open
produces the tooltip shown in Figure 14.6.

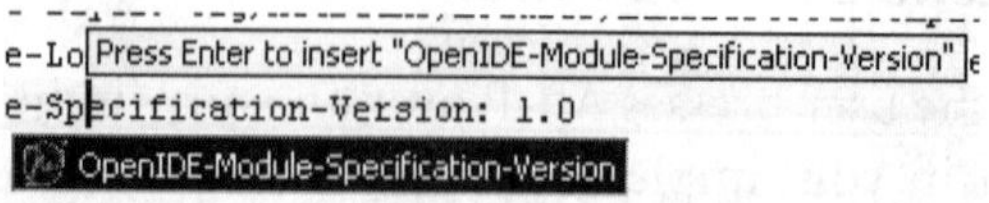

```
e-Lo Press Enter to insert "OpenIDE-Module-Specification-Version" e
e-Specification-Version: 1.0
 OpenIDE-Module-Specification-Version
```

Figure 14.6: A tooltip over the manifest code completion box

CHAPTER FIFTEEN

Component Palettes

15.1   Introduction

Speed, accuracy, and efficiency are three primary concerns when you use an IDE to create an application. In this context, code snippets that can be dragged and dropped into a document can be very helpful. For example, when you open a JSP file in the IDE, a palette with items representing common JSP tags is displayed on the right side of the IDE. When you want to add a table to the JSP file, you don't need to type the tags by hand. You can simply drag a table item from the palette and drop it in the JSP document. When you do so, a dialog box appears where you can fill in the desired number of rows and columns, as well as other properties such as the table's border width and cell spacing. When you click **OK**, the tags defining the table are created for you by the IDE. In the same way, when you provide support for a new file type as described in Chapter 10, you can help your users by including a component palette with items that are useful when creating and editing documents of that type.

However, component palettes are not only useful in the context of file types and editors. When you create a custom component extending the Net-Beans API `TopComponent` class, as described in Chapter 8, a component palette might also be useful. A rich client application that lets the user create graph-oriented models, for example, might also rely on a component palette. In this case, the component palette could contain icons that the user can drag

307

from the palette and place in the graph. As in the case of JSP documents, this would speed up the process of prototyping a graph, make it more accurate, and increase the efficiency of the development process.

Another scenario involving component palettes is the one in which a component palette already exists, but does not provide all the items that your users need. For example, even though the IDE comes with a component palette for HTML files, you might want to enrich it with additional items. You could provide additional items yourself, or you could let the user add items to the palette on the fly. Both these scenarios are described in the sections that follow.

This chapter discusses a variety of aspects worth considering when working with component palettes. It includes a wide range of practical examples that aim to help you in doing so.

15.1.1   Understanding the Component Palette

The first step in working with a palette is to insert a `PaletteController` instance in a `TopComponent`'s `Lookup`.[1] For information on `Lookups`, see Chapter 5. A palette controller provides access to categories and items in a palette. The palette controller is provided by the NetBeans API `PaletteController` class, which belongs to the Palette API. The `PaletteController` class provides the methods listed in Table 15.1.

The result of associating a palette controller with a `TopComponent` is that when the `TopComponent` opens, the palette should open too. Therefore, you should implement the palette controller by adding it to the `TopComponent`'s `Lookup`. Do this by calling a method in the `TopComponent`'s constructor. The method should return the palette controller.

---

1. For text-based editors in 6.0, you can register a palette in the `layer.xml` file for a given MIME type.

Table 15.1: Methods in the `PaletteController` class

Name	Description	Related section
`addPropertyChangeListener()`	Listens to the palette for changes.	15.4.3
`removePropertyChangeListener()`	Removes an added property change listener.	–
`getSelectedItem()`	Retrieves the selected palette item.	15.4.3
`setSelectedItem()`	Selects a palette item.	–
`getSelectedCategory()`	Retrieves the selected palette category.	–
`clearSelection()`	Clears the selection, so that no category or item is selected.	–
`refresh()`	Refreshes the list of categories and items—for example, when conditions set by the palette filter have changed.	15.4.2
`showCustomizer()`	Opens the **Palette Manager**.	15.4.5
`getRoot()`	Retrieves the root node. This node is only visible in the **Palette Manager**, not in the palette itself.	15.4.5

```
private MyTopComponent() {
  initComponents();
  setName(NbBundle.getMessage(MyTopComponent.class,
                   "CTL_MyTopComponent"));
  setToolTipText(NbBundle.getMessage(MyTopComponent.class,
                      "HINT_MyTopComponent"));
  associateLookup( Lookups.fixed( new Object[] {
             PaletteSupport.createPalette() } ) );
}
```

In the program listing above we see that after the user interface components are initialized, their names and tooltips are set. Next, the `associateLookup()` method is called, creating a new palette. This is the typical pattern when dealing with palettes in the context of `TopComponents`. Often, the new object created in the `associateLookup()` method is provided by a method in a separate class, here called `PaletteSupport`. Of course, this could also be an inner class. In either case, the `createPalette()` method returns the palette controller from the NetBeans API `PaletteFactory` class. The `PaletteFactory` class has one method, as shown in Table 15.2.

Table 15.2: Method contained in the `PaletteFactory` class

Name	*Description*
`createPalette()`	Creates a new palette controller instance from the given root node. Provides parameters for custom actions, a palette filter for dynamically hiding categories and palette items, and a custom drag-and-drop handler.

A palette factory creates new instances of a palette controller. The palette factory is provided by the NetBeans API `PaletteFactory` class, which belongs to the Palette API.

You define a hierarchy of folders and files in the module layer file. (The layer file is discussed in Chapter 6.) The folders under the palette's root folder represent categories. The files within the category folders are palette items. The NetBeans Platform converts the module layer file's hierarchy into nodes and displays it in the palette. This is rather convenient because very little coding is required to set up the palette. The top folder is returned as the first argument in the `PaletteFactory`'s `createPalette()` method. In the example below, the top folder is called `Cards`:

```
public static PaletteController createPalette() {
  try {
      return PaletteFactory.createPalette("Cards",
                                  new MyActions(), null,  null );
  } catch (IOException ex) {
      ex.printStackTrace();
  }
  return null;
}
```

The `createPalette()` method has three additional arguments:

- **Actions.** This argument supplies additional buttons for the **Palette Manager** and additional menu items for the contextual menu provided by a palette, its categories, its items, or combinations of these. Also, it lets you set the action invoked when the user double-clicks an item. It is implemented by the `PaletteActions` class. It cannot be set to `null`; at the very least, skeleton methods need to be defined for each of this class's abstract methods. See Section 15.4.1.

- **Filter.** This is an optional filter that can dynamically specify categories and items, implemented by the `PaletteFilter` class. It can be set to `null`. See Section 15.4.2.

- **Drag-and-drop handler.** This handles the drop of new items into the palette and adds custom data flavors to the transferable of items being dragged from the palette to editor window. It is implemented by the `DragAndDropHandler` class and can be set to `null`.

Each of these arguments are dealt with later in this chapter. Until we go into more detail later, we use skeleton implementations of these arguments.

15.1.2   Creating Your First Palette

In this section, you work with the principles discussed in Section 15.1.1. After creating a module project, you create a folder hierarchy in the layer file (for details on the layer file, see chapter Chapter 6) to initialize the palette. Then you create a `TopComponent` and add a palette with empty categories to the `TopComponent`'s `Lookup`.

1. Create a new module project. Add the following hierarchy to the layer file:

```
<folder name="Cards">
  <folder name="Hearts">
  </folder>
  <folder name="Diamonds">
  </folder>
  <folder name="Clubs">
  </folder>
  <folder name="Spades">
  </folder>
</folder>
```

2. Use the **New Window Component** wizard (**File | New File**) to create an implementation of the NetBeans API `TopComponent` class. Name it `MyTopComponent`.

3. Add a dependency on the Nodes API and the Common Palette API.[2] (Right-click the **Libraries** node, choose **Add Module Dependency**, and select the modules from the list.)

4. In the `TopComponent`'s source view, add the palette to the `TopComponent`'s `Lookup`:

```
associateLookup( Lookups.fixed( new Object[] {
  PaletteSupport.createPalette() } ) );
```

Add an `import` statement for the `org.openide.util.lookup.Lookups` package.

5. Create a Java class and call it `PaletteSupport`. Add the method that returns a palette controller for the `Cards` hierarchy that we created in the layer file:

```
public static PaletteController createPalette() {
  try {
    return PaletteFactory.createPalette("Cards",
                        new MyActions(), null, null );
  } catch (IOException ex) {
    ex.printStackTrace();
  }
  return null;
}
```

---

2. In 5.5, this API is called Core—Component Palette.

Add an import statement for `org.netbeans.spi.palette.`
`PaletteController`, `org.netbeans.spi.palette.PaletteFactory`,
and `java.io.IOException`.

6. Add a dummy implementation of the `MyActions` argument:

```
private static class MyActions extends PaletteActions {

  public Action[] getImportActions() {
    return null;
  }

  public Action[] getCustomPaletteActions() {
    return null;
  }

  public Action[] getCustomCategoryActions(Lookup lookup) {
    return null;
  }

  public Action[] getCustomItemActions(Lookup lookup) {
    return null;
  }

  public Action getPreferredAction(Lookup lookup) {
    return null;
  }
}
```

Add import statements for `javax.swing.Action` and
`org.netbeans.spi.palette.PaletteActions`.

7. Install the module. Under the **Window** menu, you should be able to find
a new menu item. When you choose the new menu item, the
`TopComponent` opens, together with its palette, as shown in Figure 15.1.

Notice that our categories have been sorted alphabetically by the NetBeans
Platform. In the following section, we add items to our palette.

15.2 Adding Items to a Palette

Now that you have created a palette, you will want to fill it with items that the
user can drag and drop. Palette items are loaded into a palette by the palette

Figure 15.1: Your first palette

factory's `createPalette()` method. This method loads palette items from the layer file. The hierarchy's top folder is the first argument returned:

```
return PaletteFactory.createPalette("Cards",
                    new MyActions(), null, null );
```

Also, you need to create a data loader implementing the Data Systems API. Your new data loader lets the application recognize the palette items registered in the layer file. When you use the **New File Type** wizard, creating a basic data loader is very easy. The **New File Type** wizard can create a data loader based on a file extension. You need to create a set of files of the specified extension. Add the information you want the palette item to provide to the files. Next, you register the files in the layer file. When you install the module, the data loader loads the files via their registration entries in the layer file. The next example outlines this scenario in detail.

15.2.1   Adding Items to Your First Palette

In this section, we add new entries in the layer file for our palette items. We create a new file type for the palette items and add the data we want to drag and drop from the palette. For example, each palette item should have data representing a display name and icon. We then create a data loader to recognize the new file type and load the items registered in the layer file into the palette. Details on each of these tasks are provided in the steps that follow.

1.   In the layer file, add three items to the hierarchy that you created in the previous example:

```
<folder name="Cards">
  <folder name="Hearts">
    <file name="PaletteItem_1.myitem"
          url="palette/jackOfHearts.myitem" />
  </folder>
  <folder name="Diamonds">
    <file name="PaletteItem_2.myitem"
          url="palette/jackOfDiamonds.myitem" />
    <file name="PaletteItem_3.myitem"
          url="palette/kingOfDiamonds.myitem" />
  </folder>
  <folder name="Clubs">
  </folder>
  <folder name="Spades">
  </folder>
</folder>
```

2. Install the module and notice that the empty palette items have been loaded, as shown in Figure 15.2.

Figure 15.2: Empty palette items

We need to create a data loader that recognizes the file extension .myitem. The data loader should look for the palette items jackOfHearts.myitem, jackOfDiamonds.myitem, and kingOfDiamonds.myitem in a subfolder named palette.

3. Right-click the module and choose **New | File Type**. Set the MIME type to text/x-myitem. Set the extension to myitem. Click **Next**. Set the

class name prefix to `Card`. Browse to an icon with a dimension of 16×16 pixels. Add `.palette` to the package name, for example `org.netbeans.modules.myfirstpalette.palette`. Click **Finish**.

4. The IDE generates several files. One of them is called `CardTemplate.myitem`. Make a copy of this file and paste it in the `palette` package. Change its name to `jackOfHearts.myitem`. Create two more copies and name them `jackOfDiamonds.myitem` and `kingOfDiamonds.myitem`.

5. Install the module again. Notice that the data loader correctly identifies the three items you created and registered, because the data loader's icon is shown instead of the blank white icon that you saw in step 2. The data loader's icon is the 16×16 icon that you selected in step 3. Depending on the icon that you chose, the palette should now look as in Figure 15.3.

Figure 15.3: Palette items with data loader's image

However, instead of the data loader's icon, you want to show a distinct icon per item. You also want the label to be meaningful. These are the areas that we work on in the next steps.

6. Add two image files for each of the three items in the palette package: one 32×32 pixels and the other 16×16 pixels in size. The palette has two modes, one with large icons and the other with small icons, therefore it makes sense to provide a separate icon for each mode. Once you have the six icons, add key/value pairs to each of the item files. For example,

change the content of `jackOfDiamonds.myitem` to the following, then
do the same for the other two:

```
id=id1
displayName=Jack of Diamonds
icon16=org/netbeans/modules/myfirstpalette/palette/↵
jack-diamonds.16.png
icon32=org/netbeans/modules/myfirstpalette/palette/↵
jack-diamonds.png
comment=This is the Jack of Diamonds
```

Once you have added appropriate content to each of the three item
files, you need to add code for loading the information into the palette.
We will do this in the next step.

7. Create a new Java class and call it `MyItemData`. Add getters and setters
    for each of the properties defined in the items. The class also needs to
    be able to load the images. The listing below shows all the code needed
    for this step:

```java
public class MyItemData {
  private Properties props;

  private Image icon16;
  private Image icon32;

  public static final String PROP_ID = "id";
  public static final String PROP_NAME = "displayName";
  public static final String PROP_COMMENT = "comment";
  public static final String PROP_ICON16 = "icon16";
  public static final String PROP_ICON32 = "icon32";

  /** Creates a new instance of MyItemData */
  MyItemData( Properties props ) {
    this.props = props;
    loadIcons();
  }

  public String getId() {
    return props.getProperty( PROP_ID );
  }

  public String getDisplayName() {
    return props.getProperty( PROP_NAME );
  }
```

```
public String getComment() {
  return props.getProperty( PROP_COMMENT );
}

public Image getSmallImage() {
  return icon16;
}

public Image getBigImage() {
  return icon32;
}

public boolean equals(Object obj) {
  if( obj instanceof MyItemData ) {
    return getId().equals( ((MyItemData)obj).getId() );
  }
  return false;
}

private void loadIcons() {
  String iconId = props.getProperty( PROP_ICON16 );
  icon16 = Utilities.loadImage( iconId );
  iconId = props.getProperty( PROP_ICON32 );
  icon32 = Utilities.loadImage( iconId );
}
}
```

8. The icons, labels, and tooltips in the palette are provided by the data loader's `DataNode`. Therefore, you need to decorate the `DataNode` with the properties set for each item. Open the `DataNode` class and change it so that it has the following content:

```
public class CardDataNode extends DataNode {

  private MyItemData data;

  public CardDataNode(CardDataObject obj, MyItemData data) {

    super( obj, Children.LEAF );
    this.data = data;
    setName( data.getId() );
    setShortDescription( data.getComment() );
  }
```

```
public Image getIcon(int i) {
  if( i == BeanInfo.ICON_COLOR_16x16 ||
      i == BeanInfo.ICON_MONO_16x16 ) {
    return data.getSmallImage();
  }
  return data.getBigImage();
}

public String getDisplayName() {
  return data.getDisplayName();
}
}
```

9. Finally, we use the `DataObject` to load the properties into the data loader. We can take a number of different approaches here. In this example, we load the data from a properties file. Change the `DataObject` class as follows:

```
public class CardDataObject extends MultiDataObject {

  private MyItemData data;
  public CardDataObject(FileObject pf,
      CardDataLoader loader) throws
      DataObjectExistsException, IOException {

    super(pf, loader);
    InputStream input = pf.getInputStream();
    Properties props = new Properties();
    props.load( input );
    input.close();
    data = new MyItemData( props );

  }

  protected Node createNodeDelegate() {
    return new CardDataNode(this, data);
  }
}
```

10. Install the module again and notice that now, each item's properties are displayed in the palette, as shown in Figure 15.4.

Figure 15.4: Palette items with distinct icons

Right-click on a palette item and choose **Show Big Icons**. The small icons are replaced by their 32×32 pixel alternatives, as shown in Figure 15.5.

Figure 15.5: Palette items with 32×32pixel icons

Notice that you can also right-click on an item and choose additional options, such as **Sort by Item Name** and **Hide Item Names**. When you drag an item over the `TopComponent`, you are not allowed to drop it and the cursor changes as shown in Figure 15.6.

Figure 15.6: Not allowed to drop item

In the next section we enable drag-and-drop support for the component palette.

15.2.2   Letting the User Add Items to the Palette

Instead of defining all the palette items in the layer file, you can let the user dynamically add items to the palette. In a text-based editor, you can let the user right-click on some selected text and choose **Add to Palette**. The text is then added to the palette as a code snippet. For more details, see Section 15.5.4 which discusses text-based editor scenarios. In the context of a `TopComponent`, you can let the user generate an XML file in the palette hierarchy in the user directory. As soon as a file with the extension recognized by your data loader is found in the user directory, it is loaded in the palette. The code snippet below explains how to do this. The code below could be found within the `actionPerformed()` event of a `JButton`, for example.

```
// First we set our properties, which includes the FileObject
// "cardsFolder" retrieving the root folder "Cards"
// from the user directory's config folder:
Properties settings = new Properties();
FileObject cardsFolder = Repository.getDefault().
  getDefaultFileSystem().getRoot().getFileObject("Cards");

// A user-provided String (from a dialog box, for example),
// sets the suit, such as "Hearts", which is a subfolder
// of our "Cards" root folder:
String selectedSuit = cardSuit.getSelectedValue().toString();

// A user-provided String determines the name of the card:
```

```
String CARD_BASE = cardName.getText().trim();
String CARD_EXTENSION = "myitem";
FileObject selectedSuitFolder = Repository.getDefault().
  getDefaultFileSystem().getRoot().getFileObject("Cards/" +
  selectedSuit);

if (cardsFolder == null) {
  // No Cards folder is found, so we create one:
  try {
      cardsFolder=Repository.getDefault().getDefaultFileSystem().
        getRoot().createFolder("Cards");
  } catch (IOException ex) {
      ex.printStackTrace();
  }
}

// No suit subfolder is found, so we create one:
if (selectedSuitFolder == null) {
  try {
      selectedSuitFolder=Repository.getDefault().
        getDefaultFileSystem().getRoot().
        createFolder("Cards/" + selectedSuit);
  } catch (IOException ex) {
      ex.printStackTrace();
  }
}

// We create the card if it does not exist:
try {
    FileObject cardFile = selectedSuitFolder.getFileObject(
                          CARD_BASE,CARD_EXTENSION);
    if (cardFile==null) {
      cardFile = selectedSuitFolder.createData(
                  CARD_BASE,CARD_EXTENSION);
    }
    FileLock lock = cardFile.lock();
    OutputStream out = cardFile.getOutputStream(lock);
    // Write the icon that the user selected
    // to the card file:
    settings.storeToXML(out,cardImage.getText());
    out.close();
    lock.releaseLock();
} catch (IOException ex) {
    ex.printStackTrace();
}
```

Above, we use `Repository.getDefault().getDefaultFile-System().getRoot()` to create a palette hierarchy in the user directory if it does not already exist. We obtain the name of the suit and the name of the card from the user. Next, we create a file to represent the card and write the value of the image to the file. We could also write other values here with the intention of transferring them from the palette to the component. Since the file has the extension `myitem`, it is recognized by our data loader (created in the previous section). The file is found in the palette hierarchy that our previously-defined palette factory recognizes, because the root folder is `Cards`. The palette item is immediately loaded into the palette.

15.3   Dragging and Dropping Palette Items

When explaining the concepts involved in data transfer via drag and drop, the Swing Tutorial introduces the diagram shown in Figure 15.7. The NetBeans Platform, based on Swing, uses the same approach to drag and drop. The component palette is equivalent to `JComponent A` in the diagram. The component palette's drag functionality is enabled by the component palette itself. Therefore, you do not need to create a transfer handler for the component palette, since everything necessary for the drag event is provided out of the box by the component palette itself. You need only concern yourself with the drop event.

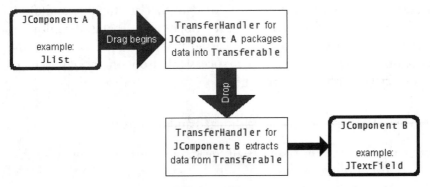

Figure 15.7: Swing drag-and-drop diagram

By default, when an item is dragged from a palette, it cannot be dropped onto a component. You must explicitly define a component as a drop target, otherwise it cannot be a recipient of a palette item's drop event. You can let the user drop an item in one or more of the following ways:

- Drag an item from the palette and drop it on the component. Implementing this behavior is the focus of this section.

- Select an item in the palette and click on the component. You need a property change listener to implement this behavior. See Section 15.4.3.

- Double-click an item in the palette; the item then appears on the component. For this behavior, you need to implement the `PaletteActions.getPreferredAction()` method described in Section 15.4.1.

A basic understanding of the Swing Drag and Drop specification is required before you work through this section. As a refresher, here are some common terms from the specification that are applicable to this section:

Drag source   The entity responsible for the initiation of the drag-and-drop operation.

Drop target   Encapsulates all of the platform-specific handling of the drag-and-drop protocol with respect to the role of the recipient or destination of the operation.

Transferable   Represents the object(s) or data that are the operand(s), or the subject(s), of the drag-and-drop operation—that is, the information that will subsequently be passed from the `DragSource` to the `DropTarget` as a result of a successful drop on the component associated with that `DropTarget`.

Data flavor   The type of data being dragged and dropped.

`DragGestureEvent`   Encapsulates all the information on the gesture that has just been recognized.

15.3.1   Defining a Drop Target

Any Swing component can be the "drop target"—the recipient of a drag-and-drop gesture. In the example that follows, we add a `JPanel` to our `TopComponent`. Next, we assign a `setDropTarget()` method and create a new `DropTargetListener` on the `JPanel`. In this example, we define dummy methods, just to make our sample compilable. After installing the module again, drag an item and notice that the cursor changes when the item is dragged over the drop target.

1. Drag a `JPanel` onto the `TopComponent`. Name it `dropPanel`.

2. At the end of the `TopComponent`'s constructor, add the following:

```
dropPanel.setDropTarget(new DropTarget(
                        dropPanel, new DropTargetListener() {
    public void dragEnter(DropTargetDragEvent dtde) {
      doDragOver( dtde );
    }
    public void dragExit(DropTargetEvent dte) {
      }
    public void dragOver(DropTargetDragEvent dtde) {
      doDragOver( dtde );
    }
    public void drop(DropTargetDropEvent dtde) {
      doDrop( dtde );
    }
    public void dropActionChanged(DropTargetDragEvent dtde) {
      }
}) );
```

Add the necessary import statements.

3. For our first implementation of drag-and-drop support, we just add dummy implementations:

```
private void doDragOver( DropTargetDragEvent dtde ) {
  dtde.acceptDrag( DnDConstants.ACTION_COPY_OR_MOVE );
}

private void doDrop( DropTargetDropEvent dtde ) {
  dtde.acceptDrop( DnDConstants.ACTION_COPY_OR_MOVE );
}
```

4. Install the module again. When you drag an item over the `dropPanel`, the cursor changes, indicating that the item is acceptable to the component, as shown in Figure 15.8.

Figure 15.8: Allowed to drop item

However, since we have not filled out the `doDragOver()` event and the `doDrop()` event, the drag-and-drop action is not handled.

15.3.2 Defining a Drag Image

A drag image is an image that appears at the cursor as the user drags an item. By default, no drag image appears. If you want to provide a drag image, the first thing to think about is what you would like that image to be. Typically, you would want the user to see the image of the item to be dropped on the drop target. By this, you're giving feedback to the user, reassuring them that the correct item is being dragged.

1. Define a new data flavor, representing the type of data you want to drag:

```
public static final DataFlavor MY_DATA_FLAVOR =
    new DataFlavor(MyItemData.class,"Data");
```

Note that our new data flavor makes use of the `MyItemData` class which is where the data is defined.

2. In the data node, define the `drag()` method, so that the item can be dragged from the palette:

```
public Transferable drag() throws IOException {
  ExTransferable retValue =
    ExTransferable.create( super.drag() );
  // Add the data to the transferable:
  retValue.put( new ExTransferable.Single(
                    PaletteSupport.MY_DATA_FLAVOR ) {
    protected Object getData() throws IOException,
        UnsupportedFlavorException {
      return data;
    }
  });
  return retValue;
```

3. Define the Swing component that you would like to create on the
   `TopComponent` when you drop the item. Here we create a `JLabel`.

```
public class ItemDataDisplayer extends JLabel {
  private MyItemData data;

  public ItemDataDisplayer( MyItemData data ) {
    super( "" );
    this.data = data;
    setIcon( new ImageIcon( data.getBigImage() ) );
    setToolTipText( data.getComment() );
  }

  public MyItemData getData() {
    return data;
  }

}
```

4. In the `TopComponent`, define the `doDragOver()` method:

```
private void doDragOver( DropTargetDragEvent dtde ) {

  MyItemData data = null;
  try {
      data = (MyItemData) dtde.getTransferable().
        getTransferData(PaletteSupport.MY_DATA_FLAVOR);
  } catch (IOException ex) {
      ex.printStackTrace();
  } catch (UnsupportedFlavorException ex) {
      ex.printStackTrace();
  }
```

```
ItemDataDisplayer displayer = new ItemDataDisplayer( data );
Image dragImage = displayer.getData().getBigImage();

Graphics2D g2 = (Graphics2D) dropPanel.getGraphics();
Rectangle visRect = dropPanel.getVisibleRect();
dropPanel.paintImmediately(visRect.x, visRect.y,
                           visRect.width, visRect.height);
g2.drawImage(dragImage,
  AffineTransform.getTranslateInstance(
  dtde.getLocation().getX(), dtde.getLocation().getY()),
  null);

dtde.acceptDrag( DnDConstants.ACTION_COPY_OR_MOVE );
}
```

5. Install the module again and drag a palette item over the drop target. Notice that an image appears at the cursor, as shown in Figure 15.9.

Figure 15.9: Dragging with icon

15.3.3   Defining a Drop Event

In Section 15.3.1, we defined a drop target event to listen to events during the drop. One of these events was the drop event where we called the custom doDrop() method. Below is that method, with comments embedded in the code:

```
private void doDrop( DropTargetDropEvent dtde ) {
  // First, check if we support this type of data:
  if( !dtde.isDataFlavorSupported(
      PaletteSupport.MY_DATA_FLAVOR ) ) {
    dtde.rejectDrop();
    return null;
  }

  // Accept the drop so we can access the Transferable:
  dtde.acceptDrop( DnDConstants.ACTION_COPY_OR_MOVE );
  MyItemData data = null;
  try {
      // Get the dragged data from the transferable:
      data = (MyItemData) dtde.getTransferable().getTransferData
        (PaletteSupport.MY_DATA_FLAVOR);
  } catch (IOException ex) {
      ex.printStackTrace();
  } catch (UnsupportedFlavorException ex) {
      ex.printStackTrace();
  }

  dtde.dropComplete( null != data );
  if( null != data ) {
    // Find the displayer for the data,
    // for which you need to declare
    // private Map displayers = new HashMap()
    // at the top of the file:
    ItemDataDisplayer displayer =
      (ItemDataDisplayer)displayers.get( data );
    if( null == displayer ) {
      // It's a drop from the palette and the data is not
      // in our list yet:
      displayer = new ItemDataDisplayer( data );

      // This is where the drag gesture recognizer belongs;
      // we will add it in the next section.

      dropPanel.add( displayer );
      displayer.setSize( displayer.getPreferredSize() );
      displayers.put( data, displayer );
    }

    // update displayer's location from the drop point:
    displayer.setLocation( dtde.getLocation() );
  }
}
```

Above, we check whether the data provided by the item is already in our list. If it is not in our list, we display the item on the drop target. Therefore, unless you want to prevent the user from dropping more than one instance of an item, remove the final `if` clause. Then, as many instances of the item as desired can be dropped onto the drop target.

15.3.4   Defining a Drag Gesture

The drag gesture lets you handle the movement of an item when, after it has been dropped, the user makes a drag movement with the mouse over the item. To implement a drag gesture, you need to first implement the `DragGestureListener` class. You also need a transferable for dragging the item. When the application recognizes your gesture as a drag gesture, it needs to get the displayer defined earlier and then start the drag. When you drop the item, the drop event that you defined earlier is called again.

1. Change the signature of the `TopComponent` to implement `DragGestureListener`.

2. Add an import statement for `java.awt.dnd.DragGestureListener`.

3. Fill out the `dragGestureRecognized()` method as follows:

```
public void dragGestureRecognized(DragGestureEvent dge) {

    // First, check which object is to be dragged:

    if( dge.getComponent() instanceof ItemDataDisplayer ) {
        ItemDataDisplayer displayer =
            (ItemDataDisplayer)dge.getComponent();

        // Get the data from the displayer and create a new
        // transferable for dragging:
        dge.startDrag( null, new ItemDataTransferable(
                                displayer.getData()) );
    }
}
```

4. Define the data transferable:

```
private static class ItemDataTransferable
    implements Transferable {

  private MyItemData data;

  public ItemDataTransferable( MyItemData data ) {
    this.data = data;
  }

  public DataFlavor[] getTransferDataFlavors() {
    return new DataFlavor[] { PaletteSupport.MY_DATA_FLAVOR };
  }

  public boolean isDataFlavorSupported(DataFlavor flavor) {
    return PaletteSupport.MY_DATA_FLAVOR.equals( flavor );
  }

  public Object getTransferData(DataFlavor flavor)
      throws UnsupportedFlavorException, IOException {
    if( !isDataFlavorSupported( flavor ) ) {
      throw new UnsupportedFlavorException( flavor );
    }
    return data;
  }

}
```

5. Add the drag source gesture recognizer to the `doDrop()` event, at the place indicated in the code in the previous section:

```
DragSource.getDefaultDragSource().
  createDefaultDragGestureRecognizer( displayer,
  DnDConstants.ACTION_COPY_OR_MOVE, this );
```

15.4 Adding Supporting Features to a Palette

Beyond allowing you to drag an item from a palette and drop it onto a drop target, the Palette API provides facilities to extend a palette's functionality. First, each palette has a contextual menu that appears when the user right-clicks in the palette. A different contextual menu appears when the user right-click within a category. Yet another contextual menu appears when the user right-clicks an item. Each of these contextual menus can be extended to offer additional menu items to the user. Second, you can add a filter to the palette so that palette items, as well as whole categories, can be shown or hidden as needed, on the fly, based on the user's actions. By default, all categories and items are shown. Third, the Palette API provides a property change listener allowing you to determine whether an item has been selected in the palette and provide appropriate actions in response. Fourth, you can set a number of attributes on a palette, as well as on its categories and items, to, for example, prevent a category or item from being deleted, which is possible by default. Finally, when you create a palette for your users, a **Palette Manager** is automatically included, so that the user can hide the categories and items that are provided by you but not needed by the user. All these supporting features are described in the sections that follow.

15.4.1   Adding Actions to the Palette

When the user right-clicks in the palette, in a category, or in an item, a set of contextual menu items appears. The methods provided by the `PaletteActions` class let you add new menu items to those that already exist. Also, you can add new buttons to the **Palette Manager**. Finally, you can specify which action is the preferred action invoked when the user double-clicks an item. The methods provided by this class are shown in Table 15.3.

Specify what should happen when an item is double-clicked. If `null` is returned, nothing happens.

A skeleton implementation of this class is as follows:

```
private static class MyPaletteActions extends PaletteActions {

  public Action[] getImportActions() {
    return null;
  }

  public Action[] getCustomPaletteActions() {
    return null;
  }

  public Action[] getCustomCategoryActions(Lookup lookup) {
    return null;
  }
```

Table 15.3: Methods contained in the `PaletteActions` class

Name	Description	Related section
`addPropertyChangeListener()`	Listens to the palette for changes.	15.4.3
`removePropertyChangeListener()`	Removes an added property change listener.	–
`getSelectedItem()`	Retrieves the selected palette item.	15.4.3
`setSelectedItem()`	Selects a palette item.	–
`getSelectedCategory()`	Retrieves the selected palette category.	–
`clearSelection()`	Clears the selection so that no category or item is selected.	–
`refresh()`	Refresh the list of categories and items—for example, when conditions set by the palette filter have changed.	15.4.2
`showCustomizer()`	Opens the **Palette Manager**.	15.4.5
`getRoot()`	Retrieves the root node. This node is only visible in the **Palette Manager**, not in the palette itself.	15.4.5

```
public Action[] getCustomItemActions(Lookup lookup) {
  return null;
}

public Action getPreferredAction(Lookup lookup) {
  return null;
}
}
```

When you define the palette controller, one of the arguments you need to define is the `PaletteActions` class. It cannot be `null`. For example, assigning the `PaletteActions` class to the palette controller might look as follows:

```
controller = PaletteFactory.createPalette( "root",
                new MyPaletteActions(), null, null );
```

After you fill out the methods in this class, the result should look similar to the following:

```
class MyPaletteActions extends PaletteActions {

  // Define the double-click action on item-level:
  public Action getPreferredAction(Lookup lookup) {
    // Get the item node from the Lookup:
    Node itemNode = (Node)lookup.lookup( Node.class );
    // Send the item node to a new action for further processing:
    if( null != itemNode ) {
      return new InsertItemAtDefaultLocationAction( itemNode );
    }
    return null;
  }

  public Action[] getCustomItemActions(Lookup lookup) {
    Node itemNode = (Node)lookup.lookup( Node.class );
    if( null != itemNode ) {
      return new Action[] {
        new CustomizeItemAction( itemNode )
      };
    }
    return null;
  }

  public Action[] getCustomCategoryActions(Lookup lookup) {
    Node categoryNode = (Node)lookup.lookup( Node.class );
    if( null != categoryNode ) {
      return new Action[] {
        new CustomizeCategoryAction( categoryNode )
      };
    }
    return null;
  }
```

```
public Action[] getImportActions() {
   return new Action[] { new ImportItemsFromAction() };
}

public Action[] getCustomPaletteActions() {
   return null; // no custom actions for palette's root
}
}
```

15.4.2   Adding a Filter and Refreshing the Palette

By implementing the `PaletteFilter` class, you are able to show or hide categories and items in a palette. Whether a category or item is shown depends on whether it is valid or not.

Both these methods are called when the palette is initially created and when `refresh()` is called on the palette controller. Therefore, when the filter's conditions change, you need to call `controller.refresh()` in order for the palette filter's methods to be triggered. Here is a basic implementation of the `PaletteFilter` class:

```
private static class MyPaletteFilter extends PaletteFilter {

   public boolean isValidItem(Lookup lookup) {
      // Get the Item node from the Lookup:
      Node itemNode = (Node)lookup.lookup( Node.class );
      // Send the Item node to the isItemVisible() method in the
      // TopComponent for further processing:
      return MyTopComponent.findInstance().isItemVisible(
                                       itemNode );
   }

   public boolean isValidCategory(Lookup lookup) {
      // Get the Category node from the Lookup:
      Node categoryNode = (Node)lookup.lookup( Node.class );
      // Send the Category node to the isCategoryVisible()
      // method in the TopComponent for further processing:
      return MyTopComponent.findInstance().isCategoryVisible(
                                       categoryNode );
   }

}
```

One area where a palette filter might be useful is providing a category specifically for advanced users. You might implement this so that, by default, only a **Basic** category is shown, as in Figure 15.10.

Figure 15.10: **Basic** category in palette

Then, if a certain checkbox is selected by the user (or some event occurs), the **Expert** category appears, as in Figure 15.11.

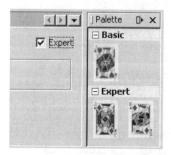

Figure 15.11: **Expert** category in palette

This scenario is implemented as follows.

1. In the `TopComponent`, define a checkbox with a `ItemStateChanged` event that returns a Boolean to a method in the filter:

```
private void expertCheckBoxItemStateChanged(
    java.awt.event.ItemEvent evt) {
  PaletteSupport.MyPaletteFilter.setCategoryExpertVisible(
    expertCheckBox.isSelected());
}
```

2. Define the filter. In addition to the two methods required by the
   PaletteFilter class, we also create a method called
   setCategoryExpertVisible() to receive the Boolean from the checkbox in the TopComponent. The refresh() method on the palette controller calls the isValidCategory() and isValidItem() methods, as
   shown below:

```
public static class MyPaletteFilter extends PaletteFilter {

    // Initial value of the Boolean is set to false:
    static boolean isCategoryExpertVisible = false;

    // Depending on the received Boolean,
    // change the initial value to the received value:
    public static void setCategoryExpertVisible(
                        boolean isCheckedOrNot){
      if( isCategoryExpertVisible != isCheckedOrNot ) {
        isCategoryExpertVisible = isCheckedOrNot;
        // Refresh the palette, by triggering the
        // Palette Filter's methods:
        controller.refresh();
      }
    }

    // If the display name of the category is "Expert"
    // and if the checkbox is selected, return False
    // so that the category is hidden,
    // otherwise return True so that the category is shown:
    public boolean isValidCategory(Lookup lookup) {
      Node categoryNode = (Node)lookup.lookup( Node.class );
      String categoryDisplayName = categoryNode.getDisplayName();
      if (categoryDisplayName.equals("Expert") &&
          !isCategoryExpertVisible) {
        return false;
      }
      return true;
    }
```

```
// In this case, we don't need a filter on the item,
// because we are only interested in showing or hiding
// a specific category:

public boolean isValidItem(Lookup lookup) {
    return true;
}


}
```

3. Finally, you need to assign the filter to the controller you defined earlier, as shown below:

```
controller = PaletteFactory.createPalette(
    "abcde", new MyActions(), new MyPaletteFilter(), null );
```

15.4.3   Adding a Property Change Listener

The palette controller's property change listener is typically used to detect when an item is selected in the palette. By default, when an item is selected, nothing happens. When you add a property change listener, you can define what the application should do when an item is selected. In the example below, the item's node is retrieved from the `Lookup`. The node's image and display name are sent to the `setCard()` method in the `TopComponent`, where further processing takes place.

```
public static PaletteController createPalette() {

  try
  {
    controller = PaletteFactory.createPalette(
                    "Cards", new MyActions(), null, null );
  }
  catch (IOException ex)
  {
    ex.printStackTrace();
  }
```

```
controller.addPropertyChangeListener(
            new PropertyChangeListener() {
    public void propertyChange(PropertyChangeEvent evt) {
       if( PaletteController.PROP_SELECTED_ITEM.equals(
                              evt.getPropertyName() ) ){
          Lookup selItem = controller.getSelectedItem();
          if( null != selItem ) {
            Node selNode = (Node)selItem.lookup( Node.class );
            if( null != selNode ) {
              Image selImage =
                selNode.getIcon(BeanInfo.ICON_COLOR_32x32);
              String selName = selNode.getDisplayName();
              MyTopComponent.findInstance().setCard(selName,
                                              selImage);

            }
          }
       }
    }
  });
  return controller;
}
```

For example, in the `TopComponent`, the `setCard()` method could be defined as follows:

```
public void setCard(String displayName, Image image){
  ImageIcon myIcon = new ImageIcon(image);
  jLabel1.setIcon(myIcon);
  jLabel1.setText(displayName);
}
```

15.4.4   Setting Palette Attributes

The `PaletteController` class provides six attributes that you can set on a root node, category node, an item node, or a combination of these. The attributes determine the initial state of a palette. Table 15.4 presents the name of the attribute, its value, description, and default value.

Table 15.4: Attributes for the `PaletteController` class

Name	Value	Description	Default
`iconSize`	`int`	Set this attribute to change the default icon size.	
`isExpanded`	`Boolean`	Set this attribute on a category to make it initially expanded or collapsed.	`False`. Collapsed, except for the first category which is expanded by default.
`isReadonly`	`Boolean`	Set a category or item to be deletable.	`False`. By default, a category or item can be deleted.
`isVisible`	`Boolean`	Make a category or item visible or invisible.	`True`. By default, all categories and items are visible.
`itemWidth`	`int`	Set this attribute to an integer number to define the width of items in the palette. This is useful if you want to have only a single column of palette items.	
`showItemNames`	`Boolean`	Set this attribute to show or hide item names.	`True`. By default, item names are shown.

The initial state of the palette can be changed in the palette's contextual menu, the category's contextual menu, and the item's contextual menu. Each contextual menu provides menu items applicable to the specific context, be it the entire palette, a category, or an item. For example, the user can right-click on a category and choose **Hide Item Names**, which overrides the `showItemNames` attribute set on the category. In the layer file, the attributes are set as attribute tags, as shown below:

```
<para><folder name="MyModulePalette">

  <attr name="showItemNames" stringvalue="false"/>

  <folder name="Category1">
    <attr name="isReadonly" stringvalue="true"/>
    <file name="PaletteItem_1.myitem"
          url="palette/PaletteItem_1.myitem" />
    <file name="PaletteItem_2.myitem"
          url="palette/jackOfDiamonds.myitem">
      <attr name="isReadonly" stringvalue="false"/>
    </file>
    <file name="PaletteItem_3.myitem"
          url="palette/PaletteItem_3.myitem" />
  </folder>

  <folder name="Category2">
    <attr name="isVisible" stringvalue="false"/>
    <file name="PaletteItem_4.myitem"
          url="palette/PaletteItem_4.myitem" />
    <file name="PaletteItem_5.myitem"
          url="palette/PaletteItem_5.myitem" />
    <file name="PaletteItem_6.myitem"
          url="palette/PaletteItem_6.myitem" />
  </folder>

</folder>
```

In the example above, all the item names are initially hidden; the first category cannot be deleted, except for the second item within the first category; and the second category is not visible. (Next, you would implement the `PaletteFilter` class to show the hidden second category, based on something done by the user.)

15.4.5 Providing a Palette Manager

When you define a palette, the NetBeans Platform provides a **Palette Manager** so that the user has a way to choose and organize the categories and items that are shown in the palette. Items in the **Palette Manager** can also be dragged from the **Palette Manager** and dropped in the palette. In the IDE, **Palette Managers** are accessed under the **Tools | Palette Manager** menu. By default, the **Palette Manager** for Swing/AWT Components and HTML/JSP Code Clips is always provided. To give a consistent user experience to the users of your palette, you should add a menu item for your palette's manager there too. To create this menu item, take the following steps:

1. Right-click the project and choose **New Action**.

2. In the **Action Type** panel, choose **Always Enabled (use CallableSystem-Action)**. Click **Next**.

3. In the **GUI Registration** panel, make the choices shown in Figure 15.12.

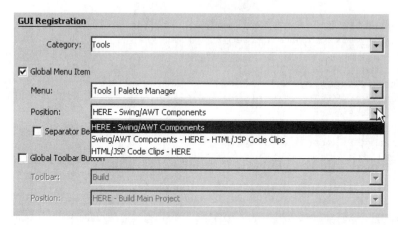

Figure 15.12: Creating an action to show the **Palette Manager**

In the **Position** drop-down list shown in Figure 15.12, choose an appropriate place to add your menu item. Click **Next**.

4. Specify a class name, display name, and package, and click **Finish**.

5. In the `performAction()` event, add the following line:

```
MyTopComponent.createPalette().showCustomizer();
```

6. Install the module again. Go to **Tools | Palette Manager** and notice the new menu item. Choose it to open your palette's manager, as shown in Figure 15.13.

You can change two aspects of the **Palette Manager** programmatically:

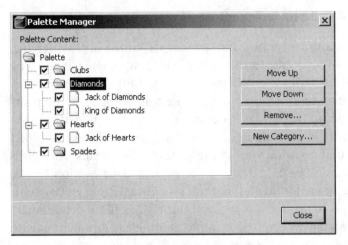

Figure 15.13: Opened **Palette Manager**

- You can add new buttons to the right of the **Palette Content** list. See the discussion of the `PaletteActions` class in Section 15.4.1.

- You can change the display name and icon of the palette root node. As shown in Figure 15.13, the display name of the palette root node is `Palette`. The root node is shown in the **Palette Manager**, but not in the palette. In the palette, it would take up too much space and not serve much purpose, which is why it is not displayed there. By calling `PaletteController.getRoot()`, you can get the `Lookup` of the palette root. For example, to change the palette root display name to `Root`, you would add the code snippet below to the `createPalette()` method:

```
public static PaletteController createPalette() {
  try {
     controller = PaletteFactory.createPalette(
                   "Cards", new MyActions(), null, null );
     Lookup myLookup = controller.getRoot();
     Node nd = (Node)myLookup .lookup(Node.class);
     nd.setDisplayName("Root");
     return controller;
  } catch (IOException ex) {
     ex.printStackTrace();
  }
  return null;
}
```

15.5 Creating a Palette for a Text-Based Editor

When you create an editor for a new file type (as described in Chapter 10), one of the features you can add to the editor is a component palette. The palette has the same appearance as the palette created for `TopComponents`. However, in the context of an editor, when an item is dropped, some post-processing may need to take place before the code is added to the editor. For example, the code may need to be formatted before it is added to the editor. For that reason, you implement the NetBeans API class `org.openide.text.ActiveEditorDrop`, as explained in Section 15.5.2. The palette items are defined in XML files that have `editor_palette_item` as their document type. In this section, we look at this XML file in detail. Apart from these differences, the procedure for implementing a component palette for editors is the same as for `TopComponents`.

15.5.1 Associating a Palette with a Text-Based Editor

1. Create the infrastructure for an editor for your file type, as described in Section 12.4.

2. Within the class, you need to extend `CloneableEditor`. One of the methods in this class associates a palette with the `TopComponent`, as shown below:[3]

```
void associatePalette(MyJavaEditorSupport s) {
  DataObject dataObject = s.getDataObject();
  if (dataObject instanceof MyJavaDataObject) {
    try {
      // Get the palette from the palette factory
      // (see next step):
      PaletteController pc =
        MyJavaPaletteFactory.getPalette();
      Lookup pcl = Lookups.singleton(pc);
      Lookup anl = getActivatedNodes()[0].getLookup();
      Lookup actionMap = Lookups.singleton(getActionMap());
      ProxyLookup l = new ProxyLookup(
        new Lookup[] { anl, actionMap, pcl });
      associateLookup(l);
```

---

3. For text-based editors in 6.0, you can register a palette in the `layer.xml` file for a given MIME type.

```
    } catch (IOException ioe) {
        // TODO exception handling
        ioe.printStackTrace();
    }
  }
}
```

For details on `DataEditorSupport` and `CloneableEditor`, along with examples of their implementation, see Section 12.4.

3. Initialize the palette by calling this method from the `CloneableEditor`'s constructor:

```
private void initialize() {
  Node nodes[] = {((DataEditorSupport)
    cloneableEditorSupport()).getDataObject().
    getNodeDelegate()};
  setActivatedNodes(nodes);
  associatePalette((
    MyJavaEditorSupport)cloneableEditorSupport());
}
```

4. Add a palette factory, where the palette controller is retrieved by the method in step 2. The palette controller gives you access to the root node, categories, and items in the palette. For details on this class and its arguments, see Section 15.1.1. For example, if the root folder to be retrieved is named `JavaPalette`, the palette factory could be implemented as follows:

```
public class MyJavaPaletteFactory {
  public static final String JAVA_PALETTE_FOLDER =
    "JavaPalette";

  private static PaletteController palette = null;

  public static PaletteController getPalette()
    throws IOException {

    if (palette == null)
      palette = PaletteFactory.createPalette(
        JAVA_PALETTE_FOLDER, new MyActions(),null,null);

    return palette;
  }
```

```
private static class MyActions extends PaletteActions {

  public Action[] getImportActions() {
    return null;
  }

  public Action[] getCustomPaletteActions() {
    return null;
  }

  public Action[] getCustomCategoryActions(Lookup lookup) {
    return null;
  }

  public Action[] getCustomItemActions(Lookup lookup) {
    return null;
  }

  public Action getPreferredAction(Lookup lookup) {
    return null;
  }
}
}
```

5. Add a category hierarchy to the layer file. Make sure that the folder name of the root folder matches the palette folder name specified in the palette factory. In the palette factory, we referred to a root folder called JavaPalette. Therefore, in the layer file, we would define a hierarchy similar to the following:

```
<folder name="JavaPalette">
  <folder name="My Snippets">
    <file name="hello.xml" url="items/hello.xml" />
  </folder>
</folder>
```

This hierarchy would create a palette with a single category called My Snippets. Within the category, a single item is found, defined in a file called hello.xml which is in a package called items, in a source structure relative to the package where the layer file is found. The definition of the XML file is discussed in the next section.

15.5.2   Adding Items to a Text-Based Editor's Palette

Each item in an editor's palette is defined in an XML file using a
NetBeans-specific DTD,[4] for example:

```
<?xml version="1.0" encoding="UTF-8"?>

<!DOCTYPE editor_palette_item
  PUBLIC "-//NetBeans//Editor Palette Item 1.0//EN"
  "http://www.netbeans.org/dtds/editor-palette-item-1_0.dtd">

<editor_palette_item version="1.0">
  <class name=
    "org.netbeans.modules.mymodule.myActiveEditorDropImpl" />
  <icon16 urlvalue=
    "org/netbeans/modules/mymodule/resources/icon16.png" />
  <icon32 urlvalue=
    "org/netbeans/modules/mymodule/resources/icon32.png" />
  <description
    localizing-bundle="org.netbeans.modules.mymodule.Bundle"
    display-name-key="NAME_key"
    tooltip-key="HINT_key" />
</editor_palette_item>
```

The elements in the XML file are outlined in Table 15.5.

Table 15.5: Elements of the editor palette XML file

Element	Description
class	Name of class that extends `ActiveEditorDrop`. This class is dealt with later in this section.
icon16	A 16×16 icon to be displayed in the palette.
icon32	A 32×32 icon to be displayed in the palette.
description	A bundle file containing key/value pairs for the palette item's label and tooltip.

---

4. In 6.0, this DTD is more flexible than shown here, because it does not rely on resource
bundles for the description and icon location.

A simpler approach, one that does not require you to create a class that extends `ActiveEditorDrop`, is to define the XML file as follows:

```xml
<?xml version="1.0" encoding="UTF-8"?>

<!DOCTYPE editor_palette_item
  PUBLIC "-//NetBeans//Editor Palette Item 1.0//EN"
  "http://www.netbeans.org/dtds/editor-palette-item-1_0.dtd">

<editor_palette_item version="1.0">

  <body>
    <pre>
      <p>hello</p>
    </pre>
  </body>

  <icon16 urlvalue=
    "org/netbeans/modules/mymodule/resources/icon16.png" />
  <icon32 urlvalue=
    "org/netbeans/modules/mymodule/resources/icon32.png" />
  <description
    localizing-bundle="org.netbeans.modules.mymodule.Bundle"
    display-name-key="NAME_key"
    tooltip-key="HINT_key" />

</editor_palette_item>
```

Notice that instead of a reference to a Java class, this XML file has this section:

```xml
<body>
  <pre>
    <p>hello</p>
  </pre>
</body>
```

When the item is dropped, the text `<p>hello</p>` appears in the editor. The disadvantage of this approach is that you have no control over the dropped text. If, for example, you want the user to be able to specify the value of attributes before the text is dropped, you need to create a class that extends `ActiveEditorDrop`, such as the following:

```java
public class Hello implements ActiveEditorDrop {

  public Hello() {
  }

  // Set the text that should be returned,
  // which is called from the handleTransfer() method:
  private String createBody() {
    String HelloItem = "<p>hello</p>";
    return HelloItem;
  }

  // Handle the transfer:
  public boolean handleTransfer(JTextComponent targetComponent) {
    // Optionally, here we can call a dialog box
    // where attributes can be set:
    Customizer c = new Customizer(this);
    boolean accept = c.showDialog();
    if (accept) {
      String body = createBody();
      try {
        // Insert the text at the caret position
        // without formatting:
        int p = targetComponent.getCaretPosition();
        try {
          targetComponent.getDocument().insertString(
                                         p, body, null);
        } catch (BadLocationException ex) {
          ex.printStackTrace();
        }
        // Alternatively, we can send the text to be dropped,
        // along with the current document,
        // to a separate class for formatting
        // (see the next section for details):
        // JavaPaletteUtilities.insert(body, targetComponent);
      } catch (BadLocationException ble) {
        return false;
      }
    }
    return accept;
  }
}
```

This is the class that you need to reference in the XML file described earlier. Install the module; the palette factory creates the palette and loads the items from the layer file. The palette provides all the functionality you need for dragging the item. If the item is defined in an XML file with the correct DTD, the editor accepts the drop and the text is added to the document.

15.5.3   Formatting Dropped Items in a Text-Based Editor

In the previous section, the palette item was dropped at the caret position in the editor. However, you may want the tags in the item to be formatted correctly. The code below serves that purpose. It receives the text to be dropped and the document where the drop should take place.

```
public static void insert(String s, JTextComponent target)
    throws BadLocationException {
  insert(s, target, true);
}

public static void insert(String s, JTextComponent target,
    boolean reformat) throws BadLocationException {

  if (s == null)
    s = "";

  Document doc = target.getDocument();
  if (doc == null)
    return;

  if (doc instanceof BaseDocument)
    ((BaseDocument)doc).atomicLock();

  int start = insert(s, target, doc);

  // Format the inserted text
  if (reformat && start >= 0 && doc instanceof BaseDocument) {
    int end = start + s.length();
    Formatter f = ((BaseDocument)doc).getFormatter();
    f.reformat((BaseDocument)doc, start, end);
  }

  if (doc instanceof BaseDocument)
    ((BaseDocument)doc).atomicUnlock();

}
```

```
private static int insert(String s, JTextComponent target,
    Document doc) throws BadLocationException {

  int start = -1;
  try {

      // First, find selected text range
      Caret caret = target.getCaret();
      int p0 = Math.min(caret.getDot(), caret.getMark());
      int p1 = Math.max(caret.getDot(), caret.getMark());
      doc.remove(p0, p1 - p0);

      // Replace selected text by the inserted text
      start = caret.getDot();

      doc.insertString(start, s, null);
  } catch (BadLocationException ble) {}

  return start;
}
```

15.5.4 Letting the User Add Items to a Text-Based Editor's Palette

When an XML file that conforms to the NetBeans Editor Palette Item DTD is found in the palette hierarchy loaded by `PaletteFactory.createPalette()`, the item described by the file is immediately added to a text-based editor's palette. Therefore, following the example introduced in Section 15.5.1, if the file below is found in the user directory's `JavaPalette` folder, an item with the referenced image, name, and hint defined in the specified `Bundle` file is loaded in the palette:

```
<?xml version="1.0" encoding="UTF-8"?>

<!DOCTYPE editor_palette_item
   PUBLIC "-//NetBeans//Editor Palette Item 1.0//EN"
   "http://www.netbeans.org/dtds/editor-palette-item-1_0.dtd">

<editor_palette_item version="1.0">

  <body>
    <pre>
      <p>hello</p>
    </pre>
  </body>
```

```
<icon16 urlvalue=
  "org/netbeans/modules/mymodule/resources/icon16.png" />
<icon32 urlvalue=
  "org/netbeans/modules/mymodule/resources/icon32.png" />
<description
  localizing-bundle="org.netbeans.modules.mymodule.Bundle"
  display-name-key="NAME_key"
  tooltip-key="HINT_key" />
```

```
</editor_palette_item>
```

When the item defined by the above XML file is dragged and dropped into the text-based editor, the text

```
<p>hello</p>
```

appears in the editor. Here is an example of how you might write the above file to the user directory:

```
// Here we're not creating anything, just initializing variables:
FileObject javaFolder =
  Repository.getDefault().getDefaultFileSystem().getRoot().
  getFileObject("JavaPalette");
String paletteCategory = "Java";
FileObject JavaCategoryFolder =
  Repository.getDefault().getDefaultFileSystem().getRoot().
  getFileObject("JavaPalette/" + paletteCategory);

// Here we create the file with the label and content
// specified by the user:
try {
    FileObject javaFile =
      JavaCategoryFolder.getFileObject(getLabel(), EXTENSION);
    if (javaFile==null) {
      javaFile =
        JavaCategoryFolder.createData(getLabel(), EXTENSION);
    }
    lock = javaFile.lock();

    OutputStream fout = javaFile.getOutputStream(lock);
    OutputStream bout= new BufferedOutputStream(fout);
    OutputStreamWriter out =
      new OutputStreamWriter(bout, "UTF-8");
    out.write("<?xml version=\"1.0\" ");
    out.write("encoding=\"UTF-8\"?>\r\n");
    out.write("<!DOCTYPE editor_palette_item PUBLIC ");
```

```
    out.write("\"-//NetBeans//Editor Palette Item 1.0//EN\" ");
    out.write("\"http://www.netbeans.org/dtds/editor-palette-↵
item-1_0.dtd\">\r\n");
    out.write("<editor_palette_item version=\"1.0\">\r\n\r\n");
    out.write("<body>\r\n");
    out.write("<pre><\r\n");
    out.write(getContent()+"\r\n");
    out.write("</pre>\r\n");
    out.write("</body>\r\n\r\n");
    out.write("<icon16 urlvalue=\"org/netbeans/modules/mymodule/"
                + getImage() + "16.png\" />\r\n");
    out.write("<icon32 urlvalue=\"org/netbeans/modules/mymodule/"
                + getImage() + "32.png\" />\r\n");
    out.write("<description localizing-bundle=\"org/netbeans/↵
modules/mymodule.Bundle\"\r\n");
    out.write("display-name-key=\"" + getLabel() + "\"\r\n");
    out.write("tooltip-key=\"" + getLabel() + "\"/>\r\n\r\n");
    out.write("</editor_palette_item>\r\n");
    out.flush();  // Don't forget to flush!
    out.close();

    lock.releaseLock();
} catch (IOException ex) {
    ex.printStackTrace();
}
```

CHAPTER SIXTEEN

Hyperlinks

16.1 Introduction

Hyperlinks in the Source Editor provide a simple yet powerful mechanism for navigating through code. When the user holds down the Ctrl key and moves the mouse over an identifier, the identifier turns blue and is underlined, much like a hyperlink on a Web page. The cursor becomes a hand, again matching the user experience in a Web browser (Figure 16.1).

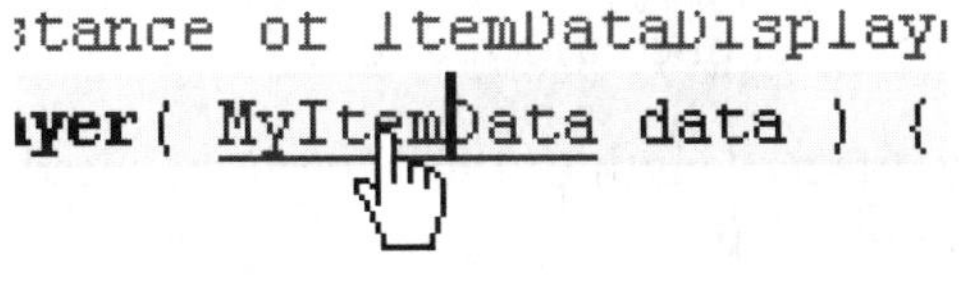

Figure 16.1: Example of a hyperlink

When a hyperlink is clicked, the corresponding identifier is found—either in the current file or in a different file, depending on how the hyperlink is defined. For example, when a Java variable name is displayed in the Source Editor, the user can jump to the variable's declaration by using it as a hyperlink.

The NetBeans APIs allow you to easily provide hyperlinking capabilities. Though the focus of this chapter is on hyperlinks in the manifest file editor, the same principles could be applied to editing other types of files, such as Java source files, XML files, and JSP files.

16.1.1   Preparing to Provide Hyperlinks

Before you begin creating hyperlinks, consider what areas in your code are interrelated. Ask yourself where the user would want to navigate after completing a section of code. Analyze how elements relate to each other and how the user could most efficiently navigate between them. Hyperlinking might not be the best solution in all situations, but often it provides a helpful mechanism for bringing users where they want to be.

16.1.2   The `HyperlinkProvider` Class

The NetBeans API class that is responsible for providing hyperlinks is called `HyperlinkProvider`. This is the main NetBeans API class that you work with when providing a hyperlink. The `HyperlinkProvider` class provides the following methods:

`isHyperlinkPoint()`   Returns `true` if the text under the cursor fulfills the definition of the token that serves as the hyperlink. For example, returns `true` if `<h1>` is under the mouse when the Ctrl key is clicked and `<h1>` is the token that has been defined as hyperlink token.

`getHyperlinkSpan()`   Returns the integer length of the hyperlink, based on the offsets provided by the token in the `isHyperlinkPoint()` method.

`performClickAction()`   Contains the action that should happen when the hyperlink is clicked. For example, this method could find the linked file, open it, and position the cursor on the link destination in that file.

16.1.3   Getting Started Really Quickly

Instead of going through this chapter step by step, you might be tempted to review (online or in the NetBeans source code repository) the existing implementations of the `HyperlinkProvider` class, looking for one that almost matches your needs and can be adapted to your purposes. Go right ahead! NetBeans is an open source project and developers are free to look through the source code for examples. At the time of writing, `JSFHyperlinkProvider`, `StrutsHyperlinkProvider`, and `WicketHyperlinkProvider` exist.

As you cut and paste code from an existing `HyperlinkProvider` to your own, or even incorporate it wholesale into your own module, you might come across things that you don't fully understand. Or, you might be curious about why something works the way it does. In that case, feel free to use this chapter as a reference rather than an implementation guide.

16.2   Preparing to Work with the `HyperlinkProvider` Class

1. **A module project.** Use the **Module Project** wizard to define a new module project named `ManifestHyperlinking`, with `org.netbeans.modules.manifesthyperlinking` as the code name base. When you complete the wizard, you will have an empty module project. It contains a `Bundle.properties` file and a module layer file, as described in Chapter 6.

2. **Module dependencies.** The `HyperlinkProvider` class belongs to the Editor Library API. Before working with the class, you need to declare a dependency on that API. In addition, you need dependencies on the following modules:

   - Datasystems API
   - Dialogs API
   - File System API
   - I/O API
   - Nodes API
   - Text API
   - UI Utilities API

- Utilities API
- Window System API

3. **A file type for which you want to create hyperlinks.** As described in Chapter 10, you can use the **New File Type** wizard to create a data loader for the file type of your choice. Since this chapter focuses on manifest files, use the **New File Type** wizard to create a data loader for the MIME type `text/x-java-jar-manifest`. This MIME type will apply to any files that have `mf` or `MF` as filename extension.

   In the code listings that follow, you are assumed to have specified `Manifest` as the class name prefix in the **New File Type** wizard. As a result, you will have files with names such as `ManifestDataObject` and `ManifestDataNode`. These are the filenames referenced in the code listings in the following sections.

4. **A** `HyperlinkProvider` **implementation class.** Create a class called `ManifestHyperlinkProvider`. Change the signature so that `HyperlinkProvider` is implemented.

5. **A registration entry in the layer file.** You need to register your implementation of the `HyperlinkProvider` class in the layer file, as shown below:

```
<folder name="Editors">
  <folder name="text">
    <folder name="x-java-jar-manifest">
      <attr name="SystemFileSystem.localizingBundle"
        stringvalue=
        "org.netbeans.modules.manifesthyperlinking.Bundle"/>
      <folder name="HyperlinkProviders">
        <file name="ManifestHyperlinkProvider.instance">
          <attr name="instanceClass"
            stringvalue="org.netbeans.modules.manifesthyper↵
linking.ManifestHyperlinkProvider"/>
          <attr name="instanceOf" stringvalue="org.↵
netbeans.lib.editor.hyperlink.spi.HyperlinkProvider"/>
        </file>
      </folder>
    </folder>
  </folder>
</folder>
```

The file registered in the layer file above must be the class that extends the `HyperlinkProvider` class.

You now have the start of your hyperlink support module. In the following section, we will look at how to create a hyperlink that lets the user navigate from a manifest file to one of the files referenced in it.

16.3   Hyperlinks in Manifest Files

The hyperlink that you will create in this section allows the user to navigate from certain values in manifest files to the files referenced by the values. For example, when the user holds down the Ctrl key and moves the mouse over the value of the `OpenIDE-Module-Layer` key, a hyperlink appears, as shown in Figure 16.2.

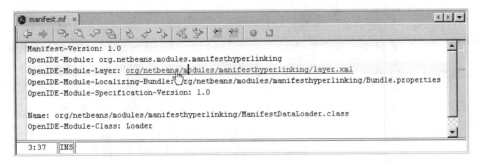

Figure 16.2: Hyperlink in a manifest file

The class that implements `HyperlinkProvider` works with the following initial values:

```
private Document lastDocument;
private int startOffset;
private int endOffset;
private String identifier;
private static TextAction focusedComponentAction;
private static RequestProcessor OPEN
            = new RequestProcessor("ManifestOpen");
```

16.3.1 Identifying Hyperlinks

The `isHyperlinkPoint()` method determines whether there should be a hyperlink at the given offset within the given document. The inline comments in the method below, as well as in the code in the remainder of this tutorial, serve to explain the purpose of the code.

```java
public boolean isHyperlinkPoint(Document doc, int offset) {

  if (!(doc instanceof StyledDocument)) {
    return false;
  }

  StyledDocument bdoc = (StyledDocument) doc;
  JTextComponent target = getFocusedComponent();

  // We want to work only with the open editor,
  // and the editor must be the active component:

  if ((target == null) || (target.getDocument() != bdoc)) {
    return false;
  }

  Element lines = NbDocument.findLineRootElement(bdoc);
  int cnt = NbDocument.findLineNumber(bdoc, offset);
  Element line = lines.getElement(cnt);
  String text;

  try {
      text = doc.getText(line.getStartOffset(),
               line.getEndOffset() - line.getStartOffset());
  } catch (BadLocationException ex) {
      ErrorManager.getDefault().notify(ex);
      return false;
  }

  int after = text.indexOf(':');
  if (after == -1) {
    return false;
  }
```

```
identifier = text.substring(after + 1).trim();
if (identifier.endsWith("layer.xml")
        || identifier.endsWith(".properties")
        || identifier.endsWith(".class")) {
    startOffset = line.getStartOffset() + after + 1;
    endOffset = line.getEndOffset() - 1;
    lastDocument = bdoc;
    return true;
} else {
    return false;
}

}
```

16.3.2   Setting the Length of a Hyperlink

This `getHyperlinkSpan()` method determines the length of the hyperlink:

```
public int[] getHyperlinkSpan(Document doc, int offset) {

  // First, check that we are working with a StyledDocument:
  if (!(doc instanceof StyledDocument)) {
    return null;
  }

  StyledDocument bdoc = (StyledDocument) doc;
  JTextComponent target = getFocusedComponent();

  // We want to work only with the open editor,
  // the editor must be the active component,
  // and the document must be the same as that used
  // in the isHyperlinkPoint method:
  if ((target == null) || (lastDocument != bdoc)) {
    return null;
  }

  // Return the position that we defined in the
  // isHyperlinkPoint method:
  return new int[] { startOffset+1, endOffset };

}
```

16.3.3   Opening the Referenced Document

The `performClickAction()` method determines what happens when the hyperlink is clicked. In general, a document should open, the cursor should move to a certain place in a document, or both.

```java
public void performClickAction(Document doc, int offset) {

  // First, check that we are working with Document:
  if (!(doc instanceof Document)) {
    return;
  }

  JTextComponent target = getFocusedComponent();

  // We want to work only with the open editor,
  // the editor must be the active component,
  // and the document must be the same as that used
  // in the isHyperlinkPoint method:
  if ((target == null) || (lastDocument != doc)) {
    return;
  }

  //Open the file:
  String fileName = identifier;

  String fileName1 = fileName.replace(".class", ".java");

  Object obj =
    doc.getProperty(Document.StreamDescriptionProperty);

  if (obj instanceof DataObject) {
    OpenFile run = new OpenFile((DataObject)obj, fileName1);
    OPEN.post(run);
  }
}
```

The token identified in the `isHyperlinkPoint()` method is received by the `OpenFile` inner class. Then the token is analyzed to see whether it contains a slash, which indicates that it is a relative link. In that case, the file object is extrapolated from the URL to the file. Otherwise, the file object is created from the token itself. Next, the document with the name of the file object is opened and the cursor is positioned at the H2 tag, if found. Paste the code below into the class where the `HyperlinkProvider` is implemented, or into a separate class:

```
class OpenFile implements Runnable {

  private DataObject obj;
  private String identifier;

  public OpenFile(DataObject obj, String identifier) {

    super();
    this.obj = obj;
    this.identifier = identifier;

  }

  public void run() {

    FileObject root = obj.getPrimaryFile().getParent();
    FileObject fo = root.getFileObject("src/" + identifier);

    if (fo == null) {
      StatusDisplayer.getDefault().setStatusText(
        "Cannot open src/" + identifier + " from " + root);
      return;
    }
    DataObject dObject;

    try
    {
      dObject = DataObject.find(fo);

      OpenCookie o =
        (OpenCookie)dObject.getCookie(OpenCookie.class);
      if (o != null) {
        o.open();
        return;
      }

      EditCookie ec =
        (EditCookie)dObject.getCookie(EditCookie.class);
      if (ec != null) {
        ec.edit();
        return;
      }
    }
```

```
   catch (DataObjectNotFoundException ex)
   {
     ex.printStackTrace();
   }
   StatusDisplayer.getDefault().setStatusText(
                            "Cannot open " + identifier);
  }

}

private static JTextComponent getFocusedComponent() {

  /** Fake action for getting the focused component */
  class FocusedComponentAction extends TextAction {

    FocusedComponentAction() {
      super("focused-component");
    }

    /** Adding this method because of protected final
     * getFocusedComponent */
    JTextComponent getFocusedComponent2() {
      return getFocusedComponent();
    }

    public void actionPerformed(ActionEvent evt){}

  };

  if (focusedComponentAction == null) {
    focusedComponentAction = new FocusedComponentAction();
  }

  return ((FocusedComponentAction)focusedComponentAction).
          getFocusedComponent2();

}
```

16.3.4   Finishing Up

Once the `HyperlinkProvider` is coded and registered in the layer file, you can install the module and try out your new hyperlinks. Hold down the Ctrl key and move the mouse over one of the referenced files in a manifest file, as shown at the start of this chapter. You now see a hyperlink (Figure 16.3).

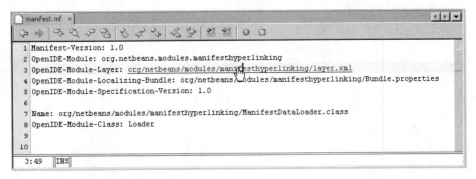

Figure 16.3: Your first hyperlink

When the hyperlink appears, you can click it and let the IDE navigate to the referenced file.

CHAPTER SEVENTEEN

Annotations

17.1 Introduction

As the user edits files in your application's *text-based editor*, you can use marks in the Source Editor and its sidebars to *annotate* code. You do this by providing an *annotation* which consists of an underline or highlight in the editor together with a *glyph* in the left sidebar, or a *mark* in the right sidebar, or both. When the user hovers over the glyph or mark, they display a tooltip with some information about the annotation. The mark in the right sidebar can be clicked to navigate quickly to the line where the annotation occurred. By providing annotations, you can enable users, for example, to fix errors in the code as they happen, instead of browsing a long list of compilation errors at the end. Promptly informing users of their errors speeds up development by reducing the likelihood of bottlenecks at the end of the cycle.

In this chapter, we'll discuss how to extend support for editing manifest files by providing error annotations. When the user enters an incorrect key/value pair, a red underline appears accompanied by the tooltip text "Incorrect format!" In the screenshot in Figure 17.1, the user did not type a space after the colon in line 3 and, as a result, that line is underlined in red.

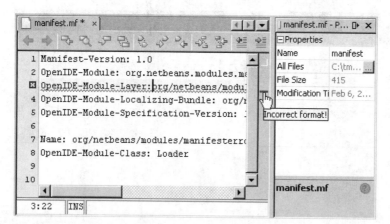

Figure 17.1: Example of an error annotation

In addition, Figure 17.1 shows an error glyph in the left sidebar and an error mark in the right sidebar. When the user hovers the mouse over the error mark, the cursor becomes a hand, and the error mark can be clicked to navigate to the line with the error.

17.2   Preparing to Create an Error Annotation

Use the **Module Project** wizard to define a new module project named `ManifestEditorAnnotation` with `org.netbeans.modules.` `manifesterrorannotation` as the code name base. When you complete the wizard, you have an empty module project. It contains a `Bundle.properties` file and the module layer file, as described in Chapter 6. You are now ready to begin creating an error annotation.

17.3   Creating an Error Annotation

The default display of an error annotation is defined in an XML file conforming to the DTD at `http://www.netbeans.org/dtds/` `annotation-type-1_1.dtd`. In particular, the DTD lets you specify whether annotated lines are highlighted, or underlined with a red wavy line, or both.

To define the error annotation's default settings, create an XML file named `org-netbeans-modules-manifest-syntax-error.xml` in the module project's main package. It could be named anything you like, but this is the name we use in this example. Paste the following example default annotation definition into the XML file:

```
<folder name="Editors">
<?xml version="1.0" encoding="UTF-8"?>
<!DOCTYPE type PUBLIC
"-//NetBeans//DTD annotation type 1.1//EN"
"http://www.netbeans.org/dtds/annotation-type-1_1.dtd">

<type name="org-netbeans-modules-manifesterrorannotation"
      visible="true"
      description_key="LAB_Error"
      localizing_bundle="org.netbeans.modules.manifesterror↵
annotation.Bundle"
      glyph="nbresloc:/org/netbeans/modules/manifesterror↵
annotation/resources/error-glyph.gif"
      waveunderline="#ff0000"
      type="line"
      browseable="false"
      severity="warning"
/>
```

As indicated in the XML definition above, you need to define the annotation's description key in the `Bundle.properties` file. Do that as follows:

```
LAB_Error=Manifest Syntax Error
```

The description key that you define in the `Bundle.properties` file is shown in the **Advanced** section of the **Options** window, as discussed in the next section.

The definition of the `glyph` attribute above indicates that you have a glyph in a subpackage called `resources`. The sample that is provided on the accompanying CD includes a `resources` folder with a number of glyphs that you can use. More glyphs can be found in the NetBeans sources.

17.3.1   Understanding the Error Annotation DTD

The Error Annotation DTD, `http://www.netbeans.org/dtds/annotation-type-1_1.dtd`, handles a variety of aspects of the definition of an error annotation. In this section, all the attributes declared in the DTD are listed and discussed. As you read the descriptions of these attributes below, consult the example definition in the previous section for an illustration.

name   Specifies the annotation's name. The name must match the `String` returned by `Annotation.getAnnotationType()`, as discussed in Section 17.5.1.

visible   Specifies whether the error annotation is visible in the **Advanced Options** window, as shown in Figure 17.2. This determines whether the user is able to customize the display of the error annotation.

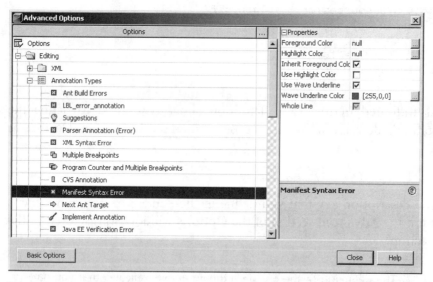

Figure 17.2: **Advanced Options** window entry for annotation

localizing_bundle   Specifies the bundle where the `description_key`, described below, is found.

`description_key`   Specifies a label shown in the **Advanced** section of the **Options** window, if `visible` is `true`. In Figure 17.2, the label is `Manifest Syntax Error`.

`glyph`   Specifies the icon shown in the left sidebar of the editor. In the example in the previous section, the `error-glyph.gif` icon (Figure 17.3) is used, provided on the accompanying CD. Figures 17.4 to 17.6 show the other glyph icons included with the sample together with their names. To use any of them, refer to its fully qualified location, as shown in Section 17.3.

Figure 17.3: `error-glyph.gif`

Figure 17.4: `implement-glyph.gif`

Figure 17.5: `override-glyph.gif`

Figure 17.6: `warning-glyph.gif`

highlight   Specifies the color of the highlight that extends across the length of the annotated code. In Figure 17.7, a red highlight is shown.

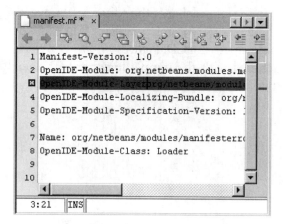

Figure 17.7: The highlight attribute

foreground   Specifies the color of the font applied to the line of code that is annotated. If you define a red foreground attribute, the font is displayed in red, as shown in Figure 17.8.

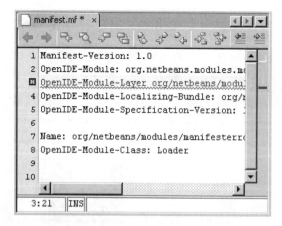

Figure 17.8: The foreground attribute

`waveunderline`   Specifies the color of the underline marking. For example, in Figure 17.8 you can see a red `waveunderline`.

`actions`   Specifies the name of a folder in the layer file containing one or more actions that you want to display in the left sidebar of the editor. For example, if you define `some-action` as the value of this attribute, you would need to create an entry similar to the following in the `Editors/AnnotationTypes` folder in the layer file:

```
<folder name="Editors">
  <folder name="AnnotationTypes">
    <folder name="some-action">
      <file name="org-netbeans-modules-manifesterror↵
annotation-SomeAction.instance"/>
    </folder>
  </folder>
</folder>
```

Then, if an action is declared in the layer file, the left sidebar would contain a submenu with the name defined by the `description_key`. Within that submenu, you would find the menu item registered in the layer file, as shown in Figure 17.9.

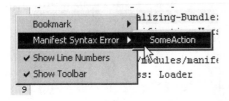

Figure 17.9: Example of an action in the left sidebar of the editor

`severity`   Specifies the color of the error mark on the right side of the editor. In Figure 17.9, `warning` is set, so the color of the error mark is yellow. If `error` is set, the color of the error mark is red, if `ok` is set, the color is green, and `none` means no error mark is shown.

This attribute can be overridden by setting the `use_custom_side_bar_color` attribute, together with the `custom_sidebar_color` attribute. Both are discussed below.

`use_custom_sidebar_color`   Specifies (as `true` or `false`) whether a custom color should be used in the editor side bar. If set to `true`, the `custom_sidebar_color` attribute, defined below, determines the custom color.

`custom_sidebar_color`   Specifies the custom color for the error mark on the right sidebar of the editor. Valid values are of the form `0xRRGGBB`, where `RR`, `GG`, `BB` are hexadecimal numbers. The default is no color, which means that the `severity` attribute determines the color of the error mark.

For example, if `use_custom_side_bar_color` is `true` and `custom_sidebar_color` is set to `#0033FF`, the error mark (in the right sidebar of the editor) is blue, as shown in Figure 17.10.

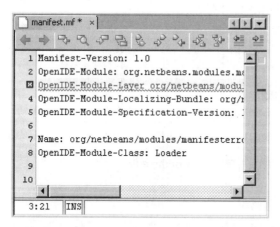

Figure 17.10: Blue error mark in the right sidebar of the editor

`browseable`   Specifies whether the Alt-Shift-N keybinding can be used to jump from annotation to annotation, if the Jump to Next Error Action module is installed.

`priority`   Specifies the priority level of the annotation. The lower the number, the higher the priority. Default is 0. If a line or part of a line would be annotated by more than one annotation, the annotation with the lowest priority number is displayed first.

17.3.2   Registering an Error Annotation

In the layer file, register the error annotation in the `Editors/AnnotationTypes` folder.

```
<folder name="Editors">
  <folder name="AnnotationTypes">
    <file name="org-netbeans-modules-manifesterrorannotation.xml"
          url="org-netbeans-modules-manifest-syntax-error.xml"/>
  </folder>
</folder>
```

When you register the error annotation in the layer file, it is reflected in the layer file's visual representation (Figure 17.11). You can see and explore the visual representation by expanding the module project's **Important Files** node and then the layer file's node, followed by the <**this layer**> node. Expand the **Editors** node and then the **AnnotationTypes** node. The XML file that you registered above is now visible. If, instead of <**this layer**>, you expand <**this layer in context**>, you can see all the annotation types provided by all

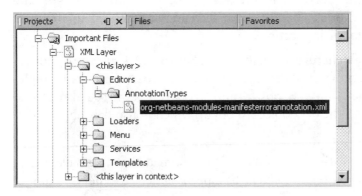

Figure 17.11: Annotation in layer file

the modules that make up the application. Within that node, expand **Editors** and then **AnnotationTypes**. You will see a long list of annotations provided by other modules.

17.3.3   Installing an Error Annotation

After you create and register an error annotation it, you can install it. Right-click the module project and install it. In the **Advanced Options** window, you should now see the error annotation (Figure 17.2).

17.4   Preparing to Use an Error Annotation

Before beginning to use an error annotation, you need to have the following:

- **A file type that you want to annotate.** As described in Chapter 10, you can use the **New File Type** wizard to create a data loader for the file type of your choice. Since this chapter focuses on editing manifest files, use the **New File Type** wizard to create a data loader for the MIME type `text/x-java-jar-manifest`. This MIME type applies to files that have `mf` or `MF` as filename extension.

  In the code listings that follow, it is assumed that you have specified `Manifest` as the class name prefix in the **New File Type** wizard. As a result, you have files with names such as `ManifestDataObject` and `ManifestDataNode`. These are the filenames referenced in the code listings in the following sections.

- **An editor infrastructure.** As described in Section 12.4, an editor's infrastructure consists of a class that extends `DataEditorSupport` and implements `OpenCookie`, `EditCookie`, and `EditorCookie`. You also need to add the editor to the data object's `Lookup` which is also described in that section.

  In the code listings that follow, it is assumed that you have a class called `ManifestEditor` which has been added to the `Lookup` of `ManifestDataObject`.

Once you have created the above items, as well as the XML file describing your annotation (Section 17.3), your **Projects** window should look as in Figure 17.12.

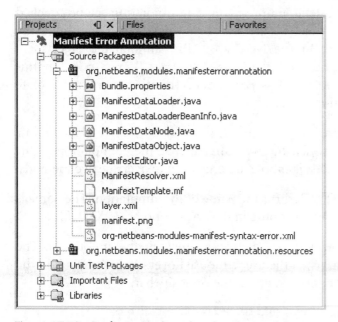

Figure 17.12: **Projects** window showing the module

You are now ready to use your error annotation in your code, as described in the next section.

17.5   Using an Error Annotation

Using our error annotation means that we must first describe it in Java code. We do so by referring to the definition of the error annotation in the layer file. Once we have described the annotation, we can attach it to a line that matches a pattern. All these steps are described below.

17.5.1   Describing an Annotation

The `org.openide.text.Annotation` class describes an annotation in Java code. For example, it defines the tooltip text that appears when the user's mouse hovers over an error mark in the right sidebar. If you want to provide annotations, you must extend `Annotation`. The annotation can be attached to an annotatable object—that is, an object implementing the `Annotatable` interface. In the NetBeans APIs, annotatable objects are `org.openide.text.Line` and `org.openide.text.Line.Part`. In this example, we annotate the `Line` class. For a brief description of how to annotate a part of a line, see Section 17.5.4.

First, we extend the `org.openide.text.Annotation` class in our `ManifestEditor` class. Next, we implement the annotation. Our implementation of this class is simple; we only need to override two methods:

`getAnnotationType()`   Returns the name of the annotation. The name is defined by the `name` attribute in the error annotation XML file.

`getShortDescription()`   Gets the tooltip text for the annotation. The tooltip is shown when the user's mouse hovers over the glyph in the left sidebar or the error mark in the right sidebar.

```
private static final class ManifestErrorAnnotation
    extends Annotation {

  static final ManifestErrorAnnotation DEFAULT =
    new ManifestErrorAnnotation();

  public String getAnnotationType() {
    return "org-netbeans-modules-manifesterrorannotation";
  }

  public String getShortDescription() {
    return "Incorrect format!";
  }

}
```

However, in addition to these two methods, the `Annotation` class provides several others. Of the methods below, we will use `attach()` and detach() when we attach and detach the annotation to and from a line of code:

addPropertyChangeListener(PropertyChangeListener l)   Listens for changes to the annotation's properties.

attach(Annotatable anno)   Attaches the annotation to an annotatable object.

detach()   Detaches the annotation.

firePropertyChange()   Fires a property change to registered listeners.

getAttachedAnnotatable()   Gets the annotatable object to which this annotation is attached.

moveToFront()   Moves annotation covered by other annotations on the same line in front of others.

notifyAttached(Annotatable toAnno)   Notifies the annotation that it was attached to the annotatable.

notifyDetached(Annotatable fromAnno)   Notifies the annotation that it was detached from the annotatable.

removePropertyChangeListener(PropertyChangeListener l)
    Removes listeners on changes of annotation properties.

17.5.2   Attaching and Detaching Annotations

We are going to attach and detach annotations in two ways. Using the first approach, described in this section, you attach or detach an annotation whenever a change is made to the document. For this, we use a DocumentListener. We use the DocumentListener's methods insertUpdate(), removeUpdate(), and changedUpdate() to check whether a line matches a pattern. If a mismatch is identified, the annotation is attached to the line. If there is no mismatch, the annotation is removed. Since this happens whenever a change is made to the document, the error check blocks all other activities. This limitation and its solution are discussed in Section 17.5.3.

```java
// Here we define what a "good line" is.
// A good line is one that uses any character for the key,
// followed by a colon and a space,
// followed by any character for the value:
private static Pattern GOOD_LINE =
  Pattern.compile(" *|[\\p{Alnum}-._]+: *[\\p{Alnum}-/._]+");

// Method handled by Runnable:
final void checkErrors() {
  StyledDocument d = getDocument();
  if (d == null) {
    // If there is no document, detach annotations
    ManifestErrorAnnotation.DEFAULT.detach();
    return;
  }
  String txt;
  try {
      txt = d.getText(0, d.getLength());
  } catch (BadLocationException ex) {
      LOG.log(Level.WARNING, null, ex);
      return;

  }
  InputStream is = new ByteArrayInputStream(txt.getBytes());
  try {
      new Manifest(is);
      // If parsing succeeds, there is no error
      ManifestErrorAnnotation.DEFAULT.detach();
      return;
  } catch (IOException ex) {
      // Failure; we need to place the annotation somewhere.
      // The code that follows applies to this catch block.
  }

  String[] lines = txt.split("\n");
  for (int i = 0; i < lines.length; i++) {
    String line = lines[i];

    if (!GOOD_LINE.matcher(line).matches()) {
      ManifestErrorAnnotation.DEFAULT.attach(
        getLineSet().getCurrent(i));
      return;
    }
  }
}
```

```
// Method from DocumentListener:
public void insertUpdate(DocumentEvent e) {
  checkErrors();
}

// Method from DocumentListener:
public void removeUpdate(DocumentEvent e) {
  checkErrors();
}

// Method from DocumentListener:
public void changedUpdate(DocumentEvent e) {
  checkErrors();
}
```

17.5.3   Defining a Request Processor Task

Thanks to the code you implemented in the previous sections, an error check is performed whenever the user types a new character. The error check blocks all other activities. For example, if the code needs to be parsed, the error check is performed first. To prevent blocking the AWT thread in this way, you can use the NetBeans API class `org.openide.util.RequestProcessor`. This class executes requests in dedicated threads. One of its uses is having a `RequestProcessor.Task` done periodically in a thread, using its `schedule()` method. In our implementation below, we schedule the error check to occur half a second after the user stops typing, instead of after every key stroke.

First, change the signature of the `ManifestEditor` class so that it implements `Runnable`. Next, create a task that is run by the `RequestProcessor`. Create the task in the constructor. Then, set the priority of the task to the lowest level, so that all other activities take precedence. Schedule the task to be run every 0.5 seconds. The request cancels all previous calls to schedule, so that there is no queue. Finally, use the `Runnable` interface's `run()` method to make the call to the `checkErrors()` method.

After implementing `Runnable`, your code should look like this:

```
// Declare new request processor:
private static RequestProcessor RP =
  new RequestProcessor("findError");

// Declare new task:
final RequestProcessor.Task findError;

// Constructor creates the request processor
// and sets the lowest priority:
private ManifestEditor(ManifestDataObject obj) {
  super(obj, new MyEnv(obj));
  findError = RP.create(this, true);
  findError.setPriority(Thread.MIN_PRIORITY);
}

// Change this method from DocumentListener:
public void insertUpdate(DocumentEvent e) {
  findError.schedule(500);
}

// Change this method from DocumentListener:
public void removeUpdate(DocumentEvent e) {
  findError.schedule(500);
}

// Change this method from DocumentListener:
public void changedUpdate(DocumentEvent e) {
  findError.schedule(500);
}

// Call checkErrors() in the run() method from Runnable:
public void run() {
  checkErrors();
}
```

17.5.4   Annotating Part of a Line

The previous sections assumed that you want to annotate entire lines. Sometimes, however, you may want to annotate only a part of a line, such as a particular word, method, or attribute value. For example, the open source NBTapestrySupport project displays an error annotation if the `inject` element's `object` attribute is incorrect, as shown in Figure 17.13.

Figure 17.13: Line part error annotation

Notice that here the wavy red underline does not span the entire line but only applies to a specific part of it. To make this possible, you need to attach an annotation to a part of a line, using `Line.createLinePart()`. This method takes the column where the line part starts as well as its length.

17.6   Finishing Up

Install the module and open a manifest file. As soon as you make a mistake by, for example, not adding a colon between a key and a value, you should see the error annotation.

In the **Advanced** section of the **Options** window, note that your annotation is registered under the name specified in the localizing bundle, as shown in Figure 17.14.

The properties displayed in Figure 17.14 match several of the properties that you defined in the error annotation XML file. For example, the `highlight` attribute in the XML file defines the default highlight state of the annotation; users can customize the highlight by changing the property in the **Advanced** section of the **Options** window (Figure 17.14).

This chapter should have given you a basic understanding of how to define error annotations, how to register them in the layer file, and how to use them in your code.

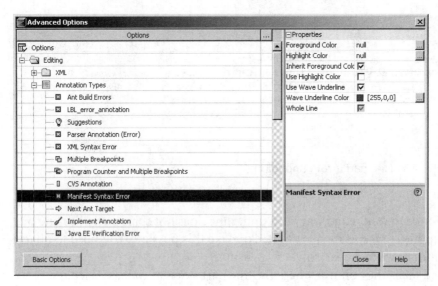

Figure 17.14: **Advanced Options** window entry for annotation

CHAPTER EIGHTEEN

Options Windows

18.1 Introduction

The **Options** window provides a centralized location for the user to change an application's configurable settings. For example, in the IDE, the user changes keyboard shortcuts in the **Options** window, under the **Tools** menu. When you provide a new module for the IDE, you can extend the **Options** window so that the user can configure the options relevant to your module. The **Options** window is part of the NetBeans Platform and, therefore, such a window is provided out of the box for all NetBeans applications. Just as you can extend the IDE's **Options** window, you can extend a standalone application's **Options** window too.

An **Options** window can be extended in one of two areas. You can let the user configure your module's settings either in the **Miscellaneous** panel or in a new panel within the **Options** window. If you extend the **Miscellaneous** panel in the IDE, you add a new category in the panel where the **Ant** and **GUI Builder** categories are found by default, as shown in Figure 18.1.

18.1.1 Your First Options Window Extension

The IDE provides a template that you can use for creating an extension to the **Options** window. In this first encounter with **Options** window extensions,

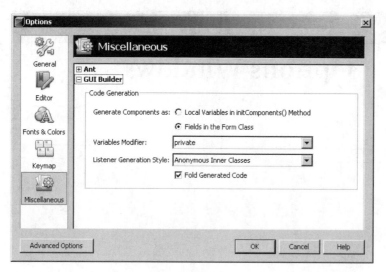

Figure 18.1: **Miscellaneous** panel in IDE

we will use the template. After that, we will discuss the files and code created by the template.

1. Create a module project. Right-click the module project and choose **New | File/Folder**. In the **New File** wizard, choose **NetBeans Module Development** in **Categories** and **Options Panel** in **File Types**. You should now see Figure 18.2.

2. When you click **Next**, you see Figure 18.3.

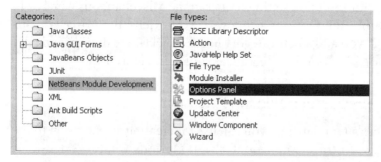

Figure 18.2: **Options Panel** template in the **New File** wizard

Figure 18.3: Selecting the type of **Options** window extension

Two types of **Options** window extensions are supported, as reflected in Figure 18.3:

- **Miscellaneous panel.** An extension to the existing **Miscellaneous** panel.

- **Primary panel.** A new panel, on the same level as the **Miscellaneous** panel.

In this case, we will extend the **Miscellaneous** panel.

3. Type `New Options Panel Extension` in the **Title** field. Then, type `Tooltip for My Options Panel Extension` in the **Tool Tip** field.

   Click **Next**. Type a class name prefix and a package where the **Options** window extension files will be stored. Click **Finish**.

4. Three new files shown in Table 18.1 are now added to the package that you specified in the previous step.

   In addition, the module layer file contains the following entries:

```
<folder name="OptionsDialog">
  <folder name="Advanced">
    <file name="org-yourorghere-mymodule-MymoduleAdvanced⏎
Option.instance"/>
  </folder>
</folder>
```

Table 18.1: Files generated by the **Options Panel** template

Name	Superclass	Description
xxxAdvanced- Option.java	AdvancedOption	Represents one category in the **Miscellaneous** panel.
xxxOptionsPanel- Controller.java	OptionsPanel- Controller	Creates the visual panel and manages the communication between the panel and the **Options** window.
xxxPanel.java	JPanel	Represents a visual panel for the **Options** window extension.

5. Open the `xxxPanel.java` class in the GUI Builder's **Design** mode. Drag and drop a panel and use the **Properties** window to set a titled border with the text "New category".

6. Install the module. In the **Options** window, you should now see Figure 18.4.

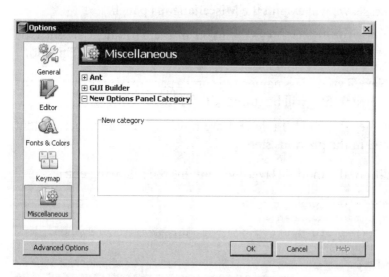

Figure 18.4: **New category** in **Miscellaneous** panel

Now that you have seen how easy it is to extend the **Options** window, we will discuss each of the generated files in detail. Then we will add some settings to the new panel and use them in our module.

18.2   Looking at the Options Window Extension Files

In this section, we look at each of the methods provided by the wizard. These are the methods that you typically work with when extending the **Options** window.

18.2.1   The AdvancedOption Class

The AdvancedOption class provides the following methods:

getDisplayName()   Returns the name of the category used in the **Miscellaneous** panel of the **Options** window.

getTooltip()   Returns the tooltip to be used in the category name.

create()   Returns the OptionsPanelController class for the category. The OptionsPanelController class creates the visual panel to be added to the **Miscellaneous** panel.

For example, this is the AdvancedOption class created by the **Options Panel** wizard that you used in the previous section:

```
public final class MymoduleAdvancedOption
                   extends AdvancedOption {

  public String getDisplayName() {
    return NbBundle.getMessage(MymoduleAdvancedOption.class,
                               "AdvancedOption_DisplayName");
  }
  public String getTooltip() {
    return NbBundle.getMessage(MymoduleAdvancedOption.class,
                               "AdvancedOption_Tooltip");
  }
  public OptionsPanelController create() {
    return new MymoduleOptionsPanelController();
  }
}
```

18.2.2   The `OptionsPanelController` Class

The `OptionsPanelController` class provides the following methods:

`update()`   Loads the settings. You should not perform any time-consuming operations in the constructor, because it blocks initialization of the **Options** window. Instead, initialization should be implemented here, in the `update()` method.

`applyChanges()`   You can use this method to store settings, because this is called when the **Options** window's **OK** button is clicked.

`cancel()`   This method is called when the **Options** window's **Cancel** button is clicked.

`isValid()`   Should return `true` if some option value in this category is valid.

`isChanged()`   Should return `true` if some option value in this category has been changed.

`getLookup()`   Supports communication between categories in the **Options** window. Each category in the **Options** window can provide a `Lookup`.

`getComponent()`   Returns the visual component representing this options category. This method is called before the `update()` method.

`getHelpCtx()`   Returns help context associated with the panel.

`addPropertyChangeListener()`   Registers a new property change listener.

`removePropertyChangeListener()`   Deregisters a property change listener.

For example, this is the `OptionsPanelController` class created by the **Options Panel** wizard that you used in the previous section:

```
final class MymoduleOptionsPanelController
              extends OptionsPanelController {

  private MymodulePanel panel;
  private final PropertyChangeSupport pcs =
                  new PropertyChangeSupport(this);
  private boolean changed;

  public void update() {
    getPanel().load();
    changed = false;
  }

  public void applyChanges() {
    getPanel().store();
    changed = false;
  }

  public void cancel() {
    // Need not do anything special, if no changes have been
    // persisted yet
  }

  public boolean isValid() {
    return getPanel().valid();
  }

  public boolean isChanged() {
    return changed;
  }

  public HelpCtx getHelpCtx() {
    return null;
    // New HelpCtx("...ID") if you have a help set
  }

  public JComponent getComponent(Lookup masterLookup) {
    return getPanel();
  }

  public void addPropertyChangeListener(
                                    PropertyChangeListener l) {
    pcs.addPropertyChangeListener(l);
  }
```

```
public void removePropertyChangeListener(
                                PropertyChangeListener l) {
    pcs.removePropertyChangeListener(l);
}

private MymodulePanel getPanel() {
    if (panel == null) {
        panel = new MymodulePanel(this);
    }
    return panel;
}

void changed() {
    if (!changed) {
        changed = true;
        pcs.firePropertyChange(
            OptionsPanelController.PROP_CHANGED, false, true);
    }
    pcs.firePropertyChange(
        OptionsPanelController.PROP_VALID, null, null);
}
}
```

18.2.3   The Visual Options Panels

The `JPanel` that provides the visual component of the **Options** window extension must interact with the `OptionsPanelController`. For this reason, the `JPanel` that is created when you use the **Options Panel** wizard provides the following methods:

```
final class MymodulePanel extends javax.swing.JPanel {
    private final MymoduleOptionsPanelController controller;

    MymodulePanel(MymoduleOptionsPanelController controller) {
        this.controller = controller;
        initComponents();
        // TODO: listen to changes in form fields and call
        // controller.changed()
    }

    void load() {
        // TODO: read settings and initialize GUI
        // Example:
        // someCheckBox.setSelected(Preferences.userNodeForPackage(
        //    MymodulePanel.class).getBoolean("someFlag", false));
```

```
  // or:
  // someTextField.setText(SomeSystemOption.getDefault().
  //    getSomeStringProperty());
}

void store() {
  // TODO: store modified settings
  // Example:
  // Preferences.userNodeForPackage(MymodulePanel.class).
  //    putBoolean("someFlag", someCheckBox.isSelected());
  // or:
  // SomeSystemOption.getDefault().setSomeStringProperty(
  //    someTextField.getText());
}

boolean valid() {
  // TODO: check whether form is consistent and complete
  return true;
}

}
```

18.3   Creating a Primary Panel

Instead of extending the **Miscellaneous** panel, you can provide a completely new panel of your own. This is called a *primary panel*. If your module comes with a lot of configurable settings, or if you are creating a standalone application rather than extending the IDE, you might want to provide primary panels.

18.3.1   Your First Primary Panel

The code required for a primary panel is not very different from that of an extension to the **Miscellaneous** panel. As before, select the **Options Panel** template from the **New File** wizard. In the first panel, type the title and label for the new primary panel and specify a 32×32 pixels icon. For example, if you are creating a new primary panel for a module that integrates support for HTML Tidy, specify the settings shown in Figure 18.5.

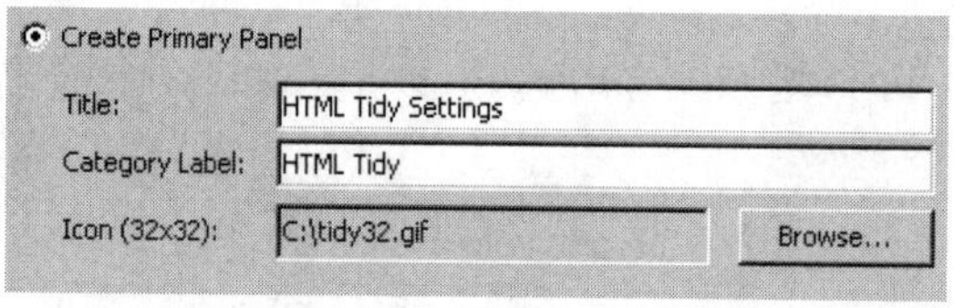

Figure 18.5: New primary panel

When you complete the wizard, drag a panel from the component palette and drop it on the visual panel in **Design** mode. After you change the background color, add a titled border with the text "Settings," and install the module, you see Figure 18.6 in the **Options** window.

In your code, the only difference between a primary panel and an extension to the **Miscellaneous** panel is that the primary panel extends `OptionsCategory` instead of `AdvancedOption`:

```
public final class MymoduleOptionsCategory
                      extends OptionsCategory {

  public Icon getIcon() {
    return new ImageIcon(Utilities.loadImage(
                "org/yourorghere/mymodule/tidy32.gif"));
  }

  public String getCategoryName() {
    return NbBundle.getMessage(MymoduleOptionsCategory.class,
                          "OptionsCategory_Name");
  }

  public String getTitle() {
    return NbBundle.getMessage(MymoduleOptionsCategory.class,
                          "OptionsCategory_Title");
  }

  public OptionsPanelController create() {
    return new MymoduleOptionsPanelController();
  }
}
```

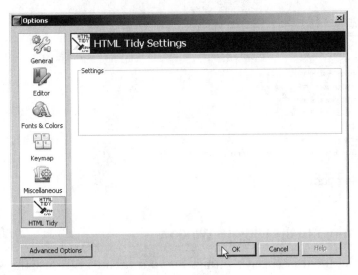

Figure 18.6: Installed primary panel

Also note that the `OptionsCategory` is not registered within an `Advanced` folder in the layer file, as was the case with the **Miscellaneous** panel extension:

```
<folder name="OptionsDialog">
  <file name="org-yourorghere-mymodule-MymoduleOptionsCategory.↵
instance"/>
</folder>
```

18.3.2   Reordering Options Panels

When you expand the module project's **Important Files** node, you can expand the layer file node. Two subnodes are found, the second one called <**this layer in context**>. When you drill down to the `OptionsDialog` folder, you see Figure 18.7.

When you drag and drop items in this view, related XML tags are generated in the layer file. You do not need to type these yourself. Instead, you can use this drag-and-drop interface to position the panels exactly to your liking.

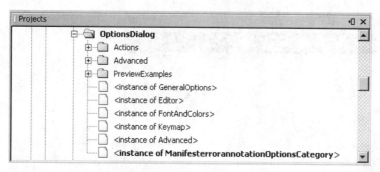

Figure 18.7: Reordering panels

18.4   Adding Settings to the Options Window

The easiest way to let the user specify settings for your module is to use the
JDK's Preferences API. According to the Preferences API Javadoc, "the
`java.util.prefs` package provides a way for applications to store and retrieve user and system preference and configuration data. The data is stored
persistently in an implementation-dependent backing store. There are two
separate trees of preference nodes, one for user preferences and one for system
preferences."

In the context of user settings for NetBeans modules, only the tree of user
preferences is applicable. For information on the user preferences tree provided by the Persistence API, see the freely available documentation for the Persistence API. In NetBeans 6.0, a NetBeans-specific Persistence API will be
provided. Using this API, you will be able, for example, to store preferences
directly in the NetBeans user directory, rather than the location used by your
Java installation.

18.4.1   Example: Using the Preferences API

In the visual panel that the **Options Panel** wizard created for you, notice the
`load()` and `store()` methods. These are called from the palette controller's
`update()` and `applyChanges()` methods to load and store settings, respectively. Plug your calls to the Preferences API into the `load()` and `store()`
methods. For example, putting this line in the `load()` method will load the
value of `jTextField1` from a key called `SOME_KEY`.

```
jTextField1.setText(Preferences.userNodeForPackage(
  MymodulePanel.class).get("SOME_KEY", ""));
```

Next, if you put this line into the `store()` method, you will put the value of `jTextField1` into the `SOME_KEY` key:

```
Preferences.userNodeForPackage(MymodulePanel.class).put(
  "SOME_KEY", jTextField1.getText());
```

Now that you have created the key and assigned it a value, you can retrieve the value wherever you need to use it. For example, in a `TopComponent`'s constructor, you might have these lines to set a field called `jTextField2` with the value obtained from the key:

```
Preferences pref =
  Preferences.userNodeForPackage(MymodulePanel.class);
String s = pref.get("SOME_KEY", "");

pref.addPreferenceChangeListener(new PreferenceChangeListener() {
  public void preferenceChange(PreferenceChangeEvent evt) {
    if (evt.getKey().equals("SOME_KEY")) {
      jTextField2.setText(evt.getNewValue());
    }
  }
});

jTextField2.setText(s);
```

Preferences are even more integrated into NetBeans 6.0. Since that version, they are the preferred way of storing private settings of your module. There is a new `org.openide.util.NbPreferences` class with factory methods that create a `Preferences` node stored in the System Filesystem. That is why in 6.0 the usual code to obtain a preference node would be:

```
NbPreferences.forModule(MymodulePanel.class);
```

CHAPTER NINETEEN

Web Frameworks

19.1 Introduction

A Web framework is a set of development and runtime constructs that simplify Web development. Examples include Java Server Faces (JSF) and Struts. Instead of hand-coding a Web application's navigation and validation, you can use a framework that provides this kind of standard infrastructure out of the box. Many different frameworks exist, but the approach to supporting them in the IDE is the same.

When you add support for a Web framework in the IDE, you provide tools such as wizards and extensions to the Source Editor. For example, the IDE's support for the Struts framework includes a wizard that creates a Struts action. Such tools simplify and speed up the creation of the framework's artifacts. For example, framework support could include a wizard that sets up a project's source structure so that it complies with the structure that a particular Web framework requires. Or you may want to provide specific refactoring for the artifacts of a Web framework. A NetBeans module can be written that contains these features. The range of support that you can provide for your Web framework is endless, but the very first step is always to register the Web framework with the IDE.

In this chapter you will do the following:

- Add new entries to the **Frameworks** panels of the **New Project** wizard and **Project Properties** dialog box.

- Programmatically create a source structure for a Web framework.

- Extend the **Frameworks** panel to provide settings for the customization of the source structure generated to support the Web framework.

- Add the Web framework's JAR files to the Web application's classpath.

At the end of this chapter, you will have the beginnings of a framework support module for the Wicket framework. Wicket is a Java Web application framework that focuses on simplicity, separation of concerns, and ease of development. Wicket pages can be mocked up, previewed, and later revised using standard WYSIWYG HTML design tools, while dynamic content processing and form handling is all done in Java code using a first-class component model. For more information, see the Wicket Web site.[1] An extensive NetBeans module that supports the Wicket framework is also available.[2] In this chapter, we recreate a small subset of the NetBeans Wicket module. As with all other samples discussed in this book, it is available on the accompanying CD.

19.1.1　Preparing to Provide Support for a Web Framework

Before you begin registering your Web framework, it is a good idea to analyze the framework support that you would like to provide. After all, the IDE might already have adequate support for what you need. For example, when thinking about the source structure that you would like to provide, there is no need to create a `web.xml` file, because the IDE already creates that for you. One approach at this preparatory phase might be to use the IDE to create a basic application that uses your Web framework and to note all the manual steps that you take. For example, notice that you need to manually add the framework's JAR files to the application. You might also need to add servlet entries in the `web.xml` file. There could be XML configuration files specific to your Web framework that you need to create manually. There might also be a stylesheet or some standard tags in a JSP file. Once you have taken all the

---

1. `http://wicket.sourceforge.net`

2. NetBeans Wicket module homepage (`https://nbwicketsupport.dev.java.net`).

typical steps that a user would take when using your framework, continue with this chapter to begin automating these manual steps.

19.1.2   The `WebFrameworkProvider` Class

The NetBeans API class that is responsible for registering Web frameworks is called `WebFrameworkProvider`. This class is a Service Provider Interface (SPI) and belongs to the Web APIs. This is the only NetBeans API class you need to extend when registering a new Web framework in the IDE. After registration, you will need other NetBeans API classes, such as classes providing hyperlinking in the Source Editor, or a component palette with items that can be dragged and dropped. The `WebFrameworkProvider` class contains the following methods:

`extend()`   Creates the source structure, consisting of packages and files, as well as entries or changes to existing files, such as the `web.xml` file.

`getConfigurationFiles()`   Returns the configuration files, if any, which are specific to your Web framework.

`getConfigurationPanel()`   Provides a configuration panel, which becomes the lower half of the **Frameworks** panel, with settings specific to your Web framework.

`getDescription()`   Gets the description of the Web framework. Alternatively, you can use the constructor to refer to a key in the `Bundle.properties` file.

`getName()`   Gets the display name, used in the **Frameworks** panels, for the Web framework. Alternatively, you can use the constructor to pass the name and description that will be returned by the default implementation of this method.

`isInWebModule()`   Checks if the given Web application has already been extended with this framework. Used by the **Frameworks** panel in the **Project Properties** dialog box to determine whether a Web framework should be listed as already used in the project.

19.1.3   Getting Started Really Quickly

Instead of going through this chapter step by step, you might be tempted to review (online or in the NetBeans source code repository) the existing implementations of the `WebFrameworkProvider` class, looking for one that almost matches your needs and can be adapted to your purposes. Go right ahead! That is what open source is all about. At the time of writing, `JSFFrameworkProvider`, `StrutsFrameworkProvider`, and `Wicket-FrameworkProvider` exist. At the same time, `WebFrameworkProvider` classes are being written for several other frameworks, including Tapestry and Spring.

As you copy and paste code from an existing `WebFrameworkProvider` to your own, or even incorporate it wholesale into your module, you might come across things that you don't fully understand. Or, you might be curious about why something works the way it does. In that case, feel free to use this chapter as a reference rather than an implementation guide.

19.1.4   Example: Basic Registration

The first example provides the absolute minimum of what an implementation of the `WebFrameworkProvider` should contain. It just passes to the constructor the name and description, which will be displayed in the **Frameworks** panel in the **New Project** wizard and **Project Properties** dialog box. Once the user has selected the entry, nothing more can be done because the `extend()` and `getConfigurationPanel()` methods are not implemented yet. You have not provided a configuration panel, and the `getConfigurationPanel()` method returns `null`, so the lower half of the **Frameworks** panel in the **New Project** wizard and the **Project Properties** dialog box is empty. At this stage, you do not need to do anything, just read the `WicketFrameworkProvider` below. In the next section, you will work with this code.

```java
public class WicketFrameworkProvider extends
                                    WebFrameworkProvider {

  // Creates a new instance of WicketFrameworkProvider
  public WicketFrameworkProvider() {
    super(NbBundle.getMessage(WicketFrameworkProvider.class,
          "WicketFramework_Name"),
          NbBundle.getMessage(WicketFrameworkProvider.class,
          "WicketFramework_Description"));
  }

  // Empty for now, but this is where all the artifacts
  // are created:
  public Set extend(WebModule webModule) {
    return null;
  }

  // If true, the Project Properties dialog box will show that
  // the framework is selected.
  public boolean isInWebModule(WebModule webModule) {
    return true;
  }

  // Return the configuration files, if any.
  // Here we return an empty array:
  public File[] getConfigurationFiles(WebModule webModule) {
    return new File[0];
  }

  // Returns the lower part of the New Project wizard or
  // the Project Properties dialog box, where the user can
  // specify settings that are specific to your framework.
  // Here, nothing is returned:
  public FrameworkConfigurationPanel getConfigurationPanel(
                                    WebModule webModule) {
    return null;
  }

}
```

19.2 Preparing to Work with the `WebFrameworkProvider` Class

To register support for a Web framework, you need to create the following:

1. **A module project.** Use the **Module Project** wizard to define a new module project named `WicketWebFrameworkSupport`, with `org.netbeans. modules.web.wicket.framework` as the code name base. When you complete the wizard, you have an empty module project. It contains a `Bundle.properties` file and the module layer file, which is described in Chapter 6.

2. **Module dependencies.** Before working with the `WebFrameworkProvider` class, you need to declare a dependency on the following modules:

   • Utilities API
   • Web APIs

   The `WebFrameworkProvider` class belongs to the Web APIs. You need the Utilities API so that you can work with the localizing file `Bundle.properties`.

3. **A `WebFrameworkProvider` implementation class.** Create a Java class called `WicketFrameworkProvider`. Copy and paste the code from Section 19.1.4 into the class.

4. **New keys/value pairs in the `Bundle.properties` file.** Add the keys mentioned in the constructor to the `Bundle.properties` file and define the values that are meaningful to your Web framework. This is the definition of the constructor, showing the keys:

```
public WicketFrameworkProvider() {
  super(NbBundle.getMessage(WicketFrameworkProvider.class,
        "WicketFramework_Name"),
      NbBundle.getMessage(WicketFrameworkProvider.class,
        "WicketFramework_Description"));
}
```

5. **A registration entry in the layer file.** Make sure that the layer file registers the `WebFrameworkProvider` class correctly, as shown below:

```
<folder name="j2ee">
  <folder name="webtier">
    <folder name="framework">
      <file name="org-netbeans-modules-web-wicket-framework-⏎
WicketFrameworkProvider.instance"/>
    </folder>
  </folder>
</folder>
```

The file registered in the layer file above must be the class that extends the `WebFrameworkProvider` class, such as the one used in the example in the previous section.

Once you have created the items above, do the following:

1. Build the module and install it into the current development IDE or in a target platform. To do this, right-click the module and choose **Install/Reload in Development IDE** or **Install/Reload in Target Platform**. The former installs the module in the current IDE. The latter will start up a new instance of the IDE and install the module there.

2. Use the **New Project** wizard to create a new Web application and notice that the **Frameworks** panel has an entry for your new Web framework, as shown in Figure 19.1.

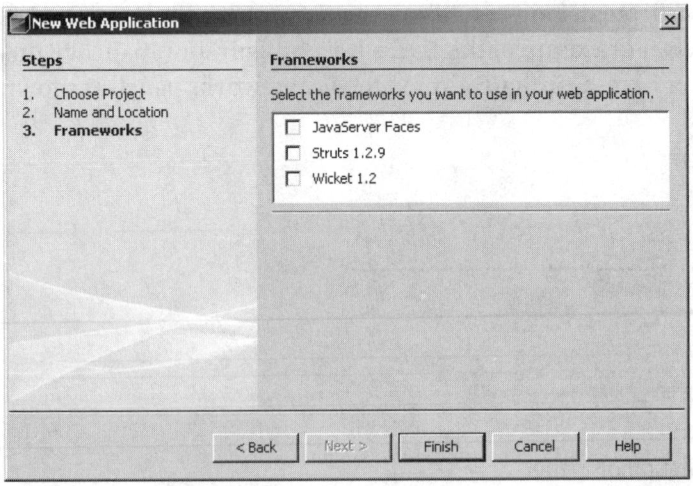

Figure 19.1: Newly registered Web framework

If you do not see your framework in the **Frameworks** panel, look in the layer file and make sure that the fully qualified `WebFrameworkProvider` class name is registered there, as shown earlier in this section.

You now have the start of your Web framework support module. In the following sections, we will look at how to add a configuration panel, how to create a source structure and files, how to add the framework's JAR files to the application's classpath, and how to check if a Web application has been extended with a framework.

19.3   Providing a Framework Configuration Panel

You can provide a configuration panel to let the user specify the preferences that impact the artifacts created by the `extend()` method, which we will look at in detail later. Even though a configuration panel is optional, it is generally a good idea to provide one. Without a configuration panel, you cannot give the user any options at all.

The configuration panel is the lower part of the **Frameworks** panel, below the Frameworks list. It is integrated into the panel where the **Frameworks** list is found, but is actually a separate panel. In each case, the configuration panel starts with the name of the Web framework, followed by the word "Configuration." This is hardcoded and results in the same look and feel for all configuration panels. For example, the IDE's JSF configuration panel begins at the text **JavaServer Faces Configuration** in the **Frameworks** panel, as shown in Figure 19.2.

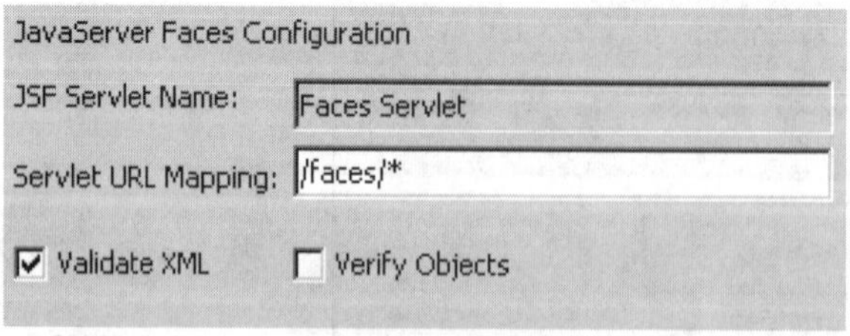

Figure 19.2: JSF configuration panel

For both JSF and Struts, the IDE provides a number of options in the configuration panel. For example, when the user selects the JSF entry in the **Frameworks** panel, the servlet URL mapping can be set. Similarly, when the user selects Struts, an application resource bundle can be entered. In the former case, the `extend()` method uses the servlet URL mapping to add entries to the `web.xml` file. In the latter case, it creates a resource bundle in the given package.

19.3.1   Creating the Configuration Panel

A configuration panel consists of two classes: a class that provides the user interface of the configuration panel (usually by extending `JPanel`) and a class that implements `FrameworkConfigurationPanel`. You can use the IDE's **New Wizard** wizard to generate skeletons for both these classes in one operation. Once you have generated the skeletons, you need to modify and extend them to create a configuration panel for your Web framework.

Do the following:

1. Right-click the package where you want the panel to be created and choose **New | File/Folder**. In the **NetBeans Module Development** category, choose **Wizard**. Click **Next**.

2. In the **Wizard Type** panel, keep the default **Registration Type** and **Wizard Step Sequence**. Type 1 in the **Number of Wizard Panels** field. You should now see Figure 19.3. Click **Next**.

3. Type `Wicket` as the prefix of your class. Check that it will be created in an appropriate package. Click **Finish**.

4. Delete the `WicketWizardAction` class, because you do not need it in this scenario.

You now have two new classes. One is called `WicketWizardPanel1` and the other, `WicketVisualPanel1`. Next, you need to modify and extend them, as described in the steps below.

1. Right-click each of the new classes, choose **Refactor**, and change the names to something more meaningful for your context, such as `WicketConfigurationPanel` and `WicketConfigurationPanel-Visual`.

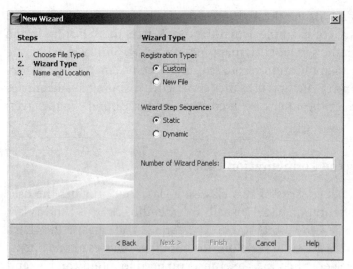

Figure 19.3: Wizard for configuration panel

It is a good idea to attempt to maintain the naming structure used by existing framework support modules. The JSF implementations of these two classes are named `JSFConfigurationPanel` and `JSFConfigurationPanelVisual`. The Struts implementations are named `StrutsConfigurationPanel` and `StrutsConfiguration-PanelVisual`.

2. Use the GUI Builder to design `WicketConfigurationPanelVisual`. For now, we will create a very simple configuration panel, shown in Figure 19.4.

The completed **Wicket Configuration** panel is far more detailed, as shown in Figure 19.5.

Once you have completed this chapter, you can have a look at the sample on the CD to learn more about the details of the completed configuration panel. For now, our panel will include only a `JLabel` and a `JTextField`. The `JTextField` is named `appClassTextField`.

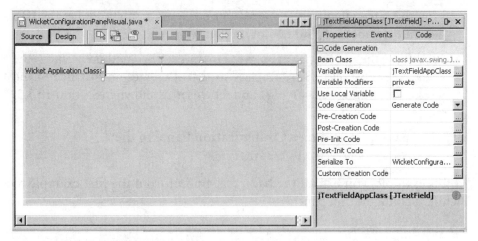

Figure 19.4: A simple **Wicket Configuration** panel

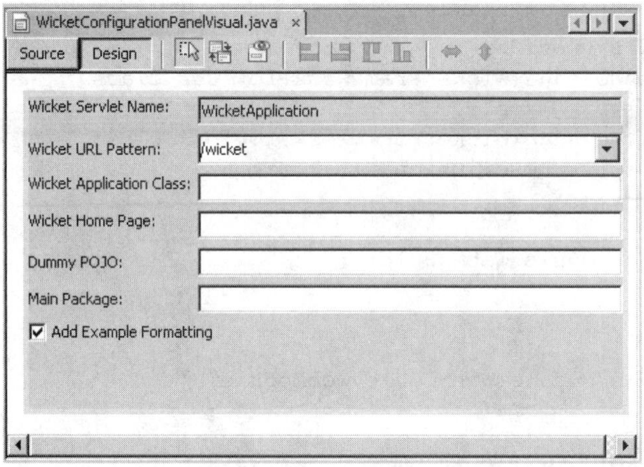

Figure 19.5: A finalized **Wicket Configuration** panel

3. Open the `WicketConfigurationPanel` class and notice that it implements a class from the NetBeans Wizard API. Change the implementation
so that `FrameworkConfigurationPanel` is implemented instead. Press
Alt-Shift-F to fix the import statements. When you click on the editor

hint, the IDE generates the `enableComponents()` method. Let the IDE generate the method, but do not implement it yet.

4. Modify the `getConfigurationPanel()` method in the `WicketFrameworkProvider` class so that it creates an instance of the `WicketConfigurationPanel` and returns it, as shown in Section 19.3.2.

19.3.2   Example: Adding a Configuration Panel to the `WebFrameworkProvider`

In this example, you extend the basic registration from the first example to include a configuration panel.

```
public class WicketFrameworkProvider extends
                                        WebFrameworkProvider {

  // Declare the configuration panel:
  private WicketConfigurationPanel panel;

  public WicketFrameworkProvider() {
    super(NbBundle.getMessage(WicketFrameworkProvider.class,
        "WicketFramework_Name"),
        NbBundle.getMessage(WicketFrameworkProvider.class,
        "WicketFramework_Description"));
  }

  public Set extend(WebModule webModule) {
    return null;
  }

  public boolean isInWebModule(WebModule webModule) {
    return true;
  }

  public File[] getConfigurationFiles(WebModule webModule) {
    return new File[0];
  }

  // Returns the lower part of the New Project wizard or
  // the Project Properties dialog box, where the user can
  // change settings specific to your framework.
  // The class returned here must implement
  // FrameworkConfigurationPanel. The class returned here is
  // the nonvisual side of the configuration panel:
```

```
public FrameworkConfigurationPanel getConfigurationPanel(
                                   WebModule webModule) {
  panel = new WicketConfigurationPanel();
  return panel;
}

}
```

After you have added the configuration panel to the `WebFramework-`
`Provider` implementation class, you can install the module again. In the
Frameworks panel, notice that when you select the framework's checkbox,
the lower part of the **Frameworks** panel shows the configuration panel
(Figure 19.6).

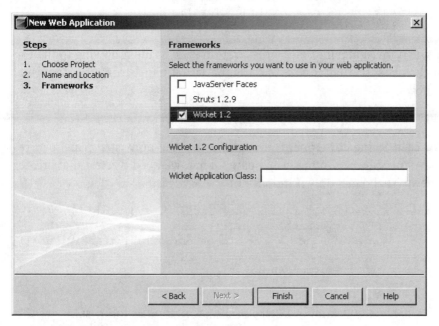

Figure 19.6: Installed **Wicket Configuration** panel

19.3.3   Coding the Configuration Panel

In your `WicketFrameworkProvider` class, the `extend()` method needs to
be able to access values from the configuration panel. For example, when a

Java class is created, the `extend()` method needs to know the class name that the user specified in the configuration panel. Therefore, you need to take some steps to prepare the panel for interaction with the `extend()` method.

Do the following:

1. In the visual panel, create getters and setters for all fields with which the user should interact. In our simple example, where we only want to create a single class, create a getter and setter as follows:

```
public String getAppClass(){
  return appClassTextField.getText();
}

public void setAppClass(String appClass){
  appClassTextField.setText(appClass);
}
```

2. In the nonvisual panel, add a declaration such as the following to the top of the class, so that you can access the visual panel from the nonvisual panel:

```
private WicketConfigurationPanelVisual configurationPanel;
```

3. For each Swing component, make sure that the nonvisual panel can retrieve the value set in the visual panel. First, we need a getter that creates a new visual panel only if it does not already exist:

```
private WicketConfigurationPanelVisual getTypedComponent() {
  if (configurationPanel == null) {
    configurationPanel = new WicketConfigurationPanelVisual();
  }
  return configurationPanel;
}
```

Change the default `getComponent()` method as follows:

```
public Component getComponent() {
  return getTypedComponent();
}
```

The `getTypedComponent()` method returns the visual panel, just as `getComponent()` does by default. However, for `getTypedComponent()`, the return type is `WicketConfigurationPanelVisual`, so that getAppClass() can be called on it. This is because in JDK 1.4 it is not possible to use a subtype instead of the original return type of a method when implementing or overriding it. It is, however, possible in JDK 1.5, so if you compile for this version, you can just implement getComponent() as follows:

```
WicketConfigurationPanelVisual getComponent() {
  if (configurationPanel == null) {
    configurationPanel = new WicketConfigurationPanelVisual();
  }
  return configurationPanel;
}
```

And then you would replace all usages of getTypedComponent() with getComponent().

The example on the CD provides further details on how the interaction between visual and nonvisual panels can be implemented.

4. Next, create getters and setters in the nonvisual panel for retrieving the class name from the visual panel as follows:

```
public String getAppClass(){
  return getTypedComponent().getAppClass();
}

public void setAppClass(String resource){
  getTypedComponent().setAppClass(resource);
}
```

You are now ready to complete the example in this chapter. For further guidance on coding the panel, look in the NetBeans sources and inspect JSFConfigurationPanel, JSFConfigurationPanelVisual, Struts-ConfigurationPanel, and StrutsConfigurationPanelVisual. In addition, you can inspect the Wicket implementations of these files on the CD.

19.4   Creating a Source Structure

The heart of the WebFrameworkProvider interface is the extend() method. It is the extend() method that determines the source structure and files that your NetBeans module will create.

19.4.1   Preparing to Use the `extend()` Method

Before you begin working on the `extend()` method, you need to declare some new dependencies. The following APIs must be included in the **Libraries** panel, which is in the module project's **Project Properties** dialog box:

- File System API
- Project API
- External Libraries
- Java Project Support

Next, create a Java file called `WicketConfigUtilities`, for some of the utility methods that you will use in this section. Similarly, the JSF framework module has a file called `JSFConfigUtitilies`, Struts has `StrutsConfigUtilities`.

19.4.2   Example: Defining the `extend()` Method

In this example, you study the `extend()` method provided by the `WicketFrameworkProvider` class. The `extend()` method works with a `WebModule` object, which represents the current Web application. This is the complete content of the `extend()` method:

```
public Set extend(WebModule webModule) {

  FileObject documentBase = webModule.getDocumentBase();
  Library lib = LibraryManager.getDefault().getLibrary(
              WicketConfigUtilities.LIB_WICKET_NAME);

  if (documentBase != null && lib != null) {
    Project project = FileOwnerQuery.getOwner(documentBase);
    ProjectClassPathExtender cpExtender =
      (ProjectClassPathExtender) project.getLookup().lookup(
      ProjectClassPathExtender.class);

    if (cpExtender != null) {
        try {
            cpExtender.addLibrary(lib);
        } catch (IOException ioe) {
            ErrorManager.getDefault().notify(ioe);
        }
```

```
    } else {
        ErrorManager.getDefault().log(
           "WebProjectClassPathExtender not found in the " +
           "project lookup of project: " +
           FileUtil.toFile(project.getProjectDirectory())));
    }

  FileObject webInf = webModule.getWebInf();
  if (webInf != null) {
    try {
        FileSystem fs = webInf.getFileSystem();
        fs.runAtomicAction(new CreateWicketFiles(webModule));
    } catch (IOException exc) {
        ErrorManager.getDefault().notify(exc);
        return null;
    }
  }
 }

  return null;
}
```

Notice this line in the listing above:

```
Library lib = LibraryManager.getDefault().getLibrary(
             WicketConfigUtilities.LIB_WICKET_NAME);
```

We want to ensure that the framework's source structure is only created if an appropriate library with JAR files is available in the **Library Manager**. Therefore, you need to define the name of the library in the WicketConfigUtilities class as follows:

```
public static final String LIB_WICKET_NAME = "Wicket";
```

As a result of the above lines, the JARs that you want to have added to the application's classpath must be in a library named Wicket. It must be registered in the **Library Manager**. A more user-friendly approach to ensuring that the required JARs are on the classpath is discussed in Section 19.5.

Next, notice this snippet from the listing above:

```
FileObject webInf = webModule.getWebInf();
if (webInf != null) {
  try {
      FileSystem fs = webInf.getFileSystem();
      fs.runAtomicAction(new CreateWicketFiles(webModule));
  } catch (IOException exc) {
      ErrorManager.getDefault().notify(exc);
      return null;
  }
}
```

The content of your application is sent to the `CreateWicketFiles` class as a parameter. This class creates the source structure's files. You will create this class in the following sections. To ensure that the activities involved in the creation of the new files are treated as one logical unit, the class does its work within an atomic action. However, the method is atomic only in the sense that no filesystem events will be fired during the atomic action. It is not atomic in the database sense, that is, partial results will not be rolled back if an exception is thrown in the middle of the atomic action.

19.4.3   Creating Templates

The `CreateWicketFiles` class, referred to in the previous section, makes use of templates when generating your source structure. This is the approach taken by all equivalent classes in framework support modules. The templates contain macros, which are automatically filled with the values that the user enters in the configuration panel.

19.4.4   A Template for Creating a Java File

A template can contain as much or as little as you would like to make available to your users. There are no restrictions. The values specified by the user in the configuration panel determine the content generated in the macros. Here is an example of a template file in the Wicket module. It is called `WicketApplication.template` and provides the application class, with application-wide settings such as the application's homepage:

```
/*
 * __NAME__.java
 *
 * Created on __DATE__, __TIME__
 */

package __NAME_OF_PACKAGE__;

import wicket.protocol.http.WebApplication;
/**
 *
 * @author __USER__
 * @version
 */

public class __NAME__ extends WebApplication {

  public __NAME__() {
  }

  public Class getHomePage() {
    return __NAME_OF_HOME_PAGE__.class;
  }
}
```

You can use this template file to create a file. Do the following:

1. Create a subpackage named `resources`.

2. Right-click the `resources` package, choose **New | File/Folder**, and choose **Empty File** in the **Other** category.

3. Name the file `WicketApplication.template` and click **Finish**.

4. Paste the template code above into the new file.

Repeat the process above for each artifact that you want to create programmatically. For example, the Wicket module's content is shown in Figure 19.7.

19.4.5   Preparing to Use a Template to Programmatically Create a Java File

In this section, you will learn how to make use of the template discussed in the previous section. First, you need to be able to access the template. The template is in a subpackage called `resources`. Therefore, you will send the

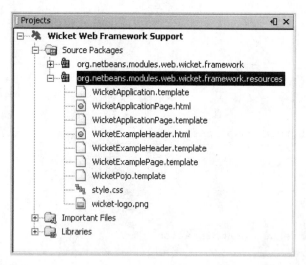

Figure 19.7: Resources package in the Wicket module

name of the template to the `readResource()` method, which will get the template from the `resources` package:

```
private String readResource(String name) throws IOException {
  return readTextResource(getClass().getResourceAsStream(
    "resources/" + name), ENCODING);
}
```

Next, you need to be able to read the template. The utility method below creates a `StringBuffer` made up of the lines in the template:

```
private static String readTextResource(InputStream is,
                       String encoding) throws IOException {
  StringBuffer sb = new StringBuffer();
  String lineSep = System.getProperty("line.separator");
  BufferedReader br =
    new BufferedReader(new InputStreamReader(is, encoding));
  try {
      String line = br.readLine();
      while (line != null) {
        sb.append(line);
        sb.append(lineSep);
        line = br.readLine();
      }
```

```
} finally {
    br.close();
}
return sb.toString();
}
```

Finally, you will need to be able to write files, using the code below:

```
private static void createFile(FileObject targetFolder,
    String name, String content) throws IOException {
  FileObject file = FileUtil.createData(targetFolder, name);
  writeFile(file, content, ENCODING);
}

private static void writeFile(FileObject file, String content,
    String encoding) throws IOException {
  FileLock lock = file.lock();
  try {
      BufferedWriter bw = new BufferedWriter(
        new OutputStreamWriter(file.getOutputStream(lock),
                               encoding));
      try {
          bw.write(content);
      } finally {
          bw.close();
      }
  } finally {
      lock.releaseLock();
  }
}
```

Most of the code in this section is just standard Java. Paste all of these utility methods into your `WicketFrameworkProvider` class. You will need them in the following section. Remember to declare the encoding:

```
private static final String ENCODING = "UTF-8";
```

19.4.6   Using a Template to Programmatically Create a Java File

In this section you use the `CreateWicketFiles` class to create a Java file. As discussed earlier, the class is called in an atomic action from the `WebFrameworkProvider`'s `extend()` method. Here the focus is on creating just one class, the `WicketApplication.java` file, used to change application-wide settings for applications that use the Wicket framework. The sample on the CD shows similar approaches for creating an HTML file, a CSS file, and an image.

```java
private class CreateWicketFiles implements
                                FileSystem.AtomicAction {

    private WebModule wm;
    private FileObject documentBase;
    private Project project;

    private FileObject targetFolder;

    private Map defaultArgs;

    public CreateWicketFiles(WebModule wm) {
        this.wm = wm;
    }

    // This is the method that creates the class:
    private void createAppClass() throws IOException {

        // First we obtain our template from the 'resources' folder,
        // using our 'readResource' utility method:
        String template = readResource("WicketApplication.template");

        // Next, we obtain the name of the class
        // from the WicketConfigurationPanel:
        String appClassName = panel.getAppClass();

        // We append '.java' to the class name:
        String appClassFileName = appClassName + ".java";

        Map args = new HashMap(defaultArgs);
        args.put("NAME", appClassName.replace('.', '/'));
        String content = formatTemplate(template, args);
        createFile(targetFolder, appClassFileName, content);
    }

    private String formatTemplate(String template, Map args) {
        MapFormat formatter = new MapFormat(args);
        formatter.setLeftBrace("__");
        formatter.setRightBrace("__");
        formatter.setExactMatch(false);
        return formatter.format(template);
    }
```

```java
public void run() throws IOException {
  documentBase = wm.getDocumentBase();
  if (documentBase == null) {
    return;
  }
  project = FileOwnerQuery.getOwner(documentBase);
  if (project == null) {
    return;
  }
  SourceGroup[] sourceGroups = ProjectUtils.getSources(project).
    getSourceGroups(JavaProjectConstants.SOURCES_TYPE_JAVA);
  if (sourceGroups.length == 0) {
    return;
  }

  // We obtain the root folder, which we need
  // so that we can write our file to our package:
  FileObject targetRoot = sourceGroups[0].getRootFolder();

  // Here we hard code the main package:
  String mainPackage = "org.example";

  // We create the target folder using the root folder
  // and with the hard-coded main package:
  targetFolder = FileUtil.createFolder(targetRoot,
    mainPackage.replace('.', '/'));

  // Here are the values that will replace the macros in
  // the template. Notice that, to keep the example simple,
  // we hardcode the name of the package and the name of
  // the home page; normally you would let the user set these
  // in the configuration panel.
  defaultArgs = new HashMap();
  defaultArgs.put("USER", System.getProperty("user.name"));

  defaultArgs.put("DATE", DateFormat.getDateInstance(
    DateFormat.LONG).format(new Date()));
  defaultArgs.put("TIME", DateFormat.getTimeInstance(
    DateFormat.SHORT).format(new Date()));
  defaultArgs.put("NAME_OF_PACKAGE", "org.example");
  defaultArgs.put("NAME_OF_HOME_PAGE", "home");

  createAppClass();
}

}
```

19.4.7 Trying Out the Framework Support Module

You can already try out your module! Install it again.

Before going further, remember that the extend() method expects a library called Wicket to be available in the **Library Manager**. Later in this chapter, we will discuss an approach that will allow the user to use the **Frameworks** panel to add a Wicket library to the **Library Manager**. However, for now, you must add Wicket to the **Library Manager** yourself, otherwise the extend() method will fail.

Once the **Library Manager** has a library called Wicket, create a new Web application and type WicketApplication in the **Wicket Configuration** panel, as shown in Figure 19.8.

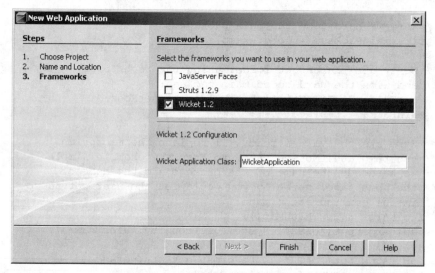

Figure 19.8: Configuration panel with the name of application class

After you click **Finish**, you will see your new file created within a package with the name that you hardcoded in the extend() method. Since you have not created the home.class, which you also hardcoded in the extend() method, you will see a red underline mark in the editor (Figure 19.9).

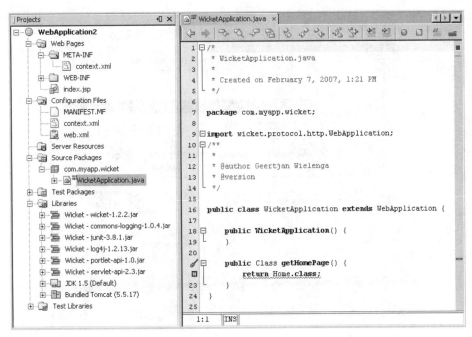

Figure 19.9: Your first generated Java file

19.5   Letting the User Select a Library in the Frameworks Panel

Instead of expecting the user to have the Web framework's JAR files in the **Library Manager**, which is the case in the `extend()` method discussed earlier, you can provide an alternative configuration panel where the JAR files can be selected from disk. First, you would need to test whether the JAR files are available in the **Library Manager**. If they are not, the alternative configuration panel would be displayed, allowing the user to browse for the JAR files.

In the Wicket module, the user does this by using the alternative configuration panel shown in Figure 19.10.

Once an appropriate folder has been selected, the standard configuration panel is shown. If an appropriate folder is not selected, the standard configuration panel is **not** shown, so that the user cannot complete the wizard. This

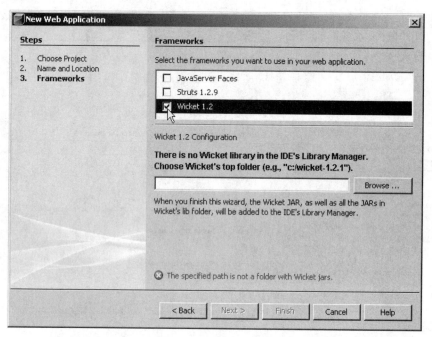

Figure 19.10: Selecting a library

ensures that when the wizard is completed, the JAR files are guaranteed to be on the classpath.

To implement this scenario, you will need to create two panels, instead of just the one described above. One provides the standard configuration panel and the other, the alternative configuration panel. Using CardLayout makes this possible, as shown in Figures 19.11 and 19.12.

Only when the JAR files are not in the **Library Manager** you need the alternative configuration panel to appear. All the code needed for this scenario is provided with the related sample on the CD.

19.6   Project Properties Dialog Box and Web Frameworks

When the user clicks **Finish** at the end of the **New Project** wizard, a Web application with a source structure that complies with the selected Web

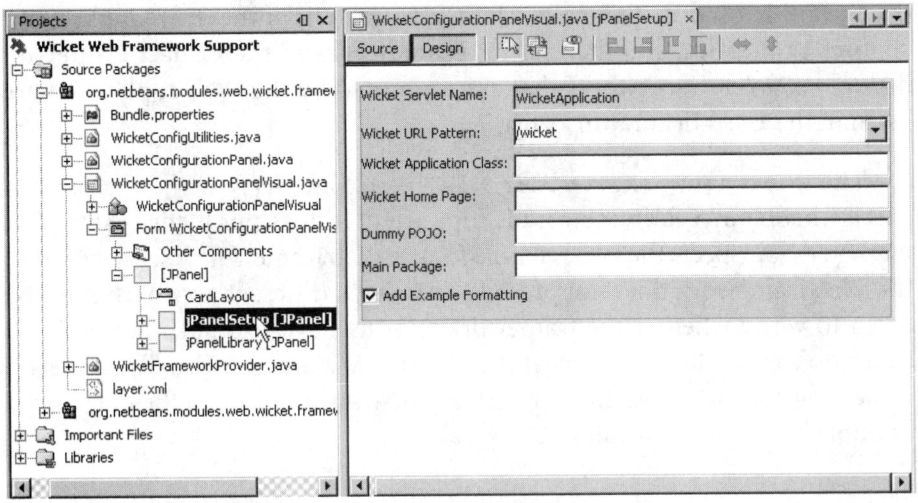

Figure 19.11: First panel

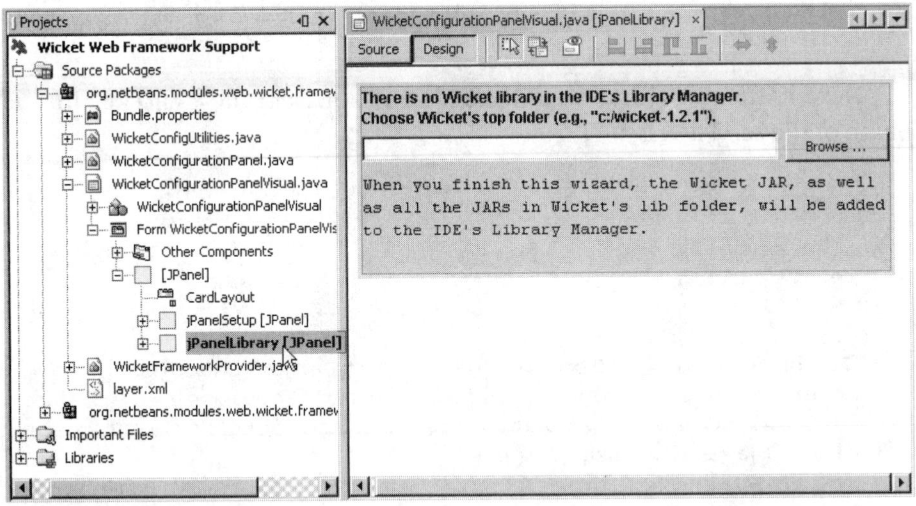

Figure 19.12: Second panel

framework is created. However, the user can choose to select a different Web framework. Or, if no Web frameworks were selected in the **New Project** wizard, one can be selected afterwards. A Web application's **Project Properties** dialog box is used in this case. The user right-clicks the Web application, chooses **Properties**, and then selects **Frameworks** in the **Project Properties** dialog box. Web frameworks that are supported by the Web application are listed in the **Used Frameworks** list.

The `WebFrameworkProvider`'s `isInWebModule()` method is used to check whether a Web framework is supported. It does this by delegating to a method that inspects the `web.xml` file for the Web framework's servlet entries. If a Web framework does not provide a servlet, a different approach must be taken to verify whether the framework is in use. For example, the project's classpath can be checked to see if the JAR files are present. Usually, however, inspecting the `web.xml` file for servlet entries should be sufficient, as the example below demonstrates.

19.6.1   Example: `isInWebModule()` Method

```
public boolean isInWebModule(WebModule webModule) {
  return (WicketConfigUtilities.getActionServlet(
    webModule.getDeploymentDescriptor()) == null) ? false : true;
}
```

Next, in the configuration utilities file, the `web.xml` file is checked for the name of the servlet class:

```
public static Servlet getActionServlet(FileObject dd) {

  if (dd == null) {
    return null;
  }
  try {
    WebApp webApp = DDProvider.getDefault().getDDRoot(dd);
    return (Servlet) webApp.findBeanByName("Servlet",
      "ServletClass", "wicket.protocol.http.WicketServlet");
  } catch (java.io.IOException e) {
    return null;
  }

}
```

19.7   Finishing Up

You have registered your Web framework and enabled your users to generate a source structure with artifacts that are relevant for the framework. You now have a very basic support for your framework. However, it is probably already quite useful. Find some users interested in the framework and ask them to test the support that you created! Their feedback will help you plan the next steps to take to further develop the module.

To extend the module, consider implementing some of the following features: syntax highlighting, code completion, hyperlinking, component palette with drag-and-drop items, multiview editors, error annotations, **Options** window extensions, and JavaHelp documentation.

CHAPTER TWENTY

Web Services

20.1 Introduction

Java API for XML Web Services (JAX-WS) 2.0—JSR 224—is an important part of the Java EE 5 Platform. A follow-on release of Java API for XML-based RPC 1.1 (JAX-RPC), JAX-WS simplifies the task of developing Web services using Java technology. It addresses some of the issues in JAX-RPC 1.1 by providing support for multiple protocols such as SOAP 1.1, SOAP 1.2, XML, and by providing a facility for supporting additional protocols along with HTTP. JAX-WS uses JAXB 2.0 for data binding and supports customizations to control generated service endpoint interfaces. With its support for annotations, JAX-WS simplifies Web service development and reduces the size of runtime JAR files.

This chapter takes you through the basics of creating an application that consumes a Web service. To do so, you start by using a powerful wizard, found in the IDE, which creates a JAX-WS Web service client in a Java application project. A Web service is represented in the IDE by nodes in the **Projects** window, each node corresponding to an operation of the Web service. You will learn how to invoke a Web service operation, which in our example returns definitions for a given word.

Once you have tested your simple client, you create a JAR file from it and wrap it in a library wrapper module project. You then attach this project to a module suite, along with a functionality module that provides a user interface.

Next, exclude the IDE's modules, because what we want to create is not an IDE-like application but a standalone application that only uses the NetBeans Platform. In this chapter, we add a functionality module that provides a window component where the user can type a word and see the returned definitions.

The procedure described in this chapter is the same as you would use with any other NetBeans module when you want to consume a Web service.

20.2 Creating and Testing a Web Service Client

In this section we create a JAR file containing a Web service client. We will need it in the next section where we will create a dependency from our module on the JAR file via a library wrapper module. Then we will call the Web service from our module, using the functionality provided by the JAR file.

Before we begin creating NetBeans projects, let's test the URL to the Web service. Once we know the Web service works, we will integrate it into NetBeans.

1. Paste the URL below into a Web browser:

   ```
   http://services.aonaware.com/DictService/DictService.asmx?
   op=Define
   ```

   The test site for the `DictService`'s `Define` operation opens in your browser. Type `and` into the **word** field. The Web browser should now display Figure 20.1.

2. Click **Invoke**. The browser displays definitions for the word "and" retrieved from the Web service, in XML format, as shown in Figure 20.2.

   Now that we know the Web service is up and running, we will create a simple client that calls the Web service and invokes its `Define` operation.

1. Create a Java application project and name it `Dict`.

2. Right-click the `Dict` project node and choose **New | File/Folder**. In the **New File** wizard, choose **Web Service Client** from the **Web Services** category. Click **Next**.

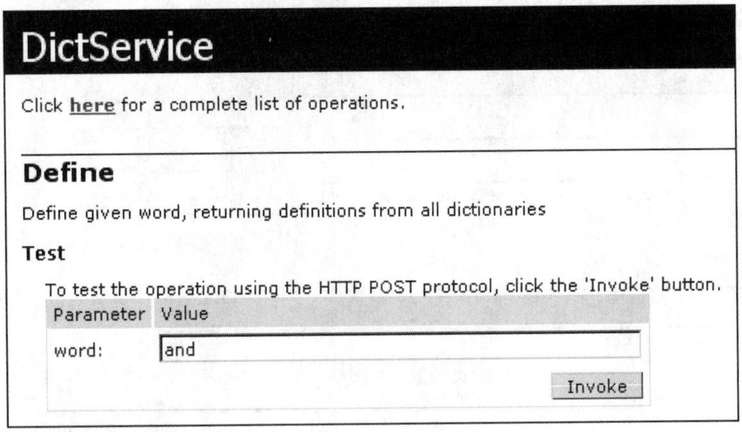

Figure 20.1: Testing the Web service

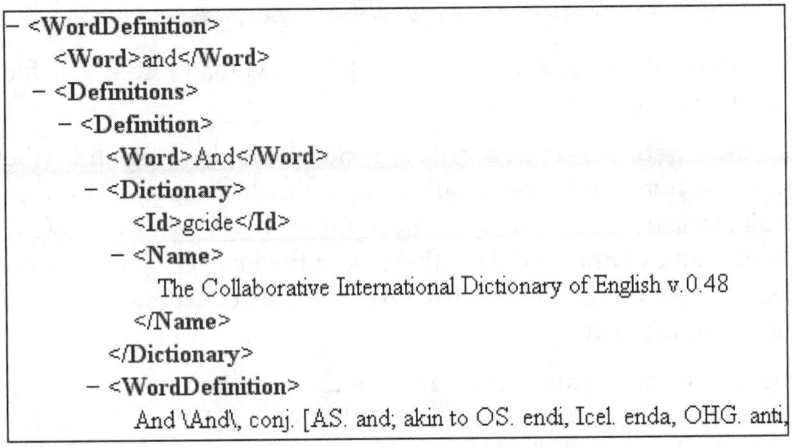

Figure 20.2: Result of testing the Web service

3. Click **WSDL URL**. Paste this WSDL URL in the **WSDL URL** text field:

```
http://services.aonaware.com/DictService/DictService.asmx?⏎
WSDL
```

4. Type `cli` in the **Package** text field.

   You should now see Figure 20.3.

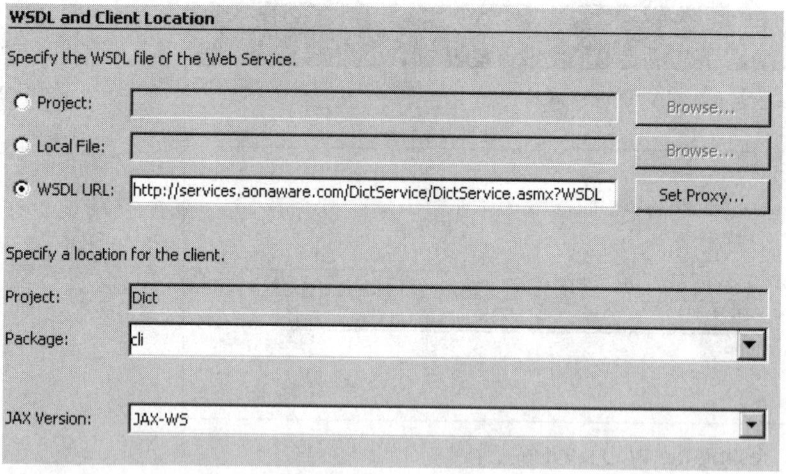

Figure 20.3: **Web Service Client** wizard

Click **Finish**. Wait a moment while the IDE downloads the WSDL file and generates stubs for the client.

5. Within the `Web Service References` node, expand the `DictService.asmx` node and its subnodes in the **Projects** window. Notice that all the operations made available by the Web service are represented as nodes. You can drag and drop them from the **Projects** window into your code, as shown in Figure 20.4. We will use this drag-and-drop functionality in the next step.

6. In the `Dict` project, expand the `Source Packages` node, then expand the `dict` package. Open `Main.java` in the Source Editor. Drag the `Define` method from the **Projects** window and drop it in the `public static void main(String[] args)` method.

The IDE generates code for you. This code is sufficient for contacting the Web service and retrieving values. However, we need to process the returned values. A `java.util.List` is returned from the Web service, because more than one definition can be returned per word. We will process the returned `java.util.List` in the next step.

Rewrite the method as follows (the additions and changes are in bold in the code listing below):

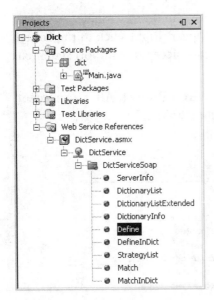

Figure 20.4: Web service in **Projects** window

```
public static void main(String[] args) {
   try { // Call Web Service Operation
       cli.DictService service = new cli.DictService();
       cli.DictServiceSoap port = service.getDictServiceSoap();
       // TODO: initialize WS operation arguments here
       java.lang.String word = "and";
       // TODO: process result here
       cli.WordDefinition result = port.define(word);

       ArrayOfDefinition list = result.getDefinitions();
       List def = list.getDefinition();
       // We iterate through the returned List
       // and display the definition:
       Iterator it = def.iterator();
       while(it.hasNext()){
           Definition one = (Definition) it.next();
           String onedef = one.getWordDefinition();
           System.out.println(onedef);
       }
   } catch (Exception ex) {
       // TODO: handle custom exceptions here
   } // TODO: code application logic here
}
```

Make sure that you define a word for the `word` variable, as shown above. Several red underline markings appear. Right-click in the Source Editor and choose **Fix Imports**. In each case, accept the import statement suggested.

7. Right-click the `Dict` project and choose **Run Project**. After a moment, the **Output** window should appear (Figure 20.5).

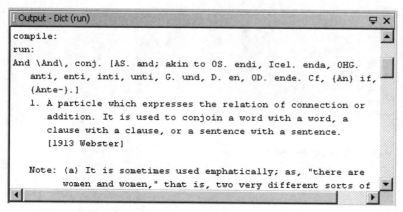

Figure 20.5: Web service results in **Output** window

If the **Output** window shows something similar to Figure 20.5, you have successfully tested your Web service client and are ready to continue with this chapter.

> If you do not get a response from the Web service and if you are behind a firewall, check that your proxy settings are correct. To check your proxy settings, choose **Options** under the **Tools** menu. Alternatively, the Web service might be down, or it might have been removed by its owner.

8. Right-click the `Dict` project and choose **Build Project**. In the **Files** window, look in the `dist` folder. You should see Figure 20.6.

Figure 20.6: Built JAR in **Files** window

Notice the project's JAR file, called `Dict.jar`. Also notice a folder called `lib`. The JARs in the `lib` folder are needed by `Dict.jar`. In the next section, we will wrap `Dict.jar` in one library wrapper module and the JAR files in the `lib` folder in another library wrapper module.

20.3   Integrating the Web Service Client

In this section, we create a module suite project to contain our module project, as well as two library wrapper modules for the Web service client functionality. We also create a module project containing our module's functionality. We use the JAR files to call the Web service from our functionality module. The functionality module allows the user to type a word, sends it to the Web service, and displays the returned definitions.

1.   In the **New Project** wizard, choose the **Module Suite** project type from the **NetBeans Plug-in Modules** category. Name it `DefineWordsSuite`.

We need to use the module suite project because we want to create a standalone application. We need to deploy two library wrapper modules, which we will create below, together with our functionality module.

These modules all depend on each other, so we need to create dependencies between them.

2. Create a library wrapper module project that contains the `Dict.jar` that you built in the previous section. To create a library wrapper module project, expand the `DefineWordsSuite`, right-click the `Modules` node, and choose **Add New Library**. Next, browse to the JAR file and complete the wizard.

3. Create another library wrapper module project for all the JAR files in the `dist/lib` folder. You can use Shift-Click to select all the JARs.

4. Create a new module called `DefineWords`. Make sure it belongs to the module suite. The easiest way to do this is to right-click the `Modules` node again and choose **Add New**.

Now the module suite project should look like Figure 20.7.

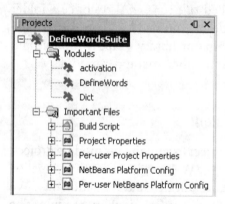

Figure 20.7: Module suite project

5. In the `DefineWords` module, create dependencies on both library wrapper modules. Also, set a dependency in the `Dict` project on the library wrapper module project that wraps the `dist/lib` folder.

6. In the `DefineWords` module, create a new window component, with `Define` as its class name prefix, and design it as shown in Figure 20.8.

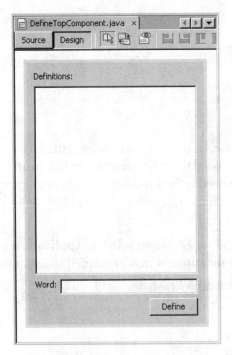

Figure 20.8: Designing the window component

In the code snippet that follows, the name of the `JTextArea` is `displayArea` and the name of the `JTextField` is `entryField`.

7.   Define the `performAction()` event as follows, using the same code as in the Java application project's Web service client created earlier:

```
displayArea.setText("");
try { // Call Web service operation
    cli.DictService service = new cli.DictService();
    cli.DictServiceSoap port = service.getDictServiceSoap();
    // TODO: initialize WS operation arguments here
    java.lang.String word = entryField.getText();
    // TODO: process result here
    cli.WordDefinition result = port.define(word);
    ArrayOfDefinition list = result.getDefinitions();
    List def = list.getDefinition();
    // We iterate through the returned List
    // and display the definitions:
    Iterator it = def.iterator();
```

```
      while(it.hasNext()){
        Definition one = (Definition) it.next();
        String onedef = one.getWordDefinition();
        displayArea.setText(onedef);
      }
} catch (Exception ex) {
    displayArea.setText("Failed");
}
```

Next, we brand the module suite. In this step, we exclude the IDE's modules from the suite—we do not need them because we are not creating an IDE-like application. All we need is the functionality provided by the modules we have created in this chapter, together with the NetBeans Platform that provides the application's framework.

8.   Right-click the module suite and choose **Properties**. In the **Application** panel, click **Create Standalone Application**. When prompted to do so, click **Exclude** to remove the IDE's modules from your application. You can also specify a title for the application's title bar, as shown in Figure 20.9.

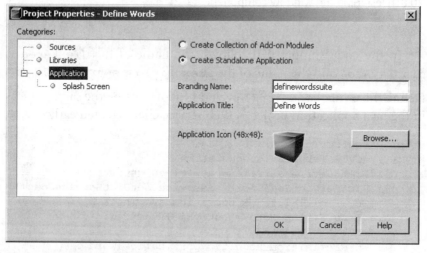

Figure 20.9: Branding the application

9. Run the module suite project. The NetBeans Platform starts up. The three modules in the module suite are installed in the NetBeans Platform.

10. You should now see your newly created window. Type a word in the text field and click **Define**. After a pause, you should see the definitions of the typed word, as shown in Figure 20.10.

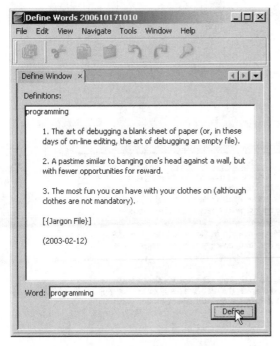

Figure 20.10: Definitions of "programming"

 If the Web service fails to return definitions, check your proxy settings in the **Options** window, which you can access from the **Tools** menu. Remember also that the Web service might be down or that it might have been removed by its owner.

Now you can reimplement this Web service in a variety of ways. For example, you can create a code completion box for text files, with entries retrieved from a file selected in the **Options** window. The code completion item's documentation task can retrieve the definitions of the current entry in the code completion box from the Web service, as shown in Figure 20.11.

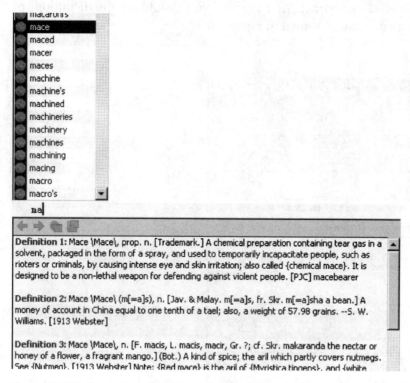

Figure 20.11: Rendering of Web service results

Chapter 14 provides all the details you need for creating a code completion box.

CHAPTER TWENTY-ONE

JavaHelp Documentation

The JavaHelp system is an open source project and a JSR reference implementation that can add a built-in set of HTML help topics to your NetBeans Platform applications. Each NetBeans module can provide its own JavaHelp *help sets*. However, within a NetBeans Platform application, it is more common to have a single module that provides JavaHelp documentation for the whole application. The IDE merges the individual help sets into a single whole. You can use a template in the IDE to generate a minimal help set, after which you can extend it by adding HTML help topics.

In this chapter, you will learn how to create a JavaHelp help set. You will use the IDE's template, add a few help topics, and hook them to elements in your application's user interface. You will also see how to customize the JavaHelp infrastructure that the IDE provides.

For more general information on JavaHelp documentation, see the JavaHelp User Guide.[1]

---

1. http://java.sun.com/products/javahelp/download_binary.html

21.1   Creating a Help Set

The starting point for creating your application's help set is to use a template. Let's do it—and then add a few sample help topics to the help set that the IDE generates.

1. Use the **JavaHelp Help Set** wizard to create a new help set, as shown in Figure 21.1.

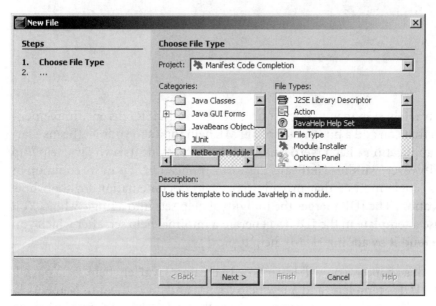

Figure 21.1: Creating a JavaHelp help set

The **JavaHelp Help Set** template creates a set of files for you to edit including, for example, the help set's table of contents and index. It also creates an initial help topic for you and registers it in the table of contents.

2. Click **Next**. The second step in the wizard lists the files it created with their locations (Figure 21.2).

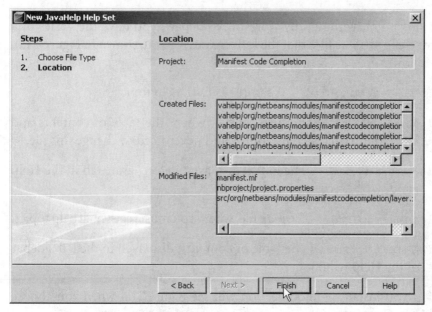

Figure 21.2: Final step of the **JavaHelp Help Set** template

3. Click **Finish**. In the **Projects** window, you now have a new help set (Figure 21.3).

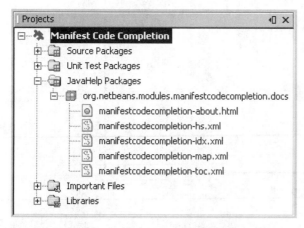

Figure 21.3: New help set in the **Projects** window

At this point, without any work on your part, you have the basics of a JavaHelp help set. The files that the IDE creates for you, shown in Figure 21.3, are as follows:

ModuleName-about.html   A sample HTML help topic.

ModuleName-hs.xml   The help set file, where the table of contents and index file are registered. You should never need to change this file.

ModuleName-idx.xml   The index, displayed in a separate tab in the **Help** window.

ModuleName-map.xml   The map file, where you must register all help topics.

ModuleName-toc.xml   The table of contents, displayed in the left sidebar of the **Help** window.

After you install the module, you will see Figure 21.4 when you choose **Help | Help Contents**.

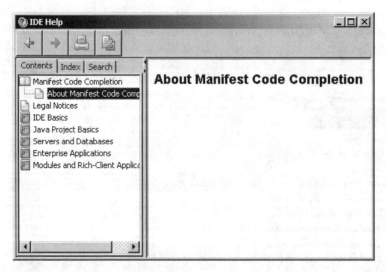

Figure 21.4: Newly installed help set

The remainder of this chapter focuses on adding help topics and the various ways in which you can tweak the help set.

21.1.1 Adding New Help Topics

In this section, you will add your first new help topic to the help set.

1. In the **Projects** window, right-click the package that contains the help files generated by the IDE. Choose **New | File/Folder**. Under **Categories**, choose **Other**. Under **File Types**, choose **HTML File**. Click **Next**. Name the HTML file and click **Finish**.

2. To register the new HTML file in the help set, open the file that ends in "-map.xml". Add an entry for the new HTML file.

3. To include the new HTML file in the table of contents, open the file that ends in "-toc.xml". Add an entry for the new HTML file. Make sure the map ID matches the ID of the entry registered in the map file.

4. To include the new HTML file in the index, open the file that ends in "-idx.xml". Add an entry for the new HTML file. Make sure that the map ID matches the ID of the entry registered in the map file.

5. Install the module again and notice that your help set has a new topic.

 You can also use the map file to match help topics with parts of the UI, so that an appropriate topic is displayed when a user clicks a **Help** button (or presses F1). There are several ways to assign an ID to a UI component. The most straightforward way is to use the `org.openide.util.HelpCtx` class. `HelpCtx` can create an ID from the UI component's fully qualified class name, or you can specify a string for the ID. For more complex scenarios, refer to the related Javadoc.[2]

---

2. Connecting Help in NetBeans: From Help Set Installation to Hooking up Context-Sensitive Help (`www.netbeans.org/download/dev/javadoc/org-netbeans-modules-javahelp/org/netbeans/api/javahelp/doc-files/help-guide.html`).

21.2   Removing the IDE's Help Sets

Several modules in the IDE—for example, the module that lets users create Web applications—provide their own help sets. It is not a problem if the module that you are working on is intended to extend the IDE, because your module's help set simply supplements the existing help sets in the IDE. However, if you are creating your own application on top of the NetBeans Platform and want to include a module's functionality without its help sets, this section describes how to remove the IDE's help sets from your application.

 If you want to exclude a module completely—that is, together with its help set—use the **Module Manager** under the **Tools** menu.

Like most other parts of your application that impact the user interface, JavaHelp help sets are registered in the module layer file, in the `Services/JavaHelp` folder. You can manually delete help sets provided by other modules by appending the "_hidden" tag to the name of the file that registers the files in the help set. For example, if you want to hide a help set with the set registration file called `org-netbeans-modules-j2ee-helpset.xml`, edit the module layer file as follows:

```
<?xml version="1.0" encoding="UTF-8"?>
<!DOCTYPE filesystem PUBLIC "-//NetBeans//DTD Filesystem 1.1//EN"
  "http://www.netbeans.org/dtds/filesystem-1_1.dtd">
<filesystem>
  <folder name="Services">
    <folder name="JavaHelp">
      <file name="org-netbeans-modules-j2ee-helpset.xml_hidden"/>
    </folder>
  </folder>
</filesystem>
```

However, this method assumes that you know the name of the help set file used by a different module. That is not always the case. For this reason, the IDE provides a user interface that displays, among other things, the help sets that are available to an application.

1. Expand the module suite's **Important Files** node, then expand the **XML Layer** node. Notice the <**this layer in context**> node, shown in Figure 21.5.

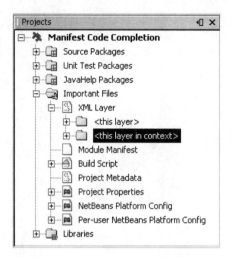

Figure 21.5: This layer in context

Within this node you find visual representations of all entries registered in all the modules that make up your application.

2. Expand the **<this layer in context>** node. Within it, find the **Services** node. There, find a node named **JavaHelp**. When you right-click an entry within this node, you can delete the node, as shown in Figure 21.6.

When you choose **Delete** for any of the entries in the **JavaHelp** node, the IDE creates "_hidden" entries in the layer file. For example, if you delete all the entries that the IDE provides by default in NetBeans IDE 5.5, the layer file will contain the following entries:

```
<?xml version="1.0" encoding="UTF-8"?>
<!DOCTYPE filesystem
  PUBLIC "-//NetBeans//DTD Filesystem 1.1//EN"
  "http://www.netbeans.org/dtds/filesystem-1_1.dtd">
<filesystem>
  <folder name="Services">
    <folder name="JavaHelp">
      <!--All 9 subhelpsets will be hidden: -->
      <file name="com-sun-enterprise-tools-studio-j2ee-⏎
helpset.xml_hidden"/>
```

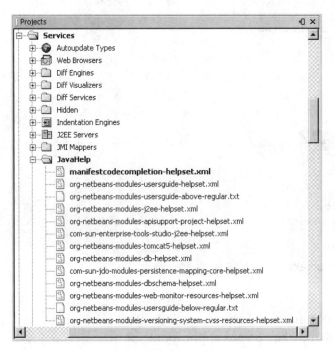

Figure 21.6: Deleting a help set

```
        <file name="org-netbeans-modules-j2ee-helpset.xml_↵
hidden"/>
        <file name="org-netbeans-modules-usersguide-helpset.↵
xml_hidden"/>
        <file name="org-netbeans-modules-apisupport-project-↵
helpset.xml_hidden"/>
        <file name="org-netbeans-modules-web-monitor-↵
resources-helpset.xml_hidden"/>
        <file name="org-netbeans-modules-db-helpset.xml_↵
hidden"/>
        <file name="org-netbeans-modules-tomcat5-helpset.↵
xml_hidden"/>
        <file name="org-netbeans-modules-dbschema-helpset.↵
xml_hidden"/>
        <file name="org-netbeans-modules-versioning-system-↵
cvss-resources-helpset.xml_hidden"/>
    </folder>
  </folder>
</filesystem>
```

You can rearrange the order of help sets by dragging and dropping the entries in the **JavaHelp** node. Again, the IDE creates corresponding entries in the layer file.

21.3   Branding the Help Set's Default Texts

By default, the title bar of the help set in your application contains the text "IDE Help." This makes sense in the context of the IDE, but if you are creating your own application, you probably want the title bar to display the name of your own application. In addition, the **JavaHelp Help Set** has a default topic that you probably do not want in your own help set (Figure 21.7).

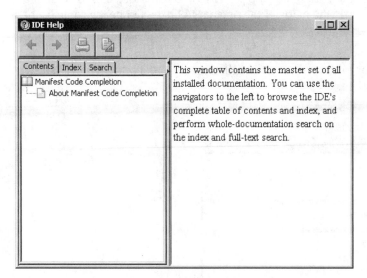

Figure 21.7: Default title bar and help topic

In this section, we will brand the default title bar and help topic. Branding is done in a folder called `branding`, which the IDE creates for you when you indicate that your module suite is going to provide an application, rather than a deployment unit for a collection of related modules.

1. First, we let the IDE create our `branding` folder. Right-click the module suite and choose **Properties**. In the **Project Properties** dialog box, choose the **Application** category. Select **Create Standalone Application**. Click **Exclude**. Click **OK**. You have now excluded all the IDE's modules—and thus all the help sets that accompany them. Close the **Project Properties** dialog box.

2. Open the **Files** window. Expand the module suite node. Notice that you have a folder called `branding`.

3. In the `branding/modules` folder, create a folder called `org-netbeans-modules-javahelp.jar`. Create a chain of nested subfolders `org/netbeans/modules/javahelp/resources` within this new folder.

 The path *must* match the path in the original JAR, as shown above. However, the name of the original JAR need not be the same as the folder name.

Within that folder, create a file called `masterHelpSet.xml`, as shown in Figure 21.8.

Figure 21.8: Branded `masterHelpSet.xml`

4. Copy the XML content below and paste it in the `masterHelpSet.xml` file. Alternatively, get the original file, which you can find in the NetBeans sources, within the folder structure shown in Figure 21.8. In particular, notice the following tags:

`<TITLE tag>`   The content of this tag, as shown in the example below, is `IDE Help`. This is the default title of the help set.

`<homeID tag>`   The content of this tag, as shown in the file below, is `org.netbeans.api.javahelp.MASTER_ID`. This is the map ID of the default topic.

```xml
<?xml version="1.0" encoding="UTF-8"?>
<!DOCTYPE helpset PUBLIC "-//Sun Microsystems Inc.//↵
DTD JavaHelp HelpSet Version 2.0//EN"
  "http://java.sun.com/products/javahelp/helpset_2_0.dtd">

<helpset version="2.0">
  <title>IDE Help</title>
  <maps>
    <homeID>org.netbeans.api.javahelp.MASTER_ID</homeID>
    <mapref location="masterHelpMap.jhm"/>
  </maps>
  <view mergetype="javax.help.UniteAppendMerge">
    <name>TOC</name>
    <label>Contents</label>
    <type>javax.help.TOCView</type>
    <data>masterHelpToc.xml</data>
  </view>
  <view mergetype="javax.help.SortMerge">
    <name>Index</name>
    <label>Index</label>
    <type>javax.help.IndexView</type>
  </view>
  <view>
    <name>Search</name>
    <label>Search</label>
    <type>javax.help.SearchView</type>
  </view>
```

```
   <presentation default="true" displayviews="true"
               displayviewimages="false">
     <name>main window</name>
     <toolbar>
       <helpaction image="helpviewer_back">javax.help.↵
BackAction</helpaction>
       <helpaction image="helpviewer_forward">javax.help.↵
ForwardAction</helpaction>
       <helpaction image="helpviewer_print">javax.help.↵
PrintAction</helpaction>
       <helpaction image="helpviewer_page-setup">javax.↵
help.PrintSetupAction</helpaction>
     </toolbar>
   </presentation>
   <presentation displayviews="false">
     <name>NBSecondaryWindow</name>
     <size width="600" height="400"/>
     <location x="200" y="200"/>
   </presentation>
</helpset>
```

5. Run the application. After you open the help set, the title bar will display whatever value you set for the <title> element, as shown in Figure 21.9.

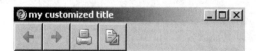

Figure 21.9: Customized help title

Similarly, if you changed the value of the <homeID> element to the map ID of one of your own help topics, you will see the default help topic changed accordingly.

CHAPTER TWENTY-TWO

Update Centers

22.1   Introduction

The IDE's **Update Center** wizard lets the user update the IDE's installed modules. When the user runs the **Update Center** wizard to connect to an update center, the IDE checks if there are new modules or new versions of already installed modules available. If new or updated modules are available, the user can select, download, and install them. You can incorporate this functionality from the IDE into your own application based on the NetBeans Platform. Before we look at how to do that, let's see what an update center is and how it is used.

An update center is nothing more than an XML file known as the *autoupdate descriptor* together with the NetBeans modules that it describes. The autoupdate descriptor lists all the NetBeans modules that you would like to distribute. For each module, the descriptor provides information such as its name, description, and a list of modules that it depends on. Most importantly, the autoupdate descriptor specifies a URL for each module that it describes. Each module, in the *NetBeans Module (NBM)* packaging format, must be accessible to clients, generally over HTTP. The autoupdate descriptor itself must also be accessible. The descriptor and the modules it refers to may all reside on the same server, or they may be spread across multiple servers if that is more convenient to the publisher. After the autoupdate descriptor and its associated modules have been published to a server, you make the modules available to your users via a URL. The URL points to the autoupdate descriptor and must be registered in the user's application. This can be done in one of two ways:

- **Automatically.** You can provide a module that registers the URL to the update center. This module can be generated in the IDE, without any coding on your part. When the user installs the module, the URL is automatically registered.

- **Manually.** You must tell the user what the URL to your autoupdate descriptor is. Then, the user needs to register the URL to your autoupdate descriptor. This can be done manually in the **Options** window.

Once the URL to the update center is registered, your users can download and install your modules via the **Update Center** wizard found under the IDE's—or under your own application's—**Tools** menu. Not only new modules, but new versions of existing modules can be distributed in this way.

In this chapter, we will look at how you can leverage this mechanism in your own applications built on top of the NetBeans Platform.

22.2   Adding the IDE's Update Center Functionality

When you first create a new application, there is no **Update Center** menu item under the **Tools** menu. For example, after creating a standalone project named TestApp, as described in Section 1.2.2, you will have an application similar to that in Figure 22.1.

The **Update Center** menu item is absent because, when you make a suite a standalone application and exclude the IDE's modules, the autoupdate module is also excluded. You need to tell the application to include the module that provides the NetBeans IDE's **Update Center** wizard, as well as its supporting functionality—the menu item and the **Module Manager**. Close the TestApp application and go back to the IDE.

1. Right-click the **TestApp** node in the **Projects** window. Choose **Properties**. In the **Libraries** panel, expand the **platform6** node. Select **Auto Update**. Click **OK**.

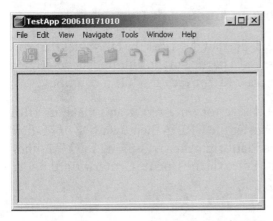

Figure 22.1: Empty NetBeans Platform application

2. Right-click the **TestApp** node and choose **Clean and Build All**. Right-click the **TestApp** node and choose **Run**.

   The application starts up again.

3. After the application has started, open the **Tools** menu (Figure 22.2).

   Now the **Update Center** menu item is available. In addition, you see the **Module Manager** menu item, which is used for installing, uninstalling, enabling, and disabling modules. You can use either of the two menu items to install modules from someone's update center.

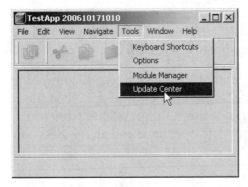

Figure 22.2: Menu item for the **Update Center** wizard

22.3   Creating and Distributing an Autoupdate Descriptor

An autoupdate descriptor is an XML file that describes the NBM files that you want to make available to your users. In particular, an autoupdate descriptor specifies a name, a description, and a URL for each module it describes.

After you put an autoupdate descriptor on a server and make its URL available to your users, they can register the URL in their own IDE or in their application built on the NetBeans Platform. After registering the URL, they can download and install your NBM files via the **Update Center** wizard under the **Tools** menu.

22.3.1   Using the IDE to Create an Autoupdate Descriptor

1. Add a few modules to the TestApp module suite by right-clicking the module suite's **Modules** node and choosing **Add New**, **Add New Library**, or **Add Existing**. For example, add three modules, called module1, module2, and module3. Once you have a few modules, continue with the next step.

2. In the **Projects** window, right-click the module suite's project node. Choose **Create NBMs**, as shown in Figure 22.3.

 If you do not see the **Create NBMs** menu item shown above, you are using NetBeans IDE 5.0 without the Module Development Update 1 module. Either install that module from the update center, or upgrade to NetBeans IDE 5.5 (or later).

The IDE builds the NBM files in the module suite project. The IDE also creates a file called updates.xml, which is the autoupdate descriptor. To see it, look in the **Files** window (Ctrl-2) as shown in Figure 22.4.

Tweak the autoupdate descriptor, if needed. For example, customize the distribution attribute for each module, so that the URL to the NBM file is correct. By default the distribution attribute uses a simple relative path, which will be correct if you publish the autoupdate descriptor and all the NBMs in the same folder (base URL).

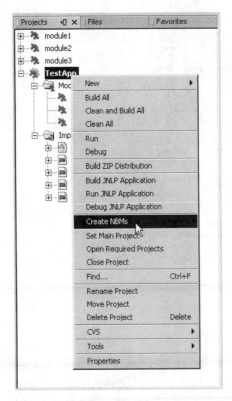

Figure 22.3: Menu item for creating NBM files

If, instead of a rich client application, you are working with a single module, you can also let the IDE generate the autoupdate descriptor for you. Just add the module to a module suite, use the **Create NBMs** menu item, and then use the menu item again whenever you want to rebuild the descriptor to publish a new version of the module.

22.3.2   Uploading the Autoupdate Descriptor and NBM Files

Now that you have an autoupdate descriptor and one or more NBM files, place them on a server of your choice. Make sure that the distribution attribute for each module listed in the autoupdate descriptor correctly points to the location of the NBM file. Once your autoupdate descriptor and NBM files are on the server, tell your users where that server is. More precisely, all you need

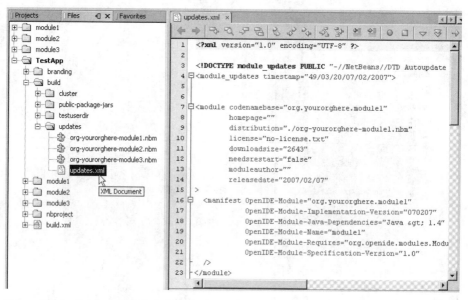

Figure 22.4: Autoupdate descriptor

to do is provide the URL to the autoupdate descriptor. Once that URL is registered in your application, the user can run the **Update Center** wizard to access the autoupdate descriptor, download the NBM files it specifies, and install them in your NetBeans Platform application.

22.4   Distributing the URL to the Autoupdate Descriptor

Your application's users need to register the URL to your autoupdate descriptor. You can provide a module that they can install through the **Update Center** wizard. Once the module is installed, the URL to the autoupdate descriptor is registered in the application. The module is very easy to create; the **Update Center** wizard can do all the work, so you don't even need to do any tweaking or post-processing. Alternatively, you can just tell your users what the URL to the autoupdate descriptor is, so they can manually register the URL in the application. Both approaches are described below.

22.4.1 Generating a Module for Registering an Autoupdate Descriptor

1. Create a new module project and add it to your module suite project. In the **Projects** window, right-click the new module project's node. Choose **New | File/Folder**. Then, in the **NetBeans Module Development** category, choose **Update Center**. Click **Next**.

2. In the **URL to Update Descriptor** field, type the URL to the autoupdate descriptor.

3. In the **Display Name** field, type the name that you want to have displayed when the user runs the **Update Center** wizard. The end result should be similar to Figure 22.5.

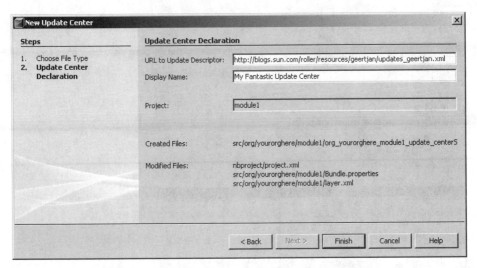

Figure 22.5: **Update Center** wizard

4. Click **Finish**. The wizard creates a file and adds entries to other files. You do not need to look at these or tweak them at all; no post-processing is necessary. You can create the NBM file right away, as described in the next step.

22.4.2   Making the User Manually Register an Autoupdate Descriptor

If you do not provide a module for installing your update center, you need to tell your users how to register your autoupdate descriptor by hand. The steps below describe how manual registration of an autoupdate descriptor is done in the IDE. However, the process is the same for any application built on top of the NetBeans Platform.

1. In the application, choose **Tools | Options**. The **Options** window appears.

2. In the **Options** window, click **Advanced Options** in the bottom left corner. In the **IDE Configuration** node, expand the **System** node.

3. In the **System** node, right-click **Autoupdate Types**, and choose **New | General Update Center**, as shown in Figure 22.6.

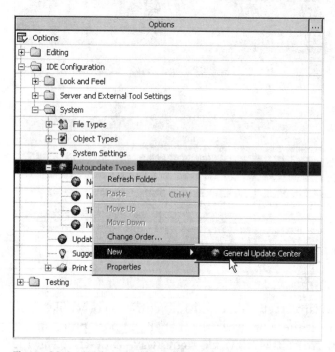

Figure 22.6: Registering a new update center

The **General Update Center** dialog box appears.

4. Type the name of the update center. The name can be anything you like. It is displayed in the **Update Center** wizard and is used to identify the update center. Click **Finish**.

5. Expand the **Autoupdate Types** node, select the newly created node for the update center, and enter the URL to the autoupdate descriptor in the **Server URL** field, on the right side of the **Options** window. Press Enter in the field. Click **Close**.

You have now manually registered the autoupdate descriptor's URL. To verify what you have done, continue with the next section.

22.5   Downloading NBM Files from an Update Center

A rich client application's **Update Center** wizard allows users to update the application's installed modules dynamically. When the user connects to your autoupdate descriptor, the application uses the NetBeans Platform support to check if there are new modules or new versions of already installed modules available. If new or updated modules are available in the update center, users can select, download, and install them.

Do the following:

1. Choose **Tools | Update Center** from the main menu to open the **Update Center** wizard.

2. Select the update centers that you wish to check for modules and click **Next** to connect to them.

3. In the **Select Modules to Install** panel, select the modules that you require. Version information and module descriptions for the selected modules are displayed in the pane below.

4. Click the > button to add the desired modules to the **Include in Install** panel. Then click **Next**. Complete the remaining pages of the wizard to install the modules.

5. If you receive the "Unable to Connect to the Update Center Server" error message, this may mean that you need a proxy to be configured to access the server. Click **Proxy Configuration** in the wizard and enter a proxy

host and port number. After entering the proxy information, click **OK** to set the values and continue with your update.

22.6   Publishing Updates to Existing Modules

After publishing an initial version of a set of modules, you will probably keep changing and enhancing the modules in various ways. How to make these changes available to your users? Right-click any module that you have significantly changed, choose **Properties**, and increment the specification version in the **API Versioning** panel shown in Figure 22.7.

When you change the specification version and click **OK**, the manifest file's `OpenIDE-Module-Specification-Version` key changes. Create the module's NBM file and update the autoupdate descriptor again as described in Section 22.3.1. Then publish the new NBM file and the autoupdate descriptor. When the user runs the **Update Center** wizard to access your update center, the changed specification version ensures that the module will be displayed in the **Update Center** wizard.

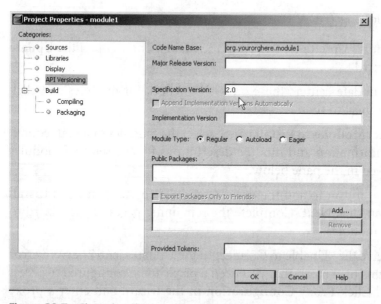

Figure 22.7: Changing the specification version

CHAPTER TWENTY-THREE

Use Case 1:
Jens Trapp on
NetBeans Module
Development

23.1 Introduction

When adding new features to the NetBeans IDE, you do not always need to start from scratch. Often you are able to build upon code developed by others. For example, there are lots of free tools available as open source projects for programmers or Web designers. It would be nice to include some of these in the IDE. One example is HTML Tidy that can be used to correct and format the markup in HTML files. In this chapter, we will encapsulate it as a NetBeans module, showing how easy it is to integrate existing tools and functionality into the IDE.

The focus of this chapter is on the integration of tools that do not require a graphical user interface. If a tool is written in Java, it is easy to integrate it simply by using it as a library and calling its methods from a separate functionality module. However, it is also easy to integrate tools that are available in binary form—if they are callable from the command line. There are many interesting tools that fall under the latter category, such as compilers, spell checkers, or code validators.

In this chapter we will integrate the well-known HTML Tidy utility by Dave Raggett. HTML Tidy consists of a parser and a converter for HTML files. It has the ability to check and clean HTML markup. It can also give hints on the correct usage of tags, as well as convert a document into different styles, including XHTML (XML-compliant HTML). After the integration of the module described in this chapter, you will be able to check, clean, and convert HTML and JSP files in the IDE's Source Editor or **Project** window. Therefore, aside from showing how tools can be integrated, this chapter also provides a very useful piece of functionality that is otherwise not supported in the IDE by default.[1]

HTML Tidy is written in C/C++. There are binaries available for almost every existing platform. There is also a pure Java version of it, but it is slightly outdated. Our module provides the integration of the native version using an external process call to HTML Tidy's executable. The binaries and a lot of documentation are available for download from http://tidy.sourceforge.net.

HTML Tidy is typically used in noninteractive mode, called from the command line. The result is either written back to the file or sent to the standard output stream. If errors or warnings occur, they are printed to the standard error stream. When used from the command line, both output and error streams are printed to the console. For our purposes, it would be good to be able to separate these streams. So, while HTML Tidy is executed as an external process, we connect its input and output streams to user interface components in the IDE. We then parse the output to retrieve error information, allowing the user to jump between error messages and the Source Editor showing the line that caused the error or warning. Finally, we implement a simple graphical user interface to control the conversion of the input file. This allows parameters to be passed directly to the command line of HTML Tidy.

To accomplish the tasks described above, we divide the integration of HTML Tidy into the Netbeans IDE into the following steps:

1. **Calling the external tool.** Simple error checking with HTML Tidy is implemented by using the **New Action** wizard and the Execution API. Files are accessed through the Nodes API.

2. **Handling the output.** The program output is parsed and the mapping between the errors in the output and their targets in the Source Editor is

---

1. There used to be a Tidy module in an older version of the IDE. That module integrated JTidy, a pure Java clone of HTML Tidy. JTidy is outdated and its future is not clear. For that reason, the module is currently in an unsupported state.

established. This step uses the Editor API and the I/O API. In an additional step, the Annotation API is used to mark errors and warnings in the Source Editor.

3. **Configuring the tool.** Loading and storing the tool's settings, such as the path to the executable, is implemented. The Options API and the **Options Panel** wizard are used.

4. **Formatting and converting files.** HTML Tidy's ability to fix and reformat code is integrated into Netbeans. Manipulating files has to be done carefully. To change the content of files, the Source Editor and Nodes API are used again.

5. **Controlling the conversion.** A wizard is added to provide a more convenient interface for specifying parameters for file conversion.

Each step listed above requires a fully-functional module, starting with a rather simple integration and developing towards a complete front-end tool to HTML Tidy. Aside from developing the graphical user interface in the final step, the steps involved in this process are generic and you can easily adapt them for other tools.

23.2 Calling the External Tool

We begin by simply calling HTML Tidy and starting it in an external process. To prevent the IDE from blocking during execution, we run the tool in a separate thread. The output is redirected so that it is visible in the IDE's **Output** window.

23.2.1 Creating the Tidy Error Check Action

After the NetBeans module project is set up, we can start with the integration of HTML Tidy. View Section 1.2.1 for instructions on how to set up a module project. In the IDE, actions are used for handling user interaction with the IDE. Creating an action has been described in more detail in Section 1.2.3. For the integration of HTML Tidy, an action should be added to the context-sensitive menus of the Source Editor and the explorer in the **Projects** window, allowing syntax checking on HTML files.

The goal of this section is to provide a new menu option, **HTML Tidy Error Check**, for the right-click menu of the Source Editor, as shown in Figure 23.1.

Figure 23.1: **HTML Tidy Error Check** menu item

You can create the menu item by following these steps:

1. Create a new module. (See Section 1.2.1 for instructions on how to create a new module.) Once you have a new module, open the **New File** wizard. Under **Categories**, select **NetBeans Module Development**. Under **File Type**, select **Action**. Click **Next**.

2. In the **Action Type** panel, select **Conditionally Enabled (use CookieAction)**. Select **DataObject** in the **Cookie Class** combo field, because this allows us to interact with the content of files. Also select the **User May Select Multiple Nodes** radio button to allow for multiple files to be processed at once. Click **Next**.

3. In Step 3, **GUI Registration**, the action can be assigned to a category. For our purposes, the **Tools** category is the best fit. To prevent the main menus

from becoming cluttered, we will place the action only in the context-sensitive menus—that is, only where they will be useful to the user. Therefore, make sure the **Global Menu Item** and **Global Toolbar Button** checkboxes are deselected, then select the **File Type Context Menu Item** and **Editor Context Menu Item** checkboxes. Under the **File Type Context Menu Item**, choose **text/html** from the **Content Type** drop-down list. You may want to place the menu for the **File Type Context Menu** below the menu item <**separator**>—**HERE**—**Tools**, so select it from the **Position** drop-down list. Likewise, for the **Editor Context Menu Item**, choose **format**—**HERE**—<**separator**>. Click **Next**.

4. In the wizard's final step, **Name, Icon, and Location**, enter `TidyErrorCheckAction` for **Class Name**. For **Display Name**, enter `HTML Tidy Error Check`. Click **Finish**.

The wizard creates an empty `performAction()` method in the `TidyErrorCheckAction` class. This method is called when the action is triggered. In order to add functionality, this method needs to be edited. It is good practice to have long-running events handled in a separate thread. This is especially true for HTML Tidy, since it runs in an external process. By doing this, we eliminate the possibility of the IDE freezing during the execution of the action. Otherwise, if the external program has a problem, it may stop the execution of the IDE. When the process is started as a separate thread, it runs in the background and the user may continue working on other tasks. If an error does arise in the external process, the user can simply kill the process without affecting the IDE.

The NetBeans Platform provides the infrastructure for starting tasks with the Execution API. In most cases, you should use the `RequestProcessor` class to start new threads, as shown in the following examples. For simplicity, however, a slightly different approach is taken here. If you are running third-party code that you cannot change, you can use `ExecutionEngine` to encapsulate the called method. It acts as a shell. If `System.exit()` is called from within the thread, `ExecutionEngine` prevents it from stopping the whole process, which in this case would include the NetBeans process itself. It also automatically redirects the output of the thread so that it is printed to the IDE's **Output** window rather than to the console. This latter property is the reason for our use of `ExecutionEngine` in the first step.

To start a new thread for the action, modify the `performAction()` method in `org/yourorghere/nbtidyintegration/TidyErrorCheck-Action.java` as follows:

```
public final class TidyErrorCheckAction extends CookieAction {

  protected void performAction (Node[] activatedNodes) {
    ExecutionEngine engine = ExecutionEngine.getDefault();
    engine.execute(getName(), new TidyRunnable (
                              activatedNodes, "-e"), null);
  }

  ...
}
```

Since the actual work is delegated to a different class running in its own thread, the method is rather short. Any class that implements the `java.lang.Runnable` interface may be passed to the execution engine and executed in a separate thread. Additionally, a name must be specified that will be used to reference the process internally. The `getName()` method already returns the action name, so we also use it for referencing the process.

The action class is obviously not compilable yet, because the `TidyRunnable` class still needs to be implemented. This is described in the following sections. The function of this class is to encapsulate the call to HTML Tidy. To make the class reusable, the actual command-line argument for error checking (`"-e "`) is passed in the constructor. When the action is triggered, the `run()` method, declared by the `Runnable` interface, is invoked after the thread is started.

23.2.2   Retrieving the Filename

The action defined in the previous section provides access to selected nodes within your project. Nodes are used to reference the internal structure of a project. This is described in greater detail in Chapter 9. For this example however, it is only necessary to know how to retrieve the filenames of the selected files. We can access the filenames from the `DataObjects` that are associated with the nodes through the use of cookies. This is shown in the excerpt from `org/yourorghere/nbtidyintegration/TidyRunnable.java` below:

```
DataObject dataObject =
  (DataObject)nodes[i].getCookie(DataObject.class);
FileObject fileObject = dataObject.getPrimaryFile();
File file = FileUtil.toFile(fileObject);
System.out.println(
  "File: "+file+" - Size: "+file.length()+"...");
```

In general, `DataObjects` can reference more than one file. For example, `DataObjects` for Java classes cover both the source and compiled class files. For the HTML object type used here, there is only one file to reference. The method `getPrimaryFile()` returns a `FileObject` to it. The filename can then be retrieved using the `FileUtil` class. It may seem a bit complicated to retrieve filenames in three steps, but the node, data, and file objects offer a rich variety of access options for the various representations of files inside the IDE. This becomes increasingly important in the steps that follow.

23.2.3 Running HTML Tidy

As mentioned above, the class `TidyRunnable` is called through the `ExecutionEngine` and therefore needs to implement the `java.lang.Runnable` interface. To comply with this interface, the `run()` method needs to be implemented. The `run()` method loops over the selected nodes asking for their associated files and executes HTML Tidy on each file.

While the `ExecutionEngine` class launches *internal* threads, HTML Tidy needs to be called in an *external* process. This is supported by the standard `NbProcessDescriptor` mechanism provided by the same Execution API package. It provides functionality similar to the `ProcessBuilder` class from the `java.lang.*` package, but allows a more convenient way of passing arguments to it. Once a process is described, it can be executed by calling the `exec()` method which returns an instance of the `Process` class. The `Process` instance is then used to access the input or output stream of the external process. In the case of HTML Tidy, we are only interested in the error stream, which is read by the `readOutput()` method. The method simply sends the process output to the `System.out` stream, and the execution engine takes care of redirecting it to the output panel.

```
NbProcessDescriptor desc = new NbProcessDescriptor(
  tidyExecutable, commandLineArgs + " \"" +
  file.getAbsolutePath() + "\"");
Process process = desc.exec();

readOutput(process.getErrorStream());
process.waitFor();
```

So far, the path to the executable has been hardcoded. This is not optimal because, for example, if the module is later distributed, the executable could be stored in a different location. We need to provide some configuration support for the pathname to make the module generally usable. This is addressed later in this chapter.

The command-line arguments for the process call have to be built for the process descriptor. In this case, the option `"-e"` for error checking and the filename need to be concatenated. Since spaces are permitted in the filename, we have to treat the filename in a special way so that the tool can handle it. The `NbProcessDescriptor` class is capable of reading arguments the same way as UNIX Bourne Shell, so we can put the filename in quotes (escaped by the backslash: `\"`).

In order to implement the `TidyRunnable` class, use the **New File** wizard again (Ctrl-N):

1. Select a plain **Java Class** from the **Java Classes** category. Click **Next**.

2. Enter `TidyRunnable` into the **Class Name** for the next step of the wizard. If you work with more than one project, make sure that you add the class to the correct project. Also, check that the package name matches your project's root package. In our case, this is `org.yourorghere.nbtidyintegration`. Click **Finish**.

When the wizard finishes, the code for `TidyRunnable` is generated, as listed below:

```java
public class TidyRunnable implements Runnable {
  Node[] nodes;
  String commandLineArgs;
  String tidyExecutable = "c:\\Programme\\Utils\\tidy.exe";

  /** Initialize HTML Tidy runnable.*/
  public TidyRunnable(Node[] nodes, String commandLineArgs) {
    this.nodes=nodes;
    this.commandLineArgs=commandLineArgs;
  }

  /** Perform error check on all nodes;
      this is called in its own thread.*/
  public void run() {
    if (new File(tidyExecutable).exists()) {
      // Check if executable exits
      try {
          for (int i =0; i<nodes.length; i++) {
            DataObject dataObject = (DataObject)nodes[i].
              getCookie(DataObject.class);
            processDataObject(tidyExecutable, dataObject);
          }
      } catch(InterruptedException ex) {
          ErrorManager.getDefault().notify(ex);
      } catch(IOException ex) {
          ErrorManager.getDefault().notify(ex);
      }
    } else {
        System.out.println(
          "Executable not found at "+tidyExecutable +".");
    }
  }

  /**
   * Perform error checking on a single data object.
   * @param executable Absolute path to the executable
   * @param dataObject Data Object that is processed
   * @throws java.lang.InterruptedException
   * @throws java.io.IOException
   */
```

```java
void processDataObject(final String executable,
    final DataObject dataObject)
    throws InterruptedException, IOException {

  FileObject fileObject = dataObject.getPrimaryFile();
  File file = FileUtil.toFile(fileObject);
  System.out.println(
    "File: "+file+" - Size: "+file.length()+"...");

  NbProcessDescriptor tidyProcessDesc =
    new NbProcessDescriptor( executable, getCommandLineArgs() +
    " \"" + file.getAbsolutePath() +"\"");
  Process process = tidyProcessDesc.exec();
  readOutput(process.getErrorStream());
  process.waitFor();
  System.out.println("Exit: "+process.exitValue());
}

/**
 * Parse the output.
 */
static void readOutput(InputStream errStream) {
  try {
      BufferedReader error =
        new BufferedReader(new InputStreamReader(errStream));
      String errString = null;
      while ((errString = error.readLine()) != null) {
        System.out.println(errString);
      }
  } catch (Exception e) {
      System.out.println("Could not read Process output " +e);
  }
}
}
```

If HTML Tidy is used in error checking mode, the warning and error messages only appear in the error stream. The output stream is used only when the HTML files are modified, as demonstrated later in this chapter. To keep the example simple, only the error stream is read here. In Section 23.5.1 we will see how to read both streams simultaneously.

23.2.4 Resolving Dependencies

After adding the above lines of code to the `TidyErrorCheckAction` and `TidyRunnable` classes, the project is still unable to compile if you have not yet resolved all imports and dependencies. In the Source Editor, errors may be visible, which need to be fixed prior to compiling the project. Some dependencies have already been defined when the action class was originally generated. But now, because several additional classes have been used which belong to other API's, we need to declare new dependencies. We can do so by opening the **Project Properties** window (choose **Properties** from the right-click menu of the project node in the **Projects** window). All dependencies can be declared in the **Libraries** category. To add a new dependency, click **Add . . . .** The **Add Module Dependency** wizard opens to assist you in finding the correct module. You can then specify the name of the class used in the project, and a list of all modules containing this class is presented. For this example, we need to declare dependency on the Filesystems API, because we used the `FileObject` and `FileUtil` classes. Since we also used the `NbProcessDescriptor` and `ExecutionEngine`, the Execution API is required as well.

After adding dependencies, we must return to the Source Editor to fix imports. This can be done by choosing **Fix Imports** from the Source Editor's right-click menu, or simply by using the keystroke Alt-Shift-F. This is required for both `TidyErrorCheckAction` and `TidyRunnable`. As there are more than one options available for the `File` class, you have to select the correct package (`java.io.File`) from a dialog that pops up when you attempt to fix the import.

23.2.5 Running the Example

When all dependencies have been declared and imports fixed, the project can compile. It can be loaded and installed into the current IDE by choosing **Install/Reload in Target Platform** from the right-click menu of the project node in the **Projects** window. Before you do this, however, you may want to add some information to the project in the **Project Properties** window, such as a description or license file. You can also specify a version number to be able to track the different versions of the module. To access the **Project Properties** window, choose **Properties** from the right-click menu of the project node in the **Projects** window.

When the module is installed in the running IDE, it can be used to check HTML files. If an HTML file is opened, the corresponding action appears in the Source Editor's right-click menu, as shown in Figure 23.1. To open a file in the Source Editor, type Ctrl-O. A file browser opens, allowing you to choose a file from a local directory.

If you have HTML files inside your opened NetBeans project, the menu item also appears in the context-sensitive menus of the **Projects** and **Files** windows when the selected node is an HTML file. If the action is selected, HTML Tidy is executed. The result is printed in the **Output** window, as shown in Figure 23.2.

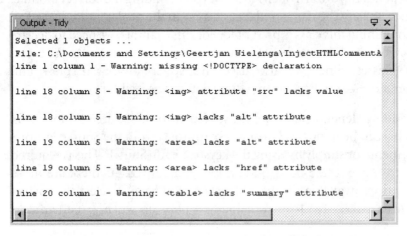

Figure 23.2: HTML Tidy output printed in the **Output** window

Since the action has been bound to the HTML MIME type, in its current state it only supports HTML files—but not JSP files. One way to add support for JSP files is by defining a completely separate action using the wizard again. However, if the actions performed on HTML and JSP files should be the same, this would just duplicate the boilerplate code. It is simpler to edit the XML layer and copy the configuration to other MIME types, as shown below for JSP files. This is easy to do even without knowing too much about XML grammar. For more information on the XML layer, see Chapter 6.

```xml
<?xml version="1.0" encoding="UTF-8"?>
<!DOCTYPE filesystem PUBLIC "-//NetBeans//DTD Filesystem 1.1//EN"
  "http://www.netbeans.org/dtds/filesystem-1_1.dtd">
<filesystem>
  <folder name="Actions">
    <folder name="Tools">
      <file name="org-yourorghere-nbtidyintegration-TidyError↵
CheckAction.instance"/>
    </folder>
  </folder>
  <folder name="Editors">
    <folder name="text">
      <folder name="html">
        <folder name="Popup">
          <attr name="format/org-yourorghere-nbtidyintegration-↵
TidyErrorCheckAction.shadow" boolvalue="true"/>
          <file name="org-yourorghere-nbtidyintegration-Tidy↵
ErrorCheckAction.shadow">
            <attr name="originalFile"
                stringvalue="Actions/Tools/org-yourorghere-↵
nbtidyintegration-TidyErrorCheckAction.instance"/>
          </file>
          <attr name="org-yourorghere-nbtidyintegration-Tidy↵
ErrorCheckAction.shadow/SeparatorAfterFormat.instance"
                boolvalue="true"/>
        </folder>
      </folder>
      <folder name="x-jsp">
        <folder name="Popup">
          <attr name="format/org-yourorghere-nbtidyintegration-↵
TidyErrorCheckAction.shadow" boolvalue="true"/>
          <file name="org-yourorghere-nbtidyintegration-Tidy↵
ErrorCheckAction.shadow">
            <attr name="originalFile"
                stringvalue="Actions/Tools/org-yourorghere-↵
nbtidyintegration-TidyErrorCheckAction.instance"/>
          </file>
          <attr name="org-yourorghere-nbtidyintegration-Tidy↵
ErrorCheckAction.shadow/SeparatorAfterFormat.instance"
                boolvalue="true"/>
        </folder>
      </folder>
    </folder>
  </folder>
</filesystem>
```

23.3   Handling the Output

So far we have only provided a very basic integration of our external tool. It is a one-way integration: When HTML Tidy is called on a file, warnings and errors are printed, but there is no link back to the source from the generated output. In modern IDEs, one would expect to be able to jump directly to the error inside the Source Editor. In NetBeans, this can be achieved with the use of hyperlinks, so that by clicking on the error message in the **Output** window, the error in the file is brought into focus in the Source Editor with the cursor positioned directly on the line responsible for that error.

23.3.1   Printing the Output

In the previous example, we took a simple approach to handling the output. The `System.out.println()` was used for printing and the `ExecutionEngine` took care of sending the output to the **Output** window. To interact with the output, however, we need to handle this ourselves, rather than letting the `ExecutionEngine` do it for us. Previously, the engine created the **Output** window, but we can also provide our own **Output** window in order to have more control over the output. To create an **Output** window, we can use the `IOProvider` class.

The `getIO()` method of the `IOProvider` can be used for creating a new **Output** window with a given name. If a window with the given name does not already exist, a new window is generated. It should be noted, however, that if the second argument to `getIO()` is `null`, a new tab is generated even if a window with the same name already exists. The window itself is represented by the `InputOutput` class. By calling `select()` on the `InputOutput` class, the window is activated. If it was previously hidden, it is made visible. To print to the window, we need to use the `OutputWriter` class. For this example, we will change the signature for the `TidyRunnable` constructor by adding a writer object to it. If we then replace all `System.out.println()` method calls by calls to the writer object in the `TidyRunnable` class, we get exactly the same result as before. The changed methods of the `org/yourorghere/nbtidyintegration/TidyRunnable.java` class are listed here:

```java
/**
 * Perform error check; this is called in its own thread.
 */
public void run() {
  InputOutput io = IOProvider .getDefault().getIO(NbBundle.
    getMessage(getClass(), "TidyOutputTabLabel"), false);
  io.select(); // Tree tab is selected
  OutputWriter writer = io.getOut();

  try {
      writer.reset(); // Clean the output window
      writer.println("Selected "+nodes.length+" objects ...");

      if (new File(getTidyExecutable()).exists()) {
          // Check if executable exits
          for (int i =0; i<nodes.length; i++) {
            DataObject dataObject =
               (DataObject)nodes[i].getCookie(DataObject.class);
            processDataObject(writer, getTidyExecutable(),
                             dataObject);
          }
      } else {
          writer.println("Executable not found at "+
            getTidyExecutable() + ". Please select " +
            "a valid path in the Options panel.");
      }

  } catch (Exception ex) {
      ErrorManager.getDefault().notify(
                                  ErrorManager.WARNING, ex);
  }
  writer.close();
}

/**
 * Perform external program with this data object.
 * @param executable Absolute path to the executable
 * @param writer Writer for the output tab
 * @param dataObject Data Object that is processed
 * @throws java.lang.InterruptedException
 * @throws java.io.IOException
 */
```

```
void processDataObject(final OutputWriter writer,
    final String executable, final DataObject dataObject)
    throws InterruptedException, IOException {

  FileObject fileObject = dataObject.getPrimaryFile();
  File file = FileUtil.toFile(fileObject);
  writer.println(
    "File: "+file+" - Size: "+file.length()+"...");

  NbProcessDescriptor tidyProcessDesc =
    new NbProcessDescriptor( executable,
    getCommandLineArgs() +" \"" + file.getAbsolutePath() +"\"");
  Process process = tidyProcessDesc.exec();
  readOutput(writer, process.getErrorStream());
  process.waitFor();
  writer.println("Exit: "+process.exitValue());
  writer.flush();
}

/**
 * Parse the output.
 */
static void readOutput(OutputWriter writer,
                       InputStream errStream) {
  try {
    BufferedReader error =
      new BufferedReader(new InputStreamReader(errStream));
    String errString = null;
    while ((errString = error.readLine()) != null) {
      writer.println(errString);
    }
  } catch (Exception e) {
    writer.println("Could not read Process output " +e);
  }
}
```

The **Output** window has some additional options which, although they are not used here, are worth mentioning. As the class name `InputOutput` implies, the class also provides an input field. It is not visible by default, but may be shown by calling `io.setInputVisible(true)`. Another way to interact with the window is by providing Swing actions. These Swing actions are added when calling the `select()` method. If they are added, they appear along the left side of the **Output** window. For example, in NetBeans IDE 6 this feature is used for presenting "stop" and "rerun" buttons for the build process. Please read the API documentation for IOProvider for more information.

Since we can now handle the output ourselves, we do not need the implicit redirection that the ExecutionEngine provides for us. Therefore, we can exchange the lines that created the new thread in the action class with the standard mechanism:

```
public final class TidyErrorCheckAction extends CookieAction {
  static RequestProcessor processor = null;
  protected void performAction (Node[] activatedNodes) {
    if(processor==null)
      processor = new RequestProcessor("TidyErrorCheck",1,true);
    processor.post(new TidyRunnable (activatedNodes, "-e"));
  }
  ...
```

23.3.2   Listening to the Output

So far, we have only rebuilt our example without adding any new features. Now, as we can handle the output ourselves, we can take advantage of this by creating hyperlinks in the **Output** window. The hyperlinks to be created in the generated output are provided through the OutputListener interface from the I/O API. If an object that implements the interface is passed to the println() method, the line in the **Output** window will display as a hyperlink. It is underlined and uses a different color, similar to hyperlinks in a Web browser. When hovering over the link, the pointer changes to indicate that the link is active.

```
writer.println (errMessage, listener);
```

The listener can only be applied to the println() method, so this approach is slightly different from that in HTML pages where several hyperlinks can appear within one line. For our purposes, however, this is exactly what is needed. The OutputListener interface acts as a callback function. When a user clicks on the hyperlink in the **Output** window, the outputLineAction() method is invoked on the listener object. In order to handle the click action that occurs on the link, a new class that implements the OutputListener interface is defined in the file org/yourorghere/nbtidyintegration/ TidyOutputListener.java:

```
public class TidyOutputListener implements OutputListener {
  public static String PATTERN_STRING = "\\s*line\\s*([0-9]+)\\⌐
s*column\\s*([0-9]+)\\s*-\\s*([^ :]+):\\s+(.+)";
  public static Pattern PATTERN =
    Pattern.compile(PATTERN_STRING);
  DataObject dataObject;

  public TidyOutputListener(DataObject dataObject) {
    this.dataObject = dataObject;
  }

  /** Open the line in HTML file that caused the error.*/
  public void outputLineAction(OutputEvent outputEvent) {
    String lineString = outputEvent.getLine();
    Matcher matcher = PATTERN.matcher(lineString);
    if (matcher.matches()) {
      int lineNumber = Integer.parseInt(matcher.group(1));
      int columnNumber = Integer.parseInt(matcher.group(2));
      LineCookie lc =
        (LineCookie) dataObject.getCookie(LineCookie.class);
      Line l = lc.getLineSet().getOriginal(lineNumber-1);
      l.show(Line.SHOW_GOTO, columnNumber-1);
    }
  }

  /** Nothing to do here.*/
  public void outputLineCleared(OutputEvent outputEvent) {
  }

  /** Nothing to do here.*/
  public void outputLineSelected(OutputEvent outputEvent) {
  }
}
```

The outputListenerAction() method is able to access information on
the hyperlink the user clicks on. In this case, the hyperlink is parsed to retrieve
the line and column number. This is described in the following section. Once
the line number is retrieved, we need to create a reference to the actual line in
the Source Editor. To interact with the files loaded in the IDE, we rely on the
DataObject class that has been passed as an argument to the constructor.
From there, we get the object representing a line in the DataObject with the
help of a LineCookie. The cookie mechanism is the same as that described
in the action handler class from the previous step. The LineCookie offers
access methods for the lines in the DataObject. However, the file may have

been modified, and the line numbers might therefore have changed. This often occurs when the user fixes errors from top to bottom: The line numbers for the error messages at the bottom of the document may not match the actual line numbers in the Source Editor. To remedy this, the IDE stores the line number information for the last saved version of the file. By calling the `getOriginal()` method, the correct line is returned. In HTML Tidy, line numbers start at index 1, while in the IDE, as in other Java-based programs, numbering starts with a 0 index. Therefore, we need to subtract 1 when using the line and column numbers from the HTML Tidy output. With the `Line` object at hand, it is easy to open the Source Editor and set the cursor to the right position:

```
l.show(Line.SHOW_GOTO, columnNumber-1);
```

SHOW_GOTO[2]   Opens the Source Editor if necessary, shows the line, and takes focus.

SHOW_SHOW[3]   Opens the Source Editor if necessary and shows the line.

SHOW_TOFRONT[4]   Same as SHOW_GOTO, except that the Window Manager attempts to front the Source Editor (i.e., make it the topmost window).

SHOW_TRY_SHOW[5]   Shows the line only if the Source Editor is open.

23.3.3 Parsing the Output

When invoking the listener, we need to specify the target. In our case, this is the file represented by the `DataObject` that we stored in the listener object. We also need the position of the error or warning in order to set the cursor

2. www.netbeans.org/project/www/download/dev/javadoc/org-openide-text/org/openide/text/Line.html#SHOW_GOTO

3. www.netbeans.org/project/www/download/dev/javadoc/org-openide-text/org/openide/text/Line.html#SHOW_SHOW

4. www.netbeans.org/project/www/download/dev/javadoc/org-openide-text/org/openide/text/Line.html#SHOW_TOFRONT

5. www.netbeans.org/project/www/download/dev/javadoc/org-openide-text/org/openide/text/Line.html#SHOW_TRY_SHOW

position in the Source Editor. Since we have not yet retrieved the cursor position, we must do so from the error message itself. In the case of HTML Tidy, this information is encoded at the beginning of each error or warning message (see Figure 23.2). To obtain this information, these lines need to be parsed. The most powerful way to parse text is through the use of *regular expressions*, a pattern matching language originally developed for UNIX shell programming. Ever since Java 1.4.2, regular expressions have been bundled with the Java 2 Standard Edition. The following pattern can be used to parse the output received from HTML Tidy:

```
"line ([0-9]+) column ([0-9]+) -\ ([^ :]+): (.+)"
```

It is beyond the scope of this chapter to offer a detailed explanation of the expression, so only some aspects are explained here. The lines that we are trying to match are shown in Figure 23.2. If a line matches the expression used above, we want to extract some values from it. In the regex pattern language, this can be reflected by *match groups* which are surrounded by parentheses. The first two match groups "([0-9]+)" grab the line and column number. The plus sign in the pattern indicates that the expression within brackets (in this case, a numerical character between 0 and 9) has to appear at least once. The third match group "([^ :]+)" grabs the next part of the string, ending just before the colon ": ", which specifies the reason the line has been flagged—that is, Warning or Error. The fourth and final match group "(.+)" reads the remainder of the message, which represents an explanation of the error or warning.

When using regular expressions it is always safer to replace the spaces in the pattern with a predefined character set, "\s", which matches spaces and tabs. When using this in Java, the backslash must be escaped by another backslash, resulting in "\\s". It is also a good idea to allow an arbitrary number of spaces to occur. It is not easy to count white spaces, and if you miss one, the pattern match fails. This is expressed by appending either a plus (+) or an asterisk (*) to the match group. The plus symbol requires at least one occurrence of the match group; the asterisk represents any number of occurrences, possibly zero. The expression described here has been implemented in the TidyOutputListener class, as displayed above.

To separate the error and warning messages from other output, the messages from HTML Tidy should be checked against the regular expression. A listener is only registered in the `writeln()` method, provided the line matches the pattern. All other lines are not displayed as hyperlinks, and are printed without a listener attached to them.

To implement the listener, we need to modify the `readOutput()` method in `org/yourorghere/nbtidyintegration/TidyRunnable.java`. Since the listener class requires the data object, we need to pass it as additional argument to the method:

```
static void readOutput(OutputWriter writer,
    DataObject dataObject, InputStream errStream) {
  TidyOutputListener listener =
    new TidyOutputListener(dataObject);
  try {
    BufferedReader error = new BufferedReader (
      new InputStreamReader (errStream));
    String err = null;
    while ((err = error.readLine ()) != null) {
      Matcher matcher = TidyOutputListener.PATTERN.matcher (err);

      if (matcher.matches ()) {
        writer.println (err,listenet);
      }
      else {
        writer.println (err);
      }
    }
  }
  catch (Exception e) {
    writer.println ("Could not read Process output " +e);
  }
}
```

After this has been done, the module needs to be compiled and reloaded into the target platform so that the changes are included.

Now, a more user-friendly integration of the HTML Tidy is available. With hyperlinks pointing to the code in the Source Editor, it is much easier to take a closer look at the errors and warnings generated in the output (Figure 23.3).

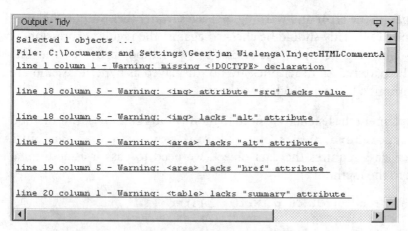

Figure 23.3: HTML Tidy output with hyperlinks

23.3.4   Annotating Errors in the Source Editor

To take the integration a little further, it is also possible to mark the errors
and warnings found by HTML Tidy directly in the Source Editor. This can be
achieved using the NetBeans Annotation API (not to be confused with Java 5
annotations!). Annotations are widely used within the IDE, for example to
show where compile errors arise in code. All lines containing errors are consequently linked to an annotation. Annotations are also employed when the
user sets a breakpoint. Annotated lines are highlighted in the Source Editor.
Since all lines may not fit on the screen, the annotated lines are also marked
in the error strip which is visible on the right side of the Source Editor adjacent
to the scrollbar. On the left side of the Source Editor, icons are displayed
showing the annotation type. A tooltip can be revealed by hovering the
pointer over an icon.

To add annotation support, take the following steps:

- Add a Java class representing the annotation.

- Add an annotation UI declaration file, which specifies the highlight color
  and icon. Since HTML Tidy distinguishes between errors and warnings,
  two annotation types are declared using separate configuration files.

- In the XML layer, declare the representation of the annotation inside the UI.

- When printing HTML Tidy's output, parse the lines to find the information required for annotations.

- To free system cache and eliminate the possibility of conflicts arising from previously existing annotations, clean any old annotations before running HTML Tidy.

The annotation class can be quite simple. It has to extend the abstract class `org.openide.text.Annotation` by implementing the methods `getAnnotationType()` and `getShortDescription()`. The type is basically a unique identifier that can be chosen by the programmer. It only has to match the type string used for the declaration in the XML layer. In the case of HTML Tidy, we want to distinguish warnings from errors, so we define two annotation types. Depending on the severity of the instance, either a `warning` or `error` annotation type is returned. The short description is assembled from the column number and cause of the error. These values are set in the initializer.

Since the IDE does not keep track of annotations, we are responsible for maintaining their lifecycle and removing them once they become invalid. In order to keep track of them, all annotations are collected in a list. To enforce this, the initializer is made private, and the only way to create a new instance is by using the `create()` method. A `clear()` method is also provided to remove all annotations:

```
public class TidyAnnotation extends Annotation {

  private static List<Annotation> annotations =
    new ArrayList<Annotation>();
  private static String[] annoType = {
    "org-yourorghere-nbtidyintegration-tidyerrorannotation",
    "org-yourorghere-nbtidyintegration-tidywarningannotation"
  };

  private String reason;
  private int column;
  private int severity = 0;
```

```
public static TidyAnnotation create(
    String severity, int column, String reason) {
  TidyAnnotation annotation =
    new TidyAnnotation(severity, column, reason);
  annotations.add(annotation);
  return annotation;
}

public static void clear() {
  for (Annotation annotation : annotations)
  {
    annotation.detach();
  }
}

public static void remove(TidyAnnotation annotation) {
  annotations.remove(annotation);
}

/**
 * Create a new instance of TidyErrorAnnotation
 */
private TidyAnnotation(String severity,
                       int column, String reason) {
  this.severity = severity.contains("Err")?0:1;
  this.reason=reason;
  this.column=column;
}

/**
 * Define the Tidy Annotation type
 *
 * @return Constant String "TidyErrorAnnotation"
 */

public String getAnnotationType() {
  return annoType[severity];
}

/** Provide the Tidy error message as a description.
 * @return Annotation Reason */
public String getShortDescription() {
  return reason+ " ("+ "Column: "+column+")";
}
```

```
/** Create an annotation for a line from a match string */
public static void createAnnotation(
    final LineCookie lc, final Matcher matcher)
    throws IndexOutOfBoundsException, NumberFormatException {
  String lineNumberString = matcher.group(1);
  int lineNumber = Integer.parseInt(lineNumberString)-1;
  String columnNumberString = matcher.group(2);
  int columnNumber = Integer.parseInt(columnNumberString)-1;
  String severity = matcher.group(3);
  String reason = matcher.group(4);
  final Line line = lc.getLineSet().getOriginal(lineNumber);
  final TidyAnnotation annotation =
    TidyAnnotation.create(severity, columnNumber, reason);

  annotation.attach(line);
  line.addPropertyChangeListener(new PropertyChangeListener() {
    public void propertyChange(PropertyChangeEvent ev) {
      String type = ev.getPropertyName();
      if ((type == null) ||
          type.equals(Annotatable.PROP_TEXT)) {
        // User edited the line, assume error should be cleared
        line.removePropertyChangeListener(this);
        annotation.detach();
        TidyAnnotation.remove(annotation);
      }
    }
  });
}
}
```

The Java class does not store any UI-specific information, such as the highlight color or icon. This information is taken from an XML configuration file, which is included in the NetBeans configuration filesystem. For this example, we distinguish between warnings and errors by using two separate annotation declarations. Both are implemented in the same class, but each uses its own color, icon, and label. Each annotation type is declared in its own file in the project's root directory (the directory that also includes the XML layer). The warning annotation is created in the file TidyWarningAnnotation.xml. The XML file can be created by using the **New File** wizard (press Ctrl-N or click on its menu item in the **File** menu). Select **XML** under **Categories** and **XML Document** from **File Types**. Once the file is generated, match its contents accordingly:

```
<?xml version="1.0" encoding="UTF-8"?>
<!DOCTYPE type PUBLIC
  "-//NetBeans//DTD annotation type 1.0//EN"
  "http://www.netbeans.org/dtds/annotation-type-1_0.dtd">
<type
  name="org-yourorghere-nbtidyintegration-tidywarningannotation"
  description_key="TidyWarningLabel"
  localizing_bundle="org.yourorghere.nbtidyintegration.Bundle"
  visible="true"
  glyph="nbresloc:/org/yourorghere/nbtidyintegration/↵
nbtidywarning.png"
  highlight="#FFBBBB"
  type="line"
  severity="warning" />
```

In a similar manner, the error annotation type is stored in TidyErrorAnnotation.xml:

```
<?xml version="1.0" encoding="UTF-8"?>
<!DOCTYPE type PUBLIC
  "-//NetBeans//DTD annotation type 1.0//EN"
  "http://www.netbeans.org/dtds/annotation-type-1_0.dtd">
<type
  name="org-yourorghere-nbtidyintegration-tidyerrorannotation"
  description_key="TidyErrorLabel"
  localizing_bundle="org.yourorghere.nbtidyintegration.Bundle"
  visible="true"
  glyph=
    "nbresloc:/org/yourorghere/nbtidyintegration/nbtidyerror.png"
  highlight="#FF5555"
  type="line"
  severity="error"/>
```

The icons we declared in the files need to be created and copied to the specified locations manually. The labels defined in the configuration files must now be added to the Bundle.properties file:

```
TidyErrorLabel=Tidy Error
TidywarningLabel=Tidy Warning
```

Next, the annotation declarations must be registered with the NetBeans Platform. This is performed in the XML layer. The following lines need to be added to the already existing Editors folder (<folder name="Editors">...</folder>):

```
<folder name="AnnotationTypes">
  <file name="org-yourorghere-nbtidyintegration-TidyWarning⏎
Annotation.xml"
        url="TidyWarningAnnotation.xml"/>
  <file name="org-yourorghere-nbtidyintegration-TidyError⏎
Annotation.xml"
        url="TidyErrorAnnotation.xml"/>
</folder>
```

The names match the current directory structure, with slashes replaced by dashes.

The annotations are now ready for use. To integrate them into the example, the readOutput() method from the TidyRunnable class must be modified. If the output line matches the pattern from the regular expression, an annotation is created. The pattern then extracts all required information for displaying the annotation.

```
static void readOutput (OutputWriter writer,
    DataObject dataObject, InputStream errStream) {
  LineCookie lc =
    (LineCookie) dataObject.getCookie (LineCookie.class);
  TidyOutputListener listener =
    new TidyOutputListener(dataObject);
  try {
    BufferedReader error =
      new BufferedReader (new InputStreamReader (errStream));
    String err = null;
    while ((err = error.readLine ()) != null) {
      Matcher matcher = TidyOutputListener.PATTERN.matcher (err);

      if (matcher.matches ()) {
        TidyAnnotation.createAnnotation(lc, matcher);
        writer.println (err,listener);
      }
      else {
        writer.println (err);
      }
    }
  }
  catch (Exception e) {
    writer.println ("Could not read Process output " +e);
  }
}
```

Adding annotations is only half of the problem; we also need to remove them if the error or warning has been corrected in the Source Editor. For the purposes of this example, we can manage this quite easily by removing annotations as soon as the lines they reference are changed. We do not check if the changes actually make the lines valid. Furthermore, the `clear()` method in the initializer of the `TidyRunnable` class is called each time the action is performed, thereby removing all previously created annotations (Figure 23.4).

```
/** Initialize HTML Tidy runnable.*/
public TidyRunnable(Node[] nodes, String commandLineArgs) {
  TidyAnnotation.clear();
  this.nodes=nodes;
  this.commandLineArgs=commandLineArgs;
}
```

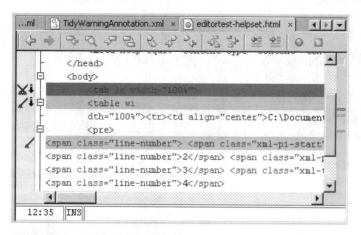

Figure 23.4: HTML Tidy annotations

Annotations are an easy way to mark areas in the Source Editor. For further information on annotations, consult the chapter on error annotations (Chapter 17).

23.4 Configuring the Tool

In its current state, our HTML Tidy module runs fine in the IDE. However, it might not run on every machine because the path to the executable has been hardcoded. This is commonly considered bad practice and ought to be changed before the module can be published. The user should be able to configure the path of the executable. As described in Section 18.1, the NetBeans Platform provides central configuration functionality, as well as an easy way to plug module-specific configurations directly into the platform. Configuration functionality is accessible through **Tools | Options** from the IDE's main menu.

The **Options** window opens in standard mode where frequently accessed parameters can be set (see Figure 23.5). Options are grouped into categories, each category being displayed in its own panel. There is also a **Miscellaneous** category grouping all options that cannot be classified into the given categories. We will use the **Options Panel** wizard which allows us to integrate the module's configuration settings into the **Options** window.

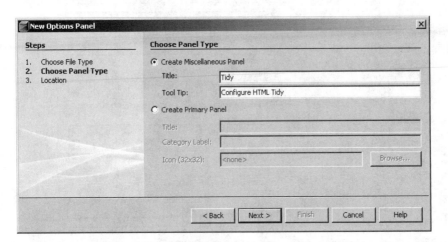

Figure 23.5: HTML Tidy configuration

23.4.1 Extending the Options Window

It is possible to generate a new category for the **Options** window, with a corresponding icon in the left sidebar. Otherwise, new configuration settings can simply be added to the **Miscellaneous** category. If you have a lot of settings to add, it is probably best to group them into a separate category. For HTML Tidy, however, we only need to set one parameter, so it makes sense to add it to the **Miscellaneous** category.

To add new configuration settings to the **Options** window, start by opening the **New File** wizard (Ctrl-N):

1. Select **NetBeans Module Development** under **Categories**, then select **Options Panel** under **File Types**. Click **Next**.

2. In **Choose Panel Type**, make sure the **Create Miscellaneous Panel** radio button is selected. This specifies that a new subcategory within the **Miscellaneous** panel must be generated. Enter a meaningful name and tooltip for the new panel, as displayed in Figure 23.6. Click **Next**.

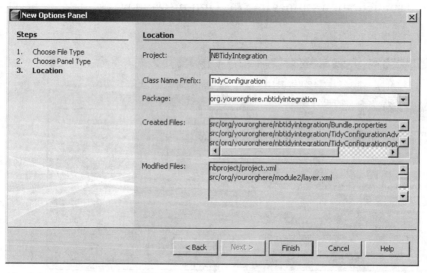

Figure 23.6: **Options Panel** wizard, step 2: **Choose Panel Type**

3. In Step 3, **Location**, you can specify a name and location for the generated classes. Leave all the defaults to allow the IDE generate the new panel for the NBTidyIntegration module. All files created or modified by the

wizard are listed here, giving you an overview of how the project is affected (see Figure 23.7). Note that three Java files are generated, as well as a form that we need to design in order to specify its appearance in the **Miscellaneous** panel.

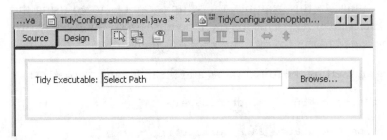

Figure 23.7: **Options Panel** wizard, step 3: **Location**

When designing the panel, the GUI Builder (also known as Matisse) can be used. With the GUI Builder, the panel can be created quickly and efficiently without requiring a lot of knowledge of the underlying code. For more information, consult Chapter 11. For our purposes, what is required is a simple form to capture user input for the path to HTML Tidy executable. Use Figure 23.8 as a guideline.

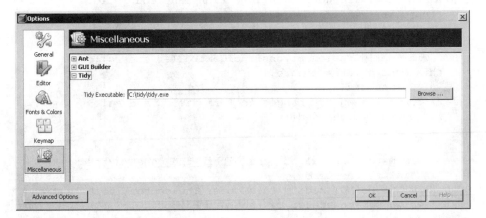

Figure 23.8: Designing the **Options** panel

23.4.2   Persisting the Options

In order to permanently store the options set by the user, the `load()` and `store()` methods of the `TidyConfigurationPanel` class are called by the NetBeans Platform. When this panel class was created by the wizard, skeletons for these methods were also generated, including some suggestions on how to handle the settings. In this example, the settings can be stored using the standard Java Preferences API. This may well be the easiest way, as only two lines need to be added to the `load()` and `store()` methods.

For loading and setting the initial value, add the following to `load()`:

```
String defaultValue = NbBundle.getMessage(
  TidyErrorCheckAction.class,
  "AdvancedOption_Executable_Path_Default");
executableTextField.setText(Preferences.userNodeForPackage(
  TidyConfigurationPanel.class).get(
  TidyRunnable.EXECUTABLE_KEY, defaultValue));
```

For storing the value after it has been changed, add the following to `store()`:

```
Preferences.userNodeForPackage(TidyConfigurationPanel.class).
  put(TidyRunnable.EXECUTABLE_KEY,
    executableTextField.getText());
```

The complete listing for the `TidyConfigurationPanel` class is below:

```
final class TidyConfigurationPanel extends javax.swing.JPanel {
  private final TidyConfigurationOptionsPanelController
    controller;

  TidyConfigurationPanel(
      TidyConfigurationOptionsPanelController controller) {
    this.controller = controller;
    initComponents();
    // TODO: listen to changes in form fields and call
    // controller.changed()
  }

  /** This method is called from within the constructor to
   * initialize the form.
   * WARNING: Do NOT modify this code. The content of this method
   * is always regenerated by the Form Editor.
   */
```

```java
// <editor-fold defaultstate="collapsed"
//             desc=" Generated Code ">
private void initComponents() { ... } // </editor-fold>

private void configurationChangePerformed(
    java.awt.event.ActionEvent evt) {

  String defaultValue=NbBundle.getMessage(
    TidyErrorCheckAction.class,
    "AdvancedOption_Executable_Path_Default");
  String storedValue = Preferences.userNodeForPackage(
    TidyConfigurationPanel.class).
    get(TidyRunnable.EXECUTABLE_KEY, defaultValue);
  if (!executableTextField.getText().equals(storedValue))
    controller.changed();
}

private void executableBrowseButtonActionPerformed(
    java.awt.event.ActionEvent evt) {

  String filename = executableTextField.getText();
  JFileChooser chooser = new JFileChooser(new File(filename));

  // Show open dialog; this method does not return until
  // the dialog is closed
  int result = chooser.showOpenDialog(this);

  // Determine which button was clicked to close the dialog
  switch (result) {
    case JFileChooser.APPROVE_OPTION:
      File selectedFile = chooser.getSelectedFile();
      executableTextField.setText(
        selectedFile.getAbsolutePath());
      controller.changed();
      break;
    case JFileChooser.CANCEL_OPTION:
      // Cancel or the close-dialog icon was clicked
      break;
    case JFileChooser.ERROR_OPTION:
      // The selection process did not complete successfully
      break;
  }
}
```

```
void load() {
  String defaultValue=NbBundle.getMessage(
    TidyErrorCheckAction.class,
    "AdvancedOption_Executable_Path_Default");
  executableTextField.setText(Preferences.userNodeForPackage(
    TidyConfigurationPanel.class).get(
    TidyRunnable.EXECUTABLE_KEY, defaultValue));
  // or:
  // someTextField.setText(SomeSystemOption.getDefault().
  //   getSomeStringProperty());
}

void store() {
  Preferences.userNodeForPackage(TidyConfigurationPanel.class).
    put(TidyRunnable.EXECUTABLE_KEY,
        executableTextField.getText());
  // or:
  // SomeSystemOption.getDefault().setSomeStringProperty(
  // someTextField.getText());
}

/** check whether form is consistent and complete*/
boolean valid() {
  String path = executableTextField.getText();
  return new File(path).exists();
}

// Variable declarations - do not modify
private javax.swing.JButton executableBrowseButton;
private javax.swing.JLabel executableLabel;
private javax.swing.JTextField executableTextField;
private javax.swing.JScrollPane jScrollPane1;
private javax.swing.JTextArea jTextArea1;
// End of variable declarations
}
```

Further information on the Options API can be found in Section 18.1

23.5   Formatting and Converting Files

So far, our module only offers error checking. After it is run, the files remain unmodified and the user must fix any errors himself. But the HTML Tidy tool can do much more than this! It is capable of fixing HTML syntax errors automatically. The file can be reformatted, tags can be cleaned or simply converted to uppercase. It would be nice if all these features were available in the IDE as well. In HTML Tidy, the user specifies the conversion using command-line parameters. We can integrate this functionality into the IDE.

23.5.1   Manipulating Files

Before we consider performing a conversion on a file, there are two issues that need to be addressed. The first is how to handle unsaved modifications. The second is, whether it is possible to undo changes. Unsaved modifications occur when the user does not save the file while editing it. When the HTML Tidy action is run, it processes the actual file content from the last save. For the error checking described in the first part of this chapter, any unsaved changes made by the user would be ignored. Fortunately, since we did not modify anything, no harm was done. In the worst case scenario, wrong error messages could appear, or the line numbers could be shifted. However, if a file is converted, any unsaved changes will be lost.

There are two approaches to handling unsaved changes. The system can be forced to save the file automatically. For example, this can be done before a project is compiled. Prior to saving a file, the DataObject is checked to see whether it has been modified. If so, a save() method is provided in the SaveCookie class (see Chapter 4 for more information on cookies), as shown in Example 23.1.

Example 23.1: Forcing a file to be saved automatically

```
/** Save the DataObject if it has been modified */
void forceSave(DataObject dataObject) throws IOException {
  if (dataObject.isModified()) {
    SaveCookie cookie =
      (SaveCookie)dataObject.getCookie(SaveCookie.class);
    if (cookie!=null) {
      cookie.save();
    }
  }
}
```

After the file has been saved, its path may be passed to the external process as an additional command-line parameter, as we did in the first steps of the integration (see Section 23.2.1). The compile and build actions of the IDE work like this; they force the modified files to be saved before the compiler is started. Users, however, may sometimes not expect this behavior, so it is a good idea to notify the user and ask for permission prior to writing any changes to disk.

Another approach is to directly retrieve the content from the Source Editor and pass it to the external process. In this case, the content of the file is written directly to the input stream of the external process. The external process is usually able to read its input from the standard input stream. This is true for HTML Tidy, but also for many other tools, especially those that were originally developed for UNIX platforms. The following code shows how to retrieve the content of a `DataObject` from the Source Editor:

```
public static StyledDocument getDocument(DataObject dataObject) {
    final EditorCookie edit =
      (EditorCookie)dataObject.getCookie(EditorCookie.class);
    if (edit == null) {
      ErrorManager.getDefault().log(ErrorManager.USER,
                                    "no editor cookie!");
      return null;
    }
    return edit.getDocument();
  }
```

The two approaches discussed above handle their conversion results differently. In the first case, the result is written back to file. The NetBeans Platform automatically recognizes the changes and updates the file in the Source Editor, if it is already opened. In the second case, the external process typically writes the result to its output stream. The module then needs to capture that stream and display it in the Source Editor. The file in the Source Editor remains unsaved, if not explicitly saved. And, since in the second case the Source Editor is involved, it is possible to revert back to the original contents simply by selecting **Undo** (Ctrl-Z) from the **Edit** menu.

So, which approach to choose—save the files automatically or manipulate the Source Editor? This depends on the tool that you are running externally. HTML Tidy supports both options, but not all tools do. You may be forced to use one of the solutions. It is also possible to use a combined approach where the content is read from file but the result is captured and pasted directly into the Source Editor. From a usability perspective, the first approach is preferable in cases where many files need to be processed. For example, consider a scenario in which all HTML files in a project require conversion. Since external changes cannot be undone from within the IDE, it could be helpful to store a copy of the file or to print the result to a different file or directory.

While the next section offers an example of the first approach, the second one is preferable for this section, because only one file is to be converted. The `ConvertToUpperAction` class should therefore be restricted from selecting more than one file. This can be set in the **New Action** wizard. Also, the action should only be registered for the **Editor Context Menu Item**, since the way it is implemented requires that the file is opened in the Source Editor.

The `TidyRunnable` class from the example above uses the filename in the command line to specify the files to be checked. When working with the contents rather than the filename, the behavior needs to be changed. Each external process may use three standardized input/output streams to communicate. These streams are easy to access by the Java API. In the first example, the error stream of the process is accessed by calling `process.getErrorStream()` (see Section 23.2.1). Now, we also need to access the other two—the standard input and standard output streams. Being treated here as an external process, `process.getInputStream()` returns an input stream that we can print to. The content is not read from file, but taken directly from the Source Editor. Once the external process is created, the content is written to its input stream. If no filename is specified in the command line, HTML Tidy, like most command-line tools in UNIX, expects to receive content from the input stream. In UNIX, this can be used to combine several commands into one command line by connecting the output stream of one command with the input stream of the next. After the call, we need to read the output stream of the external process to get the results back. In the previous examples, only the error stream was of interest. It was redirected to the **Output** window and we keep this behavior here. Additionally, the modified content is printed to the standard output of the process. We get access to that content by reading from `process.getOutputStream()`. Reading both error and output streams simultaneously has to be done carefully. One reader may potentially block the other, resulting in a deadlock in the IDE. To prevent this from happening, access to the external process' input and output streams is managed in separate threads.

Writing the editor content to the process input stream is handled in a straightforward manner by implementing the `Runnable` interface:

```
public class PrintInputStreamRunnable implements Runnable {
  String content;
  OutputStream out;
  public PrintInputStreamRunnable(OutputStream outStream,
                                  String content) {
    this.out=outStream;
    this.content=content;
  }

  public void run(){
    try {
        out.write(content.getBytes());
        out.close();
    } catch (IOException ioe) {
        ErrorManager.getDefault().notify(
          ErrorManager.WARNING, ioe);
    }
  }
}
```

The stream and the content are passed in the initializer, because the `run()` method of the `Runnable` interface does not allow for arguments. After writing the content, the stream should be closed, which prevents the external process from trying to listen for more content.

The code for reading content is done in a similar manner. The received content is stored in a `StringBuilder` variable. To retrieve it, the `getResult()` method is called:

```java
public class ReadOutputStreamRunnable implements Runnable {
  Reader reader;
  StringBuilder result = new StringBuilder();

  public ReadOutputStreamRunnable(Reader reader) {
    this.reader = reader;
  }

  public void run() {
    char[] cbuf = new char[8192];
    int read;

    try {
      while ((read = reader.read(cbuf)) != -1) {
        result.append(cbuf, 0, read);
      }
    }
    catch (IOException ex) {
      // Stream closed
    }
  }
  public String getResult()  {
    return result.toString();
  }
}
```

The external process can be called via several helper classes, as demonstrated in the following example. To reuse as much code as possible from the first examples, the previously used `TidyRunnable` class is extended by changing the behavior of the `processDataObject()`. Since the extended class is used to perform conversions by HTML Tidy, the class is called `TidyConversionRunnable`. It calls the external process in the same way the `TidyRunnable` did, but before that, it grabs the contents from the Source Editor. It then reads the results of the process back from HTML Tidy using the `ReadOutputStreamRunnable` class described above. This is performed as an external task. To make sure all content has been read, it waits for the task to finish before reading the result. The old content from the Source Editor is then replaced by the retrieved content. Since the Source Editor is aware of this change, the undo methods may be used to revert the changes made by HTML Tidy.

```java
package org.yourorghere.nbtidyintegration;

...

public class TidyConversionRunnable extends TidyRunnable {
  private static RequestProcessor processor = null;
  /** Initialize the HTML Tidy runnable.*/
  public TidyConversionRunnable(Node node,
                                    String commandLineArgs {
    super(new Node[] {node}, commandLineArgs);
  }

  /**
   * Run external program with this data object.
   * @param executable Absolute path to the executable
   * @param writer Writer for the output tab
   * @param dataObject the data object that is processed
   * @throws java.lang.InterruptedException
   * @throws java.io.IOException
   */
  @Override
  void processDataObject(final OutputWriter writer,
      final String executable, final DataObject dataObject)
      throws IOException {
    try {
      writer.println("Running: "+executable+ " Arguments: "+
                    getCommandLineArgs());
      StyledDocument doc = getDocument(dataObject);
      String content = doc.getText(0, doc.getLength());

      NbProcessDescriptor tidyProcessDesc =
        new NbProcessDescriptor(executable,
                                getCommandLineArgs());
      Process process = tidyProcessDesc.exec();
      if(processor==null)
        processor =
          new RequestProcessor("ConversionRunnable",1,true);
      processor.post(new PrintInputStreamRunnable(
        process.getOutputStream(), content));
      BufferedReader outReader = new BufferedReader(
        new InputStreamReader(process.getInputStream()), 8192);
      ReadOutputStreamRunnable outRunnable =
        new ReadOutputStreamRunnable(outReader);

      Task outTask = processor.post(outRunnable);
      readOutput(writer, dataObject, process.getErrorStream());
```

```
          process.waitFor();
          outTask.waitFinished(10000);
          String result = outRunnable.getResult();
          try {
            outReader.close();
            process.getErrorStream().close();
          }
          catch (IOException ioe) {
            // Stream already closed, this is fine
            ErrorManager.getDefault().notify(
              ErrorManager.WARNING, ioe);
          }

          doc.remove(0, doc.getLength());
          doc.insertString(0, result, null);
        }
      catch (BadLocationException e) {
        ErrorManager.getDefault().notify(ErrorManager.WARNING, e);
      }
      catch (InterruptedException e) {
        ErrorManager.getDefault().notify(ErrorManager.WARNING, e);
      }
      return;
    }

  public static StyledDocument
      getDocument(DataObject dataObject) {
      final EditorCookie edit =
        (EditorCookie)dataObject.getCookie(EditorCookie.class);
      if (edit == null) {
        ErrorManager.getDefault().log(ErrorManager.USER,
                                      "no editor cookie!");
        return null;
      }
      return edit.getDocument();
    }
  }
}
```

To complete this example, the conversion should be connected to the IDE. The following Action performs formatting of the HTML tags. HTML Tidy has a set of rules which it applies by default. Through the use of command-line arguments, various settings can be chosen. In this example, we convert all tags to uppercase. Upon converting the document, we write the result back to the Source Editor by using TidyConversionRunnable.

```
public final class ConvertToUpperAction extends CookieAction {
  private static RequestProcessor processor = null;
  protected void performAction(Node[] activatedNodes) {
    if(processor==null)
      processor =
        new RequestProcessor("ConvertHTMLUpper",1,true);
    TidyConversionRunnable runnable = new TidyConversionRunnable(
      activatedNodes[0], "-upper");
    processor.post(runnable);
  }
}
```

23.5.2   Seeing the Difference

Another useful feature would be a **Diff** window displaying the original and modified versions side by side. The IDE's **Diff** window, typically used to display changes in files under version control, can be applied here. The user can then decide whether to accept or reject any changes. All this can be achieved with minor modifications to the above code.

```
if (diff(before, rewritten, mime)) {
  doc.remove(0, doc.getLength());
  doc.insertString(0, rewritten, null);
}
```

Since the action cannot be completed before the user decides how to proceed, the **Diff** window needs to be displayed in a notifier. For this, the following `diff()` method must be added to the `TidyConversionRunnable` class:

```
boolean diff(String before, String after, String mime) {
  Diff diff = Diff.getDefault();
  JPanel panel = new JPanel();
  Component tp = null;
  StringReader bReader = new StringReader(before);
  StringReader bAfter = new StringReader(after);
  try
  {
    tp = diff.createDiff("DiffBefore", NbBundle.getMessage(
      getClass(),"TidyDiffBeforeTitle"), bReader, "DiffAfter",
      NbBundle.getMessage(getClass(),"TidyDiffAfterTitle"),
      bAfter, mime);
    tp.setMinimumSize(new Dimension(320,600));
    panel.setMinimumSize(new Dimension(320,600));
  }
```

```
catch (IOException ioex)
{
  ErrorManager.getDefault().notify(ioex);
  return false;
}
panel.add(tp);
DialogDescriptor d = new DialogDescriptor(
  tp, NbBundle.getMessage(getClass(), "TitleDiff"));
d.setModal(true);
d.setMessageType(NotifyDescriptor.PLAIN_MESSAGE);
d.setOptionType(NotifyDescriptor.DEFAULT_OPTION);
Dialog dlg = DialogDisplayer.getDefault().createDialog(d);
dlg.pack();
dlg.setSize(new Dimension(800,600));
dlg.setVisible(true);
return (d.getValue() == NotifyDescriptor.OK_OPTION);
}
```

The **Diff** window (Figure 23.9) is a fine example of how one can very easily reuse tools that are already available somewhere in the NetBeans ecosystem.

23.6   Controlling the Conversion

HTML Tidy is very powerful. There are many file conversion options. The previous section only implemented one of them—converting tags to uppercase. It is possible to define actions, similar to what was accomplished in the previous example, for other conversions as well. This would be a rather tedious approach, however. It's much better to implement a graphical user interface, allowing the user to specify several conversion options at once. There are basically two ways to add a user interface to the platform. One is by providing a window as a `TopComponent`, the other is by offering a wizard. Since the interface should only be visible when setting up the conversion, it would be good style to provide this as a wizard.

23.6.1   Creating the Wizard

Wizards are used in IDEs for all sorts of things, and the NetBeans Platform offers basic tools for creating new wizards. There is even a **New Wizard** wizard that can be used to generate wizards. The developer only has to specify the class name prefix and the number of required steps, and a template including

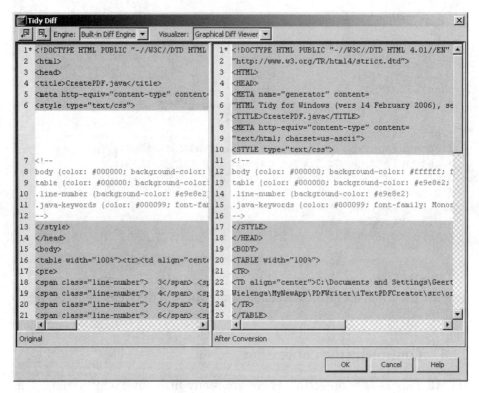

Figure 23.9: **Diff** window

the panels is generated. For the purposes of this chapter, the wizard for converting files with HTML Tidy requires two steps. In the second step of the wizard, the user specifies the command-line parameters (Figure 23.10). The third step of the wizard displays a summary list of all files that are to be modified (Figure 23.11).

For the generation of the wizard class skeleton, two classes are created for each step, one representing the visual part (the view) and the other specifying a controller. The interfaces for each step are created separately using the GUI Builder. For this example, the first panel of the wizard enables all command-line options of HTML Tidy to be generated as components to a graphical interface (Figure 23.12). The second panel has a `JList` to hold the list of selected files (Figure 23.13). This allows the user to check which files are to be modified

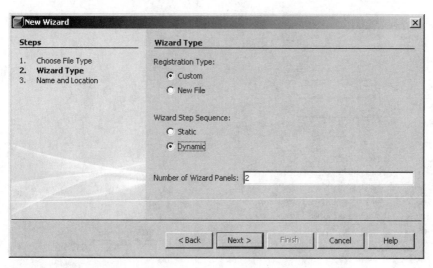

Figure 23.10: **New Wizard** wizard, step 2: **Wizard Type**

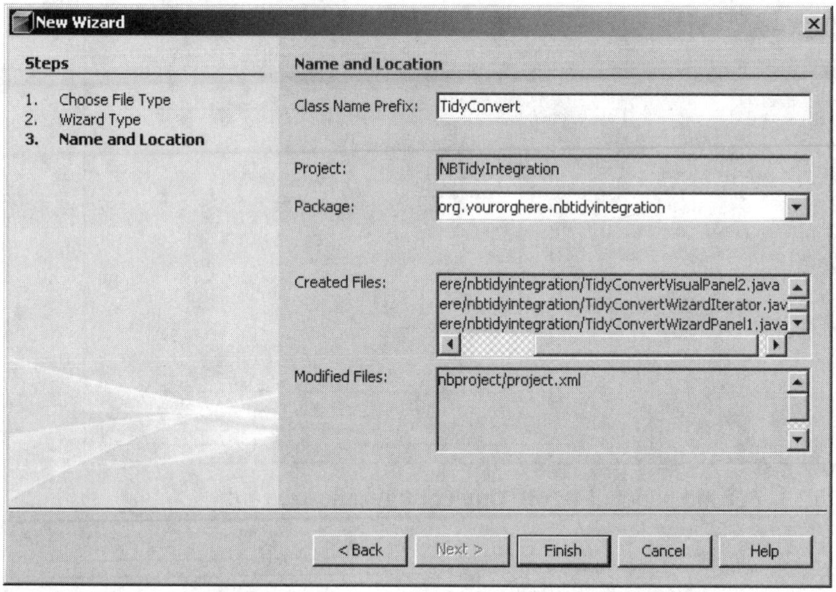

Figure 23.11: **New Wizard** wizard, step 3: **Name and Location**

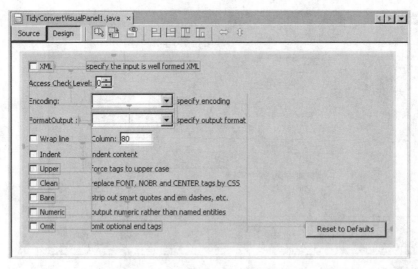

Figure 23.12: First panel of **HTML Tidy Configuration** wizard.

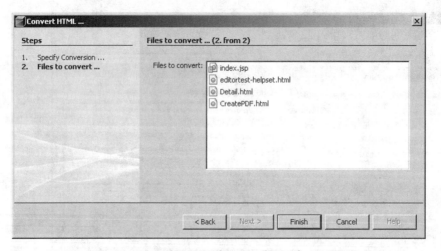

Figure 23.13: Second panel of **HTML Tidy Configuration** wizard

just prior to running the action. This behavior is similar to the **New File** wizard which we used before to generate actions and wizards.

While the `VisualPanel` and `WizardPanel` classes act as viewers and controllers, respectively, we need to add a model to represent the configuration. Here, we apply the well-known MVC pattern in which the user interface design is divided into multiple responsibilities. Therefore, a simple `TidySettings` class is created. For handling the settings, an approach similar to that of the **Options** section can be taken. If all settings are stored to the `Preferences` class, any configuration that has been previously set by the user is used once the wizard is reopened. `TidySettings` does not include any business logic, but simply provides keys for the preferences and their default values. It provides arrays with options that can be used in the wizards to offer valid values for user input. The class also supplies a method to generate the command-line arguments for the current settings (`generateCommandLineArguments()`).

As you may notice from the code, building and configuring all the keys and values for the UI is a lot of work, especially if there are so many options as in HTML Tidy. To prevent typos when reading and writing the settings, static strings should be used as keys. Furthermore, the settings need to be initialized properly, and we should provide a meaningful default value. For some options, only some values are valid and we need to specify those. It would be nice to have the bulk of this work done automatically. Eventually, the Beans Binding Framework, which is currently defined in a JSR, will make this possible. For now, however, this has to be done manually.

```
public class TidySettings {
  public static String KEY_CONVERSION_UPPER="conversion.upper";
  public static String KEY_CONVERSION_BARE="conversion.bare";
  public static String KEY_CONVERSION_CLEAN="conversion.clean";
  public static String
    KEY_CONVERSION_NUMERIC="conversion.numeric";
  public static String KEY_CONVERSION_OMIT="conversion.omit";
  public static String KEY_CONVERSION_WRAP="conversion.wrap";
  public static String
    KEY_CONVERSION_WRAP_COLUMN="conversion.wrapColumn";
  public static String KEY_CONVERSION_XML="conversion.xml";
  public static String
    KEY_CONVERSION_ENCODING="conversion.encoding";
```

```
public static String
  KEY_CONVERSION_FORMAT_OUTPUT="conversion.formatOutput";
public static String KEY_CONVERSION_INDENT="conversion.indent";
public static String KEY_CONVERSION_ACCESS_CHECK_LEVEL=
  "conversion.accessCheckLevel";

public static String CONVERSION_FORMAT_OUTPUT_ASIS = "as is";
public static String CONVERSION_FORMAT_OUTPUT_XHTML = "xhtml";
public static String CONVERSION_FORMAT_OUTPUT_HTML = "html";

public static String DEFAULT_CONVERSION_ENCODING = "ascii";
public static boolean DEFAULT_CONVERSION_INDENT = Boolean.TRUE;
public static boolean DEFAULT_CONVERSION_CLEAN = Boolean.TRUE;
public static boolean DEFAULT_CONVERSION_BARE = Boolean.FALSE;
public static boolean DEFAULT_CONVERSION_UPPER = Boolean.FALSE;
public static boolean
  DEFAULT_CONVERSION_NUMERIC = Boolean.FALSE;
public static boolean DEFAULT_CONVERSION_OMIT = Boolean.FALSE;
public static boolean DEFAULT_CONVERSION_XML = Boolean.FALSE;
public static String DEFAULT_CONVERSION_FORMAT_OUTPUT =
  CONVERSION_FORMAT_OUTPUT_ASIS;
public static boolean DEFAULT_CONVERSION_WRAP = Boolean.TRUE;
public static int DEFAULT_CONVERSION_WRAP_COLUMN = 80;
public static int DEFAULT_CONVERSION_ACCESS_CHECK_LEVEL = 0;

public static String[] ENCODINGS = {
  "raw",      // Output values above 127 are left without
              // conversion to entities
  "ascii",    // Use ISO-8859-1 for input, US-ASCII for output
  "latin0",   // Use ISO-8859-15 for input, US-ASCII for output
  "latin1",   // Use ISO-8859-1 for both input and output
  "iso2022",  // Use ISO-2022 for both input and output
  "utf8",     // Use UTF-8 for both input and output
  "mac",      // Use MacRoman for input, US-ASCII for output
  "win1252",  // Use Windows-1252 for input, US-ASCII for output
  "ibm858",   // Use IBM-858 (CP850+Euro) for input, US-ASCII
              // for output
  "utf16le",  // Use UTF-16LE for both input and output
  "utf16be",  // Use UTF-16BE for both input and output
  "utf16",    // Use UTF-16 for both input and output
  "big5",     // Use Big5 for both input and output
  "shiftjis" // Use Shift_JIS for both input and output
};
```

```java
public static String[] FORMAT_OUTPUT_OPTIONS = {
  CONVERSION_FORMAT_OUTPUT_ASIS,
  CONVERSION_FORMAT_OUTPUT_HTML,
  CONVERSION_FORMAT_OUTPUT_XHTML
};

/** Don't create an instance */
private TidySettings(){
}

public static String generateCommandLineArguments() {
  Preferences settings =
    Preferences.userNodeForPackage(TidySettings.class);
  StringBuilder sb = new StringBuilder();

  sb.append(" -").append(settings.get(KEY_CONVERSION_ENCODING,
    DEFAULT_CONVERSION_ENCODING)).append(" ");

  if (settings.getBoolean(KEY_CONVERSION_UPPER,
                          DEFAULT_CONVERSION_UPPER))
    sb.append("-upper ") ;
  if (settings.getBoolean(KEY_CONVERSION_CLEAN,
                          DEFAULT_CONVERSION_CLEAN))
    sb.append("-clean ") ;
  if (settings.getBoolean(KEY_CONVERSION_NUMERIC,
                          DEFAULT_CONVERSION_NUMERIC))
    sb.append("-numeric ") ;
  if (settings.getBoolean(KEY_CONVERSION_BARE,
                          DEFAULT_CONVERSION_BARE))
    sb.append("-bare ") ;
  if (settings.getBoolean(KEY_CONVERSION_OMIT,
                          DEFAULT_CONVERSION_OMIT))
    sb.append("-omit ") ;
  if (settings.getBoolean(KEY_CONVERSION_WRAP,
                          DEFAULT_CONVERSION_WRAP))
    sb.append("-wrap ").append(settings.getInt(
      KEY_CONVERSION_WRAP_COLUMN,
      DEFAULT_CONVERSION_WRAP_COLUMN)).append(" ");
  if (settings.getBoolean(KEY_CONVERSION_INDENT,
                          DEFAULT_CONVERSION_INDENT))
    sb.append("-indent ") ;
  if (settings.getBoolean(KEY_CONVERSION_XML,
                          DEFAULT_CONVERSION_XML))
    sb.append("-xml ") ;
```

```
    String format_output =
      settings.get(KEY_CONVERSION_FORMAT_OUTPUT,
                   DEFAULT_CONVERSION_FORMAT_OUTPUT);
    if (!format_output.equals(CONVERSION_FORMAT_OUTPUT_ASIS))
      sb.append("-as").append (format_output).append (" ") ;

    sb.append("-access ").append(settings.getInt(
      KEY_CONVERSION_ACCESS_CHECK_LEVEL,
      DEFAULT_CONVERSION_ACCESS_CHECK_LEVEL));

    return sb.toString();
  }

  public static Object[] getEncodings(){
    return ENCODINGS;
  }

  public static Object[] getFormatOutputOptions(){
    return FORMAT_OUTPUT_OPTIONS;
  }
}
```

Next, the model and the view need to be connected through the controller. The wizard panels provide a place for this with the readSettings() and storeSettings() methods. These are called when a panel is opened or stored, respectively. Specifically, readSettings() is called when a panel is displayed; previously stored settings must be read from Preferences and used to initialize the widgets. If the tool has not been used before, the default values are applied. Finally, the widgets need to be updated accordingly. Likewise, when a panel is closed, all settings must be stored back to Preferences again.

```
package org.yourorghere.nbtidyintegration;

...
public class TidyConvertWizardPanel1
    implements WizardDescriptor.Panel {
  ...

  // You can use a settings object to keep track of state.
  // Normally, the settings object will be the WizardDescriptor,
  // so you can use WizardDescriptor.getProperty & putProperty
  // to store information entered by the user.
```

```java
public void readSettings(Object settings) {
  TidyConvertVisualPanel1 c =
    (TidyConvertVisualPanel1)component;
  Preferences p =
    Preferences.userNodeForPackage(TidySettings.class);
  c.setEncoding(p.get(TidySettings.KEY_CONVERSION_ENCODING,
                TidySettings.DEFAULT_CONVERSION_ENCODING));
  c.setIndent(p.getBoolean(TidySettings.KEY_CONVERSION_INDENT,
              TidySettings.DEFAULT_CONVERSION_INDENT));
  c.setClean(p.getBoolean(TidySettings.KEY_CONVERSION_CLEAN,
             TidySettings.DEFAULT_CONVERSION_CLEAN));
  c.setBare(p.getBoolean(TidySettings.KEY_CONVERSION_BARE,
            TidySettings.DEFAULT_CONVERSION_BARE));
  c.setUpper(p.getBoolean(TidySettings.KEY_CONVERSION_UPPER,
             TidySettings.DEFAULT_CONVERSION_UPPER));
  c.setNumeric(p.getBoolean(
               TidySettings.KEY_CONVERSION_NUMERIC,
               TidySettings.DEFAULT_CONVERSION_NUMERIC));
  c.setOmit(p.getBoolean(TidySettings.KEY_CONVERSION_OMIT,
            TidySettings.DEFAULT_CONVERSION_OMIT));
  c.setXML(p.getBoolean(TidySettings.KEY_CONVERSION_XML,
           TidySettings.DEFAULT_CONVERSION_XML));
  c.setWrap(p.getBoolean(TidySettings.KEY_CONVERSION_WRAP,
            TidySettings.DEFAULT_CONVERSION_WRAP),
            p.getInt(TidySettings.KEY_CONVERSION_WRAP_COLUMN,
            TidySettings.DEFAULT_CONVERSION_WRAP_COLUMN));
  c.setAccessCheckLevel(p.getInt(
    TidySettings.KEY_CONVERSION_ACCESS_CHECK_LEVEL,
    TidySettings.DEFAULT_CONVERSION_ACCESS_CHECK_LEVEL));

  String formatOutput =
    p.get(TidySettings.KEY_CONVERSION_FORMAT_OUTPUT,
          TidySettings.DEFAULT_CONVERSION_FORMAT_OUTPUT);
  String selectedItem =
    TidySettings.CONVERSION_FORMAT_OUTPUT_ASIS;
  if ((formatOutput!=null)&&(formatOutput.length()>0)) {
    if (formatOutput.toLowerCase().contains("xhtml")) {
      selectedItem=TidySettings.CONVERSION_FORMAT_OUTPUT_XHTML;
    }
    else if (formatOutput.toLowerCase().contains("html")) {
      selectedItem=TidySettings.CONVERSION_FORMAT_OUTPUT_HTML;
    }
  }
  c.setFormatOutput(selectedItem);
}
```

```
public void storeSettings(Object settings) {
  TidyConvertVisualPanel1 c =
    (TidyConvertVisualPanel1)component;
  Preferences p =
    Preferences.userNodeForPackage(TidySettings.class);
  p.putBoolean(TidySettings.KEY_CONVERSION_BARE, c.getBare());
  p.putBoolean(TidySettings.KEY_CONVERSION_UPPER,
                c.getUpper());
  p.putBoolean(TidySettings.KEY_CONVERSION_CLEAN,
                c.getClean());
  p.putBoolean(TidySettings.KEY_CONVERSION_NUMERIC,
                c.getNumeric());
  p.putBoolean(TidySettings.KEY_CONVERSION_OMIT,
                c.getOmit());
  p.putBoolean(TidySettings.KEY_CONVERSION_WRAP,
                c.getWrapLine());
  p.putInt(TidySettings.KEY_CONVERSION_WRAP_COLUMN,
            c.getWrapLineColumn());
  p.putBoolean(TidySettings.KEY_CONVERSION_XML, c.getXML());
  p.put(TidySettings.KEY_CONVERSION_ENCODING, c.getEncoding());
  p.put(TidySettings.KEY_CONVERSION_FORMAT_OUTPUT,
        c.getFormatOutput());
  p.putBoolean(TidySettings.KEY_CONVERSION_INDENT,
                c.getIndent());
  p.putInt(TidySettings.KEY_CONVERSION_ACCESS_CHECK_LEVEL,
            c.getAccessCheckLevel());
  }
}
```

For the second panel of the wizard (step 3, **Name and Location**), all files that are to be created and modified are conveniently displayed in **Created Files** and **Modified files**, respectively. The user can then check this and potentially cancel the wizard if the correct files are not listed. In order to fill the file list once the panel is visible, the `readSettings()` method from the wizard panel is used again. It calls the `setFiles()` method to initialize the list. The nodes are taken from the properties of the `WizardDescriptor`, which holds the wizard state. When calling the wizard, we need to add the nodes as a property, as shown below:

```
package org.yourorghere.nbtidyintegration;

...

public class TidyConvertWizardPanel2 implements
  WizardDescriptor.Panel {

  ...

  public void readSettings(Object settings) {
    if (settings instanceof WizardDescriptor) {
      Object nodes =
        ((WizardDescriptor)settings).getProperty("nodes");
      ((TidyConvertVisualPanel2)component).
        setFiles((Node[])nodes);
    }
  }
  public void storeSettings(Object settings) {}

}
```

In the following listing, the method `setFiles()` is implemented. The nodes are added to a default list model. If not explicitly set, a default renderer is used to display the values of the list items. If the default renderer is used, the `toString()` method is called to represent an object from the list. Since the `toString()` method of a node does not return the display name, we need to add our own `ListCellRenderer`. If it inherits from the `DefaultCellRenderer`, only a single method needs to be overwritten. The `getComponent()` method of the renderer is responsible for generating a widget for a list item when it becomes visible. The default returns a `JLabel`. If we inherit from the default, we can reuse this label by calling the superclass method. Afterward, the `JLabel` properties are adapted to meet our requirements. The methods provided by the Nodes API are used for this purpose. The Nodes API offers the `getHtmlDisplayName()` method, which returns the filename in HTML syntax. If no HTML name is available, the standard name is used. The `JLabel` only interprets the label as HTML if the text is surrounded by the `<html> </html>` tags. For most objects it does not make a difference whether it is printed as HTML or not. But if you work, for example, with code versioning, the label color describes the state of the file, as shown in Figure 23.13: If the label is blue, the file has been modified; if it is green, it is new.

Since we have access to the data object, we may also check whether the files have unsaved changes. If so, they are marked with an asterisk ("*") similar to the tabs shown above the Source Editor. Additionally, the filename alone may not be unique within a project, and the path is consequently added as a tooltip for the user. Also, the correct icon that specifies the node type should be used. With this cell renderer, the panel has the same look as other components in the IDE.

```
package org.yourorghere.nbtidyintegration;

...

public final class TidyConvertVisualPanel2 extends JPanel {

  public String getName() {
    return NbBundle.getMessage(getClass(),
                          "CTL_TidyConversionWizardStep2");
  }
  ...

  // Variable declarations - do not modify
  private javax.swing.JLabel fileLabel;
  private javax.swing.JList fileList;
  private javax.swing.JScrollPane jScrollPane1;
  // End of variable declarations

  puic void setFiles(Node[] nodes) {
    DefaultListModel model = new DefaultListModel();

    for (int i =0; i<nodes.length; i++) {
      model.addElement(nodes[i]);
    }
    fileList.setModel(model);
    fileList.setCellRenderer(new NodeCellRenderer());
  }
```

```
private class NodeCellRenderer extends
                                    DefaultListCellRenderer {
  NodeCellRenderer() {
    super();
  }

  public Component getListCellRendererComponent(
      JList list, Object value, int index,
      boolean isSelected, boolean cellHasFocus) {
    super.getListCellRendererComponent(
      list,value,index,isSelected,cellHasFocus);
    Node node = (Node)value;

    String label=node.getHtmlDisplayName();
    if(label==null)
        label=node.getDisplayName();
    DataObject dataObject =
      (DataObject)node.getCookie(DataObject.class);
    if (dataObject.isModified()) {
        setText("<html>"+label+"*</html>");
    } else {
        setText("<html>"+label+"</html>");
    }
    FileObject fileObject = dataObject.getPrimaryFile();
    File file = FileUtil.toFile(fileObject);
    setToolTipText(file.getAbsolutePath());
    setIcon(new ImageIcon(node.getIcon(
                        BeanInfo.ICON_COLOR_16x16)));
    return this;
  }
 }
}
```

This example only demonstrates how to list the files as nodes. Since a wizards is generally only active for a short time—when the user runs it—it is not necessary to support interaction between the list and other parts of the IDE. If you want to display nodes in a TopComponent window, you should use the widgets provided by the Explorer API described in Chapter 9.

23.6.2   Connecting the Wizard

Once the wizard is complete, an action must be defined for invoking it. The action operates on the same objects as those previously described for error checking, so the first steps are the same (see Section 23.2.1). An action can be created using the **New Action** wizard, as shown previously. To start the wizard, we need to edit the `performAction()` method again. The code we have to add is slightly complicated, but, fortunately, this does not need to be done manually. When the wizard was generated by the New Wizard wizard, a `WizardIterator` class was created. It includes a sample `performAction()` method in a comment, which can be copied into the newly generated action. Since in this example, a conditionally enabled action is used, the method signature of the template might not match, but this is easy to fix. The `WizardDescriptor` holds all state information during the execution. It can also be used to pass information to, or retrieve information from, the wizard:

```
wizardDescriptor.putProperty ("nodes", activatedNodes);
```

The command-line arguments are generated in `TidySettings` from the preferences that were set in the first panel of the wizard. Unless the user clicks on the Cancel button, the conversion is started.

In previous sections, the action converted the contents of a single file opened in the Source Editor. When the wizard is run, however, the user may want to convert more than one file at once. In this case, a better approach would be to convert the stored files. If the file has unsaved changes, it should be previously saved, as described in Example 23.1. The `forceSave()` is added to the previously used class `TidyRunnable`. The class needs to be modified, so the method is called on every data object. Since in this case, the result is not written back to the Source Editor, the HTML Tidy executable needs to modify the file directly on disk. By adding the `"-m"` option to the command line, HTML Tidy is told to overwrite the file on disk without printing it to the output panel.

```
protected void performAction(Node[] activatedNodes)
{
  WizardDescriptor.Iterator iterator =
    new TidyConvertWizardIterator();
  WizardDescriptor wizardDescriptor =
    new WizardDescriptor(iterator);
  // {0} will be replaced by
  // WizardDescriptor.Panel.getComponent().getName()
  // {1} will be replaced by WizardDescriptor.Iterator.name()
  wizardDescriptor.setTitleFormat(
    new MessageFormat("{0} ({1})"));
```

```
wizardDescriptor.setTitle(getName());
wizardDescriptor.putProperty ("nodes", activatedNodes);
Dialog dialog =
  DialogDisplayer.getDefault().createDialog(wizardDescriptor);
dialog.setVisible(true);
dialog.toFront();
boolean cancelled = wizardDescriptor.getValue() !=
                    WizardDescriptor.FINISH_OPTION;
if (!cancelled)
{
  // Do something
  String commandLine =
    TidySettings.generateCommandLineArguments();
  if(processor==null)
    processor = new RequestProcessor("ConvertHTML",1,true);
  Runnable runnable =
    new TidyRunnable(activatedNodes, "-m "+commandLine, true);
  processor.post(runnable);
}
}
```

After this is completed, the wizard should appear when the module is re-compiled and run in the target platform. It should now be possible to invoke the wizard and convert files with HTML Tidy. So far, the action has been added only for HTML files, although it could be made available for JSP files as well. As described earlier, this can be achieved simply by copying the action configuration into the JSP section of the XML layer. HTML Tidy also works on XML files and can be used for reformatting purposes, provided it is copied to the XML content type section. The format, however, is slightly different from the one already offered by the standard XML reformatter.

This concludes our discussion of how external tools can be incorporated into the IDE. The module now supports the main features of HTML Tidy. It can be invoked directly from the IDE for HTML and JSP files. You can further enhance the module, but our focus has been on providing a generic example that can be reused for other tool integrations. Various techniques and technologies have been used and, hopefully, you have got ideas on how to integrate your favorite tools into the IDE.

CHAPTER TWENTY-FOUR

Use Case 2: Rich Unger on Application Development

24.1 Introduction

The AudioStation is a small but realistic example of a modular NetBeans Platform application. This application is a simple WAV file editor (Figure 24.1). It was built to work with audio clips containing speech, which would be heard over a telephone. These files use the mu-law encoding, which is commonly used in telephony applications and is natively supported by JavaSound.

What would you expect from a basic sound file editor? You can sample your voice using a microphone and view the result as the familiar waveform. You can select a portion of the waveform for cropping. The one unusual feature is the ability to view the file in the frequency domain as well (using a *fast Fourier transform*, or FFT).

In this chapter, you will learn how to:

1. Use the Datasystems API to create support for a new MIME type (`audio/wav`).

2. Use the Window System API to create a component for viewing files of the new MIME type

3. Use the MultiView Windows API to allow multiple views of the same WAV file.

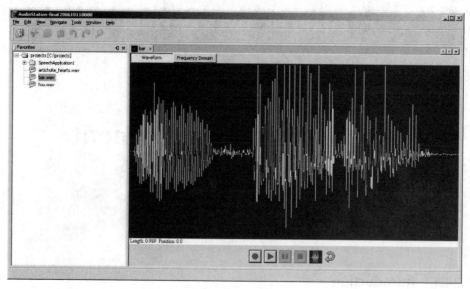

Figure 24.1: The AudioStation application

4. Use the Lookup API to expose an API hook that allows other modules to provide views into your multiview component.

5. Create a module containing one such view (the frequency-domain view).

The final source code for the AudioStation is available in the NetBeans CVS tree under `platform/samples/AudioStation`. You can browse the source code at `www.netbeans.org/source/browse/platform/samples/AudioStation`.

24.2   Getting Started

Create a module suite with the name `AudioStation`. The first thing you'll want to do with your suite is leave out all the IDE modules and use only the basic platform. To do this, right-click your project's node and select **Properties**. Under **Libraries**, uncheck all the other clusters, as shown in Figure 24.2.

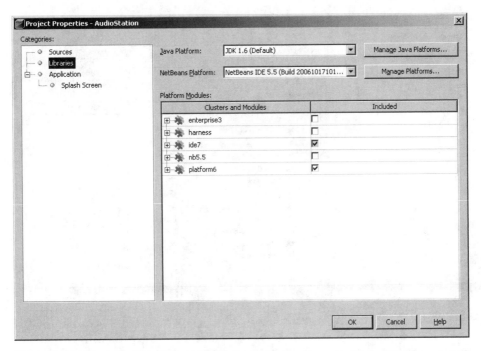

Figure 24.2: Use only the platform cluster

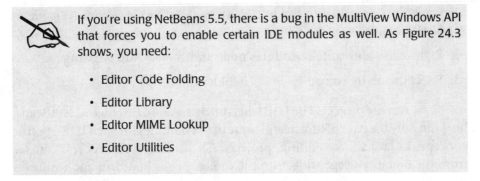

If you're using NetBeans 5.5, there is a bug in the MultiView Windows API that forces you to enable certain IDE modules as well. As Figure 24.3 shows, you need:

- Editor Code Folding

- Editor Library

- Editor MIME Lookup

- Editor Utilities

Something else you might want to do now is add the `wavutils` module from the AudioStation sample code. This module contains all the necessary JavaSound and Java2D code, as well as a set of useful icons. The easiest way to get this into your suite is:

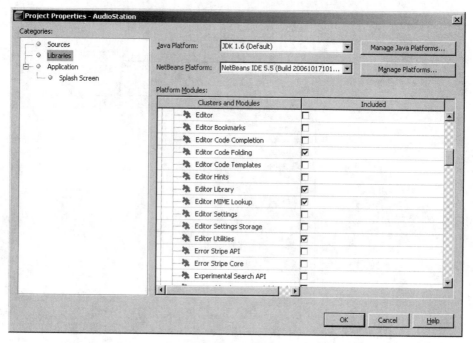

Figure 24.3: Workaround for NetBeans 5.5 bug, fixed in 6.0

1. Copy the `wavutils` folder into your `AudioStation` folder (outside of NetBeans).

2. Right-click your suite's **Modules** node and choose **Add Existing**.

3. Select the newly copied `wavutils` folder.

Now, run the project. The IDE will launch a second instance of NetBeans, but with only the bare platform and none of the modules for such IDE-specific concepts as Java source editing, projects, CVS support, etc. As you can see from the memory usage widget on the toolbar, your platform application is using just a few megabytes of memory.

There are a few things you can do with this basic platform application. You can access the **Update Center** or system options from the **Tools** menu.

The **View** menu has a simple Web browser. These can all be removed using your module's layer file, a technique that we'll get to later.

Under the **Window** menu, there's a **Favorites** item which lets you browse your hard drive. By right-clicking in the **Favorites** window, you can add new root directories to browse from. In Figure 24.4, you can see that I've added a bookmark for my `c:\projects` folder which contains some WAV files.

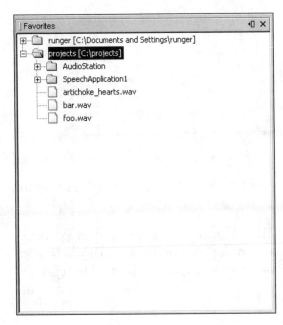

Figure 24.4: Browsing the hard drive using just the basic NetBeans Platform

At this point, NetBeans doesn't know what to do with files that end in `.wav`. If you double-click one of them, NetBeans will ask if you want to treat it as a text file.

The next step is to tell NetBeans that these files have their own MIME type and should be treated differently from plain text files.

24.3   Creating Support for the `audio/wav` MIME Type

Start by adding a new module to your suite, called `wavsupport`, and making it dependent on the `wavutils` module. This module will eventually need some other dependencies as well, so you may as well add them now:

- Core—MultiView Windows
- Datasystems API
- Dialogs API
- Editor Library
- File System API
- Nodes API
- UI Utilities API
- Utilities API
- Window System API

Now you'll want to create support for a new file type. The IDE has a wizard for this (Figure 24.5).

In the next screen, supply a MIME type of `audio/wav` and an extension of `wav` (Figure 24.6). In the final screen, supply a prefix `wav` that will be used in generating all the file names. Also, supply an icon to be used to represent WAV files. You can browse to the `wavIconSmall.gif` file supplied in the `wavutils` module.

When the wizard has finished, you've got everything you need to tell NetBeans about your new MIME type. The only thing you'll want to change is the `WavTemplate.wav` file. This is the file that's copied when a new instance of a WAV file is created. The file that was just created is a text file. You should replace it with a WAV file, such as the zero-sample file that can be downloaded from `www.netbeans.org/source/browse/platform/samples/Audio-Station/wavsupport/src/org/foo/wavsupport/WavTemplate.wav`.

Once you've done that, try running the AudioStation project again. (If your old AudioStation is already running, you can right-click the `wavsupport` module's icon and select **Install/Reload in Target Platform**, which is much

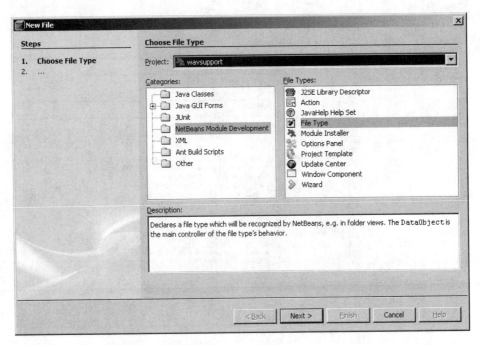

Figure 24.5: The **File Type** wizard

faster.) This time, you should see that any WAV files have the new icon (Figure 24.7).

Attempting to open these files by double-clicking them, however, generates an exception. That's because this MIME type does not yet know that it can be opened. To fix this, you must add an entry to the module's layer file. For more background on what layer files are, see Section 6.3.

To tell WAV files that they can be opened, you must add the `OpenAction` to the layer file under `Loaders/audio/wav/Actions`. Add a file to this folder called `org-openide-actions-OpenAction.instance`. Make sure it's the first action in the list—this will make it the default action (the one invoked when double-clicking a file).

Now, if you run AudioStation again, double-clicking a WAV file will no longer generate an exception. In fact, it will do nothing except beep at you.

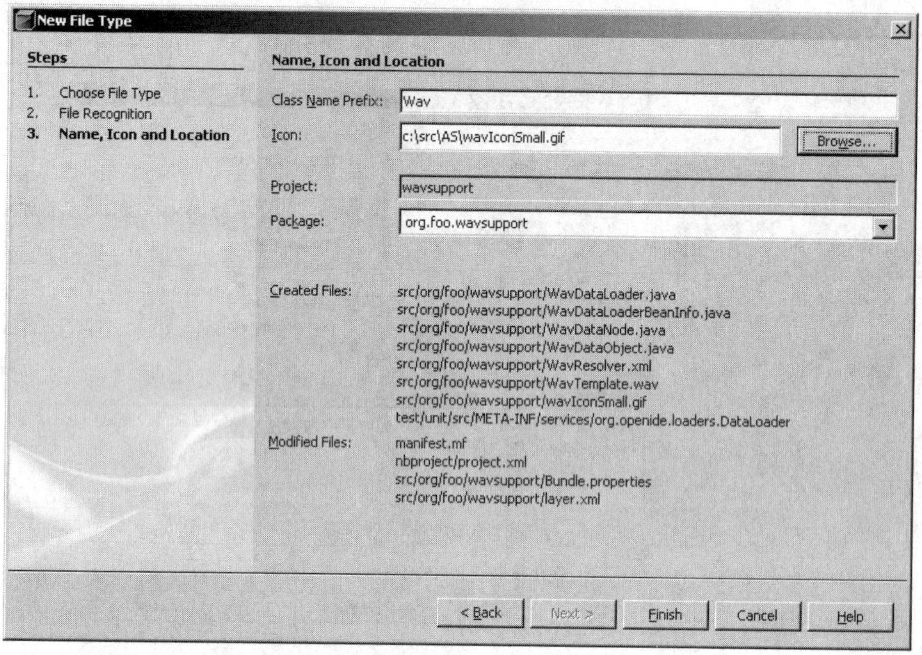

Figure 24.6: Whoa, that wizard creates a lot of files!

This is because, though a WAV file knows it can be opened, it has no idea of *how* to open itself.

`DataObjects` know how to do things like open, close, or save themselves because they contain instances of `OpenCookie`, `CloseCookie`, or `SaveCookie`.

There are certain convenience classes that take care of the common use cases for opening and closing. The class `org.openide. loaders.OpenSupport` is the best base class to use when creating an `OpenCookie` and `CloseCookie` for a nontextual file type:

```
import org.openide.cookies.CloseCookie;
import org.openide.cookies.OpenCookie;
import org.openide.loaders.MultiDataObject;
import org.openide.loaders.OpenSupport;
import org.openide.windows.CloneableTopComponent;
```

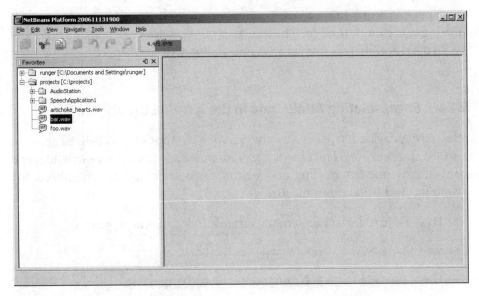

Figure 24.7: An icon for WAV files

```
public class WavOpenSupport extends OpenSupport
    implements OpenCookie, CloseCookie {

  public WavOpenSupport(MultiDataObject.Entry entry) {
    super(entry);
  }

  protected CloneableTopComponent createCloneableTopComponent() {
    // We'll implement this when we write a component class
    throw new UnsupportedOperationException(
                                "Not supported yet.");
  }

}
```

To tell the `WavDataObject` about this class, add the following line to its constructor:

```
getCookieSet().add(new WavOpenSupport(getPrimaryEntry()));
```

Now NetBeans knows how to go about opening WAV files. We're still missing two things, though. The `WavDataObject` does not actually hold any audio data, and there is not yet any component class for displaying WAV files.

24.4   Encapsulating Audio Data in the `WavDataObject`

We have provided a class (in the `wavutils` module) called `Wrapped-AudioInputStream`. This class is a JavaSound `AudioInputStream` with some convenient code for reading and writing files, selecting stream subsets for cropping, and some other niceties.

To start, just declare a member variable in `WavDataObject`:

```
private WrappedAudioInputStream audioStream;
```

Then, provide some accessors to the underlying data:

```
public AudioFormat getAudioFormat()
  {
    return getAudioInputStream().getFormat();
  }

  public WrappedAudioInputStream getAudioInputStream()
  {
    if( audioStream == null )
    {
      FileObject promptFO = getPrimaryFile();
      File promptFile = FileUtil.toFile(promptFO);
      try
      {
        audioStream =
          WrappedAudioInputStream.createFromFile(promptFile);
      }
      catch (Exception ex)
      {
        NotifyDescriptor nd = new NotifyDescriptor.Message(
          "Can't get audio stream for " + getName() +
          " because " + ex.toString());
        DialogDisplayer.getDefault().notify(nd);
      }
    }
    return audioStream;
  }
```

```
// @param is the AudioInputStream for this prompt,
// or null to revert to disk.
public void setAudioInputStream( WrappedAudioInputStream is )
{
  final WrappedAudioInputStream oldStream = audioStream;
  audioStream = is;
  // If the audio input stream is not null, the WAV file
  // is modified.
  setModified(is != null);
  firePropertyChange(PROP_WAVEFORM, oldStream, is);
}

public static final String PROP_WAVEFORM = "waveform";
```

The last thing you need to do is tell NetBeans how to save the file. This works similarly to the OpenCookie. Your WavDataObject needs a SaveCookie:

```
public class WavSaveCookie implements SaveCookie {
  private WavDataObject wav;

  public WavSaveCookie(WavDataObject wav)
  {
    this.wav = wav;
  }

  public void save() throws IOException {
    if (!wav.isModified())
      return;

    // Get the linear PCM data
    WrappedAudioInputStream pcmStream
      = wav.getAudioInputStream();

    if (pcmStream != null)
    {
      File wavFile = FileUtil.toFile(wav.getPrimaryFile());

      // Write out to mu-law format
      pcmStream.toFile(wavFile, Formats.ULAW_FORMAT,
                    AudioFileFormat.Type.WAVE);
    }
    wav.setModified(false);
  }
}
```

Now, you could add an instance of this cookie to your `WavDataObject`, as you did with `WavOpenSupport`. However, it would be better if the cookie were only present when the audio data is modified. To accomplish this, create an instance variable for the `WavSaveCookie` and add or remove it from the cookie set when the `WavDataObject` is modified:

```
private final SaveCookie saveCookie;

public WavDataObject(FileObject pf, WavDataLoader loader)
    throws DataObjectExistsException, IOException
{
  super(pf, loader);
  getCookieSet().add(new WavOpenSupport(getPrimaryEntry()));
  saveCookie = new WavSaveCookie(this);
}

public void setModified(boolean modified)
{
  super.setModified(modified);
  if (modified)
  {
    addSaveCookie();
  }
  else
  {
    removeSaveCookie();
  }
}

private void addSaveCookie()
{
  if( getCookie( SaveCookie.class ) == null ) {
    getCookieSet().add( saveCookie );
  }
}

private void removeSaveCookie()
{
  SaveCookie save = (SaveCookie) getCookie( SaveCookie.class );
  if( save != null ) {
    getCookieSet().remove( save );
  }
}
```

24.5   Creating a Component for Viewing WAV Files

The quickest way to make a GUI for WAV files is to use GUI Builder. Create a new JPanel form and call it **WavPanel**. Then draw the screen shown in Figure 24.8.

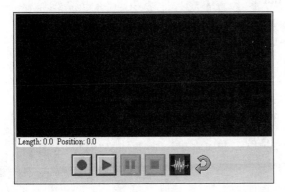

Figure 24.8: The **WavPanel** drawn with GUI Builder

The top half of this is a pre-made sampling graph which can be found in the wavutils module. It must be exported to the GUI Builder palette. You can do this from the **Tools | Palette Manager** menu.

The bottom half is just a bunch of JButtons with icons that can be found in the wavutils module.

One other quick hint: It's easier to draw the row of buttons if you put the buttons inside a JPanel, and switch the layout of that panel to FlowLayout. This makes it much easier to center the buttons horizontally.

You can use GUI Builder to add listeners for the buttons and fill in the appropriate logic for playing, pausing, recording, etc. Since none of this logic is core to the NetBeans integration aspect of AudioStation, we will refer you to the provided source code if you want to see how it works.

Once you have a JPanel you're happy with, it's time to dock the panel into the NetBeans Window System. For that, you'll need a TopComponent. A

TopComponent is just a type of JComponent that knows how to interact with the NetBeans docking framework.

It is good style to isolate your GUI and application logic outside of the TopComponent class (as you've now done with your WavPanel). This will make it easier for us to move to a multiview editor later. For now, your TopComponent can be as minimal as:

```
public class WavComponent extends CloneableTopComponent {
  private transient WavPanel wavPanel;

  public WavComponent(WavDataObject dobj) {
    wavPanel = new WavPanel(dobj);
    setLayout(new BorderLayout());
    add(wavPanel, BorderLayout.CENTER);

    setActivatedNodes(new Node[] {dobj.getNodeDelegate()});
  }
  public Image getIcon() {
    return Utilities.loadImage(
      "org/foo/wavutils/wavIconSmall.gif");
  }
}
```

Now, just return to your WavOpenSupport class and fill in the unimplemented method:

```
protected CloneableTopComponent createCloneableTopComponent()
{
  WavDataObject dobj = (WavDataObject)entry.getDataObject();
  WavComponent tc = new WavComponent(dobj);

  tc.setDisplayName(dobj.getName());
  return tc;
}
```

At this point, you should be able to run your application (Figure 24.9) and use it to create, open, edit, and save WAV files. Congratulations!

To create a new file, right-click on a folder in the **Favorites** window and select **New | All Templates | Other | Empty Wav File**.

Now, let's take your application and create an extension point that allows others to add new functionality to it.

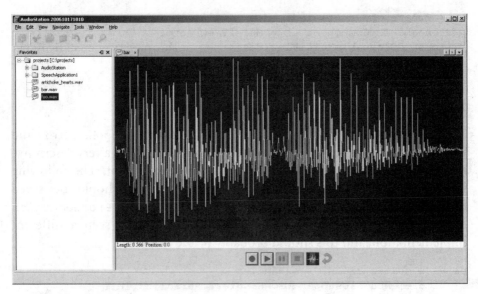

Figure 24.9: Finally, editing a WAV file!

24.6   Converting WAV Editor to Multiview

In this section, you will change the `WavComponent` into a multiview component. For a description of multiview, see Chapter 12.

The `WavOpenSupport` needs to return a multiview component instead of the current, minimal `WavComponent`.

```
protected CloneableTopComponent createCloneableTopComponent()
{
  // Create an array of MV descriptors with only one view of the
  // data (the one we've already created - the waveform view)

  WavPanelMultiViewDescriptor main =
    new WavPanelMultiViewDescriptor();
  MultiViewDescription[] descArry = { main };

  // Initialize the view with data
  WavDataObject dobj = (WavDataObject)entry.getDataObject();
  main.setWavDataObject(dobj);
```

```
// Create the multiview
CloneableTopComponent tc = MultiViewFactory.
  createCloneableMultiView(descArry, main, new CloseHandler());

tc.setDisplayName(dobj.getName());
return tc;
}
```

This introduces references to two new classes: `CloseHandler` and `WavPanelMultiViewDescriptor`. The `CloseHandler` has a very descriptive name. It handles the closing of the multiview component. The following implementation just asks the user whether the file should be saved before closing. Based on the answer, it calls either the `ProceedAction` or the `DiscardAction` on each element. We've never seen a different implementation, and this should probably be the default:

```
private static class CloseHandler
    implements CloseOperationHandler, Serializable {
  private static final long serialVersionUID = 1L;
  public boolean resolveCloseOperation(
                  CloseOperationState[] elements) {
    NotifyDescriptor nd = new NotifyDescriptor.Confirmation(
      "Save before closing?");
    DialogDisplayer.getDefault().notify(nd);

    if (nd.getValue().equals(NotifyDescriptor.YES_OPTION))
    {
      for (CloseOperationState element : elements)
      {
        element.getProceedAction().actionPerformed(
          new ActionEvent(this,
                    ActionEvent.ACTION_PERFORMED, "xxx"));
      }
      return true;
    }
    else if (nd.getValue().equals(NotifyDescriptor.NO_OPTION))
    {
      for (CloseOperationState element : elements)
      {
        element.getDiscardAction().actionPerformed(
          new ActionEvent(this,
                    ActionEvent.ACTION_PERFORMED, "xxx"));
      }
      return true;
    }
```

```
      else
      {
        // Cancel
        return false;
      }
    }
  }
}
```

The `WavPanelMultiViewDescriptor`, apart from being a factory for the `MultiViewElement`, provides a description of the view (name, icon, etc.):

```
public class WavPanelMultiViewDescriptor
    implements MultiViewDescription, Serializable {
  private static final long serialVersionUID = 1L;
  public static Image ICON =
    Utilities.loadImage("org/foo/wavutils/sampleGraph.gif");
  private WavDataObject dobj;

  public int getPersistenceType() {
    return TopComponent.PERSISTENCE_ALWAYS;
  }

  public String getDisplayName() {
    return "Waveform";
  }

  public Image getIcon() {
    return ICON;
  }

  public HelpCtx getHelpCtx() {
    return null;
  }

  public String preferredID() {
    return "wavEditor";
  }

  public MultiViewElement createElement() {
    return new WavComponent(dobj);
  }

  public void setWavDataObject(WavDataObject wav) {
    dobj = wav;
  }
```

```
private void writeObject(ObjectOutputStream out)
    throws IOException
{
  out.defaultWriteObject();
}
}
```

Now, convert the old WavComponent into a MultiViewElement. The element no longer needs to be an instance of TopComponent (though it won't hurt anything if it is).

```
public class WavComponent implements MultiViewElement {

  private static final CloseOperationState CLOSE_OPERATION_STATE
    = createCloseOperationState();
  private transient WavPanel wavPanel;

  public WavComponent(DataObject dobj)
  {
    super();
    wavPanel = new WavPanel(dobj);
  }

  public Action[] getActions() {
    return new Action[0];
  }

  public Lookup getLookup() {
    return wavPanel.getWavDataObject().getNodeDelegate().
      getLookup();
  }

  public UndoRedo getUndoRedo() {
    return new UndoRedo.Manager();
  }

  public JComponent getVisualRepresentation() {
    return wavPanel;
  }

  public JComponent getToolbarRepresentation() {
    // We don't need any widgets on the toolbar
    return new JPanel();
  }
```

```
public CloseOperationState canCloseElement() {
  if (wavPanel.getWavDataObject().isModified())
  {
    return CLOSE_OPERATION_STATE;
  }
  else
  {
    return CloseOperationState.STATE_OK;
  }
}

public void setMultiViewCallback(MultiViewElementCallback
  multiViewElementCallback) {
  // Don't need this
}

// Semantics similar to the equivalent methods in TopComponent
public void componentDeactivated() {}
public void componentActivated() {}
public void componentHidden() {}
public void componentShowing() {}
public void componentClosed() {}
public void componentOpened() {}

public Object writeReplace() {
  return null;
}

private static CloseOperationState createCloseOperationState()
{
  return MultiViewFactory.createUnsafeCloseState(
    "xxx", new ProceedAction(), new DiscardAction());
}

private static class ProceedAction extends NodeAction
{
  protected void performAction(Node[] node) {
    try
    {
      if (node != null && node.length > 0)
      {
        SaveCookie sc =
          (SaveCookie)node[0].getCookie(SaveCookie.class);
        sc.save();
      }
    }
```

```
    catch(IOException ex)
    {
      ErrorManager.getDefault().notify(ex);
    }
  }

  protected boolean enable(Node[] node) {
    return true;
  }

  public String getName() {
    return "Save";
  }

  public HelpCtx getHelpCtx() {
    return null;
  }
}

private static class DiscardAction extends NodeAction
{

  protected void performAction(Node[] node) {
    if (node != null && node.length > 0)
    {
      DataObject dobj =
        (DataObject)node[0].getCookie(DataObject.class);

      try
      {
        // Throw away what's in memory.
        // The DataObject will be recreated from disk.
        dobj.setValid(false);
      }
      catch (PropertyVetoException ex)
      {
        ErrorManager.getDefault().notify(ex);
      }
    }
  }

  protected boolean enable(Node[] node) {
    return true;
  }
```

```
    public String getName() {
      return "Discard";
    }

    public HelpCtx getHelpCtx() {
      return null;
    }
  }
}
```

At this point, you should have an editor almost exactly like that in the previous section, but in a multiview window, as shown in Figure 24.10.

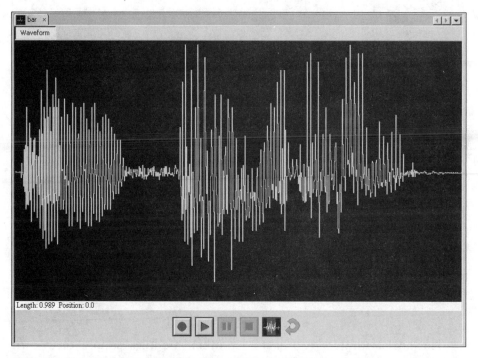

Figure 24.10: A "multiview" WAV editor, with only one view

Next, you will define an extension point to allow other modules to insert new views into your multiview.

24.7   Creating an API for Plugging in Additional Views

The first order of business in creating any API on the NetBeans Platform is to create a separate package (e.g., `org.foo.wavsupport.api`). Modules that depend on `wavsupport` should only be able to access classes in this package. To enforce this, go to `wavsupport`'s **Project Properties** and designate the package as public, as shown in Figure 24.11.

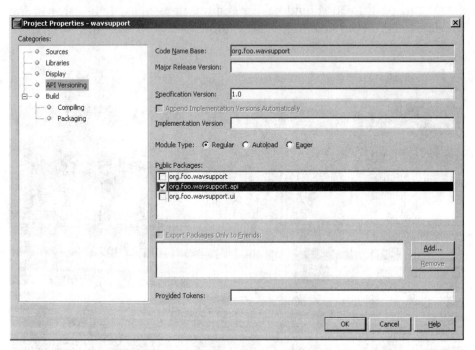

Figure 24.11: A public API package

The goal with this API is to let other modules supply their own `MultiViewDescriptions`. At the very least, that means you want to collect instances of `MultiViewDescription` from those modules and insert them into your multiview.

However, for those other modules to have enough information to create any meaningful visualizations, they need access to the WavDataObject. So, create a subinterface in your API package:

```
public interface WavViewDescriptor
    extends MultiViewDescription, Serializable {
  void setWavDataObject(DataObject dobj);
}
```

Notice that the setWavDataObject() method takes a generic DataObject instead of the more specific WavDataObject. This is because WavDataObject is not in the API package. It is cleaner to make any data required by client modules available in the DataObject's cookie set.

Create a new interface called WavCookie in the API package and move any public constants from WavDataObject to it. Also, declare any public API methods you want to expose from WavDataObject:

```
public interface WavCookie extends Node.Cookie {
  public static final String PROP_WAVEFORM = "waveform";

  AudioFormat getAudioFormat();
  WrappedAudioInputStream getAudioInputStream();
  void setAudioInputStream( WrappedAudioInputStream is );

  void addPropertyChangeListener(PropertyChangeListener l);
  void removePropertyChangeListener(PropertyChangeListener l);
}
```

Then, just make WavDataObject implement this interface:

```
public class WavDataObject extends MultiDataObject
  implements WavCookie {
  ...
}
```

Note that you do not need to explicitly add the WavDataObject to its own cookie set, as you did with the open and save cookies. This is a special case. All DataObjects are automatically in their own cookie set.

Finally, you must perform the query for instances of WavViewDescriptor to fill your multiview. In WavOpenSupport you are currently instantiating just the WavPanelMultiViewDescriptor and passing it in a one-element array to the `MultiViewFactory`. Instead, make that descriptor the first in a list of unknown size and populate the rest of the list using `Lookup` (see Section 4.3):

```
WavViewDescriptor main = new WavPanelMultiViewDescriptor();

List<WavViewDescriptor> all = new ArrayList<WavViewDescriptor>();
all.add(main);

Lookup.Template template =
  new Lookup.Template(WavViewDescriptor.class);
Lookup.Result result = Lookup.getDefault().lookup(template);
for (Object wvd : result.allInstances())
{
    all.add((WavViewDescriptor)wvd);
}
```

Then, give all the descriptors a reference to the data object:

```
for (WavViewDescriptor wvd : all)
{
    wvd.setWavDataObject(dobj);
}
```

And, lastly, convert the list to an array to pass to the `MultiViewFactory`:

```
WavViewDescriptor[] allArray = new WavViewDescriptor[all.size()];
all.toArray(allArray);

CloneableTopComponent tc =
  MultiViewFactory.createCloneableMultiView(allArray, main,
                                            new CloseHandler());
```

Now, a client module can implement the `WavViewDescriptor` interface you've exposed and, using the information from the `WavCookie`, provide a new tab in your multiview without having to edit the source code of the `wavsupport` module at all.

24.8   Implementing Your Own API to Provide a New View

Now it's time to don the hat of your potential API clients and create a module that presents a different visualization for a WAV file. For your convenience, the `wavutils` module contains a component (`FFTGraph`) that renders a frequency-domain view, based on a public domain FFT (Fast-Fourier Transform) library we found on the Web (thanks Tsan-Kuang Lee, from the University of Pennsylvania!)

Start by creating a new module in the suite called `fftview`. Don't forget to include `wavsupport` and `wavutils` in the set of modules on which it depends.

Next, create an implementation of your API interface, `WavViewDescriptor`:

```
public class FFTViewDescriptor implements WavViewDescriptor {

  private static final long serialVersionUID = 1L;
  public static Image ICON =
    Utilities.loadImage("org/foo/wavutils/sampleGraph.gif");
  private DataObject dobj;

  public int getPersistenceType() {
    return TopComponent.PERSISTENCE_ALWAYS;
  }

  public String getDisplayName() {
    return "Frequency Domain";
  }

  public Image getIcon() {
    return ICON;
  }

  public HelpCtx getHelpCtx() {
    return null;
  }

  public String preferredID() {
    return "FFT";
  }

  public MultiViewElement createElement() {
    return new FFTComponent(dobj);
  }
```

```
public void setWavDataObject(DataObject wav) {
  dobj = wav;
}

private void writeObject(ObjectOutputStream out)
    throws IOException
{
  out.defaultWriteObject();
}

}
```

Then, you need just one more class to provide the actual component:

```
public class FFTComponent implements MultiViewElement {

  private DataObject dobj;
  private final FFTGraph graph = new FFTGraph();

  public FFTComponent(DataObject dobj)
  {
    super();

    this.dobj = dobj;
    final WavCookie c =
      (WavCookie)dobj.getCookie(WavCookie.class);
    assert(c != null);

    graph.createGraph(c.getAudioInputStream());

    c.addPropertyChangeListener(new PropertyChangeListener() {
      public void propertyChange(PropertyChangeEvent evt) {
        if (evt.getPropertyName().
            equals(WavCookie.PROP_WAVEFORM))
        {
          WrappedAudioInputStream wais = c.getAudioInputStream();
          if (wais == null)
            graph.clearGraph();
          else
            graph.createGraph(wais);
        }
      }
    });
  }
```

```java
public JComponent getVisualRepresentation() {
  return graph;
}

public JComponent getToolbarRepresentation() {
  return new JPanel();
}

public void setMultiViewCallback(
  MultiViewElementCallback multiViewElementCallback) {
  // Do nothing (we don't need the callback)
}

public CloseOperationState canCloseElement() {
  // The main wav component handles asking the user to save.
  // _This_ component is OK, whatever the outcome.
  // If the main component needed to provide any visual
  // feedback before saving/closing, this component could
  // have its own Proceed/Discard actions
  return CloseOperationState.STATE_OK;
}

public void componentDeactivated() {}
public void componentActivated() {}
public void componentHidden() {}
public void componentShowing() {}
public void componentClosed() {}
public void componentOpened() {}

public Object writeReplace() {
  return null;
}

public Action[] getActions() {
  return new Action[0];
}

public Lookup getLookup() {
  return dobj.getNodeDelegate().getLookup();
}

public UndoRedo getUndoRedo() {
  return new UndoRedo.Manager();
}
}
```

The only step left is to publish the existence of this implementation so that the `Lookup` code in `WavOpenSupport` knows where to find it. The simplest way to do this is to add a file `src/META-INF/services/org/foo/wavsupport/api/WavViewDescriptor` with the contents:

```
org.foo.fftview.FFTViewDescriptor
```

Now, when you run your application, you should see two views, as shown in Figure 24.12.

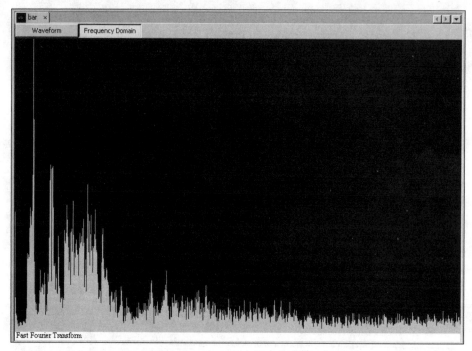

Figure 24.12: Frequency-domain view of a WAV file

This technique of querying the global `Lookup` for instances of interfaces you create as APIs is extremely useful. It is particularly well suited for situations when you have to integrate with a product or library whose API changes frequently, or with multiple products from competing vendors. Your interface becomes a stable bridge; each client module is an implementation of your interface using a particular vendor's APIs.

For example, if you are writing software for filling out tax forms, you might have an interface that allows you to query a client module about tax rates, laws, and required formatting of the forms. Then, you would supply modules for different jurisdictions. The next year, you'd only have to update those modules while the core application would work unchanged.

Advanced Module System Techniques

This appendix will cover some aspects of module configuration and design in more depth than was needed to for most of the chapters in this book. Although there are quite a few examples in those chapters, the APIs and many concepts have mostly been discussed one by one, without any orchestration. And while each of the concepts—such as organizing architecture around modules, exporting some of module's packages as public, having dependencies between modules, treating modules as regular or making them autoloads or eager ones, or using Lookup for their communication—is good and interesting and useful on its own, it is their mutual cooperation that makes these concepts shine. That is exactly why this appendix will concentrate on use cases and important scenarios, explaining how to solve them when building applications on top of the NetBeans Platform.

A.1   Hiding Implementation Details

Imagine that your goal is to develop a library for usage by other people. You know that you want to use the NetBeans runtime container as the framework. Now the question is, what is the best way to do this?

The simplest way is to start with a NetBeans module project and fill it with the library API classes and implementation. By default none of these classes are accessible from outside—and this is indeed not the purpose of the module.

That is why it is necessary to export some packages by marking them as public. Only classes in those packages will be visible by other modules.

It is good design practice to separate modules that provide a UI from those that provide an API. Consider how people might want to use such modules when assembling their own applications. While the modules that provide and register useful UI elements—menu items, toolbar buttons, etc.—are included in applications because they contribute to the visual experience of the end user, the modules that provide an API are usually included because they provide classes that other modules link against. These purposes are different and it's not good to intermingle them.

Modules with interesting UI are usually made *regular* modules, as their functionality can be enabled or disabled by the end user. For example, an end user can enable or disable support for Subversion as needed. Disabling modules that are not needed is a simple way for end users to customize and simplify the application UI. The benefits of disabling don't apply just to end users. Those that assemble applications built from modules are in a similar position. Their building blocks are modules and they can decide to either include or exclude a block. For that reason, it makes sense to ensure that each block represents just one feature and not a mix of various ones.

Those modules that serve as a library have a different purpose. Most of the time their enablement state is guided just by the fact that some other module (for example, one providing an interesting UI element) needs them. The user does not directly enable/disable the library modules, so they are not, in NetBeans terminology, regular ones. They are enabled automatically, and NetBeans calls them *autoloads*. Always make sure that if the primary purpose of a module is being a library, it is marked as an *autoload*.

Another thing that is very important when writing a library is keeping track of various versions of the API inside the library. For that, NetBeans supports a *specification version* for each module. The recommended development practice is to always increase the specification version when a new feature (class, method, externally visible change in behavior) is added into the module. Also it is very good to annotate newly added methods and classes with the `@since X.Y` tag in the Javadoc, where the `X.Y` is the first *specification version* of the module that contains the given feature. Annotating public classes this way makes it easier for readers of the Javadoc to find out which version of the API they need to depend on.

> The default way to generate Javadoc is to invoke it from the project's popup menu (**Generate Javadoc** command) or call `ant javadoc` from the command line in the module's source directory. This generates regular Javadoc for all public packages in the module.

Here is a brief summary of advice for library module writers:

- Don't mix UI and APIs in the same module. Use a separate module for each.

- Make the library modules *autoloads*.

- Choose which packages are public and which are private.

- Make sure you keep track of changes by correctly versioning your modules.

A.2   Design for Extensibility

Now imagine that your goal is not just to write a simple library (in the sense defined in Section 3.2). You also want to let others extend its functionality. What is the right architecture for this use case?

Of course using `Lookup` is the obvious choice when designing code that will run inside a NetBeans-based application, as shown in the `Validator` example in Chapter 4. However, to make the cooperation of modules that provide the extension point and those that wish to plug into it as smooth as possible, we need to think about the appropriate type for the modules— whether they should be regular, autoloads, or eager.

> Using `Lookup`, or `ServiceLoader` from JDK 1.6, is a good choice when creating a standalone application as well—assuming you can use JDK 1.6 or include the NetBeans library that provides `Lookup` (`org-openide-util.jar`) in the application.

Making both types of modules—the provider of the extension point and the modules to be plugged in it (i.e., *regular* modules)—has a potential drawback: Now the user is in charge of enabling and disabling these modules. The worst scenario is that the user might choose to disable the provider of the extension point and then reenable it. Since all the modules that want to plug into the extension point need to have a runtime dependency on the provider, the user is asked whether to also disable all these modules. If agreed, the whole tree of modules depending on the provider of the extension point gets disabled. Then, when the user decides to enable the provider of the extension point again and the consistency check is made, the system finds that it is safe to only enable the provider of the extension point and leaves all the modules that plug into it disabled. As a result, simple UI action of disabling or reenabling a module which the user may believe is "idempotent"—that is, will return the system into previous state—can produce surprising results. In some situations this may be a desirable state, but in most cases, this behavior is neither expected nor desired. Thankfully, there are design techniques provided by the NetBeans runtime container to change the enable/disable behavior.

The solution is to use other than *regular* module types for your base modules that provide extension points. For example, you can have the base module defined as *autoload* and all the other modules as *regular*. The state of an autoload module is determined by the modules that need that module, not by the user. This setup prevents the end user from changing the enablement state of the base module. The user can turn the *regular* modules—that is, those that plug into the extension point—on and off. If (and only if) all of those modules are disabled, the (autoload) base module providing the extension point automatically gets disabled as well. Similarly, enablement happens automatically on demand. As soon as the user turns on any of the modules that have dependency on the provider of the extension point, that provider module is automatically enabled to satisfy the dependency of the just enabled module. In contrast with the situation when your base module is *regular*, using an autoload module as the base guarantees that if the user disables a set of modules and reenables them, the system returns to the same state it was in the beginning. This is usually the expected behavior. However, keep in mind that *autoload* modules should not provide any important UI elements. Otherwise, as soon as such a module is not needed by any other module, it will be disabled and its UI elements will disappear, which might confuse the user.

If you want to retain idempotency (where disabling and reenabling returns the system to the same state) but want the base module to define its own UI, there is another solution: make the base module a *regular* module and turn all the modules that plug into the base module into *eager* modules. Eager modules are out of control of the user and are always enabled by the NetBeans infrastructure if they can be enabled—that is, when all their dependencies are satisfied. The user can locate the base module and disable it, which immediately results in disabling all modules that depend on it and are declared as *eager*. Similarly, when a user decides to turn the base module with extension point on, all the modules that plug into it (that is, all modules having a dependency on the base module) immediately get enabled by the infrastructure, because all their dependencies are now satisfied. This is a reasonable solution if the base module that provides the extension point has a significant UI element which the end user is expected to manipulate—for example, turn on or off.

As can be seen, there are many ways to achieve an extensibility via extension points. It is not just about using the `Lookup` design pattern, but also about giving appropriate roles to the modules that participate in mutual cooperation. For some situations, it is most practical to stick with all modules being *regular*. For other situations, it is better to choose an *autoload* or *eager* approach. All of these choices, including hybrid solutions, have their pros and cons. Choosing the best one usually depends on the particular problem you need to solve.

A.3   Splitting API and Implementation

Nearly any book about good design suggests splitting the interfaces and implementation. Such a division clears up a bunch of code and significantly contributes to good application design. This is one of the most effective ways to fight with the "object-oriented spaghetti code" as described in Section 2.3. Splitting the API and implementation is a particularly good thing in the modular world.

There are various benefits associated with splitting the API and its implementation or its user interface. For example, as shown in Section 3.2.4, there can be various different implementations of the same API. If they all comply with the spirit of the API, one can dynamically assemble a final application from various combinations of the API, its users, and its implementations.

 For example, in the NetBeans source tree there is the I/O API located in `openide/io` and a bunch of implementations (`core/output`, `core/output2`, etc.) However, just one of those implementations is bundled as part of NetBeans IDE 5.5.

To some extent this is similar to using the XML parsing API in Java. There is the general API in `javax.xml.parsers` and `org.w3c.dom` or `org.sax`, but then there are dozens of different implementations of this API. To the extent where they behave the same (e.g., for parsing trivial XML documents) you can just use the API and request the presence of *some* implementation, without caring which one it is. This is a useful design pattern in many situations. For example, NetBeans uses this API vs. implementation split for separating the API of an output window manager from its implementation. (There are actually three implementations: one based on `JList`, one based on an ANSI-compliant terminal emulator, and one based on a memory mapped file viewed through `javax.swing.Document`.) Another example is in the window manager implementation (which handles the layout of components in a NetBeans-based application, allowing it, for example, to be reorganized using drag-and-drop, etc.).

In all of these examples, the API module is an *autoload* which other modules can depend on. Usually it has a `static` getter for an implementation:

```
public class SomeAPISingleton {
  public static SomeAPISingleton getDefault() {
    return (SomeAPISingleton)Lookup.getDefault().
      lookup(SomeAPISingleton.class);
  }
}
```

Each module using the API will then request to have an API singleton class (e.g., `SomeAPISingleton`) on the classpath by specifying a module dependency on the provider of that class. It will also request an implementation of the API. The usual semantics is to ask for a "token" named exactly like the class, in this case `org.somepkg.SomeAPISingleton`, by having a tag in the manifest, for example:

```
OpenIDE-Module-Requires: org.somepkg.SomeAPISingleton
```

You do not need to edit the manifest by hand—this can all be done in the **Libraries** panel of the **Project Properties** dialog.

Modules providing the implementation of the `SomeAPISingleton` class then have to declare themselves as providers to the NetBeans runtime container. Again, this can be done by a single line in the module's manifest file:

```
OpenIDE-Module-Provides: org.somepkg.SomeAPISingleton
```

This line tells the system that whenever someone "requests" such a token, the module also gets enabled. It is wise to make the module providing the implementation *autoload*. That way, the enabled/disabled status of the implementation is under full control of the NetBeans runtime container.

In some situations it is possible to have a reasonable default implementation inside of the API that can be used as a fallback when no "real" implementation is present. This can be used to simplify dependencies between modules, as now the API can be used without its implementation. It can also be very useful for running unit tests, which just need some implementation and do not care about how trivial it is. In that case, the `getDefault()` method would be:

```
public class SomeAPISingleton {

  public static SomeAPISingleton getDefault() {
    SomeAPISingleton api = (SomeAPISingleton)Lookup.getDefault().
      lookup(SomeAPISingleton.class);
    if (api != null) {
      return api;
    }
    return new DefaultImpl();
  }

  private static class DefaultImpl extends SomeAPISingleton {
    // Some implementation
  }
}
```

NetBeans IDE 6.0 introduces another pair of tags that enhance the "provides/requires" behavior and overcome 5.5's limitations of the *requires* token. Due to "ordering" problems, it used to be impossible to make the API module request its implementation directly. Instead, every user of the API module needed to also use the `OpenIDE-Module-Requires` tag to request the implementation to be present, which was unfortunate.

Beginning with 6.0, you can use new tag `OpenIDE-Module-Needs` which behaves exactly like `OpenIDE-Module-Requires` but with the advantage that it can be used also from the API module. Thus, beginning with 6.0, each API module which requires an implementation can specify the following:

```
OpenIDE-Module-Needs: org.somepkg.SomeAPISingleton
```

And the modules using the API need only to have a module dependency on the API module. The whole system will make sure that the implementation is also enabled, as illustrated in Figure A.1.

There is a yet another useful tag in 6.0 called `OpenIDE-Module-Recommends`. Its behavior is similar to that of the "needs" tag, but the system does not report a failure when the dependency is not satisfied. The API can "recommend" its implementation to be enabled. If it also provides some reasonable default implementation itself, it tells the system that it can continue even if no recommended implementation is present.

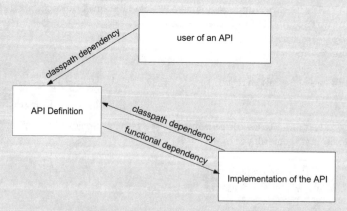

Figure A.1: Relationship between API, implementation, and user

All this is possible. There are many variants of splitting the API and implementation that can be chosen NetBeans 5.5, and even more in 6.0. All you need to remember is that separating API and implementation is, according to many design books, a good decision and that NetBeans-based applications get first-class support to do so due to module and token dependencies.

A.4   Do I Really Need Cyclic Dependency?

Often people coming to the NetBeans environment ask how they can use cyclic dependencies. The short answer is: "No, you cannot and should not use cyclic dependencies." However, not everyone likes this answer. Sometimes this is treated as a weakness of the NetBeans Module System, which isn't exactly true. In fact, disallowing cyclic dependencies is one of the biggest features of the NetBeans Module System, allowing it to fight with "object-oriented spaghetti" code. The next few paragraphs explain why providing less is, in fact, contributing to better design.

Nearly everyone knows how scary mutual dependencies within really messy object-oriented spaghetti code can get. Regardless how much people try, the "entropy of software" is always around and cannot be fully avoided. If things get out of control, each piece of a system starts to refer to every other piece—after a while you get a "complete graph" where each piece is interconnected with every other. And not only that; in still worse situations the dependencies can become bidirectional. The whole system gets progressively harder to compile, maintain, and understand. You may end up having to effectively treat the whole code base as a single package, which nullifies the benefits of having a system built of distinct components.

The NetBeans Module System and the API support for development of NetBeans extensions are carefully designed to prevent such misuse. Of course, it is not possible to completely prevent someone from shooting themselves in the foot—one can still create a single huge module and inside it worship the "spaghetti" design. But as soon as you decide to split the application into multiple modules, you get a classpath dependency graph which is acyclic.

People migrating from an existing monolithic application may need help with splitting the application into modules. So, let's practice this on the following example.

Imagine there is a legacy code base split into two packages:

```
package org.netbeans.example.arrays;
public class MutableArray {
  private byte[] arr;
  public MutableArray(byte[] arr) {
    this.arr = arr;
  }

  public void xor(byte b) { ... }
  public void and(byte b) { ... }
  public void or(byte b) { ... }

  public void encrypt(OutputStream is) throws IOException {
    Encryptor en = new Encryptor();
    byte[] clone = (byte[])arr.clone();
    en.encode(clone);
    is.write(clone);
  }
}

package org.netbeans.example.crypt;
public class Encryptor {
  public void encode(byte[] arr) {
    MutableArray m = new MutableArray(arr);
    m.xor((byte)0x3d);
  }
}
```

The example is pretty simple and a bit artificial, but it shows the point. There are two independent packages that need each other. The package for working with arrays needs to encrypt its data, for which it uses `Encryptor`. The `crypt` package then works on arrays and uses `MutableArray` to simplify its work. This is an excellent example of spaghetti object-oriented design, by the way.

Can this example be split into two NetBeans modules? Yes, it can: Just use `Lookup`! For reasons of sanity, no cyclic dependencies between NetBeans modules are allowed. If you put each package into its own module, then only one can have a compile and classpath dependency on the other. So the initial step is to decide which of the modules is going to depend on the other. In the above example, it looks like the `Encryptor` is some kind of service, so it may seem more natural to let the `org.netbeans.example.crypt` module depend on `org.netbeans.example.arrays` as mapped out in Figure A.2.

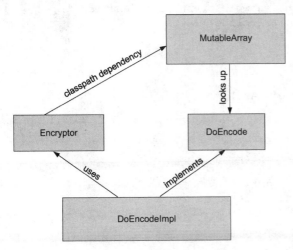

Figure A.2: Application split into two modules

As a result, no changes are needed in `Encryptor`—its use of `MutableArray` is OK as that class is on its compile and runtime classpath. However, `MutableArray` can no longer refer to `Encryptor` directly. To solve this problem, you need to create a facade and wrap the calls to the `Encryptor` in it. The facade interface will be defined in the `org.netbeans.example.arrays` module and will be implemented by the `org.netbeans.example.crypt` module. And of course, the implementation will be found using `Lookup`. Here is the rewritten code sample:

```
package org.netbeans.example.arrays;
public class MutableArray {
  private byte[] arr;
  public MutableArray(byte[] arr) {
    this.arr = arr;
  }
```

```
public void xor(byte b) { ... }
public void and(byte b) { ... }
public void or(byte b) { ... }

public void encrypt(OutputStream is) throws IOException {
  DoEncode encode =
    (DoEncode)Lookup.getDefault().lookup(DoEncode.class);
  assert encode != null :
    "We need org.netbeans.example.crypt to be enabled!";
  byte[] clone = (byte[])arr.clone();
  en.encode(clone);
  is.write(clone);
}
public interface DoEncode {
  public void encode(byte[] arr);
}
}

package org.netbeans.example.crypt;
public class Encryptor {
  public void encode(byte[] arr) {
    MutableArray m = new MutableArray(arr);
    m.xor((byte)0x3d);
  }
}

// This class has to be registered in
// META-INF/services/org.netbeans.example.arrays.DoEncode
// in order to be locatable by Lookup.getDefault()
public class DoEncodeImpl implements DoEncode {
  public void encode(byte[] arr) {
    Encryptor en = new Encryptor();
    en.encode(arr);
  }
}
```

The DoEncode interface is the facade that isolates the actual calls into the Encryptor class. Instead, the original call uses Lookup. getDefault().lookup(DoEncode.class) to locate the actual implementation of the facade and communicates with it. The implementation is provided by the org.netbeans.example.crypt module which is, obviously, able to refer to the Encryptor class. Thus, the cyclic compile-time dependency is avoided.

Of course, during runtime both modules have to be present, as they cannot work without each other—there is an `assert` check in `MutableArray.encrypt` to ensure that an implementation of the `DoEncode` facade is provided. This is an important architectural restriction, and as such it can be expressed as a module dependency using the "needs/provides" tags. The module with `MutableArray` should specify that it needs implementation of the facade by adding the following line into its manifest:

```
OpenIDE-Module-Needs: org.netbeans.example.arrays.DoEncode
```

And the module providing the `Encryptor` should tell the NetBeans runtime container that it provides the implementation:

```
OpenIDE-Module-Provides: org.netbeans.example.arrays.DoEncode
```

By doing this, the NetBeans runtime container knows that these modules need each other and always enables both of them or none.

Similar refactoring can be applied to all cyclic dependencies between modules that need each other to perform their functionality. As a result, when you migrate to the NetBeans modular architecture, you are encouraged to clean up the object-oriented spaghetti mess and replace it with cleaner module dependencies. Coding on top of the NetBeans Platform helps to improve the architecture of Java applications!

The drawback of `OpenIDE-Module-Needs` is that it is available only in NetBeans IDE 6.0. In version 5.5, each module that depends on `org.netbeans.example.arrays` also needs to specify `OpenIDE-Module-Requires: org.netbeans.example.arrays.DoEncode`, which works—but is a bit more complicated and less easy to use.

A.5   Crossing the Informational Divide

Some design decisions are tough. When coding in the modular way, the most important decision is about dependencies between modules. The more dependencies are created, the less freedom is given to people who want to assemble the modules into a final application. In fact, reducing the amount of dependencies is one of the most important tasks when writing modular code.

However, not having dependencies at all is not an option. Various, even unrelated, components need to talk to each other. The following paragraphs describe a design pattern for connecting two independent modules.

Imagine that there are two independent modules (let's call them module X and module Y) providing some interesting end-user functionality (meaning they are likely to be *regular* modules). The modules are independent, which means that they are not presented in the UI as one feature but as two independent functionalities. Indeed, this is not good, as the user is not at all interested in the underlying modular architecture. The user wants a UI that is easy to use. That means the goal is to unify the UI while not compromising the beautiful modular architecture underneath.

The solution is to create yet another module (let's call it B) that depends on X and Y and serves as a "bridge" between them. Each of the *regular* modules encapsulates the communication with the other into a *facade* which is then implemented by the bridge B. The bridge B is an *eager* module. As a result, whenever both X and Y are enabled, the system also enables B. And since B includes implementations of the facade from both of these modules, X and Y are able to communicate with each other through B. If either X or Y is missing, the dependencies of B are not satisfied and the module that is present just silently skips the communication through the facade.

This is demonstrated in Figure A.3 where module B implements an interface defined by module X and registers it as an extension point. X then finds the implementation of this interface in global `Lookup`. If not `null`, it calls it

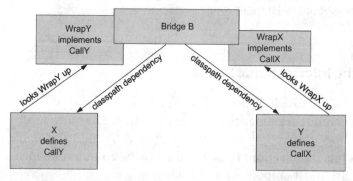

Figure A.3: Bridge module example

every time it needs some functionality from module Y. Each method call gets handled by the implementation defined in B, which can directly access the methods of Y and do whatever X requested. To handle the communication between Y and X, the situation is reversed: The module Y creates an interface, B implements it and registers it. When Y calls one of its methods, B can directly call methods in module X. Simple, type-safe, effective.

A.6   Restricting Access to Friends

Often a public package in a module is not meant for public consumption. In many examples given in this chapter, there is just one module that is allowed to compile and link against an API provided by another module. NetBeans supports this with the notion of "friend" modules.

The basic idea is that the provider of some API can choose which modules can access its API packages, thereby creating its group of "friends." Having a restricted set of users of an API is useful, for example, in refactoring—if you know all the friends, then you can update all of them at once. If the potential clients of some API are spread around the world, then refactoring often becomes unmanageable. A module can declare a list of other "friend" modules in a manifest and in the NetBeans project customizer. The build system of NetBeans IDE then verifies that only the allowed modules have a dependency on the provided API and that they refer only to the public packages of the module.

 The NetBeans project tries to protect privacy and encourage good design practices as much as it can. However, it understands that there are situations when one needs to override the default access policy and be able to access nonpublic packages of a module, or access a module even if one is not its friend. This is possible—one can use an *implementation dependency*. With it, you can access all public classes in the module, as the NetBeans classloading mechanism disables its protections against doing so. However, you need to understand that accessing internals of other modules can be dangerous, as they can change without any notice. You should always try to find a better solution than implementation dependencies with their risk of shooting yourself in the foot. And yet, if you know what you are doing—or if you are really desperate—you can use implementation dependencies as a last resort.

A.7   Having Public as Well as Friend API

Very often people who design systems using modules in the NetBeans runtime container complain about the impossibility of creating a module that would have both a public API and a friend API. Yes, such a setup is impossible in NetBeans 5.5 as well as, very likely, in 6.0 and future systems. But this shouldn't be seen as a limitation. Rather, it is a pragmatic design choice, especially given that there is a design pattern that allows you to achieve the same functionality in the current NetBeans runtime container.

Imagine a module that provides some library functionality to other modules, while it also has an API for other modules to plug in a service provider. While the library API is dedicated for public consumption, the API for service providers is immature and under development. That is why the module writer decides that only a certain list of selected modules can use this provider API. This is a common requirement. However, it faces restrictions of the NetBeans Module System: There can only be one type of exported package—either public packages or friend packages.

This restriction has its own reasonable justification. Each module has one specification version number and one major version number that are used to identify the actual version of the module. It is expected that newer versions having the same major number are compatible—that is, contain the same functionality as the older ones plus something more. If there is an incompatible change, it is expected that the major version number is increased as well. However, if two different types of API packages were allowed to be in one module, its version number would suddenly have two meanings: It would represent the version of the public packages as well as the version of the friend ones. As these packages are likely to be evolving independently—for example, the public packages are more compatible—the versioning could become un-maintainable. You cannot, for example, express that the friend API has changed incompatibly while the public packages remained compatible. That is why the scenario with different package types is not allowed.

The simplest way to overcome this restriction is to use an implementation dependency to access the friend packages. Of course, this has its own problems. The first problem is that when using an implementation dependency, the module has access not only to the friend packages, but to all classes of the module, effectively overriding any encapsulation provided by NetBeans

Module System classloading mechanisms. As a result, you could accidentally start to use implementation details of the module, gradually getting entrapped in the spaghetti coding style. The other problem is that usually the implementation dependency is expressed as a dependency on the build number, which, in turn, means that both modules need to be compiled at once. For some situations, when one needs to communicate with closely related modules, this is not a problem (for example, NetBeans IDE uses this for communication between the `projects/projectuiapi` and `projects/projectui` modules which are always built and distributed together). However, if the set of modules that need to access the friend packages is more widely spread, then we need to seek a different solution.

The general way to address the problem of two different API types in one module is to split the module into two. So, instead of having one module with public and friend packages, you could have module F (for friend packages) and module P (for public packages), as shown in Figure A.4. Module P has a compile-type dependency on module F and is declared as its friend. That means it can link against its interfaces, look them up as extension points (see Section A.2), and use them while providing its own public packages. The module F indeed declares additional friend modules which are allowed to call F's interfaces as well, but which most likely will also implement them and register them as *extension points*. The module F should be an *autoload* module, as should module P. The other modules can be either *autoload* or *regular*.

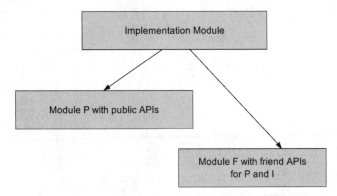

Figure A.4: Friend and public API

A.8   A Final Word on Modularity

The design examples given above are useful solution templates in situations one can face when developing modular applications. However, the most important thing to remember is that a single module does not necessarily map to a particular UI component or a unit of functionality. Projects should be carved up into whatever groupings of modules makes sense for them. Many pieces of user-visible functionality, such as XML editing, the editor itself, or Java project support in the IDE are actually implemented as many modules.

The choice of how many modules to create to implement something really depends on what you need. Generally, more modular code is likely to be more maintainable over time, so splitting your own projects into interface and implementation tends to decrease the level of coupledness between different parts of the application. When two parts of your program need to communicate in a new way and you create an API to facilitate that communication, your own code is more likely to remain maintainable. These patterns are used everywhere in NetBeans-based applications and you will face them while adding your functionality to the IDE. Of course you are encouraged to use them for your own modules as well. They will help you to create good modular designs for your applications.

Common Idioms and Code Patterns in NetBeans

This appendix is a hodge-podge of useful coding patterns that are common in NetBeans—a cookbook of sorts.

B.1 Things You Do Differently in NetBeans Than in Plain Swing Code

There are some code idioms in NetBeans modules that need to be done differently than in a regular Swing application—either because there are convenience helper classes or, in some cases, because the code in question should work with NetBeans module classloaders or branding infrastructure.

Getting a localized string

```
NbBundle.getMessage (SomeClass.class, "BUNDLE_KEY");
```

In plain Java you would use `ResourceBundle`. `NbBundle` is similar; it provides better caching mechanisms than what you get with `ResourceBundle` and works with the *branding* infrastructure, so strings retrieved from `NbBundle` can be substituted—this is why a NetBeans-based application does not show up with the word "NetBeans" in its window title and other parts of its UI. The `Class` parameter is used to discover the package in which to look for a `.properties` file. `NbBundle` always looks for a file called

`Bundle.properties` in the same package as the `Class` object passed to it.

`NbBundle` also does a few things `ResourceBundle` does not: By including integers in curly braces in the localized string, substitution can be performed. This is quite useful, because code like

```
String deleteText =
  NbBundle.getMessage(getClass(), "MSG_DELETE");
String msg = deleteText + file.getName();
```

actually does not work reliably—even if "Really delete" is a localized string fetched from `NbBundle`, not all human languages will put the name of the file at the end of the sentence. What you can do in this case is change the localized string in the resource bundle to "Really delete {0}?". The code handling this 100% correctly constructs the message:[1]

```
String msg = NbBundle.getMessage(getClass(), "MSG_DELETE",
  new Object[] { file.getName() });
```

Localized mnemonics for UI components   `org.openide.awt.Mnemonics` in the UI Utilities API considerably simplifies setting up mnemonics for components. Swing components' mnemonics are assigned using the methods `setMnemonic()` and `setDisplayedMnemonicIndex()`. This means that the index of the mnemonic and the text must somehow be supplied in the resource bundle that provides the localized text. And asking translators to calculate integer offsets into a string to assign a mnemonic, not to mention needing three key/value pairs to do it, is not very translator-friendly.

The `Mnemonics` utility class makes this easy. Simply place a `&` character before the character in the string which should be the mnemonic. Then pass it and the UI component using it to one of the utility methods of that class, as shown below:

```
Mnemonics.setLocalizedText(someJLabel,
  NbBundle.getMessage(SomeClass.class, "LBL_Something"));
```

---

1. In NetBeans 6 there is a vararg variant, so the `new Object[] {}` part can be omitted.

The utility method will create the mnemonic (stripping out the &
character) and set the text of the component.

Loading images

```
org.openide.util.Utilities.loadImage(
    "path/to/image/in/jar.jpg");
```

In plain Swing code you would likely use `ImageIO` or `Toolkit` to
load PNG, JPG, or GIF images. The `Utilities.loadImage()`
method works with NetBeans module classloaders and the branding
mechanisms in NetBeans.

B.2   Things That Represent Files

Getting a `FileObject` for a file on disk

```
FileUtil.toFileObject ( FileUtil.normalizeFile (theFile));
```

Getting a `java.io.File` for a `FileObject`

```
FileUtil.toFile ( theFileObject );
```

This method will return `null` if the `FileObject` in question is
not actually stored on disk (for example, if it is an entry in some
module's `layer.xml`).

Getting a `DataObject` for a `FileObject`

```
DataObject.find ( theFileObject );
```

Getting a `DataFolder` for a `FileObject` that represents a folder

```
DataFolder.findFolder ( theFileObject )
```

Getting a node for a `DataObject`

```
theDataObject.getNodeDelegate()
```

Getting a `FileObject` for a `DataObject`

```
theDataObject.getPrimaryFile();
```

Getting a `DataObject` for a node

```
theNode.getLookup().lookup (DataObject.class);
```

Getting a file or folder in the System Filesystem

```
Repository.getDefault().getDefaultFileSystem().getRoot().
  getFileObject( "path/to/folder" );
```

Getting the Java object represented by a `.instance`, `.settings`, or `.ser` file in the System Filesystem

```
InstanceCookie ck =
  DataObject.find ( someFileObject ).getNodeDelegate().
  getLookup().lookup ( InstanceCookie.class );
if (ck != null) {
  Object result = ck.instanceCreate();
  // Do something with it - presumably you know the actual
  // Java type of object you are getting
}
```

If you are dealing with a folder containing multiple items, `FolderLookup` can be very handy.

Getting a `Lookup` representing the Java objects in a folder containing `.instance`, `.ser`, or `.settings` files in the System Filesystem

```
FileObject myFolder =
  Repository.getDefault().getDefaultFileSystem().
  getRoot().getFileObject( "myfolder" );
if (myFolder != null && myFolder.isFolder()) {
  // If it's null, you didn't declare it
  // or someone deleted/hid it
  DataFolder folder = DataFolder.findFolder ( myFolder );
  FolderLookup fl = new FolderLookup ( folder );
  Lookup theLookup = fl.getLookup();
}
```

B.3   **Working with** Lookup

Creating a Lookup with one object in it

```
Lookup myLookup = Lookups.singleton ( theObject );
```

Creating a Lookup whose contents never change

```
Lookup myLookup =
  Lookups.fixed ( new Object[] { obj1, obj2 });
```

In NetBeans 6, this has a varargs variant so it is not necessary to create the array.

Creating a Lookup whose contents you can change

```
InstanceContent content = new InstanceContent();
AbstractLookup myLookup = new AbstractLookup (content);
content.set ( someCollectionOfObjects );
```

B.4   **Projects**

Finding the project that owns a FileObject

```
FileOwnerQuery.getOwner ( theFileObject );
```

Getting the display name of a project

```
ProjectInformation info = theProject.
  getLookup().lookup ( ProjectInformation.class );
if (info != null) {
  String displayName = info.getDisplayName();
  // Do something with it...
}
```

Getting the compilation classpath of a project   This can be useful if you have some existing code that will process a project's sources and needs to find the JARs that make up the project's classpath. Presumably there will be only one ClassPath object in the set findClassPath() returns, but the API does not forbid there being more than one.

```java
private Set <ClassPath> findClassPath (Project project) {
  ClassPathProvider cpp =
    project.getLookup().lookup (ClassPathProvider.class);
  Set <ClassPath> result = new HashSet <ClassPath> ();
  if (cpp != null) {
    Set <FileObject> sourceDirs = getSourceDirs (project);
    for (FileObject file : sourceDirs) {
      ClassPath path =
        cpp.findClassPath(file, ClassPath.COMPILE);
      result.add (path);
    }
  }
  return result;
}

private Set <FileObject> getSourceDirs (Project p) {
  Set <FileObject> result = new HashSet <FileObject> ();
  Sources sources = p.getLookup().lookup (Sources.class);
  if (sources != null) {
    SourceGroup[] groups =
      sources.getSourceGroups(
      JavaProjectConstants.SOURCES_TYPE_JAVA);

    for (int i = 0; i < groups.length; i++) {
      SourceGroup sourceGroup = groups[i];
      result.add (sourceGroup.getRootFolder());
    }
  }
  return result;
}
```

Performance

In the dark days of the late '90s there was the idea that Swing is slow. It may have been back then. Today, Java2D is screamingly fast, and that is what Swing is based on. So, as programmers, we are out of excuses for creating poorly performing Graphical User Interface (GUI) applications.

The main arbiter of performance in a NetBeans-based application is memory usage. The first step anyone can take toward optimizing their code is to avoid using any memory until something really needs to be done, and then be efficient about what information needs to be kept around.

The second arbiter of performance in a NetBeans-based application is class loading. Class objects take up memory. In a Java VM, a `Class` object is a byte array. That byte array is not loaded until the first time some code tries to use or instantiate a class. That is good—such lazy loading of classes means nothing is loaded until someone really uses the functionality. On the other hand, it is a source of indeterminacy. We spent a lot of time in the days of NetBeans 3.5 fixing problems where, in order to decide what the display name for a menu item should be, hundreds of classes had to be loaded—the result being that as soon as the user clicks a menu, everything suddenly grinds to a halt while the Java VM loads classes, figures out that there is not enough memory allocated in the permanent generation space within the Java VM (the area where class data lives), allocates more memory in the permanent generation space, and does one or more major garbage collections to make room for all the new class byte arrays.

So, two things that you can do off-the-bat to improve performance are: Don't create any more classes than needed, and write modules so that nothing will be loaded until it's needed. It probably hasn't escaped your notice that these are contradictory requirements. In the end, you will have to make judgments and choices about where to place your code for the user to have the best possible experience with your module. At the same time, your module must be a good citizen of the environment in which it runs. There are no magic bullets when it comes to performance—once in a while you can truly improve things with a better algorithm, but other than that, performance tuning a GUI application is largely an art of moving code around, ideally so that it is timed to run when the user is paying attention to something else anyway.

While we mentioned memory allocation, it pays to remember that, for short-lived objects, modern VMs are very efficient. Allocating a new object means the VM moves a pointer by one. You can get away with amazing things that allocate objects, do something with them, and then throw them away—at very little cost. On a reasonable machine running a Java 5 VM, the garbage collector for the new generation (the memory area where the newly allocated objects live) can garbage-collect a gigabyte of RAM in less than a second. And if you're using the default settings for NetBeans, there is, at most, only 128MB of RAM on the Java heap to scan.

The problem is not so much creating garbage, but creating things that survive for a long time and *then* become garbage. The way modern VMs work, new objects are allocated in an "eden" area which can be cleaned up by the garbage collector very fast. If those objects are still there after a few rounds of garbage collection, they get copied to an area for storing longer-lived objects. And if they live for a very long time (by microprocessor, not human, standards), they get copied to the "old generation" storage which is the most expensive place to clean up.

This has parallels in the architecture of modern CPUs. They typically have a memory cache—on-chip memory that is very fast to work with. When your code asks for something that is not in the processor's cache and needs to be pulled out of main memory, that is called a *cache miss*. Going and getting that thing will be *much* slower than if it were already in the cache. Old objects, since they are stored in a different memory area, increase the likelihood of cache misses.

At the same time, NetBeans is a GUI application—by definition anything that pertains to the GUI is going to be a long-lived object, and there is not much you can do about that.

The lesson here is to write objects so they persist only the minimum information needed to reconstruct whatever data someone asks for. If you want to keep a reference to a file, keep a string path to the file—strings are cheap. Most of the time, rebuilding a data model from minimal information is as fast as dragging it out of memory, as sometimes that memory may have been swapped to disk by the operating system's memory manager.

C.1   Responsiveness versus Performance

Performance means something runs fast. Running fast is good. But it is not necessarily the holy grail. What is more important than performance for most GUI applications is responsiveness. If you are using a piece of software, you will like that software if you feel you are in control—you know what it is doing, and it is doing what you told it to in a quick responsive way.

In NetBeans 3.5, we did a huge amount of work on performance. The results were somewhat ironic—users talked about the amazing improvements in performance. But in many cases nothing had gotten faster—we had just made sure an hourglass cursor appeared any time the user did something that would take a while. In more cynical moments, we called it "NetBeans, Wait Cursor Edition." But the fact is that *responsiveness* can be more important than performance per se. If you tell someone "This will take a while, go get a cup of coffee," they may not love it—but you have not lied to them and have not lost their trust. If, however, that same user performs some gesture in the UI and the world grinds to a halt, you have lost their trust—they are not in control and do not know if they should kill the application or wait and hope that something happens. So the number one rule in performance tuning is *not* "make everything really fast" (though it's nice when you can). It's "don't lie when its going to be slow."

That's not an absolute for writing inefficient code—no matter how much everyone repeats the mantra "Premature optimization is the root of all evil," it is not an excuse for doing obviously dumb things.

C.2   Performance Tips for Module Authors

It pays to be conscious of the following things as you code:

How often will this code run?   If it is an action run from a menu item, it's probably not a place to optimize heavily—a wait cursor will do. Users won't spend all day clicking that menu item again and again.

What is my threading model?   If you're doing I/O or other expensive operations, you probably want to ensure that your code can't be called in the AWT event thread. Enforce it by throwing an exception if it is. The best approach is to dispatch work to be done later on a thread you control—you can use `org.openide.RequestProcessor` or any of the newer thread pool classes in `java.util.concurrent`. That has an additional advantage: If your code is called by some foreign code, you cannot know what locks that code holds. If you've dispatched a `Runnable` to a thread pool, you *know* exactly what locks are held when your code runs. You nearly eliminate the problem of thread deadlock in such code (and if you have a deadlock, you know who caused it).

That is *not* to say that multithreading is a panacea. If you can get work done fast in the event thread, do it in the event thread. Context switching between threads has a cost. *On a single-processor machine, multiple threads buy you nothing.* The reason to do this sort of thing is so that your code plays nicely with other code, particularly the Swing event thread, because doing anything slow there blocks painting.

How late can I load XYZ?   All of the declarative mechanisms in NetBeans are there to *avoid doing work until it is provably necessary*. The System Filesystem and the default `Lookup` are there for you to use, and their primary purpose is to allow objects to be registered but lie fallow, their classes not even loaded into the VM, until something really needs to use them.

Constructing objects should be cheap   Often, when an object from your
module is created, there is still no guarantee that it is going to be used.
A constructor for any object should do the minimum work needed to
make it possible for other code to call it, without fully initializing it
until later. This is particularly true for Nodes whose constructors often
run in the event thread. If your Node is doing a lot of work in its constructor, you are probably using it *as* a data model instead of a
presentation layer *for* a data model, which is what Nodes are for.

Profile, profile, profile   A truism of Java performance is that, where you
think the bottleneck is, is probably not where it really is. Especially
with the optimizations a modern JIT compiler can do, the work you
see happening when you look at the code may not be the work that is
actually happening.

There is no substitute for the right algorithm   Object-oriented programming emphasizes readability over efficiency. It's a reason why computers get continually faster and programs don't. Objects are a convenience for humans—computers run assembly code today as they did
fifty years ago. Objects make systems more easily programmable to
humans. A good algorithm can be encapsulated into an object that is
quite simple—just write it well and blanket it in unit tests. At their
best, objects can *make complexity simple.*[1]

C.3   Writing Modules That Are Good Citizens

The first principle in writing modules that are good citizens of their environment is to do no work until it is needed. "Work" in this case includes anything
that triggers classloading, as this makes the memory footprint of the Java VM
bigger even if you are not allocating objects yet. Hand in hand with "do no
work until needed" goes the advice: Know when that work is going to happen.

---

1. Tim Bray's excellent article, "On the Goodness of Binary Search," (www.tbray.org/
ongoing/When/200x/2003/03/22/Binary) is a case in point. Joel Spolsky's article
on the Shlemiel the painter's algorithm (www.joelonsoftware.com/articles/
fog0000000319.html) lends further weight to Bray's ideas. Often one is writing
something for which an optimally efficient algorithm exists. It pays to go find it.

The Perils of Lazy Loading

Circa NetBeans 3.2, a bunch of clever work went into making menus lazy. Startup time improved, since menus would not be loaded until first shown. This proved to be a responsiveness problem. Clicking a menu in the main window could mean a long delay—sometimes seconds—before the menu appeared, and the same was true of submenus. The source of the problem: classloading. Showing a menu could involve inadvertently loading hundreds or thousands of classes into the VM. During that time, the UI was hung. The old **Options** dialog with its tree of objects dumped into the System Filesystem had similar problems.

So sometime around NetBeans 3.4, a lot more cleverness went into making the menus all lazy. Icons and display names could be handled declaratively with file attributes in the System Filesystem, so no class needed to be loaded at all to display a menu. Displaying menus was now fast, and there was much rejoicing.

In 3.4, of course, there was a new problem. Sometimes you would click a menu item and the menu just sat there on screen for a horribly long time. The problem? Mainly classloading. Now there was a dilemma; we were trying to *improve* performance, but going back to preinitializing menus meant startup would take longer—which had been the point of lazy menus to begin with. So for NetBeans 3.5, a solution was found: A runnable runs in a background thread after the UI is shown and preinitializes the menus. Lovely lazy loading code, defeated immediately after startup.

The moral of this story is: Lazy loading is moving work around. The same work was being done either on startup, or when a menu was shown, or when a menu item was clicked. The end solution was not pretty, but *it makes it deterministic when the work happens*. There are three ways to solve this sort of problem:

1. *Do less work*—find a better algorithm, or data structure, or unnecessary work you can optimize away.

2. *Amortize the work*—divide it up so it happens in small chunks at times the user won't notice.

3. *Make when it happens deterministic*—and make "when" be sometime when it is not going to interrupt the user.

A lot of work went into making the actions, the menu system, and the old **Options** dialog as lazy as possible. That is, menus did not know what their actions were until they were shown. This was a quite clever engineering work, with display names and icons assigned in the System Filesystem so an action could be displayed fast.

A generally useful list of advice follows:

Node constructors should be fast   Nodes need to be constructed rapidly on demand from the UI.

`DataObject` **constructors should be fast**   Do not try to parse a file in the constructor for a `DataObject`! Simply create objects that will parse it on demand when something really needs programmatic access to the file's content. If accessing those objects will be slow, clearly document the threading model for them and do not permit them to be called from the event thread.

Know when you're doing I/O   And whenever possible, keep that code off the event thread.

Avoid oversynchronization   Synchronization is used for thread safety. It can be a source of deadlocks. Synchronization in Java comes with a performance penalty. Avoid repeatedly calling synchronized methods. Rather, try to lock the subsystem of the largest granularity you can lock, do your work, and then unlock it.

Avoid `ModuleInstall` **classes**   `ModuleInstall` classes run code on startup. More code running on startup means startup takes longer. Wherever possible, find or create ways to use the default `Lookup` and the System Filesystem to register objects declaratively, so that your code can look them up when needed and not before.

Index

Symbols

CD-ROM Warranty

Prentice Hall PTR warrants the enclosed CD-ROM to be free of defects in materials and faulty workmanship under normal use for a period of ninety days after purchase (when purchased new). If a defect is discovered in the CD-ROM during this warranty period, a replacement CD-ROM can be obtained at no charge by sending the defective CD-ROM, postage prepaid, with proof of purchase to:

> Disc Exchange
> Prentice Hall PTR
> Pearson Technology Group
> 75 Arlington Street, Suite 300
> Boston, MA 02116
> Email: AWPro@aw.com

Prentice Hall PTR makes no warranty or representation, either expressed or implied, with respect to this software, its quality, performance, merchantability, or fitness for a particular purpose. In no event will Prentice Hall PTR, its distributors, or dealers be liable for direct, indirect, special, incidental, or consequential damages arising out of the use or inability to use the software. The exclusion of implied warranties is not permitted in some states. Therefore, the above exclusion may not apply to you. This warranty provides you with specific legal rights. There may be other rights that you may have that vary from state to state. The contents of this CD-ROM are intended for personal use only.

More information and updates are available at:
http://www.prenhallprofessional.com/